THE
EXTREME
GONE
MAINSTREAM

PRINCETON STUDIES IN
CULTURAL SOCIOLOGY
Paul J. DiMaggio, Michèle Lamont,
Robert J. Wuthnow, and Viviana A. Zelizer,
Series Editors

A list of titles in this series appears at the back of the book

THE EXTREME GONE MAINSTREAM

Commercialization and Far Right
Youth Culture in Germany

CYNTHIA MILLER-IDRISS

Princeton University Press
Princeton and Oxford

Portions of this book derive in part from other publications.
I gratefully acknowledge permission for the adaptation of portions
of the following works:

"The Extreme Goes Mainstream? Commercialized Right-Wing
Extremism in Germany." *Perspectives on Europe* 42(1): 15–21 (2012).
Courtesy of the Council for European Studies, Columbia University.

"Marketing National Pride: The Commercialization of Right-Wing
Extremism in Germany." Pp. 149–60 in Sullivan, Gavin, ed. (2014).
*Collective Pride and Related Emotions: New Directions in Theory and
Practice.* Routledge.

"Soldier, Sailor, Rebel, Rule-Breaker: Masculinity and the Body in the
German Far Right." *Gender and Education* 29(2): 199–215 (2017).
Available online: http: //www.tandfonline.com/10.1080/09540253.2016.1274381.

"Youth and the Radical Right." Rydgren, Jens, editor. *The Oxford
Handbook of the Radical Right.* Oxford: Oxford University Press, forthcoming.

Published by Princeton University Press,
41 William Street, Princeton, New Jersey 08540

In the United Kingdom:
Princeton University Press,
6 Oxford Street, Woodstock, Oxfordshire OX20 1TR
press.princeton.edu

Jacket photograph courtesy of Markus Mandalka

Library of Congress Cataloging-in-Publication Data

Names: Miller-Idriss, Cynthia, author.
Title: The extreme gone mainstream : commercialization and far right youth culture in
Germany / Cynthia Miller-Idriss.
Description: Princeton : Princeton University Press, [2018] | Series: Princeton studies in
cultural sociology | Includes bibliographical references and index.
Identifiers: LCCN 2017016559 | ISBN 9780691170206 (hardcover : alk. paper)
Subjects: LCSH: Nationalism—Germany. | Right-wing extremists—Germany. |
Youth—Political activity—Germany. | Culture and politics—Germany.
Classification: LCC DD76 .M5452 2018 | DDC 306.20943—dc23 LC record available at
https://lccn.loc.gov/2017016559

British Library Cataloging-in-Publication Data is available

This book has been composed in Sabon Next LT Pro and Trade Gothic LT Std

Printed on acid-free paper. ∞

Printed in the United States of America

10 9 8 7 6 5 4 3 2 1

For my parents,
Lynn and Gary,
my first readers then,
and now.

CONTENTS

LIST OF ORGANIZATIONAL ACRONYMS

AfD Alternative für Deutschland (Alternative for Germany)

apabiz Antifaschistisches Pressearchiv und Bildungszentrum e.V. (Anti-fascist Press Archive and Educational Center)

BfV Bundesamt für Verfassungsschutz (Federal Office for the Protection of the Constitution)

BNP British National Party

CDU Christlich Demokratische Union Deutschlands (Christian Democratic Union)

GIRDS German Institute for Radicalization and Deradicalization Studies

ISIS The Islamic State of Iraq and Syria

KKK Ku Klux Klan

mbr Mobile Beratung gegen Rechtsextremismus (Mobile Advising against Right-Wing Extremism)

NPD Nationaldemokratische Partei Deutschland (National Democratic Party of Germany)

NPI National Policy Institute

NSDAP Nationalsocialistische Deutsche Arbeiterpartei (National Socialist German Workers Party)

NSU Nationalsozialistischer Untergrund (National Socialist Underground)

OSCE Organization for Security and Cooperation in Europe

PEGIDA Patriotic Europeans against the Islamization of the Occident

PBS Public Broadcasting System

SA Sturmabteilung (Assault Detachments)

SS Schutzstaffel (Protection Squadrons, a division of the SA)

SPLC Southern Poverty Law Center

UKIP U.K. Independence Party

ARCHIVAL SOURCES

Antifaschistisches Pressearchiv und Bildungszentrum (apabiz), Berlin

Alphabetical folders under *Skinversände* (BRD) and product collections

United States Library of Congress, Washington, D.C.

Archival sources: Prints & Photographs Division:

LOT 3633 (F), Folder: Nazi-era photographs, 1922–45
LOT 5212 (F), Folder: Souvenirs decorated with Nazi symbols
LOT 5180 (G), Folder: Kampf unter der Kriegsflagge . . .
LOT 9856 (G), Folder: Kitsch
LOT 2888 (G), Folder: Altreligiöse Ausdrucksformen des
  Schwabenlandes, 1938 . . .
LOT 7488 (H), Folder: Ordensburg Sonthofen
LOT 8398 (F), Folder: Nazi party facility in Upper Bavaria
LOT 8580 (F), Folder: Sculptured eagles designed for buildings and
  monuments, 1933–36.
LOT 2747 (F), Folder: German press photographs, 1935–44
LOT 3649 (F), Folder: Sudentenland
LOT 4589 (H), box 2 of 4, Folder: Pictoral history of the rise of the
  Nazi party in Germany, 1920–33
LOT 2685 (H), Folder: Ortsgr. Urkunden, Piltolengehaenge, Dienstkleidung
  fuer NSF-Bahnhofsd. Tuerschilder, sonstiges
LOT 2760 (H), Folder: Reichsbauernfuehrer R. W. Darre zur Errinerung
  an das Harzlager 1936
LOT 3982 (G), Folder: Album of German snapshots, 1935–40, of Nazi
  ceremonies and parades
LOT 3111 (H), Folder: Original drawings, designs and artwork for symbols
  or posters for the Gutenberg Reichsausstellung held in Leipzig
  in 1940
LOT 5083 (H), Folder: Hitler Youth and League of German Girls album,
  1933–40 (?)
LOT 3640 (F), Folder: German miscellaneous ephemeral material, 1918–45
Photo album with 60 photographic prints in Folder: Nazi gatherings,
  activities and celebrations, ca. 1934

PREFACE AND ACKNOWLEDGMENTS

> I hate this *having to pay such rapt attention to the bullies & thugs.*
> I hate how they continue to command our attention,
> I hate that the greatest revenge seems to be beyond us —
> to erase, to forget. To obliterate the memory of such evil . . .
> — Joyce Carol Oates, "Hatefugue," *New Republic*,
>   November 14, 2014

I read Joyce Carol Oates's powerful poem about the Holocaust as I was putting the finishing touches on my book proposal for this monograph, and it plaintively lodged itself in my head, constantly reminding me to attend to it. I read the poem almost daily as I wrote, holding its words close as I analyzed images and pored over interview transcripts. I felt how much she hated the attention paid to "bullies & thugs," her desire to erase and forget the Nazis. I thought about these words as I walked to campus, as I prepped for talks, as I folded laundry. "Hatefugue" kept me close to the bigger meaning of this project while I wrote, challenging me to think harder than I ever had about whether studying far right youth culture also valorizes it; whether it might be best, in the end, as Oates suggests, to erase, to forget.

During the same period that Oates's poem was banging around in my head, the media headlines were filled with horrific stories of beheadings at the hands of ISIS fighters, some of whom were young men from Europe not so different in age and circumstance from the young men I studied. Suddenly the world was captivated by the question of why European youth in particular, but also youth from the United States, Canada, Australia — relatively settled places with strong economies — would run off to ISIS to engage in terrorist violence. I couldn't help but see parallels between ISIS's propaganda about the mythological return to an Islamic caliphate and the German far right's valorization of Nordic heroes and Viking legends. I read journalists' accounts about recruits who talked about wanting to be a part of something bigger than themselves, about searching for meaning and belonging, about feeling angry at adult societies who had let them down, and I heard echoes of the same kinds of words in my interviews with German youth in and around the far right scene. For the first time in my academic career, it dawned on me, I may have learned something that might truly matter in the world—that people should listen to. After years of studying far right youth subculture in Germany, I now knew things about why youth were attracted to right-wing extremism that I felt had strong parallels to extremist recruitment and radicalization in a variety of contexts, from child soldiers in Sierra Leone to the 9/11 hijackers.

The issue—unfortunately—became ever more pressing. While I was researching and writing this book, far right wing extremists—many of whom display the kinds of symbols I discuss here—murdered seventy-seven young people in Norway, six Sikh worshippers in Wisconsin, and nine bible study participants in South Carolina. I presented some of my initial arguments about youth radicalization to a group of scholars and practitioners in London in November 2015, before we discovered on smartphones over dinner that evening that attacks were underway in Paris by Belgian recruits to ISIS. In my final year of writing, over a million Syrian refugees made their way to Germany, met with a warm welcome by the majority of Germans but also with significant episodes of violence. Meanwhile, in mid-2016, U.K. citizens responded to targeted anti-immigrant and xenophobic rhetoric and voted to exit the European Union. That summer saw terrorist attacks in Orlando, Florida, and Nice, France, followed by the election of Donald Trump to the U.S. presidency on a wave of racist, anti-Muslim, and anti-immigrant sentiment, cheered on by white supremacists and nationalist groups like the Ku Klux Klan and Robert Spencer's National Policy Institute, who tried to rebrand themselves as the "alt-right." More violence continued, as attacks at a Berlin Christmas market and an Istanbul nightclub rounded out a year of violence perpetrated almost exclusively by young men. Putting onto paper what I had learned about far right youth engagement in Germany suddenly took on an almost moral obligation for me, fueling the final weeks of my analysis and writing.

Ultimately, despite my great love for her poem, I found I disagree with Oates. I disagree because I believe that bullies and thugs are not born, but made. And I believe they are made and made anew in every generation, in every religion, in every ideology and corner of the globe. My work is animated by the firm and foundational belief that if bullies and thugs are made, then they can be *unmade*. They can be deradicalized, resocialized, rehabilitated. Succeeding at this task, however—the unmaking of bullies and thugs—requires not erasure but rather its opposite—constant vigilance. We must pay close attention to extremist hatred, decoding their signals, analyzing their symbols, and listening to their words if we ever hope to interrupt them, to capture the hearts and minds of young people before they go too far into the world of bullies and thugs.

The best revenge, in other words, is not erasure, but prevention and intervention. And these can be achieved only through understanding of the varied motivations and dynamics of the "bullies and thugs" Oates so eloquently and justifiably wishes we did not have to devote our "rapt attention" to. I find Oates's words beautifully optimistic—tinged in the assumption that erasing one set of bullies and thugs might mean we have erased the peculiar blend of rationality, irrationality, and hatred that led to the Holocaust in the first place. As the events of the past few years have shown all too well, this is not the case.

Some of the images and comments I discuss in the following book are disturbing and offensive. It wasn't always easy to look at them, nor to hear the anger and vitriol that some youth communicated when they talked about Muslims, migrants, and others. But many of the youth gave me hope, even as they struggled to understand how to negotiate an increasingly diverse world. More importantly, the hardest words to listen to are, I believe, the most important ones. It is my strongest belief that we need to understand as much as possible how young people are thinking in order to develop effective strategies to address this kind of hatred. This sometimes means studying images, interviews, and texts that one personally finds deeply offensive and troubling. It is always worth mentioning this because the act of studying such populations should not be taken as any kind of tacit approval of the beliefs or opinions represented—in fact, it is just the opposite.

Forgetting and erasing would be lovely. But it would also be dangerous. On the contrary: we are obliged to pay attention. If silence is complicity, then forgetting, I would argue, is even worse.

Perhaps more than anything else I have done in my life, this project chose me, rather than the other way around. I stumbled across the new forms of commercialization analyzed in this book while I was in Berlin in the spring of 2009, sorting through photographers' databases in search of a cover photo for my first book. I was astonished at how much had changed in German far right subculture just since I had completed my prior fieldwork five years earlier. Fascinated, I flew back to New York planning to write an article about it. But as the weeks passed after my return from Berlin, it became increasingly clear that an article wouldn't suffice. The project would not let me go; I found myself, quite literally, waking up thinking about it. This was handily the most affirming experience I have had as an academic and a scholar. Never before had I felt such a compulsion to investigate and understand a phenomenon. But it was also a pursuit that required an army of other people to embrace and support my quest to comprehend what was happening in a subcultural scene halfway around the world, because for many reasons, it was a terrible time for me to launch a new transnational empirical research project. Together with Seteney Shami at the Social Science Research Council and Mitchell Stevens at Stanford University, I was in the midst of data analysis on an ambitious research project studying university internationalization and the production of knowledge about the "rest" of the world at twelve U.S. universities.[1] We were about to sign a book contract committing me to significant data analysis and writing time. I hadn't yet earned tenure and, by all accounts, should have spent my remaining time focusing on publications rather than new data collection. And—most daunting—I had two babies still in diapers. The fact that this book even exists is a testament to dozens of people who selflessly embraced this project in a myriad of ways.

This project began as an image analysis, and I am grateful to several archivists and photographers without whom the image archive would not exist. I owe sincere thanks to archivists and researchers at apabiz-Berlin, the U.S. Library of Congress, the U.S. Holocaust Memorial Museum, the Granger Archives, EXIT-Deutschland, and the German Historical Museum/Deutsches Historisches Museum for their help in navigating collections, identifying appropriate images, and helping secure the needed permissions for reprinting images in this book. Katharina Börner painstakingly sorted thousands of images, which she then carefully coded and tagged with a codebook I devised with her input. Several activists, policy makers, and researchers who work in various capacities to monitor and combat far right extremism in Germany were tremendously helpful to me as I sought to understand the commericalization phenomenon and to analyze and decode various images. In particular, I am grateful to Winfriede Schreiber and her colleagues at the Verfassungsschutz Brandenburg; Uli Jentsch, Frank Metzger, and Michael Weiss from apabiz; Bianca Klose from Mobile Beratung Gegen Rechtsextremismus (mbr) Berlin; Annett Kahane from the Amadeo Antonio Stiftung; and Daniel Köhler, who was at EXIT-Deutschland at the start of this study and now directs the German Institute on Radicalization and Deradicalization Studies (GIRDS). I am grateful to New York University for sabbatical time in the 2011–12 academic year, which provided the time I needed to assemble and analyze the digital archive and to launch the next phase of the project, and to American University for permitting me to spend my first year on the faculty in 2013–14 on unpaid leave so that I could accept a fellowship in Germany. I owe Jonathan N. Winters—a true IT hero—tremendous thanks for years of assistance on the technical aspects of managing the large digital image archive and making it accessible from both sides of the Atlantic.

Before the digital archive phase was complete, it was clear that the image analysis wouldn't suffice to develop a fuller understanding of the commercialization phenomenon. I owe tremendous thanks to several individuals who helped make the next phase of the project possible. I am particularly grateful to Dr. Christian Magnus-Ernst at the Berliner Schulsenat, who has facilitated my research access to Berlin schools for nearly fifteen years, as I moved out of graduate school and into my first academic job, through promotion and tenure and then to a new institution. Dr. Magnus-Ernst thoughtfully and efficiently reviewed my research instruments and previewed the images, responding quickly and supportively to enable me to collect data while ensuring the ethical protections of Berlin students and teachers. He has always responded quickly and warmly to my requests, completely contradicting all expectations of the unwieldy nature of large bureaucracies. I wish I had more to give back to him and to the Berlin Schulsenat than merely a copy of this book.

The German teachers and students whose voices grace these pages gave me their time, their ideas, and their opinions generously and unreservedly. Their school principals welcomed me warmly into their school communities and were patient over the many years of data collection and analysis. They are named in this book only by pseudonym in order to protect their confidentiality—but without their time and engagement, this project could not have been.

Both phases of the research, as well as an additional year spent analyzing and writing in Cologne, were supported by several foundations, agencies, and universities who made it possible for me to travel back and forth to Germany and to archives in Washington, DC, to assemble the digital image archive and conduct interviews with young people and their teachers. This project wouldn't have happened without the generous support of the German Academic Exchange Service (DAAD), the Alexander von Humboldt Foundation, the Spencer Foundation, the Goethe Institut, New York University, American University, and the Morphomata Center for Advanced Studies at the Universität zu Köln. Two Economic and Social Research Council (ESRC) research network grants in 2013–15 (Grant Number ES/N008812/1) and 2016–18 (Grant Number ES/L000857/1) with co–principal investigators Hilary Pilkington, Graham Macklin, and Fabian Virchow, funded a regular seminar series that provided critical space for me to present exploratory analyses and learn from other scholars and practitioners across Europe and North America. Because those seminars took place under Chatham House

Rules—meaning that attributions for ideas and findings presented in seminars should not be given—I cite presentations from those seminars only with the explicit permission of the presenters.

I owe special thanks to Stephanie Grupp-Clasby and Katrin Pieper for nominating me to spend the 2013–14 year at Morphomata, and to Günter Blamberger and Dietrich Boschung for so graciously welcoming me into their fascinating community of global fellows. At Morphomata I joined scholars from across the globe who were analyzing images of death in various time periods and expressive forms. My year in residence there—where I was one of a few social scientists among a group of art historians and classicists—was instrumental in shaping how I examined the images in this book, as I detail more in the methodological appendix. While I am of course grateful for the time and space I was gifted to write during my year there, I am equally grateful for Morphomata's intellectual influence on me and on this work. Indeed, chapter 4 of this book—in which I analyze images of death in the commerical iconography of brands and products in the far right youth subcultural scene—simply would not exist without my time at Morphomata.

Other colleagues and friends in Germany were particularly helpful in facilitating access, discussing ideas, and providing feedback on the project. Stefanie Grupp-Clasby, Gesa Morassut, Georg and Ulrike Kirschniok-Schmidt, Heike and Ingo Blöink, Günter Blamberger, and Dietrich Boschung, as well as Martin Roussel, Jan Soffner, Larissa Förster, Thierry Greub, Semra Mägele, Regina Esser, and Marta Dopieralski at the Internationales Kolleg Morphomata were all especially helpful to me.

I am indebted to Katharina Börner, Annett Graefe, Christian Bracho, Liz Knauer, Stephanie Dana, Chanae Brown, and Alessandra Hodulik for research assistance at various stages of this project. I thank Steffen Geusch for his technical knowledge of the construction trades, particulately related to the translations of occupational jobs for which names do not exist in English. Katharina Börner deserves special additional mention for the years she spent managing the project as my field coordinator in Berlin, conducting interviews and observations, handling correspondence and scheduling, and helping find housing for my many short-term rental stays in Berlin. Annett Graefe took over from Katharina in 2013 and efficiently managed the remaining interview transcription and coding from NYC and Berlin and merits special thanks for her deep engagement in the analytical part of this project, including coding the transcripts, cross-checking my translations of the German interview quotes, and assembling some of the tables presented here, which not only was helpful logistically but also added much to my understanding.

Much of what I have written here had an earlier life in the form of varied presentations and drafts. Mabel Berezin, Kathy Blee, Gideon Botsch, Dana Burde, Julian Go, Arunima Gopinath, Annett Graefe, Roger Griffin, Shamil Idriss, Daniel Köhler, Helgard Kramer, Michèle Lamont, Martin Langebach, Elizabeth Luth, Graham Macklin, Gary Miller, Virág Molnár, Ann Morning, Nicole Pfaff, Hilary Pilkington, Jan Raabe, Joan Ramon-Resina, Jens Rydgren, Jan Schedler, Seteney Shami, Pete Simi, Mitchell Stevens, Fabian Virchow, Jon Zimmerman, my fellow scholars-in-residence at the Morphomata Center for Advanced Studies, and at least a few hundred workshop participants and audience members, and dozens of graduate students read or listened to earlier versions of this work and asked questions or provided formative suggestions that have much improved the final version. I owe an intellectual debt to Jon Fox for early discussions about "consuming the nation." Daniel Köhler has been generous over many years of this project, offering feedback and expert consultation as I worked to decode images and understand the German far right youth scene and most notably reading the entire draft in its entirety, and providing a detailed review as a native expert. The journalist Thomas Rogers graciously shared what he had learned through his own research on the production side as he researched and wrote pieces on the commercialization phenomenon for *Rolling Stone Magazine* and the *New Republic*.

Midway through the project, I moved from NYU to American University, where my colleagues in the School of Education and the Department of Sociology, and especially Deans Sarah Irvine Belson, Cheryl Holcomb-McCoy, Stacey Snelling, and Peter Starr offered timely and useful support to help see the project through its final months of data coding and analysis. My new colleagues in the School of Education and the Department of Sociology at AU and in the broader DC area, especially Elizabeth A. Worden, Christian Bracho, Bernhard Streitwieser, Susan Shepler, Amanda Taylor, and GWU's Dean Michael Feuer—offered a terrific new intellectual community in which to finish the book. I thank Jacqueline Garcia and Ophira Bansal for administrative support that significantly freed up my time to finish the writing. I owe tremendous thanks to Seteney Shami and Mitchell Stevens for embracing this project despite the significant delays it meant for our collective projects. Finally, I will always be grateful to the three German photographers who generously provided thousands of images for the archive: Roland Geisheimer, Markus Mandalka, and Sascha Rheker, and to the journalist Felix Heusmann and freelance photographer Kate Oczypok for their later additions of images in this book. Their generosity continues to astound me, and I am pleased that I could include some of their terrific work in this book's images with the support of a publishing subvention from American University.

Michèle Lamont has championed this project in many ways that deserve thanks, but most especially for her enthusiastic read of the book proposal, which she brought to the attention of her fellow Princeton Series in Cultural Sociology series editors, Paul J. DiMaggio, Robert J. Wuthnow, and Viviana A. Zelizer. I owe each of them thanks for their positive feedback and support of the project. My editor Meagan Levinson at Princeton University Press understood from the very beginning what I wanted to accomplish with this project; her intellectual engagement and keen editorial sense have much improved the final product. I am also grateful for production, marketing, and copyediting assistance from David Campbell, Kathleen Kageff, Sara Lerner, Samantha Nader, and Stephanie Rojas, to the Princeton University Press art department for their terrific cover design, and to the rich and thoughtful guidance of two anonymous reviewers.

The babies who were in diapers when this project began will head to middle school as this book goes to print, having lived with this project and its consequences for them for almost all their lives. I brought my daughters back and forth to Germany with me five times during the course of this project, for trips ranging from eight days to twelve months, and left them behind at home for several shorter trips. This required an army all on its own. I am forever grateful to Gary and Lynn Miller, Havva Idriss, Krystal Bordini, Vera Hellmann, and Fatima Mernissi for traveling to Berlin and Cologne to take care of my small children on various fieldwork trips, and to Zee Smith, Mollie Sheridan, Carolina Jordan, Rachel Hargraeves, Maria Esposito, Wibke Wehner, and Chloe Fatsis, who at various points cared for them in the United States and in Germany while I researched and wrote portions of this book. Others found creative ways to facilitate my travel and work around roadblocks that could have prevented me from all the juggling the travel required. Elementary school principal Gail Boyle signed off on homeschooling from Berlin for two lengthier trips that fell during the academic school year. Most significantly, my former dean Mary Brabeck made my initial 2009 trip to Berlin possible at a moment when it seemed impossible. Everything in this book is ultimately traceable to a moment in an archive on that trip, and so without Mary's intervention, this book would not have been. In a career that has had tremendous public impact, what to Mary must have seemed a small decision was one of the most consequential for me, and I am so very grateful to her.

Wonderful friends and family remain my deepest sources of support, for which words of gratitude seem wholly inadequate. Gary and Lynn Miller,

Havva Idriss, Jon Miller, Zee and Milas Smith, Reed Idriss and Meredith Renda, and my MNO tribes in Greenwich Village, Larchmont, Cologne, and DC have kept me sane and balanced. More than anything, I am grateful to Shamil, Aniset, and Nura, who have graciously tolerated uprooted lives, dozens of plane rides and rental apartments and relocations — not the least of which, for my daughters, was being plopped into German-language schools for a year without knowing the language. From my deepest core, I thank those little girls for their resilience, their joy, their embrace of adventure, their love of German playgrounds and *Wochenmärkte*, and their growing ability to sleep on red-eye flights to Europe. Shamil's convivial reaction to the logistical craziness this project brought to our lives and of what it would mean for him personally and professionally, and his complete faith and trust that the transnational travel and bilingual stress would work out just fine for the girls in the end, are unmeasurable. Even more critically for this particular book, as an intellectual partner, his deep insights from a lifetime of practical work on youth, conflict, and extremist engagement in global contexts outside of Germany shaped my thinking about far right and extremist youth in ways that have had an indeliable impact. For Shamil, as always over the past two decades, words are still entirely inadequate to express my thanks.

Finally, I would be remiss if I did not mention how fortunate I am to have become a part of a rich community of German and European scholars of the far right, who have graciously accepted me as a member of their academic tribe. Despite years of study, residence, and fieldwork in Germany, as an American I will always be an outsider in ways that inevitably impact my observations of cultural, social, and political phenomena. Any explanatory success I have in this book is due in large part to the formal and informal feedback and support I have received over the years from native German and European experts and colleagues, many of whom are named individually above. To my great surprise, they never blinked at this strange outsider who wanted to interrogate one of the darkest aspects of German history and contemporary youth subculture. It is my sincere hope that some of the findings here will be of some use to German scholars, activists, and educators who work to understand and combat far right violence every day. With that said, however, all opinions and analyses presented in this work are mine and do not necessarily reflect the opinions of any of the reviewers or funders of this work. I, of course, take responsibility for any errors.

THE
EXTREME
GONE
MAINSTREAM

INTRODUCTION
Selling the Right Wing

So join the struggle while you may.
The revolution is just a T-shirt away.

—Billy Bragg

On a hot day in late June 2010, I shaded my eyes with folded hands and peered through a locked steel-and-glass doorway into a well-lit Berlin clothing store named Trømso, after a Norwegian town with a rich Norse history.[1] A doorbell-style buzzer enabled access to the store by permission only. Although I would later go back to peruse the clothing in greater depth, on that first visit, I found myself uncharacteristically hesitant to press the button, even though I had spent months studying the brand and securing funding to go there in person from New York. Somewhat irritated with myself, and realizing there were no staff or customers visible at this midday hour, I settled for observing the store through the windowed entry, alternately peering through the glass, taking photos, and scribbling field notes under the hot sun.

What I saw was this: bamboo-colored flooring connected the entryway with the rear of the store, where stacks of neatly-folded T-shirts and sweatshirts rested on deep, bright-white shelving. Near the store's entrance, a mannequin sported a lovely, butter-yellow polo shirt and lightly distressed jeans. Boxwood topiary globes rested atop tall, woven-seagrass planters flanking the front counter, while a pair of additional small boxwood globes were centered on stone platters on each side of the register. A rubber-backed carpet protected the floor at the entryway, emblazoned with the store's name and logo in large print. To a casual observer, the store was chic and inviting, and it certainly looked no different from any other mainstream, sporty clothing shop. But in fact, as I already knew, Trømso was not any ordinary store. Along with Thor Steinar's Tønsberg shop, which had opened in February 2008 in the heart of Berlin's hippest commercial district a few kilometers away—Trømso was clear evidence of the radical, and profitable, transformation in far right youth subcultural style analyzed in this book.

Since the early 2000s, far right youth have gravitated away from the singular, hard-edged skinhead style in favor of sophisticated, fashionable, and

1

highly profitable commercial brands that deploy coded far right extremist symbols. German and American media have dubbed the youth who wear such brands "Nipsters"—Nazi hipsters.[2] By marrying right-wing ideology and symbols with popular culture and style in high-quality clothing, Thor Steinar (the parent brand of the Trømso and Tønsberg stores described above)—and similar commercial entities, such as Erik and Sons and Ansgar Aryan—have effectively created a new far right subculture. Buying a bomber jacket, shaving one's head, and donning combat boots are no longer the "entry points" to the right-wing scene. Today's far right youth can express their own individuality and still be right wing, and commercial entities are both capitalizing on this and acting as driving forces of the phenomenon.

Commercialization is not an entirely new phenomenon for the far right. The commercialization of right-wing ideology dates at least to the early 1930s, when for-profit companies began to produce a variety of souvenir-style products deploying likenesses of Hitler, symbols like the swastika, and the national colors: black, white, and red. Nazi consumers could buy children's toy soldiers, yoyos, spinning tops, playing cards and horns, chocolate candies with swastikas, clothing, accessories, and decorative items like pocket watches, busts of Hitler, collector plates, paper cups, tin pails, piggy banks, German-style suspenders, and even light bulbs with swastikas imprinted on the glass.[3] Referred to as national "kitsch," such commercial products were viewed critically by Nazi party leaders and others who felt the use of revered symbols like the swastika on commercial products was irreverent and cheapened the National Socialist ideology. "Out with National Kitsch!" declared a 1933 headline in the Cologne newspaper *Der Feuerreiter Köln*, describing the production and sale of such items as "outrageous," while a Berlin newspaper the same year referred to the phenomenon as an "industry of tastelessness."[4]

This early commercialization remained limited to touristic, decorative items using standard symbols and iconography valorizing the Nazi party during the Third Reich.[5] But in the 1980s, the commercialization of far right ideology reemerged as part of the growing popularity of the right-wing rock music scene in the United States, which spread quickly to Europe.[6] The neo-Nazi skinhead style emerged at this time, characterized by shaved heads, high black combat boots (typically worn with white laces), suspenders (braces), and bomber jackets—a working-class aesthetic adopted from British racist skinheads.[7] Right-wing youth gathered, socialized, and radicalized at global right-wing concert tours and music festivals, while music CDs were sold in mail-order catalogs, from product sheets, out of the backs of cars at concerts, on folding tables, and, eventually, on centralized clearinghouse websites. A limited range of basic product items were sold during this period, including low-budget, screen-printed T-shirts, pins, patches, and stickers with coded symbols and references to far right ideology. The product quality was rudimentary, and the coded symbols lacked the kind of sophisticated coding, complex symbol usage, and product quality that would develop in earnest a few decades later.

This all changed when Thor Steinar launched its product line with a slick mail-order catalog in 2002, offering high-quality clothing laced with sophisticated codes relying on historical, colonial, military, and Norse mythological references.[8] From the outset, Thor Steinar was significantly different from the commercialization that predated it. It crafted a new way of coding and embedding ideology, drawing on less overt references than previous products had done; even the brand's name, for example, combines reference to a Norse god and a (misspelled) name of a Nazi general. The clothing captivated a generation of far right youth who were eager to shed the social stigma of the skinhead look and avoid the legal ramifications of banned symbols, and it inspired an entire genre of extremist attire, with new brands targeting micro-subcultures within the far right spectrum. The style enabled youth to embrace more mainstream clothing and subcultural styles while still secretly conveying racist, white supremacist, and far right ideologies, including xenophobia and the valorization of violence, whiteness, and Nazi and colonial history.[9]

Within a few years, Thor Steinar had moved beyond a mail-order catalog, developing a sophisticated website that was virtually indistinguishable from high-end brands like Abercrombie and Fitch or Marc O'Polo, and began opening chic physical stores in major cities throughout Germany. The website and stores evoke sporty, fashionable, mainstream brands. The clothing is expensive (the equivalent of $30 to $40 for a T-shirt or over $100 for a pair of denim jeans). The quality of the cotton, the workmanship, and the fit is far superior, with more variety and product styles, than previous products marketed to far right youth. Product lines include men's, women's, and, children's clothing (later discontinued) as well as accessories like bags, belts, key chains, hats, and wallets.

The sweeping commercial success of the Thor Steinar brand—which by the mid-2000s was earning annual revenues of nearly €2 million[10]—rapidly and literally transformed the face of the European extreme right.[11] Other brands quickly followed in Thor Steinar's footsteps, marketing mainstream-style clothing with coded symbols that evoke, connote, or directly reference far right ideological viewpoints or mythic ideals appealing to the subculture—such as Vikings. Today, there is a diverse range of brands that are popular among youth in the far right scene, particularly within soccer and hooligan subcultures. About a dozen brands clearly dominate the scene in terms of their popularity with youth and the attention given to them through the media, monitoring from authorities, bans in stadiums and schools, and trainings for educators. Three brands—Erik and Sons, Ansgar Aryan, and Thor Steinar—initially produced the most sophisticated and comprehensive lines of clothing, but others have quickly jumped into the market as well.

The brands are distinguishable from one another in a variety of ways. Some websites sport hypermasculine, muscular models with heavy tattoos and piercings, while others are sportier and clean-cut. Some of the brands use clear and direct racist or xenophobic references, while others use a subtler approach relying on colonial, military, and mythical references and motifs. Ansgar Aryan is known among antifascist activists as a "clear neo Nazi fashion vehicle," while Erik and Sons is characterized as a less expensive and more authentic counterpart to the mainstream style of Thor Steinar.[12] At least two brands (Fourth Time and Label 23/Boxing Connection) have cornered a crossover market comprising youth at the intersection of three subcultural scenes: the far right, soccer/football hooligans, and martial arts subcultures.[13] Other brands, like Yakuza, are known primarily for their offensive and provocative iconography that includes but also extends beyond right-wing ideology, including T-shirts and hoodies with misogynistic iconography and references alongside racist, Islamophobic, anti-Semitic, and xenophobic ones. Phalanx Europa, tied to the Identitäre Movement, steers away from the dark colors and camouflage patterns popular with the early brands, marketing modern, hip clothing in bright colors with witty, intellectual iconography and commentary.[14]

The specific product images I analyze in this book draw heavily from the three major brands, but I include smaller and crossover brands in my analysis of images and commercialization as well. Regardless of their market share, what the brands share is a way of encoding historical and contemporary far right, nationalistic, racist, xenophobic, Islamophobic, and white supremacist references into iconography, textual phrases, colors, script, motifs, and product names within products that are essentially identical to other mainstream youth clothing styles. Absent the coded symbols, in other words, the new brands in the far right scene are virtually indistinguishable in style from other clothing popular with youth. This is a radical shift for a youth subculture that was virtually synonymous for two decades with its uniform, skinhead style of shaved or closely cut hair, black bomber jacket, camouflage fatigues, and high black combat boots.

It is not only the codes themselves that are fascinating, but their embeddedness in high-quality, well-made mainstream style clothing. The clothes are expensive economic objects that also act as status symbols while simultaneously embedding a nationalist, xenophobic, or extremist code in the embroidered stitching on the lapel of a $75 hooded sweatshirt. The T-shirt plays a particular role in this regard, bearing the heaviest weight of the coded messages. Long-sleeve or short-sleeve, the T-shirts (and heavier hooded sweatshirts) act as billboards, literally serving up a broad-chested message to observers. As Timo, a twenty-two-year-old scaffold builder apprentice explained, there is intentionality in T-shirt iconography and messaging: "Lots of people wear [such symbols] on a T-shirt so that it can be seen. So that you can see, OK, good, they are maybe a little *gewaltbereit* [ready to be violent]."[15] Consumers thus become literal embodiments of nationalist messages—a topic that is discussed in greater depth in chapter 6's analysis of masculinity and the body.

The brands' relationships with the far right varies. One of Thor Steinar's original owners, Axel Kopelke, reportedly had ties to the far right scene, but the brand was subsequently sold to a conglomerate based in Dubai before returning to European leadership in 2010 under CEO Marco Wäspe.[16] Its reputation today is of a brand that deliberately markets to and profits from the far right scene. Prominent neo-Nazi Patrick Schroeder told an American reporter, for example, that Thor Steinar's use of Nordic references to attract neo-Nazi consumers was an "ice-cold, political, economic calculation and it worked out for them."[17] The brand remains an identifiable symbol of far right affinity and of the modern extreme right in Germany more generally, even as over time the brand has distinctly shifted away from direct right-wing codes, relying more heavily on Nordic mythology in what antifascist activists have referred to as a "light aesthetic change."[18] Several of the other brands have explicit connections to the far right. Erik and Sons' CEO Udo Siegmund has reportedly been spotted with neo-Nazi bands and at concerts, according to antifascist news sources; the brand has sponsored bands and far right gatherings[19] and reportedly has a strong connection to the far right scene, according to one antifascist activist I spoke with. Ansgar Aryan's racist and neo-Nazi connections are fairly clear in the brand name alone.[20] Phalanx Europa, founded by Austrians Patrick Lenart and Martin Sellner, is closely tied to the far right Identitäre Movement—a hip, modern, youth-oriented subset of the far right. A pro-Identitäre website tells potential consumers that wearing the brand in your clique, at school, when you go out, or while you work out is "an aesthetic-political act: against the multi-kulti [multicultural] empire, against the action-less bourgeois and the vision-less pessimists. No to the flooding of Europe, no to dull consumption — yes to heroism."[21]

The codes themselves rely on — and market to — consumers' knowledge of far right ideology but also play on adolescent (masculine) desires related to rebellion, resistance, aggression, violence, male camaraderie, belonging, and identity.[22] Many of the symbols deployed by the brands directly reference immigrant groups and ethnic and religious minorities or express exclusionary, xenophobic, or racist ideologies. The code deployment carefully toes the line of legality in Germany, sometimes marketing directly to consumers' awareness of legal bans of particular symbols and phrases, as chapter 2 details in greater depth.

The introduction of commercial stores selling the brands in major cities, meanwhile, contributes to the broader growth of far right subculture, because the stores serve not only as sites to sell consumer products, but also as what Germans call *Verknüpfungspunkte* — "nexus points." Physical stores are gathering places for right-wing youth to share ideology and news about right-wing rock music concerts, and to plan protests, rallies, neo-Nazi marches, or other activities. Commercialization is more than merely a reflection of subcultural style, in other words. The phenomenon is rather unique to Germany, although the strategy is expanding and the largest brand, Thor Steinar, is sold in shops throughout Europe and Eastern Europe and most recently in the U.K. and North America, as chapter 5 discusses in greater detail. Thor Steinar registered a U.S. trademark and as of 2016 is selling the brand online through its U.S.-based representative, Dortrix. Aside from this development, however, the commercialization that exists in the United States is rudimentary in comparison to the European scene, and the symbol usage is much less complex; there is no comparable degree of sophistication in the American commercial market for products laced with far right wing references or codes.

Commercialization in Context

The growth of the extremist commercial market has coincided with one of the most significant waves of far right popularity in Europe in recent memory. The past several years have witnessed a steady increase in far right wing politics and social movements across Europe. In 2014, voters elected far right, anti-immigrant, Eurosceptic, and nationalist parties into parliaments in fourteen European countries, winning a quarter or more of the national vote in Denmark and France, a fifth in Austria, and more than 10 percent in Greece, Hungary, and the Netherlands (with 9.7 percent in Sweden).

Meanwhile, far right parties gained fifteen additional seats in the May 2014 European Parliament elections (for a total of fifty-two seats), while Greece's openly neo-Nazi party Golden Dawn and Germany's National Democratic Party (NPD)—a controversial but legal party—won seats there for the first time.[23] The new German far right party Alternative for Germany (AfD) has achieved surprising results across the country, winning especially high percentages of the 2016 regional elections in the state of Sachsen-Anhalt (24.3 percent), where they became the second-strongest party after the Christian Democratic Union (CDU).[24]

These electoral trends toward the far right have been punctuated by spectacular and ongoing acts of right-wing terrorist violence, as I discussed in this book's preface. Dozens of defendants from the Golden Dawn party remain on trial in Greece for a variety of criminal activities, including supporting black-clad vigilantes who have repeatedly attacked immigrants on the street. In Germany, the migrant crisis sparked a violent backlash from the extreme right, as over one thousand attacks on refugee homes took place in 2015.[25] Less violent far right actions have also increased significantly; tens of thousands of ordinary citizens have joined regular PEGIDA (Patriotic Europeans against the Islamization of the Occident) marches across Europe.

Such protests and violent episodes exist in a context in which far right, nationalist, xenophobic, anti-Semitic, Islamophobic, and racist rhetoric and discourse has risen across Europe.[26] Prominent incidences of anti-Semitic violence in the summer of 2014 in Europe led the Swiss chairman of the Organization for Security and Cooperation in Europe (OSCE) to warn that "anti-Semitism remains a challenge to stability and security in the OSCE region."[27] A recent Pew Global Attitudes survey reported high levels of anti-Muslim, anti-Roma, and anti-Jewish sentiment in several European countries; over half of those surveyed reported unfavorable views toward Muslims in Italy, Greece, and Poland, for example.[28] In Germany, the most recent "Mitte" study—a nationally representative survey conducted every two years—reported increases in resentments against asylum seekers and Muslims; fully 50 percent of respondents in 2016 reported that they "occasionally feel like a stranger in my own country because of how many Muslims there are here."[29] In their 2015 annual report, the Federal Office for the Protection of the Constitution (Bundesamt für Verfassungsschutz, or BfV) noted increases in the number of right-wing extremist individuals in general as well as in the more specifically defined groups of "subcultural right-wing extremists" and neo-Nazis.[30]

These developments pose significant challenges for countries that have spent decades rebuilding democratic societies in the post–World War II era and have firmly committed to policies and practices that protect pluralistic communities. Academics and policy makers have struggled to understand the diverse causes and dynamics that have made the far right so appealing for so many people—that appear, in other words, to have made the extreme more mainstream. Although largely stylistic, the Nipster is a consequential development for policy makers and educators who find it more difficult to recognize far right young people in time to intervene, whether in or outside of classrooms. As a recent *New York Times* article declared, the Nipster "is discomfiting for how it undermines our ability to identify a potential threat."[31] And while the brands have carefully toed the line of legality, occasionally they produce iconography or messaging that crosses the line into illegal territory. As a result, these developments in commercialization have been carefully monitored by German authorities, policy makers, educators, and antifascist activists. Thor Steinar, for example, which officially and vehemently denies far right connections, has nonetheless been widely recognized as a brand associated with the far right. The Office for the Protection of the Constitution (*Verfassungsschutz*) in Brandenburg contends that the Thor Steinar brand serves as a "scene-typical badge of recognition and demarcation."[32]

Banning is one of the primary strategies pursued by authorities in their efforts to combat the far right. Dozens of symbols, phrases, and even specific gestures are legally banned in Germany if they can be directly tied to the Nazi party. Saying "Heil Hitler" or raising one's arm in the so-called Hitler greeting are arrestable offenses under article 86a in the German criminal code (*Strafgesetzbuch*), which prevents the public use of symbols, signs, and speech acts associated with national socialist organizations (or other organizations deemed to be against the constitution).[33] Symbols like the swastika, the official Nazi flag, the "SS" runic symbol, and the civil badge of the SA (*Sturmabteilung*) are therefore all legally banned. Specific symbols associated with global pan-Aryan or racist groups such as the Celtic cross are also banned, as are symbols that are so similar to banned symbols (such as modified swastikas) they are deemed to be "equivalent" to the banned symbols.[34] Thus, the Triskele, for example, a modified swastika that was used by a division of the SS as well as the once-banned right-wing group Blood and Honour, is illegal because it is tied to a banned organization. The legal bans are limited in power, however, particularly because in recent years, the German courts have tended to rule in favor of defendants who argue for the right to use modified Nazi and far right wing symbols. Legal bans are also limited in scope because they are largely restricted to symbols proven to have a direct association with banned organizations.[35]

The key interpretive issue for courts in recent years has hinged on the concept of "association" with banned organizations—namely, whether or not any given symbol can be shown to directly reference an organization like the Nazi party. Thor Steinar's original logo is a classic case of how the courts' views on symbols are evolving. The original logo was created by combining two banned runic symbols (both of which had been used by the Nazi party) into a symbol that evoked a swastika. The logo was banned in several German states and became the subject of protracted legal disputes, until several state courts overturned the legal bans on the logo (see chapter 5 for further discussion). The courts' reversals were based on a semiotic argument: namely, that the combination of two banned symbols creates a new symbol that can no longer be understood to reference the banned organization.[36]

As I came to learn during discussions with scholars and antifascist activists, the state makes an effort to monitor new brands through the patent registration process. The German Patent and Brand Office (Deutsches Patent- und Markenamt) approves applications for new brand names once they confirm applicants are not copying existing patented brands and once they ensure that the brand's content is legal and not objectionable. This latter condition, known as *Verstoss gegen die guten Sitten*—loosely translated as "objectionable against good morals"—allows the patent office to reject applicants on moral grounds. The classic case is pornography, but right-wing extremist content is monitored as well, and brand applications are rejected when they contain clear right-wing extremist content.[37] The process is not foolproof, however: as a colleague explained to me, the new German brand Consdaple passed initial review because the reviewers did not catch the embedded code in the name—the initials of the Nazi party, NSDAP—but a few weeks later, it lost its protected brand category when the true meaning behind the brand name came to light. This means that the T-shirt can continue to be produced, but not with protected brand (*Markenschutz*) status.

While legal bans of entire brands may not be possible, it is possible to ban particular symbols if they are deployed in public—notably the swastika, but other symbols as well (see chapter 5). Moreover, dress codes and rules within private and public institutions can be implemented and are widely in use. Visitors as well as employees of the Bundestag, the federal parliament in Berlin, are prohibited from wearing Thor Steinar clothing. The brand (along with other brands, symbols, and logos) is banned in many schools, public sector buildings like the Bundestag, stadiums, and at least one university.[38]

There is also considerable attention among antifascist activists to the brands and stores. Although I found general public awareness of the commercialization phenomenon to be fairly uneven, left-wing activists are highly engaged in efforts to publicize and protest the brands, particularly when they open physical storefronts. On the June day when I first observed the Trømso store in Berlin, I noted that the store's exterior shutters and paint bore the effects of paint-bomb attacks. Remnants of splattered paint—large black blobs across the top, smaller red spatters down the creamy columns between the windows—were evidence of left-wing activists' repeated assaults. Later the same day, I observed the entrance of the Thor Steinar Tønsberg, nestled amongst chic local boutiques in Mitte's Rosa Luxemburg Strasse, an area populated heavily by tourists drawn to the neighborhood's stores, cafes, galleries, and high-end shops. The Tønsberg façade was heavily damaged, covered in red paint, with broken, cracked, and scratched windows. Two weeks later, I passed a poster with an image of a fist punching the Thor Steinar logo, under the words "Close down the Nazi-Shop Trømso" (*Naziladen Trømso dichtmachen*) (see plate 25). Across the center of the poster, two photos appear: one a photo of the broken glass of a clothing retailer's storefront, and the other of the Trømso shop. At the bottom of the poster, the phrase "Broken glass shards bring good luck!" appears in bold, red capital letters, over the address and telephone of the Trømso store.[39] Other store openings produced similar reactions and protests, as did the opening of a Thor Steinar store in London in 2014.[40] When Thor Steinar opened a store in Chemnitz named Brevik just a short time after the right-wing extremist Anders Behring Breivik murdered seventy-seven mostly young people in Norway, there was tremendous public outcry.[41]

In this book, I examine the emergence of high-quality, commercialized products laced with far right extremist codes. The case is fascinating as a study of youth subcultures and symbol usage, but it is also about much more than subcultural style. I will suggest that consumption of coded ideological symbols is a potential gateway to extremist recruitment and radicalization. The mainstreaming of extremist subcultural style has made it easier for youth to wear and consume commercialized products and clothing laced with extremist, anti-Semitic, racist, and nationalist coded symbols and references. For some youth, they are an entry point to the scene. They are products that desensitize youth, dehumanize immigrants and religious or ethnic minorities, and make light of past pogroms and tragedies. They are worthy of our serious attention.

The Empirical Base

The methodological appendix offers a full overview of the methods and data I used in my efforts to understand the transformation in far right youth subculture documented in this book. My research for this project very much followed the tenets of grounded theory, although I didn't plan it that way. In the early years of this project, my intent was to study the symbols, iconography, and codes prevalent across the new brands in the far right scene. I was focused on trying to understand how the coding worked, what symbols were being deployed, and what they meant. With the help of a native German research assistant, I digitized commercial product catalogs, took photos of clothing and products, captured screenshots from commercial websites, and sorted through thousands of photographs from three professional German photographers who follow the far right at public events such as protests, marches, festivals, and concerts. I gathered historical images where right-wing symbols were evident, so that I could trace the historical usage of codes and symbols. Ultimately, I assembled a digital archive with several thousand images and coded those images in Atlas.ti, tagging each image with multiple inductive and deductive codes that helped filter and sort the images into categories that could be analyzed in greater depth.

The images in the digital archive are drawn from four main sources, which I discuss in greater depth in the methodological appendix. Three professional photographers who follow the far right and extremist right wing in everyday settings generously granted me searchable access to their full photo archives, enabling me to search by keyword and then sort through thousands of images of youth wearing and deploying commercialized clothing and coded symbols from 2001 through 2011. In order to understand whether and how the contemporary deployment of symbols and brand consumption drew on or modified historical symbols, I gathered historical images from the 1930s–40s from the special collections of confiscated prints, photographs, and Nazi propaganda at the John W. Kluge Center at the U.S. Library of Congress, the digitized collections housed at the U.S. Holocaust Memorial Museum, and a limited number of images from the private Granger Collection. In order to capture the shift from the skinhead era to the early commercialization, I gathered more recent historical images from the 1980s and 1990s, as well as contemporary images from the past decade, from the collections at the Anti-fascist Press Archive and Educational Center in Berlin. The archive I built also includes hundreds of screen shots of the websites of several commercial brands that sell clothing and products popular with far right youth, and digital images I captured on the street in Berlin and other German cities, including images, stickers, posters, graffiti, buttons, patches, banners, flags, clothing, and other products.

The task was immense. I spent a sabbatical year building and coding the initial database and then spent another full fellowship year at the University of Cologne analyzing two categories of the images in greater depth, which resulted in chapters 3 and 4 of this book. Analyzing the images was a complicated task that led me into new methodological territory, as I drew on scholarship on iconography and iconology, art history, religion, visual culture, and national myths and as I worked to decode complex layers of symbols requiring intimate knowledge of German nationalist history, global pan-Aryanism, and violent youth cultures.

Part of what is so difficult about the decoding process is that symbols are not only multivocal, but are also sometimes ephemeral rather than concrete. In other words, they often do not convey a decisive or direct meaning, but rather an evocative one. This does not weaken their impact; indeed, symbols and myths can be very powerful even in forms that are less than full-fledged narratives. The mythical motifs that Mircea Eliade references, for example, may be present in hints, partial images, or suggestions that are evoked or alluded to indirectly in phrases, symbols, or text.[42] Thus, images that evoke Nordic imagery are just as important as ones that depict Nordic symbols or scenes directly.

But the presence of symbols that evoke rather than convey meaning directly does pose methodological challenges. When symbols *evoke* a sense of something, they elicit meaning in ways that often are abstract and dependent on an observer's own autobiography.[43] They are, as Davies explains, a "physical manifestation of ideas" that help manipulate "otherwise abstract concepts like those of kinship, manhood, womanhood, self-sacrifice, and so on."[44] The ways in which a symbol acts on an observer is highly dependent on the broader sociocultural configurations[45] in which individuals' lives are embedded; symbols are thus interpreted in light of broader social and cultural contexts and in light of individual's own life histories and experiences. An image of a father and daughter, for example, might evoke nostalgia, wistfulness, anger, tenderness, resentment, joy, yearning, grief, hopefulness, or more, depending on the observer's own filial relationships and history and the broader sociocultural norms, values, expectations, pressures, and practices related to parenthood, fatherhood, or childhood more generally. National symbols work the same way: images of national flags might evoke pride or shame or other affective reactions.[46] And these reactions vary tremendously within regional or national contexts; symbols like the Confederate flag, which many regard as a racist symbol glorifying slavery, is interpreted by others as a respectful tribute to southern heritage.[47] The interviews I conducted with fifty-one youth, in which they reviewed a subset of thirty-four of the images from the database and offered their own interpretations, were critical as checks against my own interpretations and to provide a sense of how observers react to and understand the coded symbols.

Finally, it is worth noting that the work of identifying and decoding allegorical images has many layers of complexity, particularly for someone who is working cross-culturally and crosslinguistically. In order to identify and classify allegorical images—much less interpret and analyze them—several different strategies are needed.[48] This includes a familiarity with or consultation of expert source material related to particular allegories—otherwise, as Erwin Panofsky pointed out, an observer would simply identify a painting of the Last Supper as an "excited dinner party."[49] This is very true in my own work as well, and the interpretation of these images draws not only on my own practical and subject knowledge but also on expert source consultation. I regularly consulted with scholars of the far right, antiracist activists, native German research assistants who have familiarity with far right scenes, literary and mythological sources and texts, and political and military history, particularly the period of the Third Reich, in my efforts to decode symbols and iconography.

Despite these efforts, there are no guarantees as to the "correctness"[50] of my interpretations, particularly because symbols are often multivocal and multivalent and can have ambiguous interpretations.[51] Indeed, the producers of coded T-shirts and products rely heavily on this very ambiguity to avoid legal consequences and social stigma, as I discuss more in chapter 2. Labeling any particular symbol a "right-wing" symbol is possible only in the context of other symbols and cues. I discuss this dilemma further in the appendix.

School-Based Responses to the Far Right

My original plan was to write this book based on the images, but as analysis continued, I found myself unsatisfied with my ability to answer a number of questions about the production and reception of the images. Did consumers of the commercial products understand the coded iconography and intended messages? How do they interpret the symbols? Why do they purchase the clothing, and how do they understand its meaning within and outside of the far right scene? How have schools and teachers dealt with the transformations in far right subculture? Do teachers understand the coded messages, and if so, what do they do when they encounter them? On the production side, I had questions as well: how do the designers research and deploy the coded symbols and messages? How ideologically motivated are they, and how much are they driven primarily by profit motives?

Taking on all these questions would have made an already ambitious project completely unwieldy, and so I knew I had to narrow my focus. Ultimately, I decided to study the reception side and designed a second phase to the research that involved fieldwork and interviews in two schools—known here by the pseudonyms the Flusser school and the Erker school. I chose to focus on schools for several reasons. First, I have long been interested in schools as sites where young people are socialized into broader social values, including national identities. German schools have a mandate to counteract the radical right wing and have received increasing attention as a site where right-wing extremism needs to be dealt with more seriously,[52] so they were a natural place to study how authorities were reacting to the transformations in far right subculture. Second, schools are the most frequent site where youth encounter bans on brands and symbols and are an ideal site to study the relationship between local policy decisions (like school bans) and youth resistance, shedding potential new light on the relationship between schools and youth culture. Moreover, because the vast majority of research on youth "resistance" has focused on the left,[53] we know almost nothing about how schools affect youth culture on the right. Little is known about the impact of school bans on youth consumption of extremist symbols or their commercialization. There has been some attention to right-wing extremism in the German school system[54] and specifically in vocational schools,[55] but these studies — or the research on which they are based — predate the emergence of the new commercial forms of right-wing extremist subculture, which began in earnest after 2000. Other work on far right and right-wing extremist style is not connected to schools.[56] There is anecdotal evidence that the game-playing aspect of the coded symbols are directly related to bans, as I discuss more in chapter 5. But there has been no empirical research studying how the bans are understood by far right youth; whether the bans have an influence on their consumption of coded symbols and commercial products; or whether such consumption is related to far right wing and extremist behaviors and attitudes. Most of the research on the far right wing, particularly in Germany, has focused on tracing predictors of right-wing extremism, analyzing the role of social class, gender, education, family socialization, region, employment status, exposure to foreigners, and other factors as they relate to youth's propensity to join right-wing extremist groups.[57] In sum, I hoped that by heading to schools, I would be able to shed light on the relationship between bans on symbols and the use of coded symbols in the new game-playing culture of far right wing youth.

Finally, I chose to work with schools because they are an excellent place to gain access to youth. I needed to gain access to youth who were consumers of far right clothing brands, or who at least came into frequent enough contact with the brands to be able to discuss them. Vocational schools in Germany educate the majority of German youth aged sixteen to twenty and are clustered by career field. From my previous fieldwork in German schools, I knew that vocational schools for construction trades have struggled with significant populations of far right youth, and that they would be a place where I would be able to talk to youth in and around the far right scene.[58]

I would thus be able to gain access to a population of youth who were high risk for far right and extremist participation or who had spent much of their lives around other youth who were part of those scenes.

Berlin was an appealing site because the two schools I studied are the only construction trade schools in the state, and so all youth from Berlin and much of the surrounding state of Brandenburg who want to train in a construction field end up as students at one of these two schools. In a stroke of fieldwork-design luck, one of the two schools in Berlin bans all symbols, brands, and representations that convey ideological positions, while the other does not. The schools' student populations are quite similar, drawing largely from the same region and youth backgrounds, and students do not directly choose the schools; they are assigned to one school or the other based on their selection of occupation. The similarities in the student bodies and the variation in policy decisions thus set up a naturally occurring, quasi-experimental design, providing the opportunity to examine whether and how the bans affect the use of coded symbols among youth and the participation of youth in the right wing more generally.

The Berlin schools also appealed to me because Berlin is one of only a few locations where young people can train to become scaffold builders, who I anticipated would be particularly well-informed participants. I knew from my previous research that scaffold builder classrooms were likely to have higher numbers of far right youth compared to other occupations. As Oliver, a twenty-three-year-old nearing the end of his scaffold builder apprenticeship, noted, "I've only known about brands like Thor Steinar for the past two years or so, since I started training to be a scaffold builder, where it's said that a certain ideology is represented." Moreover, the scaffold builders brought important regional diversity to the study because scaffold builder apprentices travel to Berlin for multiweek residential sessions, staying in a dormitory and attending theoretical training in school intensively before they return to their home cities for further practical training. This meant that from a base in Berlin, I was able to interview young people from cities throughout eastern Germany, such as Leipzig and Braunschweig.

I therefore aimed to oversample scaffold builders (N=9), who ultimately made up nearly 20 percent of the fifty-one youth interviewees. Concrete layer (N=7) and masonry (N=7) apprentices constituted an additional 27 percent of the final sample, with the remaining interviewees spread across a variety of construction fields, from roofing and carpentry to more specific fields related to historic preservation, building energy design, and street construction (see tables 7 and 8). All but two of the youth interviewed were born in Germany, though the two born elsewhere (in Poland and in Kazakstan) grew up in Berlin. Four youth (who were born in Germany) had names that are traditionally Turkish in origin, indicating at least partial Turkish heritage. Two of the fifty-one youth were female, which is consistent with male-dominated fields in construction. Although some of the brands have limited women's product lines, there are far fewer options, and the iconography tends to contain fewer coded symbols, compared with the men's clothing (see chapter 6 for further discussion).

Ultimately, with the help of my field coordinator and research assistant based in Berlin, I conducted sixty-two interviews in 2013–14[59] with youth (N=51) and their teachers and principals (N=11), which focused on how young people interpret the brands and symbols and the effect of school bans on the game-playing nature of coded extremist symbols. The interviews with youth aimed to understand whether young people—who were aged sixteen to thirty-nine[60] at the time of their interview, with an average age of twenty-one—own or wear any of the banned clothing, how they define their own sense of style and its meaning to them, how they feel about school bans of symbols or clothing brands, and how they interpret a series of images depicting far right symbols in clothing. Interviews with teachers and principals are supplemental, primarily providing background information on the history of the schools and local discussions about bans and their enforcement, and illustrating teachers' and principals' engagement with the issue of school bans and far right youth culture.

Thus, the empirical base for this book is a combination of the unique digital archive of thousands of historical and contemporary images, combined with sixty-two interviews conducted in 2013–14 in two German construction trade vocational schools with histories of far right extremist youth presence. The digital archive enabled me to track the emergence of the far right commercial scene and its use of symbols, while the interviews and observations traced whether and how young people in and on the periphery of the far right consume, understand, and interpret the brands and coded symbols, and how schools and educational policy makers are responding. Before I turn to an overview of the rest of this book, there are two key terms that need to be defined, because of their centrality to the book and its arguments. In the following section, I explain how I define and use the terms "youth" and the "far right."

Youth in and around the Far Right Scene

I define "youth" as encompassing the period of life from early adolescence through the midtwenties. At the early end of this phase, youth are just beginning to experience greater freedom of movement from parents and other authorities. At the latter end, most youth are transitioning into financial independence, working, studying, or training full time for future careers. It is a phase characterized by experimentation and norm breaking.[61] During this decade of life, young people develop more independent political ideas, experience romantic and dating relationships, and increasingly find peer and friendship groups to be more important to their daily lives than their familial relationships.

Youth is also a phase when their individual and collective identities are developing and changing, as young people come into contact with new people and friends, learn more about their communities and worlds, and navigate complex sets of expectations from the cultural worlds of their peers, families, and broader communities. While the term "youth" sometimes applies to younger children as well as to adolescents and young adults, I follow the general trend in the literature in a focus on "older" youth (from late adolescence to young adulthood). This period marks the primary period in which political attitudes develop and solidify[62] as well as a time when youth are experimenting with various styles, subcultures, and youth scenes. Such scenes and subcultures, notably, are not static or sealed units but adapt and change as youth enter and exit various groups.[63] Subcultures are—as Anoop Nayak skillfully describes—groups that "momentarily coalesce around a configuration of values only to transform and mutate again, in a perpetual state of flux and cultural repositioning."[64] My focus on older youth aims to capture this phase of experimentation and varied engagements with subcultures and scenes, as they explore new styles, music, hobbies, and peer groups during the transition to early adulthood.

Any discussion of youth subcultures is predicated on an understanding of the "mainstream," particularly because youth position themselves in resistance to it and as aiming to "provoke" it. It is important to note, however, that there is no single, monolithic mainstream society against which subcultures are positioned. Just like subcultures, the mainstream is not a sealed or static entity—it is, rather, a shifting spectrum against which youth in subcultural scenes position themselves. The term's analytical usefulness thus derives from its usage by youth across a wide variety of subcultural scenes as they articulate anger toward what they perceive as the "mainstream." As J. Patrick Williams explains, "young people's claims about the 'mainstream,' while deemed vague and inarticulate by many adults (including social scientists), are real for the participants themselves. And . . . that reality is powerfully linked to notions of selfhood and identity, as well as to social behavior."[65]

Defining the far right is a somewhat more complex endeavor—in part because it, like all youth subcultures—is not a single or unitary entity. I rely on the term "far right" as a way of referencing attitudes, scenes, groups, and political parties that espouse some combination of xenophobic, antidemocratic, authoritarian, anti-immigrant, anti-Semitic, antigovernment, fascist, homophobic, ethnonationalist, or racist values, beliefs, actions, and goals. The term also extends to populist and Euroskeptical political parties, parts of the U.S. Christian right, the Tea Party movement, patriot groups, the Ku Klux Klan (KKK), neo-Nazi groups, right-wing terrorist cells like Germany's National Socialist Underground (NSU), and "lone wolf" terrorists like Norway's Anders Behring Brevik or the United States' Wade Michael Page. There is significant variation in what counts as "far right" across countries, in part because of different historical and legal contexts.[66] Most research publications on the far right establish a definition for the term right at the outset—but these definitions vary to some extent.[67] Moreover, the labels are often ideologically laden (e.g., some use the term "hate groups," but far right wing groups often position others as the "haters") and are often heavily contested.[68] My use of the term "far right" aims to contextualize far right youth engagement within a broad spectrum, while acknowledging that scholars lack full agreement on what the "far right" actually is.

I regard far right youth as youth who are either actively engaged or quietly supportive of nationalist or exclusionary platforms that seek to maintain or restore national ethnoscapes[69] to reflect an idealized community based on racial, ethnic, linguistic, or national criteria. Globally, this would include youth who are white or Aryan nationalists, Ku Klux Klan members, neo-Nazi members, soccer hooligans, neofascists, racist skinheads, and members of antigovernment patriot militia or hate groups, as well as youth who express views consistent with these groups—on social media, for example—even if they are not formal members.

Finally, it is important to note that far right youth identity is not clearly bounded or monolithic. Adolescence and early adulthood are key phases of identity formation, during which youth may move in and among various subcultural communities, engaging in contradictory actions or espousing conflicting identities. They may make racist comments on social media even as they exude loyalty and friendship to classmates or teammates who are members of minority groups. The public performance of identities and attitudes may contrast sharply with privately held beliefs or what youth say or do at home. Youth who express far right political views may be "far right" during early adolescence but move away from these views in later adolescence. Or they may offer contradictory views on topics like immigration, opposing the presence of certain groups while accepting others. In many cases, there is a strong emotional core to far right identity, but an unclear or unarticulated connection to political ideology of any kind. Scholars have long understood youth identities to be fluid and complex, with boundaries that are porous rather than fixed.[70] Identification with far right scenes is no different. But while previous scholarship has shown that individuals hold multiple and sometimes conflicting identities,[71] empirical work on extremist and far right wing identity has largely positioned youth engagement in extremism as unidimensional, fixed, and unconflicted. I suggest that youth who engage in extremist movements also need to be understood as holding identities that are complex, contradictory, multiple, and varied. Identities are messy rather than clear-cut; they can surge and retreat in relevance for individuals and communities at any given time, such that their value for an individual at any one point may not be easy to consciously articulate.[72]

I have found it most accurate to speak of youth who are in and around the far right scene, which acknowledges that youth move in and out of various subcultural scenes in experimental and playful ways, shifting from core to periphery and back again. Sometimes these shifts take place over years, and sometimes the contradictions are apparent even in the course of a single interview. Across the interviews, it was rare for youth to directly volunteer that they were currently or formerly engaged with the far right. But many more expressed views consistent with right-wing ideology, making statements or agreeing with messaging in commercial products that expressed xenophobic, anti-Semitic, Islamophobic, racist, anti-immigrant, nationalist, or antigovernment ideologies. The majority had family, friends, classmates, acquaintances, or neighbors who are part of the far right or who owned clothing associated with the far right. These youth regularly engage with peers and communities that are quietly supportive or actively advocating for far right ideas.

Finally, it is critical to emphasize that even if they are experimental or contradictory, identities and actions can be dangerous and harmful, particularly when they originate in scenes where violence against others is valorized, celebrated, or encouraged; where minority religious or ethnic communities are dehumanized; and where racism and xenophobia are normalized, as is the case with many far right youth subcultural scenes and groups. Acknowledging that youth in the far right have flexible engagements in far right scenes does not therefore imply that those engagements are any less consequential or worthy of intervention.

Chapter Overview

In chapter 1, I situate the empirical base of *The Extreme Gone Mainstream* within theories of culture, nationalism, iconography, and youth extremist subcultures. I begin by describing two prevailing notions of how culture "works" — one that presents culture as a coherent meaning system and the other that characterizes it as a "tool kit" of actions and strategies. *The Extreme Gone Mainstream* highlights a mechanism that links these two theoretical approaches to culture, I suggest, by showing that symbolic codes are best understood as embedded in and constituted by meaning systems. Coded, commercialized symbols expressing far right ideology are strategies that can be understood only within the broader schematic structures that help people interpret and understand the messages those symbols convey. In this chapter, I also address theories of extremism and youth subcultures, arguing that previous research on nationalism and extremism has paid more attention to political dimensions than cultural ones. Finally, I link far right commercial symbols to recent scholarship on visual symbols, arguing that attention to the aesthetic dimensions of far right subculture is particularly overdue in light of the recent "iconic" turn in the social sciences.[73] As Dominik Bartmański and Jeffrey Alexander point out, sociologists' ongoing attention to Marxist understanding of economic objects and their relationship to class-based exploitation has led many scholars to overlook the potential for economic objects to have constitutive power for individuals' lives, identities, sense of belonging, or — in this case — the extremist participation of consumers.[74]

I turn in chapter 2 to the first of the five areas that make up the empirical core of the book. In this chapter, I focus on the ways in which symbolic codes are manipulated and deployed in the iconography and text of clothing products. The chapter focuses in particular on the use of codes that draw on alphanumeric combinations or on historical references. Such codes are seen not only on T-shirts and other clothing products but also on tattoos, license plates, accessories, and even giant Styrofoam letters in football stadium stands. Some alphanumeric and historical codes are co-opted from other popular youth cultural scenes and then stripped of their original cultural referents. I trace the game-playing aspect of the codes, by showing how young people (and commercial companies) adapt the codes and their display in order to navigate bans of particular symbols and brands. Drawing on interview data with young Germans in and around the far right scene, this chapter also looks both at whether and how youth understand and interpret embedded far right codes, and at how they consume the clothing and products more generally.

Chapter 3 undertakes a careful analysis of commercial iconography and accompanying slogans and textual references to Norse and Germanic mythology in T-shirts and other products, combined with interview data explaining how youth interpret the meaning of these symbols and myths. The chapter argues that the fantasy of Nordic heritage — and all the positive traits associated to be a part of that heritage — including loyalty, purity, beauty, integrity, and honesty — appeal to youth as a strategy for handling the uncertainty of the postmodern era. I show how fantastical myths and symbols are used to directly depict or evoke a sense of loss, a sense of a particular way of life "slipping away," or a sense of urgency around a need for preservation, survival, resurrection, or rebirth of a particular kind of nation. I argue that they help to crystallize a kind of "magical thinking" about the death (or potential death) of a blood-based ancestral group. Allegorical references — symbols that imply or convey something else — are of particular importance for how they facilitate what I call "aspirational nationhood" — fantasy expressions of a nation that never existed but that is nonetheless aspired to. Such symbols help strengthen group bonds and act as a powerful mechanism of belonging and identification for far right youth. In closing, I link these arguments to new theoretical work about the appeal of Nazism and fascism as rooted in the loss of stability in the global, postmodern era.[75]

Chapter 4 examines historical and contemporary far right wing symbols that directly depict, reference, or evoke death or dying through reference to historical myths and legends as well as contemporary acts of violence. The chapter traces three ways in which the far right deploys symbols of death: abstract death, specific deaths and death threats, and reference to the death of a civilization or entire way of life. The chapter argues that the iconography of death helps evoke fear and produce anxiety among viewers, in part by breaching societal taboos that deem death unspeakable and by evoking death and violence in the name of the nation. By linking depictions of weapons that can cause death; illustrations or references to blood, war, physical fighting or confrontation; or violence to a particular vision of the nation, I argue that such iconography makes coded or oblique references to contemporary immigration and diversity in ways that indirectly or directly threaten members of minority and nonwhite groups. Symbols of death are thus a performative strategy to demonstrate fearlessness and suggest violence as a means to achieve nationalist or extremist goals.

In chapter 5, I analyze symbols borrowed from non-German movements and global or pan-Aryan extremists. Here, I also include the appropriation of nonextremist products that have been assigned new meaning as well as symbols and codes that are in languages other than German. Drawing on interview data as well as the image analysis, this chapter highlights the multivocality of far right symbols that are simultaneously nationalist and global. This multivocality is further amplified, I suggest, by the ironies of far right youth deployment of non-German symbols such as Palestinian scarves and Che Guevara T-shirts to signify a view of themselves as "freedom fighters," while simultaneously adhering to anti-immigrant sentiments or enacting violence against ethnic and racial minorities in the name of the German nation. The chapter draws both on an analysis of images and of young people's interpretation of "global" symbols deployed in the commercialized products to argue that far right ideologies have broadened, in the global era, beyond (mere) national borders. I suggest there are parallels for how other geographically dispersed extremist ideologies—from Islamist extremism to ecoterrorism—might mobilize followers across national and linguistic boundaries. Here, I also analyze legal disputes about the bans and examine youth reactions to school bans of particular symbols and codes as well as teachers' discussions of the enforcement of those bans. Ultimately, I argue that banning policies tend to backfire, further contributing to the game-playing aspect of code modification that make the symbols appealing in the first place.

In chapter 6, I focus on how youth fashion and style serve as markers and expressions of belonging and resistance in ways that mutually reinforce masculinity and nationalism. Drawing on interview data, I show that style is deeply personal and intentional for young people. While research on young women has long discussed issues of body image, the interview data discussed here shows that clothing choices are also embedded in body image and in conceptions of masculinity for young men. The chapter focuses in particular on two emotional articulations of masculinity that are heavily marketed through the products: the desire for male comradeship and belonging, and the urge to express resistance, frustration, and anger at mainstream society. I also show how the products idealize male strength and physicality, drawing on muscular, tattooed Viking warriors with inflated biceps and hypermasculine models that may appeal to adolescent males who feel pressured to conform to scripted ideals about appropriate masculine behavior and physique.[76] Hypermasculine symbols like Viking gods, I suggest, become intertwined with youth fantasies of a romantic, pure, and untroubled past[77] in ways that may help them navigate the transition to adult life and uncertain labor markets.

In the conclusion, I tease out two sets of implications illuminated in the book: one for our understanding of culture and one for our understanding of nationalism and extremism. Both implications rest on the evidence presented in chapters 2–6 of how the use of coded symbols can serve as a mechanism both of belonging and of resistance, helping youth feel connected to other insiders in the far right scene while simultaneously expressing resistance against mainstream society. I argue that this "push and pull" of belonging and resistance ought to expand our understanding of gateways to radicalization and violence by showing how commercialized extremist products—and other "lifestyle elements" like tattoos or far right wing music—help strengthen racist, nationalist, and ideological identification and act as conduits of resistance to mainstream society. In the German case, the commercialized, coded references and symbols—many of which use humor or aggressive coded references to historical atrocities against Jews, Muslims, and others deemed not to belong—desensitize and socialize consumers and their peers and dehumanize victims. Disaffected and disenfranchised youth who enter extremist and radical scenes through their consumption of subcultural elements like tattoos, clothing, styles, or music may become gradually more involved with extremist ideologies. Far from being mere "subcultural style," commercialized extremist products can be a gateway to extremist scenes, radicalization, and violence. Style and aesthetic representation thus need to be considered more seriously for their potential role in radicalization.

I also suggest that the empirical analysis of symbolic deployment can help refine prevailing theories of culture and challenge mainstream sociologists to take economic objects more seriously not only for their exploitative power, but also for their constitutive possibilities. Developing a richer understanding "from the ground up" of the underpinnings of this particular subculture, I argue, has important implications for a range of youth extremist and radical practices globally as well as for sociologists' understandings of how culture works.

1 TRYING ON EXTREMISM
Material Culture and Far Right Youth

> The fight against right-wing extremism is also
> always a fight about symbols.
> — Thorsten Fuchs

In a recent essay titled "The Neonazi Next to Me," the German author Thorsten Fuchs recounted his discomforting experience when a moving company employee showed up at his front door dressed in a style that suggested far right affinity. Describing his struggle to decide whether to speak up or remain silent, Fuchs ultimately concludes, as the epigraph above notes, that fighting far right symbols means fighting the normalization of "clothing, symbols, sentences or words" that are eventually "regarded as normal" if they remain uncontradicted in daily life.[1] Like Fuchs, scores of social scientists have started to attend more seriously to the consequential nature of many of the aesthetic and material dimensions of social life. This recent "iconic" turn in the social sciences has shed light on the symbolic and visual dimensions of phenomena ranging from HIV statistics and September 11 to brands and to what Daniel Miller simply calls "stuff."[2] In this chapter, I argue that understandings of the far right commercialization phenomenon ought to be situated within this visual turn and in light of other recent work emphasizing the symbolic in studies of the nation and the relationship between aesthetic style, performance, and political identities.[3]

This approach differs from mainstream scholarship on the far right, which has predominantly focused on formal, political engagement through organized social movements and parties, rather than on cultural and aesthetic dimensions. There are good reasons for focusing on formal groups and political parties, of course. The recent electoral successes of far right parties and movements across Europe merit serious attention. And the official nature of parties and movements has some empirical advantages when compared to the shifting nature of subcultural scenes. The boundaries, agendas, and ideologies of official far right movements and parties, as well as electoral, polling, and survey data on voters, can be analyzed and compared across national contexts in ways that are often more challenging for subcultural settings.

The focus on formal, organized social movements and political parties, however, means that we know more about the motivations of citizens who vote for the far right at the polls than we do about individuals who engage in the far right in less formal or organized ways. My intention in this book is not to diminish the importance of studying the far right as a political movement, but rather to emphasize the need to also assess the far right as a site of cultural and subcultural engagement, particularly for youth. Far right youth subcultures are critical to understand, both because they can lead to later political engagement (through marching at demonstrations, for example) and because they are heavily associated with violence, whether through spontaneous, drunken hooligan soccer-match brawls or through premeditated violence, firebombings, or attacks on asylum seekers' homes. Perhaps most significantly for this work, the fluid nature of subcultures that I discussed in the introduction means that youth who move in and out of them can also be conduits of extremist rhetoric, ideology, views, and attitudes, bringing far right ideology back into the mainstream with them as they engage with younger siblings, classmates, or peers. The deployment within far right iconography, lyrics, or symbols of humor; game-playing codes; and clever historical and contemporary references thus have the potential to impact not only consumers of far right culture but also the broader mainstream with whom they may interact, helping desensitize observers to racism, xenophobia, and historical atrocities and helping dehumanize victims. In this sense, culture matters, rather significantly.

Approaching the far right as not only a political but also a cultural space, however, would mean that we need to pay closer attention not only to youth political attitudes and views, but also to what draws youth into the cultural aspects of the far right—what attracts them to far right music, festivals, or consumer products? We also know relatively little about the material and visual dimensions of the far right more generally. While there has been some qualitative and ethnographic work on the subcultural dimensions of the far right, scholars have pursued traditional fieldwork ethnographies that generally have not attended in depth to visual and material culture.[4] There has been some recent work on visual culture in Middle East politics and in terrorism more generally, as well as limited applied work (for example, pedagogical pamphlets on far right symbols designed for educators and law enforcement), but to date, there has been no systematic scholarship on the visual and material dimensions of far right youth culture.[5] In the following sections, I explain some of the prevailing arguments about extremist youth engagement in order to situate the discussions of symbol deployment in the remainder of this book.

Why Do Youth Engage in the Far Right?

It is impossible to pin down a single, definitive explanation for far right youth engagement. Much like school shootings in the United States or global terrorist violence, a broad cluster of individual and social factors contributes to extremist radicalization, and the resonance of any particular factor varies from case to case, depending on individuals' personal background and susceptibility. Across the bevy of research on youth violence and the far right, however, there are certain factors that appear repeatedly.

One of the factors that appears to have an impact is economic stress. Scholars hypothesize that youth become more susceptible to far right radicalism and extremism when they experience economic strain or "relative deprivation"—that is, a failure to achieve anticipated success. Some research has suggested that poor life trajectories, unmet expectations, and comparisons with peers' success may contribute to resentment and anger against perceived competitors, especially immigrants—and this may be especially true for working-class men, who are especially vulnerable to the decline of manual labor jobs in the postindustrial economy.[6] But it is also likely that economic strain plays a role because it creates opportunities for the far right to mobilize, since economic crises are often accompanied by developments like growing distrust of institutions, challenges to political legitimacy, or increasing political fragmentation.[7] Far right groups use economic crises to mobilize youth (and others) by using language about immigrants "stealing" jobs or "abusing" the social welfare system, or drawing on metaphors about "floods" of migrants and communities that are "overrun" or at a "breaking point."[8] There is some evidence showing that economic strain plays a bigger role when demographic change is taking place through immigration; Lauren McLaren's research in the 1990s in Germany, for example, showed that increasing unemployment affects right-wing violence only if the number of foreigners in the country is also increasing.[9]

The economic threat thesis is quite contentious, however. Although youth who express economic fears, insecurity, or worries are more likely to hold right-wing attitudes,[10] several scholars have argued that "cultural" threats are a stronger predictor of far right preference than are "economic" threats.[11] And there is evidence that unemployment itself is not related to far right engagement—although growing up with an unemployed parent does have an effect.[12] Thus, although economic threats and relative deprivation are frequently discussed as major contributors to xenophobia, anti-immigrant sentiment, and far right preference in general, the empirical data shows a complicated relationship.[13] It is clear that economic conditions alone cannot explain far right engagement.

Another factor is the extent to which people feel threatened by perceived changes in social norms, values, and beliefs. For example, far right rhetoric about social and legal changes such as same-sex marriage, rising single parenthood, public attention to transgender identity, the increasing percentage of Muslim citizens and residents, or globalization's impact on growing cultural and religious diversity positions such changes as a threat to local, cultural, national, or religious identity. The anti-EU rhetoric of some French farmers and periodic negative community reactions to the building of mosques or the use of nonnational or native languages on street signs are examples.[14] Whether youth are susceptible to far right rhetoric on social change, however, depends to some extent on what else is happening in the broader political and national context. Local, national, and global factors such as legal bans on symbols and organizations, domestic crime, terror attacks, migration and refugee crises, and the growth and visibility of far right political parties have an impact. Durso and Jacobs show, for example, that hate group presence increases when street crime increases, because racist groups have "successfully harnessed" the public's resentment against minority group criminal activity.[15] The rise in Islamophobia following incidences of Islamist terrorism or the rise of racism and antigovernment "Patriot Groups" after the election of the first African American president in the United States in 2008[16] and the rise in antimigrant, antirefugee, and Islamophobic rhetoric in Germany following the mass sexual assaults in Cologne and other German cities are other recent examples. In other words, the right wing becomes more attractive to individuals when the broader social and political environment is saturated with anti-immigrant or Islamophobic rhetoric. Others have shown that the presence of extreme right wing parties at the national level increases antiforeigner sentiment in individuals; this appears to be particularly true when the rhetoric of those parties espouses "culturally" racist views as opposed to "classical" racist views, as Wilkes and colleagues have argued.[17]

The cluster of factors that affect youth's engagement in the far right also includes some combination of individual personality, family background, parenting styles, peer group characteristics, gender, region of residence within a given country, ancestry, and type of community.[18] For example, in Canada, research has shown that individuals were more likely to vote for the Canadian Alliance if they were from the west of Canada, were men of northern European ancestry, or were rural women.[19] Other scholars have studied the potential role of authoritarian family background, military experience, or time in prison as an entry point for right-wing extremism.[20] Childhood experiences with xenophobic or far right parents matter as well.

Siedler's analysis of youth voter behavior in Germany, for example, shows a strong effect among youth living in west Germany whose parents express affinity with a right-wing party: such youth are significantly more likely (35 percentage points higher) to support far right wing parties.[21] Youth who grew up with a single mother are also more likely than those from two-parent families to support far right wing parties. As Siedler argues, his findings "suggest that family events during childhood such as the experience of life with a single mother or the experience of jobless parents are more important than household income in determining adult children's far right wing party affinities."[22] However, other research has shown that families play a complicated role in the development of youth political attitudes and engagements. While previous scholars had consistently posited that social marginalization or authoritarian family background underpinned youth engagement in right-wing extremism,[23] more recent work has challenged this premise. For example, Thomas Gabriel's work tracing the life narratives of far right extremist youth in Switzerland shows clearly that youth's racist attitudes are not simply passed down across generations. Family background matters, but it appears that growing up in an environment of parental nonattention, absences, and lack of communication interact with parental or family members' political orientations and attitudes in important ways. As Gabriel writes, the common ground across youth biographies "consists of a lack of significant adults who are visible, and can thus be experienced, through their interaction and affective sympathy for the adolescent."[24]

In sum, scholars have identified a cluster of factors that contribute to the appeal of the far right for youth. First, youth who are marginalized from traditional measures of economic success or who are experiencing economic crises or youth unemployment or underemployment, or who grew up with the experience of parental unemployment, may be more susceptible to the rhetoric of radical right parties and leaders. Second, societal insecurity brought on by rapidly changing demographics or societal norms and identity as well as specific global, local, and national events—like 9/11 or the 2015 Paris attacks—serve as catalysts to far right and radical right wing engagement. The broader social climate also plays a role; we see bumps in radical right participation following rises in domestic crime and when far right political parties become more visible and vocal. Finally, scholarship has identified personal and individual characteristics that make youth from certain kinds of social backgrounds more likely to espouse radical right views. For many countries, men, rural youth, youth who experienced authoritarian backgrounds, and youth who were incarcerated or in the military are all at higher risk compared to other groups.

All these factors contribute to environments that can make youth more receptive to radical right rhetoric, but they don't fully explain youth engagement in the far right. I suggest that in order to fully understand the attractiveness of the far right, we have to situate these more structural conditions within an analysis of cultural factors, especially related to the emotional underpinnings of extremist engagement.

Extremism's Emotional Pull

Although most analyses of youth engagement in extremist movements globally continue to focus on structural, political, and religious explanations for radicalization and engagement, there is growing awareness that cultural factors play a significant role. The findings I present throughout this book suggest that extremist engagement is driven at least in part by two emotional impulses that young men find especially attractive: the urge to belong and be a part of a group, and the desire to rebel and reject mainstream or adult society.[25]

On the one hand, I argue that youth are drawn to a sense of belonging and identity that they gain from the group, to the male comradeship and bonding they gain from insider status and the sense that they are contributing to something bigger than themselves. On the other hand, youth are attracted to far right, radical, and extremist groups as a space to express anger, rebellion, and resistance against the mainstream. The valorization of violence is threaded through both push and pull factors; both expressions of male comradeship (expressed for example through a sense that one's mates or peers "have my back") and expressions of anger against others (such as immigrants or authorities) frequently directly invoke or evoke physical violence.

Belonging and Comradeship

The emotional pull of extremist engagement works as a mechanism of social integration—allowing young men in particular to strengthen their sense of identity and belonging. There is good evidence that youth propensity to join far right groups, movements, and subcultures is driven in no small part by their desire to belong to a group. Scholarship in this area has largely focused on the role of national identity and nationalist fantasies, the role of peer groups, peer pressure and friendship networks, mechanisms of in-group belonging and group cohesion, and the role of masculinity and hypermasculine aspects of the far right.

Recent scholarship in this area has included for example Pete Simi's work on the performance of violent talk, Daniel Köhler's discussion of the use of humor in the far right, Jens Rydgren's work on nationalist myths and fantasies, and scholarship on the far right music scene and the impact of racist and xenophobic lyrics on recruitment and radicalization.[26] Explanations in these areas of research tend to center around the desire for a sense of belonging, identity, and what Roger Griffin labels "rootedness," combined with "a sense of harmony with the world," a "feeling that your life makes a difference," and a sense of satisfaction from participating in "some event or process larger than oneself."[27] Georg Schuppener, for example, has argued that the public display of symbols using nationalist mythological references "facilitates the production and propagation of identity and a feeling of belonging to the group."[28]

Most of these identity-based explanations rest on an understanding of identity as a major source of meaning and social integration. Belonging to a group with a shared sense of purpose, in this line of thinking, helps people navigate the disorientation of (post)modernity and gives them a sense that they are part of something larger, stronger, and more powerful than themselves.[29] Roger Griffin's work on fascism — most notably his explanation of why Nazism appealed to voters — articulates this nicely.[30] In the context of social change or disruption in modern society, Griffin argues, myths, rituals, or fantasies of a new world order, a rebirth, or a future utopia based on a fantasy of a prior stability take on particular power. The loss of the kind of unifying worldview that was held by traditional societies and that helped make the world meaningful, Griffin argues, has led to a sense of chaos, disorder, and decline for some individuals. This kind of uncertainty and chaos increases the appeal of myths, rituals, and ideas of rebirth and renewal, or the notion of a Phoenix-like rise from the ashes and the dawning of a new era in which "we" (the nation, the people, the *Volk*, etc.) will be on top again. Collective myths, in this context, suggest the possibility of a new moment in which the period of societal despair will be over, in which one is promised to be a part of something bigger and better than oneself.[31] Thus, far right engagement may be motivated by language, symbols, music, or representations that invoke a sense of national or ethnic destiny, of an awakening and renewal, a rebirth, the dawning of a new era or a new world order. Such kinds of symbols and language are peppered throughout much of the commercial clothing and products popular in far right youth scenes, for example, and they are also a part of the discourse of far right parties and election campaigns in a variety of national contexts.

Resistance and Rebellion

The emotional appeal of extremism is not only rooted in a sense of connection and comradeship or a quest for security and stability, however—it is also driven by other emotional impulses such as anger, hatred, and a rejection of societal norms or of mainstream society and its systems. We know from social movement research with other groups that social spaces and subcultural scenes can aid in enacting and expressing countercultural and oppositional cultural beliefs.[32] There is no reason why far right youth subcultures should be any different. Far right engagement may thus be thought of as a mode of resistance and cultural subversion and as a place to protest or express anger against mainstream society and its institutions.

In some cases, this anger is expressed by breaking social norms and taboos or lashing out against a mainstream society that is perceived as corrupt or as having "failed" an individual. Simi, Bubolz, and Hardman's recent work on military experience and far right terrorism, for example, finds that during the transition to far right terrorism from far right extremism, individuals develop a political framing of their own personal experiences, "reframing personal failure as 'unfair betrayal' resulting from a corrupt system."[33] In their research, the experience of involuntary exit from the military created significant anger toward an "unjust system" and helped facilitate the radicalization process toward far right terrorism.[34] The experience of involuntary separation from the military, they suggest, acts to disrupt some individuals' military identity, creating an uncertain future and anger toward a system that has failed him or her.[35] This is not a straightforward formula; rather, they find that "anger finds greater focus after the person begins affiliating with similarly situated individuals."[36] They are very cautious to point out that although a disproportionate number of convicted far right extremists in the United States possess military experience, the majority of military service personnel are not right-wing extremists. But their work shows clearly how emotional and cultural factors add nuance to a situational or structural predictor like involuntary exit from the military, helping disentangle the dynamics and mechanisms through which that predictor works.

Of course, the emotional appeal of issues of identity and belonging and issues of rebellion and resistance are not mutually exclusive. Far right wing engagement may well be a strategy through which values and beliefs are enacted, emotional and oppositional resistance is expressed, *and* identification with peers is fostered simultaneously. These are meaningful engagements that help young people feel part of something bigger than themselves. But to the extent that such groups have strict criteria for belonging in terms of definitions and performances of nationality, race, religion, masculinity, or willingness to be violent, they may also help serve as incubators for further radicalization into extremist scenes or ideologies. In this book, I argue that these two emotional impulses are key to the appeal of the coded, commercialized brands. The brands and symbols, I suggest, help facilitate the construction of far right identity by forging a connection and sense of belonging to other insiders within the scene, and by acting as a mechanism to express rage, resistance, anger, and rebellion against mainstream society, adults, and social taboos. In the second half of this chapter, I turn to the particular role that commercial brands and products are playing in articulating these two cultural aspects of youth extremist engagement: belonging and resistance. But first, I trace the value of a visual and material approach to the study of extremism and identity.

Visual Culture, Material Objects, and Identity

Attention to the aesthetic dimensions of far right subculture is overdue in light of the recent "iconic" turn in the social sciences.[37] Visual and material symbols have long been a core part of classic sociology, dating back at least to Durkheim's notion of totemism and his assertion that material objects hold symbolic power for a community.[38] Scholars have diligently traced the symbolic power that religious objects, national symbols, and other icons have for particular communities, but less attention has been paid to the symbolic power of economic objects.[39] As Bartmański and Alexander aptly note, "because social theory has preferred the trope of disenchantment over totemism, it has either disregarded or stigmatized the metaphorical and emotional power of economic objects."[40] In other words, scholars have long focused more on the Marxist understanding of material objects and their relationship to class-based, economic exploitation than on the Durkheimian approach to material objects as holders of symbolic power. As a result, with a few mostly recent exceptions,[41] scholars have largely ignored the extent to which material objects may have not only exploitative but also constitutive power, potentially shaping the perceptions, desires, engagements, understandings, identities, sense of belonging, or—in this case—extremist participation of consumers.

This constitutive power rests on an understanding of how symbols and images function, which has been well documented in the extensive scholarship in art history on iconography and iconology, but has received less attention from social scientists.[42] The key notion is the idea that images convey meaning beyond their mere aesthetic representation; rather, images and pictures are "encoded texts" that need to be carefully deciphered.[43] Thus, the study of visual culture focuses not only on images themselves, but on how those images are experienced in light of the broader social and cultural context in which they are embedded.[44] This is particularly important in the case of symbols that convey allegorical meaning, using particular iconographical images or motifs to say something about a broader idea or notion (like "the Nation") that must be detected, decoded, and interpreted.[45]

Allegorical symbols — and other symbols that function the same way — act in constitutive ways because they shape observers' understandings and perceptions of the larger idea to which they refer. So images that invoke — or evoke — particular national histories, myths, heroes, legends, or narratives do not simply act as signals of the nation; they also send specific messages about what kind of nation should be aspired to, who belongs to that nation, and what belonging entails. Symbols and images can thus help constitute particular expectations for national identity, and emotional attachments to the nation, as I will argue throughout this book.

Regardless of the precise mechanisms through which images and symbols convey meaning about the nation, it is clear that visual aspects of nationhood have become increasingly central. Historically, political and ideological messages have been conveyed through official media outlets to citizen-recipients.[46] But states have long made use of aesthetic and visual culture as part of their own political marketing, indoctrination, and propaganda; visual symbols help establish and strengthen legitimacy, loyalty, and hegemony for regimes.[47] Radical nationalist and extremist groups have done this as well — the Nazi party's use of iconography, visual culture, and symbols alone was legendary. In the contemporary extremist world, ISIS carefully stages, choreographs, and video-records gruesome beheadings, lynchings, and other executions as part of its propaganda and recruitment strategy. But it is not only formal organizations, regimes, and governments who make use of visual culture for political ends; citizens themselves have also radically transformed how ideological messages are conveyed today, as Lina Khatib argues, noting that "television and radio broadcasts are now supplemented by Internet campaigns, staged actions in public space, the wearing of symbolic attire, the production and consumption of merchandise, posters and other symbolic objects."[48] Youth — who have long been at the helm of social movements, public protests, and marches globally — are at the forefront of this transformation in the appropriation and deployment of visual culture for ideological and political ends.

The use of the body to express and display visual culture adds an additional dimension to this transformation in how symbols and images are deployed for political ends. The use of tattoos, symbolic clothing, and the body more generally for political engagement are part of a broader trend of what Lina Khatib calls the "embodied performances of protesters in public space."[49] Others have started to look more closely at the embodiment of nationalism, such as Kristin Surak's work on how the Japanese tea ceremony acts "on and through the corpus"[50] to define the Japanese nation. I extend Surak's analysis here by examining the embodiment of extremism, focusing on how subcultural style—including clothing but also haircuts, musculature, and other characteristics of physical bodies—enact and perform ideology. I submit that it is precisely at this intersection of material culture, extremist performance, and the embodiment of ideology that we can learn something new about how culture works.

How Culture Works

One of the most enduring debates in mainstream sociology has to do with whether and how cultural elements such as belief systems, values, or norms serve as potential explanations for human behavior, compared with social structural conditions like poverty, unemployment, and educational attainment. Does culture have autonomous power to shape and motivate human behavior, or is it primarily a reflection of social structure?[51] Adding to the expository dilemma is the fact that even sociologists who focus on cultural explanations for human behavior disagree about how culture should be understood and how, exactly, it might "work" as humans make decisions and choices in their daily lives.[52]

At least two dominant approaches exist, one of which presents culture as a coherent meaning system and the other characterizing it as a "tool kit" of actions and strategies.[53] These two competing notions of culture are nicely detailed in Cheris Shun-ching Chan's recent work on life insurance markets in China. On the one hand, culture is understood as a system of meaning—what Chan calls a "constellation" of shared values, meanings, taboos, folklore, moralities, and perceptions that help shape any given individual's or group's "pattern of preferences and dispositions."[54] The alternate approach typically views culture as a repertoire or "tool-kit"[55] of actions, skills, and strategies. Scholars have rather extensively disentangled various ways in which culture works within each framework in a variety of empirical and theoretical settings. I follow Chan's approach in suggesting that the action-oriented strategies of the tool kit—such as the symbol deployment discussed in this book—are best understood as embedded in and constituted by meaning systems. Cultural strategies, as Chan argues, are "anchored in shared meanings" that help determine the "matrix of possibilities."[56] In the context of my work, I argue that coded, commercialized symbols expressing right-wing extremist ideology are strategies that can be understood only within the schematic structures[57] that help people interpret and understand the messages those symbols convey.

My work thus highlights a mechanism that links these two theoretical approaches to culture by showing that symbolic codes are best understood as embedded in and constituted by meaning systems. Coded, commercialized symbols expressing far right ideology are strategies that individuals can deploy from their "tool kits," but they only work if they are interpreted within the broader schematic structures that help people understand the messages those symbols convey. I will argue that cultural symbols can and do motivate young people to engage with extremist movements. But my findings also suggest that such symbols appear to be most powerful for youth who are already marginalized in some way—economically, socially, politically, or otherwise—from mainstream society, and who seek a way of lashing out. In this case, cultural symbols act as a mechanism to radicalize and activate extremist engagement, but primarily for youth who have particular positionality vis-à-vis the social structure. Thus, my findings support the "cultural autonomy" side of the debate about the explanatory power of culture versus social structure but also suggest that culture and cultural symbols are unlikely to work in ways that are wholly independent of social structures, because social structural conditions help determine how receptive individuals are to cultural symbols and signals. I thus agree with Orlando Patterson that it is most fruitful to consider how cultural and social structural dimensions mutually interact with one another in ways that can both constrain and enable human agency.[58]

One way of thinking about how this mechanism works for different youth is through Patterson's notion of sociocultural configuration, which he defines as collections of cultural knowledge and practices that have at their core a set of values and norms that are in turn motivated by shared interests, needs, or goals.[59] Individuals are shaped by multiple configurations simultaneously—by the prevailing mainstream configuration as well as by any number of subcultural configurations or by larger national or global configurations.[60] Such configurations help individuals interpret and process quotidian interactions and make decisions about how to behave. Configurations are a useful way of thinking about how culture works in the empirical case explored in this book because they help explain how young Germans in and around the far right scene deploy the codes both as strategies to facilitate belonging to their peers and as a means to lash out against mainstream society. Youth have access to both the dominant mainstream configuration and to any given subcultural one.

But configurations are also useful because they explain why youth who in many respects appear quite similar have such varied interpretations to the symbols; some understand many layers of complexity in the coded symbols while others miss the intended meanings entirely, even when they are consumers of the products. Some agree with the intended messages while others reject and abhor them. Even among youth who consume the commercialized symbols and products studied in this book, some may become radicalized through their engagement with such symbols, while others remain detached from the ideological content, ultimately discarding or "growing out of" the far right subculture in which those symbols are embedded.

The Revolution in a T-Shirt: Branding Identity, Selling Rebellion

As Pierre Bourdieu famously argued, one's "taste" for particular kinds of clothing or products helps to create and convey social meaning.[61] Commercialized products that market ideological content might thus be understood through the lens of theoretical work on the emergence of a consumerist culture,[62] which suggests that habits of consumption and one's own personal style is interwoven with individual identity and one's sense of purpose.[63] Style is particularly central to youth and even more so to youth subcultural groups, as Dick Hebdige succinctly explained in his well-known treatise on youth subcultures, noting that "style in subculture is . . . pregnant with significance."[64] This is no less true for nationalist consumers, as I have argued previously with Jon Fox. Ordinary people are consumers of the nation, we argue, but are also "its creative producers through everyday acts of consumption."[65] Indeed, the Nazi party's projection of a "notional Aryan body and a race consciousness" onto the swastika forged a connection between image and identity that illustrates how powerful symbols—and logos—can be for the construction of identity.[66]

Recent work on brands suggests that brand names may play a constitutive role in this process. Brands are now seen not just as devices for product promotion, but also as facilitators of particular kinds of social relationships and lifestyles.[67] Eco- or green consumers thus "buy green" both as a reflection on their identity and as a means of strengthening it. Devout religious consumers buy products stamped with the approval of religious authorities in much the same way. Indeed, decisions about what kinds of products to purchase and what meanings are attached to them have been shown to reflect and reinforce identities as green consumers, as African Americans, and as other ethnic identities.[68] In this light, consumption itself can take on a centrality to one's sense of purpose.[69] Processes of circulation and exchange are thus not merely transmitters of meaning but are also "constitutive acts in themselves."[70] But despite increasing scholarship on the ways in which consumption is a constitutive act, there has been little theoretical articulation about how symbols—including but not limited to logos—play a role in such identity construction.

Clothing choices simultaneously allow youth to express and construct their own identities.[71] Brands and products within the far right scene should thus be understood as having the capacity to create community and forge or strengthen identities, rather than merely reflecting existing national identities and fantasies.[72] The brands I study here market and sell identity, complete with explanatory myths and legends told in texts on their commercial websites. As Geneviève Zubrzycki argues, "the incarnation of national mythology into cultural forms that come to life in various practices is not merely reflective of national identity, but constitutive of it. . . . National mythology can generate sentiments of national belonging."[73] This is no less true, I suggest, if nationalist mythology shows up in the form of a T-shirt than if it shows up in a textbook.

It may be that the use of coded far right symbols in commercial products is particularly compelling for certain kinds of youth in the postmodern era. Literature on the performance of symbols within youth populations would suggest that for youth, material expressions of identity are becoming more important in light of the flexible identities of (post)modernity.[74] Youth consumption of coded right-wing extremist brands may enable them to feel socially integrated and express both individual and group self-identification.[75] Symbols may provide a source of meaning in an otherwise overwhelming and disorienting world and a sense that youth are part of something larger, stronger, and more powerful than themselves.[76] The loss of identity for youth from the former east Germany, who surveys have shown have higher rates of right-wing attitudes, may have led to symbols becoming increasingly significant for youth from the former east.[77] In sum, coded symbols and other new and commercialized forms of right-wing and nationalist ideology might be attractive to youth because they strengthen their sense of connection and self-identification with an in-group. In this way, symbols and brands that market nationalist identity in Germany are not unlike John and Jean Comaroff's analysis of the commodification of Tswana heritage in South Africa, where a local newspaper op-ed argued that the marketing of "what is 'authentically Tswana' is also a mode of reflection, of self-construction, of *producing* and *feeling* Tswana-ness."[78]

This does not mean that the meaning of particular clothing choices for a given consumer can automatically be assumed, as Colin Campbell has argued; consumers choose to purchase clothing and wear clothing for a wide variety of reasons, not all of which relate to identity or the symbolic message intended for others.[79] And the ways in which subcultural styles are received and interpreted by observers and outsiders is critically dependent on context, as the youth I interviewed emphatically argue in chapter 2. But it does mean that consumption of clothing and other consumer products may have the power to shape consumers' identities in ways that we have not yet acknowledged for extremist youth cultures and scenes.

Commercial brands that deploy far right coded symbols are not only selling identity; they are also marketing rebellion and resistance to the mainstream. Symbols, logos, and brands thus do more than help forge a sense of belonging with insiders—they also act as mechanisms of resistance against mainstream society. Style can play a critical role in this regard, as Hebdige's seminal work on punk scenes and the commodification of subcultural style showed; subcultural challenges to hegemonic authorities, Hebdige argued, are expressed "obliquely, in style."[80] Symbols are also key, as James Scott contends, because it is "not the mere existence of deviant subcultural themes" that matters but "rather the forms they may take, the values they embody, and the emotional attachment they inspire."[81] Symbols—as emotionally laden visual representations—are thus a powerful form of cultural expression not only within subcultures but also between subcultures and mainstream societies. Especially in the analyses in chapters 2, 4, 5, and 6, I will show that the deployment of coded, commercialized symbols in brands popular with the far right act as a conduit of youth resistance.[82] Youth gain a sense of power, secrecy, and the appeal of resisting authority through the consumption of forbidden and banned symbols that are often undetectable by adults and outsiders.

While the symbols are important, in other words, the coding and manipulation of those symbols is even more central to the notion of oppositional resistance. Coded, commercialized symbols may act as conduits of youth resistance to a perceived pressure to conform to societal expectations about what youth should be.[83] For the largely male, working-class youth who make up the bulk of memberships and affiliations in the German far right,[84] the display of banned and abhorrent right-wing extremist symbols may thus be a form of protest and youth resistance—of what Scott called "weapons of the weak."[85] Coding and the use of cryptic symbols may enable members of a group who feel powerless to exert control through protest, both by selectively disclosing and concealing aspects of their identity[86] and by manipulating symbols and coding in reaction to both the "hard" repression of official bans and censorship and the "soft" repression of stigma, ridicule, or silencing.[87] The expression and manipulation of symbolic codes—many of which are abhorred by the general public—may create agency for youth who feel constrained by the adult world they are entering. The game-playing aspect of subverting bans can provide youth with a sense of power and secrecy; for example, when one German school banned "88" from clothing, young people began wearing T-shirts with the phrase "100–12" (one hundred minus twelve).[88] In this sense, youth's acts of consumption and bricolage—their linking together of often disparate and sometimes contradictory cultural symbols and fragments—may be understood as everyday forms of resistance.[89]

Coded symbols and other new cultural forms of extremism would thus be attractive to youth not only because of what they mean for the in-group but also because of what they mean vis-à-vis the out-group—in particular, mainstream adults and society. Such an approach to the study of symbols is an extension of prior scholarship on symbolic codes, much of which has focused on the reception by subaltern groups of dominant and hegemonic cultural codes and myths, particularly through the work of scholars at the Birmingham Centre for Contemporary Cultural Studies.[90] The Birmingham school has been critiqued, however, for overemphasizing resistance and has also tended to intentionally or inadvertently position codes as merely a "tool" to resistance efforts.[91] So where James Scott, for example, sees symbols and ideological forms as "indispensable background" to everyday resistance,[92] I hypothesize that symbols—and their manipulation—themselves can constitute a form of resistance. By focusing on the production and manipulation of codes from within subcultural scenes—and the meanings attached to those codes—the symbols therefore themselves take center stage. Thinking of symbols as having autonomous power within social movements, I would argue, also directly challenges recent critiques insisting that culture cannot have causal power.[93]

It may be hard to think of a T-shirt as an everyday form of resistance. After all, T-shirts are easily dismissed, even discarded. They are among the least expensive items of western wear, provided free with marathon registration and charity fundraisers. But as the following chapters will show, the T-shirt deserves more attention for its performative value and for forging a link among style, national(ist) belonging, rebellion, and capitalist profit.[94] As the youth themselves made very clear, T-shirts—and clothing styles more generally—are deeply intertwined with their own sense of identity and their friendship groups. Along with other elements of subcultural style and clothing, T-shirts are a medium to enact modes of belonging and resistance for youth in and around far right scenes.

Fitting In, Growing Up: Peer Groups and Extremist Style

Clothing, fashion, and style are central to youth identity and peer groups in ways that many adults overlook.[95] This is particularly true for the study of youth radicalization. While scholars who study urban gangs, skaters, preps, punks, jocks, and other adolescent peer groups have acknowledged youth style as part of subcultural scenes,[96] work on youth extremism has tended to focus more on political and ideological content and less on the role that culture and in particular subcultural style might play in extremist recruitment and radicalization.

Part of the problem is rooted in the fact that extremist engagement is highly gendered, and young men's connection to fashion, body image, and style has received far less attention in general, compared to young women. But it's also the case that researchers who work on extremist youth have focused efforts on ideological underpinnings, xenophobia, propensity to violence, and other potential explanatory variables including authoritarian background, parental education, and lack of viable employment. While there is little doubt that such factors are important conditions for extremist engagement, I suggest that subcultural style also plays an important role that has been largely overlooked. In general, I will argue, there is much to be learned about the appeal of extremist groups—whether right wing or not—from an analysis of groups' subcultural style. In the case of the far right subcultural scene, I show that style in general and clothing choices in particular foster group identification and belonging and enable the expression of resistance and anger against the mainstream. The coding and game-playing aspects of the new subcultural styles work in particular to forge insider identification, belonging, and connection to others in the scene and simultaneously perform and embody violence and aggression, acting as tools for rebellion and lashing out against societal taboos and adult authorities.

Like other subcultural groups, far right youth have historically been most identifiable by their physical appearance—through the late 1990s as skinheads, and more recently through the consumption and display of particular brand names.[97] But little is known about how, or why, extremist style is important to youth. My interviews with youth suggest there are three fundamental issues for understanding the relationship between style and extremist engagement. First, style is extremely important—even central—to young men's identity and is closely connected to their peer and friendship groups. This is especially true for far right youth, for whom subcultural style is one of the most visible characteristics of belonging—so much so that observers often refer to youth in the scene by their style (e.g., calling them "bald heads"—*Glatze*—or referring to "those with very short hair"). Second, and relatedly, youth who are or were far right noted that their peer and friendship groups and the style in general was a clear entry point into the far right scene, describing how "everyone" was wearing an Alpha Industries jacket, for example, and so they got one too and then became more embedded in far right youth culture. Finally, across the interviews, youth repeatedly emphasized that style alone does not signify far right membership or ideology, but rather, any given brand, code, symbol, or other stylistic element is multivocal and can be understood as right wing only in the context of multiple contextual clues that signify belonging to the far right.

The T-shirt itself plays an important role as a tool for communication; it is the primary commercial product through which coded messages are deployed and performed. It acts as a sort of ideological billboard, transforming the body—an especially the back of the body—into a screen.[98] Youth were often quite astute in their understanding of how T-shirts were used in this way. As the introduction explained, Timo, a twenty-two-year-old scaffold builder apprentice, argued that the display of symbols valorizing violence is intentional: "if you didn't wear it on a T-shirt, it wouldn't be visible." But people choose to wear such T-shirts, he argues, so that the symbols can be seen, and they can convey their wearers' readiness to be violent. Georg, a twenty-one-year-old scaffold builder, equated the appeal of Nordic-symbol-laden clothing to the styles of people who choose to live a "green" lifestyle, arguing that T-shirts might help people who like Nordic heritage express that identity. "My uncle also became an eco," he explains; "he only eats tofu and honey-melon and whatever, y'know? . . . If he wears a T-shirt that says 'no meat, eat plants' or whatever, he's trying to express something with that." In a discussion about school bans on clothing, Mahmut, a twenty-one-year-old technical conservation apprentice, argued that people should be able to wear what they want because clothing "represents one's character, and if one is a Nazi, good, in my opinion he should wear a Nazi-T-Shirt, I don't care."

Youth described intentional choices in their clothing and style, arguing that clothing expresses identity and reflects various phases of identity building during adolescence in particular. Dennis, a nineteen-year-old civil engineering technician apprentice, describes himself as extremely attentive to brand names, which he says developed through his friendship group. Thomas, an eighteen-year-old apprentice in building energy design, described the close interplay between peer groups and personal style: "if you dress differently, you'd get into different circles, and then those would be different friends," but he later clarifies that he thinks people choose friends first and then adapt their style to that of their friends. Either way, Thomas suggests, one's own personal style is closely related to one's broader peer groups. Martin, who self-identified as a far right nationalist, explains that he received positive feedback from peers when he wore far right clothing in ways that encouraged his consumption of the brands. "The first time I got myself a T-shirt, it was from Thor Steinar, and then I came with the T-shirt and 'oh man, what a cool T-shirt you have on,' yeah, there was positive feedback when you got something."

Young men are also hyperaware of their peers' opinions about them. Tobias, a twenty-one-year-old civil engineering technician apprentice, explained that "from about age twelve to sixteen . . . it was really crass, it was so, so important that you wore brand-name clothes, or else you always stood in the back of the line and y'know. I think, actually it's just a phase of youth . . . of growing up. Exactly in this adolescent age, when you are trying everything and doing everything and want to prove yourself and be cool." When peers engage with the far right, it becomes easy to follow the crowd. Artur, a twenty-two-year-old concrete layer apprentice, argued that becoming right wing was to some extent a matter of having the bad luck to grow up among peer groups who were right wing. "Some people just had really bad luck, I sometimes think. . . . They happened to grow up with people like that, and they don't get any other perspectives, and they don't have any chance to really think otherwise, that's what I think about some of them." Simon, a twenty-year-old studying to earn his technical high school degree, explains that youth's "small dislike for foreigners" can grow into something worse if one lands "in the wrong friendship group, [then] it escalates until at some point you shave your head." Eckart, a twenty-one-year-old masonry apprentice, reflects that "if I had grown up in a [right-wing] group, where this is always a topic . . . this Germanic culture, then we'd probably wear it too. Or if we were something like rockers, we would grow our hair out and . . . [I have] no idea what they wear [laughs]." It is abidingly clear that peer groups, ideology, and clothing choices become closely interwoven in early-to-mid adolescence. When young people's peer groups are part of extremist scenes, then, clothing choice becomes part of the embodiment of extremist ideology.[99] I return to this issue through a deeper analysis of the interview data in chapter 2.

Consuming and Performing Extremist Style

The youth interviewed for this study have grown up in home and school environments where far right attitudes and engagements were a steady presence—they are, as I described in the introduction, youth who I consider to be in and around the far right youth subcultural scene. At the time most of these youth were in early adolescence—in the mid-to-late 2000s—far right youth culture was a strong presence in several neighborhoods in east Berlin, the surrounding state of Brandenburg, and cities like Leipzig, where many of the youth interviewed for this study grew up. A March 2009 national survey published by Niedersachsen's Criminological Research Institute (Kriminologischen Forschungsinstitut Niedersachsen), based on data from nearly forty-five hundred fifteen-year-olds in Germany, reported that 5 percent of fifteen-year-old young men identified themselves as members of a far right group.[100] The same survey showed that 14.4 percent of fifteen-year-olds were "very xenophobic," while an additional 26.2 percent were "rather xenophobic."[101] Similar figures were reported in the 2016 Leipziger "Mitte" study, but with significant differences between young people in east and west Germany: 23.7 percent of fourteen- to thirty-year-olds in east Germany and 13.7 percent of fourteen- to thirty-year-olds in west Germany had xenophobic attitudes.[102]

Youth who hold xenophobic attitudes may fall into the category of young people who are "sympathizers" of far right activities, meaning that they express understanding and support for xenophobic or far right violence, even if they do not engage themselves. Despite a strong antifascist movement and ongoing state efforts to combat the far and radical right, throughout the early part of the twenty-first century, far right extremist attitudes and youth engagement remain a significant problem in parts of Germany. The young people interviewed for this book sometimes referred to far right youth in their neighborhoods in ways similar to gangs, describing groups of adolescents and young men who moved and hung out as a group around train stations, bars, and neighborhood streets. While most research on the far right studies youth who are actively engaged with or have left far right extremist groups, I argue that this broader category of youth—sympathizers, observers, and *Mitläufer* (those who run along with the crowd)—are also critical to understand. They are a part of what I call youth who are "in and around" far right scenes. These are the youth I study here.

We did not ask youth directly if they were a part of the far right scene. Only one of the fifty-one youth I interviewed came straight out and identified himself as far right during the interview (he identified as a right-wing nationalist), and one additional youth volunteered earlier active engagement with the far right, during early-to-mid adolescence. Several other youth hinted at current or former engagement with the far right scene more obliquely, explaining that their peer groups were primarily right wing or through descriptions of their clothing brands, music tastes, or activities like attending a far right demo. Still others expressed ideological views consistent with far right positions, making statements that were Islamophobic, anti-Semitic, xenophobic, anti-immigrant, racist, or nationalistic, even though those positions sometimes contradicted other statements they made. It was not uncommon, for example, for students to condemn the far right but criticize headscarves, or criticize racism but make an anti-Semitic comment. Most of these youth have been long-term observers of peers and youth they knew who were actively engaged in the far right—in their neighborhoods, in their schools and classrooms, and now, as apprentices, at their work sites. Forty-eight of the fifty-one youth had intimate knowledge of or exposure to the far right scene through either personal engagement; current or former ownership of a brand associated with the far right; family, friends, or classmates who owned such clothing; or family, friends, or classmates who they said were currently or formerly far right. While a few of the youth had never been actively or directly engaged in far right youth subculture, and did not know anyone who owns the brands, even these youth were attending schools where far right subcultures are a steady presence.

Exposure to the far right occurs in a variety of ways for these youth. Benjamin, for example, a twenty-two-year-old technical assistant apprentice who grew up in a suburb of Berlin known for its high population of far right youth, described how a right-wing extremist band had distributed their album at his school when he was younger. "You figure it out pretty quickly," he explained, "when [you're listening and] then a song comes up like 'My grandfather was a *Sturmführer* with the SS' or something like that."[103] In interviews, well over a third (twenty-one) of the youth identified friends, acquaintances, classmates, neighbors, or relatives who they knew or suspected were far right. Youth frequently mentioned other youth in their classes who wore clothing associated with the far right. In the middle of an interview, for example, Eckart, a twenty-one-year-old masonry apprentice, looked at an image of a Thor Steinar shirt and noted that one of his classmates was wearing the same shirt today. "Too bad he's not doing the interview here," he laughed, explaining that he thinks his classmate wears the clothing to "get a lot of attention to his right-wing scene." Georg looked at the same image and said, "I have that shirt hanging in my closet," while Martin simply noted, "Yeah, I know that [shirt.] A friend of mine has it."

Table 1. Youth Association with Far Right Scene*

	SELF	FAMILY/ FRIENDS	CLASSMATES/ NEIGHBOR/ ACQUAINTANCE	TOTALS AS UNIQUE INDIVIDUALS
Part of far right scene (current or former)	2	7	17	21 youth who are, were, or have family/ friends in far right
Owns/wears clothing associated with far right	25	25	30	43 youth who own, owned, or know someone who owns/ owned brands
Volunteered views consistent with far right ideology	9	N/A	N/A	9 youth
Other exposure	35	N/A	N/A	35 youth

*As evidenced through voluntary remarks in interviews. We did not ask youth directly if they were currently or formerly engaged in the far right; the two youth classified here as "part of the far right scene" volunteered this information. Others hinted at prior involvement but were not included in this cell here.

In total, twenty-one of the fifty-one youth mentioned friends, family, classmates, neighbors, or acquaintances who they identified as currently or formerly part of the far right scene. Forty-three of fifty-one were either consumers of brands known to be part of the far right or had family, friends, classmates, neighbors, or acquaintances who consumed such products. Across the interviews, forty-eight of fifty-one youth had intimate knowledge of the far right scene through either current or former ownership of a brand associated with the far right; family, friends, or classmates who owned such clothing; or family, friends, or classmates who are in the far right scene or used to be. We classified three youth as having "no exposure" based on their interviews, but even these three youth were attending schools where far right youth are a steady presence.

In sum, the youth I interviewed were all excellent informants about the far right scene, whether from within or from outside. "I know both sides," explained Dennis, a nineteen-year-old civil engineering technician apprentice; "I know a lot of foreigners, and I also know a lot of right-wing [people]." Joachim, a twenty-three-year-old masonry apprentice who implied that he had been part of the far right scene when he was younger, admits that his friendship group is "all right wing," although he says he is not. "No, I distanced myself from it, well I said to them, in their free time they should do what they want, but I don't want to know about any of that, because I also have a lot of foreign friends. . . . [My right-wing friends] are cool with that."

Nineteen-year-old Felix describes a "buddy on the *Ostsee* [Baltic Sea] who hangs out . . . with people who, well, no one is really sure if they are Nazis or not. They style themselves that way and are [open to] racists, but they also have foreign friends and behave more or less normal." Some youth related stories about far right youth in their neighborhoods who had ended up in prison or who regularly engaged in violent episodes. Tobias talked at length about growing up in Königs Wusterhausen, which he describes as having been "very, very well known" for its heavy right wing youth presence. Every Friday when he was growing up, far right youth were involved in violent fights and shootings at the disco next to the train station. After the police started to heavily monitor the region, he says, the violence significantly subsided.

Most of the youth interviewed pointed to a current friend, relative, classmate, or peer who owned or wore clothing associated with the far right. Several of them currently own one or more brands of clothing deemed a known identifier of far right subculture or mentioned that they had owned such brands when they were younger (see table 1 for a quantitative breakdown of youth association with far right scenes across the sample). However, their narratives about the clothing—how they obtained it, why they wore it, and whether they think it should be banned—tell a more complicated story than the prevailing public and media narrative about the far right brands has told. I return to this question in chapter 2.

Style as a Gateway to Extremism

One of the most frequent questions I have received over the years of working on this project is whether and how the clothing and subcultural style facilitates far right and extremist actions and engagement. People sometimes expressed skepticism that clothing could be consequential for recruitment into or radicalization within far right subcultures. How, after all, could a T-shirt or a jacket enable extremist engagement? Does the clothing actually mobilize youth to engage in the far right, or provide credibility within it?

The answer to these questions is complicated. On the one hand, there are indications that the hardest-core right-wing extremists—those who are most ideologically committed to and active in far right movements, political parties, or terrorist cells—do not adhere to far right subcultural style. For high-ranking members or deeply embedded right-wing extremists, the kinds of subcultural style discussed here may be seen as reflecting a less serious commitment to far right ideology, politics, and goals or could be at odds, as Daniel Köhler suggests, with intentional efforts to blend into or legitimize themselves within the mainstream. Köhler describes members of right-wing movements' "upper ranks" who may be in professional roles such as "lawyers, politicians, or doctors" and may be "more dangerous to society in the long run (e.g., by leading groups, bringing innovation and new recruits, and/or radicalizing others)" than more violent "foot soldiers" in the lower ranks.[104] This group of extreme far right activists and organizers may be less likely to consume the kinds of subcultural style discussed in this book. A few of the youth made this point, arguing that the clothing was unlikely to be popular with those who have official roles or very strong ideological engagements with the far right.

"Real right-wing radicals don't wear stuff like that," Georg explained, and he then contrasts what he sees as "dumb" or "naïve" teenagers with the political objectives of the National Democratic Party of Germany (NPD)—a far right party whose legitimacy is frequently debated but that remains legal.[105] "For example, I know the head of the NPD in Berlin, Udo Voigt, personally," Georg continued, launching into a brief discussion of the party before noting, "The NPD has a totally normal clothing style." Others made the distinction between serious right-wing extremist political engagement and far right subcultural style during the interviews. Artur, a twenty-two-year-old concrete layer apprentice, said "I also recently heard that the Nazis that one doesn't recognize at first glance, they are supposed to be even worse than the skinheads." Benjamin, a twenty-two-year-old technical assistant apprentice, notes that people who wear Alpha Industries jackets are sympathizers rather than politically active in far right organizations. "I think [people who wear Alpha Industries] hold the [same] opinion, crappy foreigner and fuck off and you're an Asian and . . . blah blah, pure blood . . . but if push comes to shove, I don't think they would necessarily do anything, at least I hope so." Twenty-one-year-old roofing apprentice Klaus thinks that people who "really stand for these things wouldn't dress [as if they believe that]. . . . They are smarter than that." Instead, he says, such individuals are more likely to go around "dressed just like us, totally normal" so that they could pass through society undetected, but still go to meetings where they shout "hateful things against foreigners."

The youth I interviewed for this study, however, fall into a different category than the kinds of right-wing extremists Georg, Artur, Benjamin, and Klaus are describing. These youth are not, for the most part, fully committed far right radicals. Instead, they mostly exist at the margins of the far right, occasionally moving in and out of the scene through social events and interactions with peers, classmates, and family members. Some participated in formal far right groups or scenes as younger adolescents, and others wear clothing associated with the far right, go to right-wing concerts, and socialize with friends they describe as right wing. For this group of youth — young people at the peripheries of the far right, who may move in and out of the far right scene over time — far right clothing does appear to help recruit and provide access to far right events and settings where normal attire might prevent entry. Without question, the clearest example of how this works came from Martin, who self-identified as an active right-wing nationalist. Martin described clothing as an entry ticket to concerts and events where dressing normally would raise a red flag. He explained, "When I go out the clothes are actually really important, because you won't get in to a lot of events at all if you're not dressed [as a right-wing person]." He described the challenges of gaining access to underground, word-of-mouth concerts and events that are "mostly not exactly out in the open and not officially accessible" but are rather held "somewhere in a back courtyard." If someone shows up who is dressed normally, he explains, it can be a problem: "because you never know if he's from the press or something." Later, when people start to know you, he says, it can be a different story: "man, I've seen you a lot, yeah, come on in." But "if you go somewhere alone, for the first time with normal clothes," he asserts simply, "you won't get in at all." Martin wears the clothing as a way of signaling membership to other insiders: "well, when I wear this clothing now, it's not that I'm expecting some kind of aggressive contact. I actually wear the clothing so that someone like-minded sees it. It's often said that people wear this clothing in order to provoke, but that's actually not true for us at all. We identify ourselves through the clothing. If you see someone wearing Thor Steinar, then you know, aha, that's someone who thinks the same way [ein Gleichgesinnter]." Provided it was another young person wearing the clothing, it could also facilitate a connection, but generational boundaries still prevail: "you nod at the person, but it depends. . . . If some fifty-year-old is wearing Thor Steinar, I'm not going to go up to him as a sixteen-year-old and start chatting."

Other youth mentioned situations where the clothing might act as a recruiting tool or at least as an entry point to the far right scene, or showed how such engagement could take place in a casual interaction. For example, Jan, a seventeen-year-old masonry apprentice, described a "right-wing oriented" classmate who brought a Thor Steinar catalog to school and showed it to him (in the context of showing him something he had bought). During our interview, Georg pulled out the Yakuza catalog and gave it to the interviewer, warning her not to be shocked by the "crass motifs." Rainer, an eighteen-year-old technical conservation apprentice, explained that people who wear T-shirts with these kinds of messages on them are protesting something and sending a message "to politicians." Such a T-shirt would be useful to someone "who would maybe prefer that [historical] time or another epoch more and is looking for followers." Twenty-year-old construction mechanic apprentice Niel explained that mainstream style is a strategy to recruit and gain access to youth. The far right "is blending in to what's in fashion, in order to—well, one hears that they are reaching out to youth. Yeah, 'we have nice clothing and everything, don't you want to wear something like that?'"

Timo noted that clothing doesn't automatically create entry into the far right scene, but it does facilitate access. If someone wanted to "not be an outsider anymore," for example, or wanted to "expand his friendship group," the clothing could help him get into a far right group. "You can't just wear Thor Steinar clothes and automatically be a member of the right-wing scene," he noted. "You can buy it, but then of course you have to find the people who are also part of the schema, who belong to these groups. And of course one option would be to go to a soccer stadium," he says, and walk up to "people who look a little aggressive" and talk to them. But it would help, he agreed in response to an interviewer question, if one is wearing clothing that is a part of the far right scene.

Several youth used the term *Gleichgesinnter* (like-minded person) in discussions about the purpose of the clothing, noting that the messages help create feelings of togetherness vis-à-vis other insiders and help find and identify others who think similarly. It's not always completely clear to outsiders if clothing is far right, says eighteen-year-old electrician apprentice Finn. "But they know it," he said, explaining that it helps far right youth recognize one another. Lukas, a twenty-two-year-old carpentry apprentice, also described situations where clothing can help to find friends or "like minded people" and argued that the clothing acts as a conversation starter. "You go into a bar or someplace to party, you see someone with Thor Steinar clothing on and so you think . . . oh, here, do you also have . . . and that's really cool and whatever. . . . It's strange that people get to know one another through clothing brands." He continues with an explanation of why the brands would work this way, noting that the brands might help connect people who have similar politics. It helps people recognize others who think like them, which is important, he explains, because it helps them realize "OK, maybe I'm not so alone after all or I'm not the only one who can't exactly identify with mainstream society." The clothing also likely enhances and strengthens youth's identity within the far right scene, as twenty-four-year-old carpentry apprentice Steffen explained. It provides a "group-togetherness feeling, symbolism. We are one, we wear the same thing. We symbolize Thor Steinar and Thor Steinar symbolizes right-wing ideas. . . . Well, Thor Steinar was only just an [example], could have also been Lonsdale or something."

Conclusion

While scholars have primarily attended to political motivations for extremist engagement and have spent significant time teasing out key factors in extremist radicalization—such as economic uncertainty or reactions to social change—it is clear that cultural motivations play a significant role as well. In particular, the emotional tension between the desire to belong and the desire to rebel appears to be a key factor in the appeal of the coded symbols and messaging in brands that market to the far right. In theoretical terms, it is clear that mainstream sociologists have overlooked the constitutive power that economic objects—such as the T-shirt—can have in shaping identity and even extremist engagement. These findings challenge not only how scholars have typically thought about symbols and their role in meaning making, in other words, but also how economic objects relate to identity more broadly. I return to these claims in the conclusion in a discussion of the theoretical implications of this work.

In more practical terms, developing a richer understanding of why and how youth are attracted to—and engage in—the far right is critically important. The interview data cannot draw definitive causal claims about the relationship between far right subcultural style and engagement in broader far right scenes, actions, or violence. More research with larger samples is sorely needed. But what these youth do make clear is that the clothing acts as a potential gateway to far right scenes, facilitating access, communicating political views, helping far right youth find others with similar opinions and attitudes, and providing some measure of credibility to insiders. The clothing also clearly helps strengthen identity and a sense of belonging, as I address more directly in the chapters to come.

2 BRANDING IDENTITY

Coded Symbols and Game Playing

Nazis don't look like Nazis anymore.

—Justin, seventeen-year-old carpentry apprentice

Transformations in far right style are enabling youth to blend in to the mainstream in ways that were previously unimaginable for the far right. Young people in and around the scene are well aware of this. Kevin, a thirty-nine-year-old studying for his technical high school degree, suggested that the new subcultural styles allow the far right to "present themselves in a better light." The changes help them to be a part of the mainstream rather than stay at the margins of society, he noted, giving them a more average appearance "that also comes across as friendly, not so martial and brutal, y'know?"

Far right youth today eschew the "old" neo-Nazi or skinhead style of shaved heads, bomber jackets, and high black boots that had become popular with British and German far right youth in the 1980s and 1990s. Instead, they embrace a broad array of styles and clothing with multiple coded symbols conveying varied aspects of far right ideology and beliefs.[1] The origins of this shift, which is traced in the robust German scholarship on far right youth cultures, date to the late 1990s and early 2000s.[2] Early dramatic changes came about shortly after the turn of the century with the emergence of the Autonomous Nationalist movement, which embraced the aesthetics, symbols, and protest strategies of the far left wing in a deliberate attempt to confuse authorities and counterprotesters at right-wing actions and demonstrations.[3] The all-black Autonomous Nationalist style, often paired with hooded sweatshirts with the hoods drawn over the head, sunglasses, and scarves across the lower part of the face, represented a significant shift from skinhead style in its aesthetics, but less so in its uniformity of form. Indeed, the uniformity of the style was linked to the movement's "black bloc" strategy—a social movement tactic directly lifted from leftist activists in which groups of identically dressed, disguised protesters move as a "block" against counterprotesters or police.[4]

The Autonomous Nationalist movement was and is notable because of its stark divergence from the skinhead aesthetic. But it was also important because by co-opting leftist style for the far right, the movement set a new precedent that opened the door to a broader adoption of a variety of mainstream styles. Within a few years, the aesthetic dimensions of the far right scene fragmented and expanded. Today, there are reportedly dozens of brands popular with far right youth, some dozen of which are most clearly recognizable as part of far right subculture. Some of these are brands that market products deliberately laced with overt far right references as well as carefully coded symbols and images, while others are brands that have been appropriated within the far right scene because of coincidentally symbolic logos or symbols. All the brands' appeal rests at least in part on the ways in which these coded symbols communicate meaning, express ideology, and create a sense of belonging.

Manipulating Culture: Coded Symbols and Far Right Clothing

Symbols have a long history as devices that help transmit meaning and forge emotional ties.[5] Social movement groups across the political spectrum utilize symbols as a form of performative communication, not only to express and market their ideological beliefs, but also to strengthen a sense of belonging among group members. Even before the emergence of nations, family crests, shields, coats of arms and other symbols of nobility, communities, and religions helped to distinguish tribal and regional boundaries and mark those who belong to the group.[6] The advent of nations in the seventeenth and eighteenth centuries was accompanied by a variety of new symbols, from national flags and anthems to poetic verses, all meant to evoke national feelings and emotions, creating a sense of belonging and identification with others who shared the same geographic boundaries or ethnic ties within the new "imagined community" of the nation.[7] Later, the tremendous violence and nationalism of the nineteenth and twentieth centuries rose on a tide of political symbols and military insignia—the hammer and sickle, the Christian cross, the Islamic moon and crescent, a variety of eagles, and perhaps most famously, the swastika.[8]

Such symbols—along with iconic figures or nationalist colors—became images that can be circulated and recirculated in order to convey particular messages and evoke emotional responses from viewers. The use of images to sell products—through advertisements but also as part of the product itself—is, in this light, part of a longer trajectory through which human beings have used images to promote and convey ideas, build loyalty, cultivate belonging, and distinguish themselves from others.[9] Economic objects thus need to be understood as conveyers of symbolic meaning, carrying largely unspoken, intended, and unintended messages. These messages are complex and multivocal, as Roland Barthes notes, potentially containing a "galaxy of signifiers" that have no beginning, are reversible, and are accessible in multiple ways.[10] Subcultural style—its clothing, haircuts, musculature, tattoos, and more—contain "hidden messages inscribed in code," as Dick Hebdige argues, and our task as researchers is to disentangle those codes into "maps of meaning."[11]

There are currently over 150 recognized symbols and codes associated with the extreme right wing in Germany alone, ranging from specialized tattoos and T-shirt slogans to the appropriation of non-right-wing brands like New Balance (because the "N" in the shoe's logo is meant to symbolize "Nazi" or "neo-Nazi").[12] Thor Steinar, for example, does not have official far right connections but markets to a right-wing consumer base, selling fashionable articles of clothing laced with complex historical and contemporary codes, such as a pair of €80 jeans called "Rudolf," named for Hitler's deputy Rudolf Hess.[13] Some of the commercial products exploit—and drive—the complex coding evident in the game-playing culture that characterizes the new far right scene, such as the Thor Steinar T-shirt with an image of a fox and the words "Desert Fox: Afrikakorps"—codes that refer to the nickname of Erwin Rommel, who commanded German troops in North Africa during World War II. Others are more straightforward, like the T-shirt with the word "Aryan" sold by Ansgar Aryan. As new symbols and commercial logos appear, various public and private institutions may ban them, as chapter 5 discusses in depth.[14]

The coding phenomena is not unique to the German far right, of course—prison gangs and other youth subcultural groups in the United States and elsewhere, for example, have a long history of using coded symbols. Nor is the coding an entirely contemporary phenomenon—some of the current codes in play, for example, are modified versions of Nazi symbols used in the Third Reich. And commercial right-wing products have been around from some time, as the introduction detailed, from the Nazi kitsch of the Third Reich to the patches, buttons, stickers, and T-shirts for sale through mail-order flyers and brochures or at right-wing rock concerts in the 1980s and 1990s. But the current wave of commercialization reflects a noted transformation in the ways in which cultural symbols are being not only manipulated but also packaged and sold in sophisticated consumer goods that are deliberately marketed to far right youth.

This chapter focuses in particular on how the game-playing aspect of the codes work, using two categories of codes—alphanumeric sequences and embedded historical references—to illustrate. In addition to the analysis of symbols from the image archive, I draw here on interview data with young Germans in and around the far right scene to show the extent to which they understand the codes embedded in various brands and deployed by youth. In the latter part of the chapter, I offer a summary analysis of the evolution of extremist style and its meanings for youth in and around the far right scene. First, though, I turn to a close examination of how the coded symbols and game playing work in far right youth subculture.

Alphanumeric Codes and Game Playing

One of the oldest forms of coding relies on the sequencing of alphabetical letters to form acronyms and abbreviations; far right youth take the alphabetic and acronym formation one step further by using sequences of numbers to stand for letters, or in combination with letters or mathematical equations.[15] Historically, such codes were used by imprisoned Nazis and German soldiers in order to communicate their status as Nazi party members or SS soldiers.[16] Today, youth use the codes to communicate with other insiders but also to navigate social stigma and circumvent federal and state bans on right-wing extremist symbols as well as place-specific bans and dress codes in schools and stadiums. Such alphanumeric codes tend to be widely recognized among far right researchers, educational policy makers, and activists, although they are less well known among the general public, and they undergo frequent modification. Codes are also easy to overlook when they are encountered in unexpected or new contexts.

Alphanumeric codes are ubiquitous in youth extremist scenes both within and beyond Germany, on license plates, telephone numbers, T-shirts, tattoos, and even giant Styrofoam letters in football stadium stands. The most common coded references glorify Nazi-era or contemporary extremist leaders, events, or groups. For example, the number 18 represents the first and eighth letters of the alphabet, AH, which in turn stand for Adolf Hitler, while 88 is used for HH (Heil Hitler). The number 28 is used for Blood and Honour, an organization that was banned until 2010 (see chapter 5). The number 84 stands for the letters H and D for "Heil Deutschland," while 19/8 is a stand-in for "Sieg Heil," a Nazi greeting. The number 14 is used in reference to the number of words in a quote from the late American neo-Nazi David Lane ("We must secure the existence of our people and a future for white children").[17] The number 1919 stands for SS, while 444 stands for DDD, for "Deutschland den Deutschen" ("Germany for Germans"). The code 168:1, set up like a soccer score (168 to 1), refers to the number of victims of the Oklahoma City bombing versus the U.S. government's execution of Timothy

McVeigh. The text over the numbers identifies the two parties: "McVeigh" got 168, while "the government" got only 1. But the implied parties are "us" versus "them"—by using their bodies to display the scorecard, German youth appropriate the victory and inscribe it as performance: thus, McVeigh becomes "us": "we" got 168. Pairs of combinations may also be strung together, like 1488 (which combines the codes 14 and 88). Other codes involve mathematical equations, such as the number 41, which signifies "white racist" because 23 (the letter W) plus 18 (the letter R) equals 41.[18] The code 2yt4u uses the phonetic sounds of the letters and numbers in combination to sound out "too white for you."[19]

The expression and manipulation of symbolic codes—many of which are abhorred by the general public—is a clear marker of belonging and communication among youth in the scene. Young people in interviews repeatedly described how the brands can help create groups and that schools may be interested in banning the brands in order to prevent groups or cliques from forming. But the products do more than just bond youth together. The symbols and iconography are used to make statements against mainstream society and to provoke fear and anxiety in ethnic or religious minorities. Many of the products valorize and celebrate violence against others, even when the victims are not clearly identified, using language that threatens "you" or uses epithets like "pigs" without specifying to whom the threat is actually directed. Ongoing manipulation and adaptation of codes and symbols—in part to navigate bans of brands, logos, or symbols—also lends the entire subcultural scene a game-playing dimension that can create a sense of agency, power, playfulness, and fun for young people, potentially making it more attractive to new youth.

Codes drawing on acronyms, abbreviations, or sequences of alphabetic letters are key. Lonsdale T-shirts became popular because when worn with a half-zipped bomber jacket, the LO and the LE on the far side of the logo are covered by the jacket, leaving only the center four letters displayed: NSDA, which evokes the Nazi party's initials, NSDAP. One of the earliest commercial brands, Consdaple, imitates the graphic of the Lonsdale logo, but by adding the letter "p," a half-zipped jacket can reveal the full five letters of the National Socialist party (CONSDAPLE). Other examples include the global pan-Aryan code RaHoWa (racial holy war) as well as the German adaptation HoGeSa (Hooligans against Salafists, or *Hooligans gegen Salafisten*). A wide variety of other letter and numeric codes is also in play, including some adopted from the American gang scene and other transnational white power and pro-Aryan movements (such as ACAB, for All Cops Are Bastards, AJAB, for All Jews Are Bastards, WP/WAP, for White Power/White Aryan

Table 2. Sample Far Right Coded Symbols and Their Meaning

CODES SHOWN IN IMAGES IN INTERVIEWS	INTERPRETATION
Wüstenfuchs/Desert Fox	Nickname of Erwin Rommel, who commanded Nazi troops in North Africa.
Sweet home Madagascar	Madagascar was discussed as an original "final solution" for deportation of Jews.
Good morning Angola	References either early German colonial history in what is now Angola, or to early 20th-century proposals to establish a permanent settlement for Jewish refugees in Angola.*
Svastika	Swedish spelling of the word "swastika."
Expedition Tibet	Reference to SS expeditions to Tibet led by Ernst Schäfer that were part of the broader *Ahnenerbe* movement to research the Indogermanic roots of the Aryan "race."
18	First and eighth letters of the alphabet, AH, for Adolf Hitler.
88	Eighth letter of the alphabet, HH, for Heil Hitler.
Jeans "Rudolf"	Rudolf Hess, named for Hitler's deputy Rudolf Hess.
Runic alphabet	System of symbols used among Nordic tribes; used for Nazi insignia (like the sig or "lightning bolt" rune for the SS).
168:1	Reference to the number of people killed in the 1995 Oklahoma City bombing versus the death of Timothy McVeigh through execution.
Killer Döner	Reference to right-wing terrorist (NSU) cell's murder of Döner-stand owners.
ACAB	All Cops are Bastards; affiliation across political spectrum and urban gangs.
Kategorie C	Category C is a police designation of youth known to be violent in hooligan scene; also the name of a right-wing rock band.

CODES SHOWN IN IMAGES IN INTERVIEWS	INTERPRETATION
Palestinian scarf	Seen as symbol of freedom fighters; traditionally deployed by left-wing but used occasionally by far right.
Che Guevera image	Seen as symbol of freedom fighter; traditionally deployed by leftists.
Thor's Hammer	Nordic symbol, often interpreted as valorization of violence.
14	Refers to number of words in a sentence by American neo-Nazi David Lane, "We must secure the existence of our people and a future for white children"; has become a global pan-Aryan code.
Sport Frei!	Phrase called out in east Germany to mark start of sport/gym class; known affiliation with hooligan scene as a call at soccer matches to fight fans of the opposing team; some youth interpret as general signal to start fight/be violent.
Mauljucken	Invitation to a fight/aggressive.
Various Nordic references, Viking sailor/ship	See chapter 4; links to mythical and fantastical connection between Nordic/Aryan/Germanic tribes and whiteness; used by Nazi party.
Alpha Industries logo	Popular with far right because of similarities to SA civil badge or emblem.
J . . . nited States	Anti-Semitic slur (Jew-nited States).
Thor Steinar logo	Combined two banned runic symbols into a symbol that looks like a swastika. Banned by several states (see chapter 6), but bans overturned by higher courts.
Lonsdale brand name	When worn with a half-zipped bomber jacket, NSDA (first four letters of Nazi party abbreviation) is visible.
Consdaple brand name	When worn with a half-zipped bomber jacket, NSDAP (full abbreviation of Nazi party) is visible.

* See reference material cited in chapter 2.

Power, and ZOG/JOG, for Zionist/Jewish Occupied Government). In some cases, youth convert alphabetic sequences that have become well known into numeric sequences, creating a double-coded symbol for All Cops Are Bastards, for example, by using the numeric code 1312 to stand for ACAB. Youth will also claim that ACAB simply stands for 'eight colas, eight beers' (*acht Cola acht Bier*) as a way of obscuring the true meaning of the acronym.

Label 23/Boxing Connection, a crossover brand that markets to youth at the intersection of several different subcultures, sells a T-shirt whose back depicts a helicopter and the text *Ihr könnt uns observieren aber nicht abservieren*. This is a clever play on words that uses the change of just one letter (*o* to *a*) to make a sentence that roughly translates as "You can monitor us but you can't get rid of us." The meaning is stronger in German because *observieren* is a word with formal, official tones — making clear reference to police surveillance or monitoring, while the word *abservieren* is a colloquial or slang term that refers to being brushed off or ignored, or in its most extreme usage, "killed."[20] On the front of the T-shirt, the word *abservieren* is written with modified iconography, using the A and B in uppercase letters and the rest of the word in lowercase letters, with the B written to look like the number 8. Written this way, the word *abservieren* itself becomes a code, with A8, or "Adolf Hitler," embedded in the word.

Youth also reclaim and appropriate codes that are used by authorities to categorize far right youth. For example, "Kategorie C" is a code co-opted from the German police, who track football hooligans and right-wing extremist youth and keep a list of those considered dangerous (the list is referred to as "category C"). Declaring oneself to be "Kategorie C" thus conveys a willingness to be violent and a sense of pride and ownership in that designation. A far right wing rock band has also named itself "Kategorie C," and so some T-shirts bearing the code now refer both to the band and the coded reference. Other alphanumeric codes are adopted from unrelated popular youth cultural scenes and then stripped of their original cultural referents, such as in the usage of images of a black (8) ball from a billiards game. The black billiards ball is part of the American rockabilly music scene and was appropriated by German neo-Nazis because of the symbolic meaning of the eighth letter of the alphabet. Pairs of billiard eight balls show up in tattoos, store windows, and T-shirts to refer to the code 88 (for Heil Hitler).

Youth rely on a variety of strategies to help them interpret the meaning of various brands and symbols that are at play in subcultural scenes within their broader peer groups. They describe the media, the Internet, their social studies and history classes, and discussion with friends as key sources of information about brands, banning, and the meaning of particular symbols within the far right scene. In interviews, they frequently misinterpreted codes and often described specific items of clothing as generally "racist," although it was sometimes hard for them to say why they thought so, other than their knowledge of the brands and logos. They often pointed to the ways in which the brands played on the ambiguity of phrases and images. When Gabriel, a twenty-five-year-old conservation apprentice from Berlin, examined an image of a Thor Steinar sweatshirt with the words "Expedition Antarctica: The White Continent," he said, "it has a little bit of a dual meaning, or a dual message. Yeah, with the white continent, and I don't think the reference is to the Expedition Antarctica. Well, between the lines one knows what it really means."

Justin explained how his own observation of antifascist protests helps clarify which brands belong to which scenes: among the counterdemonstrators from the far right scene, "you'd see a lot of people who were wearing Alpha Industries bomber jackets." Sometimes youth learned the meaning of particular far right codes through inadvertent experiences with the codes. Christian, an eighteen-year-old carpentry apprentice who happens to have a birth date that contains a far right number code, related his experience at the Department of Motor Vehicles, when he wanted to get a vanity license plate with his birthday on it (August 18, or 18.8), but was turned down because the combination 188 is banned. "They said . . . that 188 is not allowed, because of AHH, Adolf Hitler Heil, and also 88 is also forbidden as a license plate number . . . they told me that this combination of numbers is banned, because it's right-wing radical. And then one of my neighbors explained to me what it means." Justus, a twenty-one-year-old concrete layer apprentice, described Thor Steinar as a "racist" brand and identified the Alpha Bomber jacket as an item of clothing that "most neo-Nazis" wear, noting that "this bomber jacket was always the racists' proverb. It's always been that way. Alpha Industries . . . actually anyone who grew up in the 2000s would have to know that."

Coded symbols often draw on elements gleaned from disparate historical and contemporary contexts, stitching cultural fragments together in new ways in a form of bricolage. In some cases, youth decontextualize the original referential meaning of historical and fantastical symbols and apply them in entirely new ways, assigning, for example, new meaning to specific runic symbols in a tattoo that signifies a subsector of extremists such as Christian neo-Nazis. In other cases, youth maintain symbols' original referential meaning but reframe and reshape memory signs toward new enemies.[21] Nazi symbols are used, for example, not only to express anti-Semitic or traditional National Socialist ideologies, but also to convey animosity toward newer immigrants. Thus, images of a skull and crossbones (*Totenkopf*) that were used on Nazi military uniforms and painted on signs at Nazi concentration camps are used by contemporary right-wing extremists who rally against different immigrant groups today (see plates 1, 13, and 19 and the lengthier discussion of the *Totenkopf* symbol in chapter 4). For example, a Reconquista brand T-shirt referenced the deaths of Turkish immigrants at the hands of a German neo-Nazi terrorist cell, by substituting rotisserie-cooking skewers for the bones in the skull-and-crossbones symbol, underneath the words "Killer Döner" (see discussion of youth reactions to this T-shirt in chapter 4). Such acts of bricolage help youth to create new narrative myths out of old, forbidden legacies and work contemporary references into historical material.[22]

Finally, the game-playing aspect of the codes is also clear in the ways in which the brands carefully walk the line between legal and illegal symbol usage. Codes and coded clothing are clearly used to circumvent bans and avoid legal problems. Dennis, a nineteen-year-old civil engineering technician apprentice, argued that far right youth today wear fewer identifiable brands and have grown their hair out longer in a deliberate effort to be less noticeable by authorities. "Many of the [far right youth] who live near me . . . they are still out and about together but they are moving on thinner ice, they have criminal records, they are more careful, they don't show their opinions as publicly in order to not be sent in [to the authorities or prison]. . . . Many of the brands are suppressed, you don't see the brands as often . . . only Thor Steinar . . . it's not as obvious, sometimes it's only [a little logo] on the pants" (see plate 3).

In some cases, individual brands or their logos become symbols on their own, conveying far right, racist, or aggressive messages. In interviews, youth repeatedly identified images of Thor Steinar brand clothing as far right, even when there were no apparent far right coded symbols in the products; rather, their interpretation of particular products as far right relied on the brand name or logo. After noting that Thor Steinar "is supposed to have connections to the far right scene," Gabriel clarified that it is "the brand itself" rather than the content of a T-shirt that conveys far right ideology, arguing that "there are provocative T-shirts from a lot of different companies." Fabian, a seventeen-year-old roofing apprentice from Berlin whose knowledge about the far right comes in part from having parents who are police officers, explains that he wouldn't buy a Thor Steinar product because he doesn't like the clothes, but also because he would be "stamped" as a Nazi: "I mean just look at the logo, it's banned." Later, he looks at an image of a Thor Steinar hooded sweatshirt and says, "If you didn't see the Steinar there, I'd say it's a totally normal hoodie. Completely neutral, but it's immediately

clear because of the 'Steinar' that it's right-wing. Even if it's sport clothing."
Lukas has a right-wing-leaning father who regularly wears Thor Steinar.
He explained, "If I see a person with Thor Steinar and a shaved head, I'd
think, OK, he's right-wing . . . but it doesn't necessarily have to be so . . . it
could also just be a person who wants to provoke." Paul, a twenty-four-year-
old construction mechanic apprentice, looked at a Thor Steinar T-shirt and
simply noted, "Based on what I know Thor Steinar stands for . . . racists like
to wear it. Neo-Nazis." Later, he elaborates that he would never wear the
brand because of its "extreme" connections to Nazis. But he explains that
other brands popular with the far right also have broader appeal; he says
he sees a lot of people wearing Alpha Industries jackets every day, which he
attributes to the fact that consumers appreciate the products' high quality
and the fact that the jackets are extremely warm. Others made an effort to
point this out too, arguing that the clothing alone does not convey far right
ideology or engagement. "I know a lot [of people] who have Alpha things,
and they are stamped right away as Nazis, but that's not the case," says Finn,
an eighteen-year-old electrician trainee. "[They] are totally normal people."

Pride and Prejudice: Historical and National(ist) Codes

The game-playing aspect of symbolic codes is not limited to alphanumeric
combinations. The iconography of the clothing products as well as the products' individual names rely heavily on coded reference to historical pogroms,
German colonialism, racism, xenophobia, and the valorization of violence.
Products use references to the colonial era, to Nazi history, or to events or
military leaders from World War II and draw on symbols and modified
symbols, colors, imagery, old Germanic script, and names that evoke or
directly reference nationalist history. Other youth modify their own bodies
to become symbols themselves, tattooing images of Nazi military weaponry,
symbols, and uniforms, using hairstyles and facial hair popular during the
Third Reich, donning Nazi-era uniforms, and imitating the style of Nazi
soldiers.

As the introduction explained, Thor Steinar's logo is a combination of two
runic symbols that are each individually banned because of their association
with the Nazi party. By crossing the two runes over one another, the logo
evokes a swastika (see plates 11, 12, and 25). Thor Steinar's children's line
(now discontinued) included a sweatshirt with the runic alphabet (which
has a long history of appropriation by the far right, most famously in the
use of the "Sig" lightning-bolt rune by the National Socialist SS). Other
T-shirts sport images of Nazi U-Boots or iconographic palm trees that evoke

the historical iconography of Hitler's Afrikakorps or use the names of Nazi leaders and legends as product names—such as the "Rudolf" jeans described earlier. Erik and Sons sells a T-shirt with an image of a historical passenger ship and the text "Sweet Home Madagascar"—the island had been discussed by Nazi leaders as an original "final solution,"—a place to which European Jews could be deported—before the gas chambers of Auschwitz and Dachau were designed.[23] An Ansgar Aryan T-shirt sports text referencing the "Expedition Tibet" and Ernst Schäfer, referring to SS expeditions to Tibet—led by Schäfer—that were part of the broader *Ahnenerbe* movement to research the Indo-Germanic roots of the Aryan "race."[24] And Thor Steinar's line includes a "Good Morning Angola" shirt, featuring helicopters flying over a palm-tree-filled, sunset-lit landscape: a reference either to early German colonial history in what is today Angola, or to several early twentieth-century proposals to establish a permanent settlement for Jewish refugees in Angola.[25]

The historical references are carefully coded, embedded within the iconography in ways that make it difficult to pin down one clear interpretation. This multivocality is deliberate and appeals to youth who are keen to avoid the social stigma of the far right while still communicating with insiders. Georg, a twenty-one-year-old scaffold builder apprentice, talked at length about the Desert Fox T-shirt, which he owns, and how he finds the historical background "cool," noting that Germans were the cleverest and most intelligent warriors in the World War. When the interviewer asks whether observers understand the historical background when he wears the T-shirt, he said, "Yes, of course, of course . . . they think that I'm right with this message, because it's like that. Because we Germans were simply the cleverest and just because one person was completely mad, it doesn't mean that all other Germans also thought that." But then he acknowledges that not everyone he encounters would understand the shirt's meaning: "It's a profound background but . . . if I was out on the street and a grandma saw it, she'd see the T-shirt and think, oh, desert fox, it's so sweet and wonderful." Rainer, an eighteen-year-old technical conservation apprentice, explained that dual meanings are evoked by signals like tattoos, shaved heads, severe and black clothing, flags, symbols, logos, and gothic script. Such signals are used "when one wants to say something that is ambiguous . . . well, it's allegedly a normal sentence, but sometimes the sentences are also still linked to the past."

In June 2016, a controversy erupted among legal scholars and authorities about the permissibility of a T-shirt with the alphabetic sequence HKNKRZ—the word *Hakenkreuz*, or swastika, with its vowels removed. The T-shirt's iconography had the letters set in two columns of three large, white capital letters (with HKN over KRZ) inside two red bars—an imitation of the U.S. rap group Run-DMC's iconic logo (see plate 28). Journalist Felix Huesmann reported that several demonstrators at a June 4 Dortmund neo-Nazi march were spotted wearing the shirt; he also reported seeing a flag with the letters HTLR (Hitler) and shirts with the iconography NTNL SZLST (National Sozialist). The shirts are for sale in online shops, reports the journalist Jana Hannemann, with textual descriptions that promise the shirts are "legally clear and ready for the disco" (*anwaltlich geprüft und disco-tauglich*).[26] The legal authorities, including the local Dortmund police, did not issue citations for the HKNKRZ T-shirt, although the word *Hakenkreuz* would have been illegal—an issue I return to in chapter 5 in a discussion of German bans on symbols. In such cases, writes Hannemann, "neo-Nazis try to exploit legal gray areas."[27]

In addition to the use of modified banned symbols that are directly borrowed from the Nazi era, coded symbolic references to both the Third Reich and the colonial era abound in the commercialized clothing—eagle's wings, palm trees, military colors and camouflage, modified swastikas, and runic symbols are common. Steffen, a twenty-four-year-old carpentry apprentice who expressed enthusiasm for some of the clothing as he sorted through the images, examined a Thor Steinar shirt with modified eagle's wings and said, "No, I don't like it. . . . It's too simple. Not half, not whole. At least they should put a real *Reichsadler* [the imperial eagle used in the Third Reich] on it" (see plates 1 and 23). When the interviewer asks if he would wear it with a real *Reichsadler*, he jokes "Ha ha, did I put my address down here anywhere? No, I probably would not wear it. Well wait, maybe in a Turkish bar, at night around midnight on a Saturday, I'd march around in it." Later in the interview, he argues that he would wear such clothing first and foremost because he finds it chic but notes he would also wear it to deliberately provoke by walking around in certain neighborhoods. But then, he argues, "if they punch me in the face and I defend myself, I'm the evil German who clobbered a Turk."

More recent historical references are important as well; some of the commercialized symbols are coded with east German cultural elements, such as the phrase "Sport Frei," which was a standard opening call to physical education class in East Germany and became appropriated, after unification, by right-wing soccer hooligans who answer the "Sport Frei," which opens soccer matches, with the call, "Heil Hitler" (see plate 27). Youth sometimes explained in interviews that the phrase also conveys a readiness to fight, since when teachers called out the phrase, everyone would run into whatever gym activity was going on. Tobias, a twenty-one-year-old civil engineering technician apprentice, explains that once the phrase was called in gym class, "we were physically engaged. . . . And when I hear the *Sport Frei* in connection with Steinar I would think . . . ready to fight . . . ready to be violent." The phrase means "it's on," Georg noted succinctly, "ding dong, time to fight." Several students linked the phrase to the slang term "third halftime," which Timo explained most clearly: "in soccer there are actually only two half-times, so the third half-time means that somewhere on the field fifty [guys] meet up with fifty [guys] and have a massive fight. Or one hundred against one hundred or twenty against twenty, depending."

Symbols and references to national pride are also key. Michael Kohlstruck analyzed the use of emblems of national pride by the extreme right wing, detailing the ways in which the phrase is paired with color and script combinations that evoke historical eras.[28] On a series of emblems with the textual phrase "I am proud to be a German" that Kohlstruck analyzed, for example, he found that the color of the background, the frame, or the script itself was black, white, and red — "the colors of the North German Confederation (1867–71), the German Empire (1871–1918) and/or the Third Reich (1933–45)."[29] The combination of black, white, and red was critical to Hitler and the Nazi party, as Hitler detailed in *Mein Kampf*, noting that National Socialist flag used red to symbolize the "social idea of the movement" and white to represent "the national idea."[30] Youth are sensitive to this combination of colors. Bernd, a twenty-two-year-old concrete layer apprentice, noted the use of the black-white-red color combination on a Thor Steinar T-shirt and said he didn't think the T-shirt should be allowed to be worn. "How can I explain it? There's nothing recognizably racist about the shirt or anything, but through the use of this symbolism and through this white or black white with red here, those are all coded colors from the old Reich." Julian, a twenty-eight-year-old studying for his technical high school degree, made a similar observation about color usage in the clothing, noting, "I think it's also a little bit referencing the Aryan race, right? I'm not so well-versed in these symbols, but . . . I would think that, because the T-shirt is black and then the colors red and white, those are the colors from the flag of the German Reich." In discussing the brand Thor Steinar, Kevin noted that lots of nations use wings or coats of arms, which are "always a signal of some kind of strength," but "the colors, white, black, red, the combination is fairly clear." T-shirts in color combinations of black, white, and red are popular across the brands, often embedded with other codes or vague references to violence, culture, preservation, or survival. Label 23/Boxing Collection, for example, sells a white T-shirt with black and red iconography whose texts include phrases like "Fight for Survival" and "Culture Club." The use of animals on coats of arms with pride slogans also link to the historical past, imitating the imperial eagle of the German Empire or the coat of arms eagle of the Third Reich.[31]

As I have argued previously,[32] expressions of national pride are an easy way of rebelling against authority figures and breaking taboos in Germany.[33] Simon, a twenty-year-old studying for his technical high school degree, raised the issue of national pride in a discussion of a jacket his brother-in-law wears that expresses pride in being from Berlin, which led to an explanation of the complications of pride in Germany. "I am also proud to be German. But I'm not a right-wing radical. I just simply have a certain national, well, national pride; if I would say that in a group, I'd be stamped as a Nazi right away. . . . Here in Germany, without question, immediately. If you say you're proud of Germany or proud to be German, you're stamped right away. It doesn't matter what friendship group you're in."

National pride slogans are a key part of marketing and branding strategies both for formal political parties and for commercial entities. As I noted in previous work, badges with the phrase "I am proud to be a German" have been sold on right-wing party websites, and the NPD has handed out stickers with the slogan at information stands.[34] One right-wing group advertised a perfume called Walküre, describing it as "the flowery scent for today's national woman," promising female customers that "with this perfume you are guaranteed to be attractive to every patriot."[35] PEGIDA — Patriotic Europeans against the Islamization of the Occident — has organized weekly protest marches since 2014, which grew from 350 people in the first Dresden gathering to nearly twenty thousand marchers by early 2015.[36] National pride is a tremendous motivating force for the far right.

Commercial companies use national pride to market to the far right in several ways. Some, like Ansgar Aryan, directly reference pride; Ansgar Aryan's tagline on its website and product catalogs is "Patriotic Ink." Others use the concept of the nation to foster a sense of belonging and identity, drawing on national references from the colonial era as well as more recent historical military references. Thor Steinar uses eagles, military symbols, and runic symbols to evoke historical national eras, particularly the Third Reich. Others use colors, modified eagle's wings, colonial and military motifs and iconography, and slogans and text that evoke or directly reference ideas like European brotherhood and "us/them" rhetoric. One T-shirt displays the words "German, proud and loyal" across the top of the back of the shirt and underneath states: "our music radical, our hearts national, the flames of freedom newly kindled, German, proud and loyal, white power!"[37]

Like the alphanumeric codes adapted from the Lonsdale and New Balance brands, some codes are drawn from mainstream brands and logos because of their coincidental symbolic value vis-à-vis historical references. The brand Fred Perry, for example, has a long history of being used by far right youth because its logo—a wreath of laurel branches—evokes military insignia used by the NSDAP. On some Fred Perry polo shirts, moreover, the collar has black, red, and white stripes—colors that, as detailed above, are popular with far right youth for their historical significance with nationalist movements and regimes in Germany, including the Nazis.[38] Alpha Industries, an American brand founded in 1957 to produce outerwear for the U.S. Department of Defense and later a popular commercial brand, became similarly popular among far right youth because its "Flying A" logo bears some resemblance to the banned civil badge symbol (*Zivilabzeichen*) of the Sturmabteilung (SA), a division of the SS (see plates 15 and 16 for an illustration).[39]

Alpha Industries is regularly monitored and banned for its connection to right-wing extremist groups. Its logo, for example, is one of several logos pictured in the student handbook (*Hausordnung*) as a banned symbol in one of the two schools I studied. Alpha jackets were repeatedly mentioned by youth as an item of clothing they owned or had worn when they were younger, frequently because all their friends also wore the jackets. Klaus, who at twenty-one is training to be a roofer, identified the brand on the list of banned brands for his school and explained that he owned an Alpha Industries jacket and wore it in early adolescence, around ages thirteen to fifteen. "Everybody wore one back then, because it was somehow fashion; I mean everyone had an Alpha jacket." He noted that "all the German rappers" wear Alpha jackets but said they are also popular with the far right, which he described euphemistically as "people with very short hair . . . who are tattooed from top to bottom and look by nature aggressive." Dennis said that although "everyone" had an Alpha jacket a few years ago, in his neighborhood now, "you don't see any right-wing extremists with [an Alpha] jacket anymore, only foreigners." But in school, he notes, the right-wing extremist connotation still holds for the Alpha jacket: after wearing his Alpha jacket to school, he was warned that the next time he did so, he'd be sent home. He expressed his sense of injustice at this intervention, explaining that the entire brand Alpha Industries doesn't represent the far right—"only the bomber jackets stand for the right wing. I was wearing a coat." Other students frequently linked Alpha Industries jackets to the far right scene, sometimes in combination with other brands. In a discussion about the brands Alpha Industries and Pit Bull, Rainer explained that if you see someone with one of those jackets, "they don't come across as very nice." But Georg, who of all the youth interviewed was one of the most informed about current trends in extremist youth scenes, scoffed at the notion that today's far right youth wear Alpha jackets. "It's out. Alpha Industry is out; no one wears it anymore." Conveniently, Alpha Industries started producing jackets with a logo that is attached by Velcro, which makes it removable—an option apparently intended to allow customers to add their own patch in its place, advertised as an option to "customize your flight jacket with our removable Alpha logo Velcro patch."[40] For German far right youth, the removable logo had an additional appeal; youth removed the logo and turned it around. Upside-down, the "Flying A" resembled a "V," which youth noted is meant to stand for *Vaterland* and which is understood to stand for a willingness to be violent or to fight (*gewaltbereit* or *kampfbereit*). Several youth mentioned the removable label, though there were slight variations in their interpretations of the positions of the removable logo. Paul, a twenty-four-year-old construction mechanic apprentice, described the upside-down symbol as a "Bosscode" symbolizing the idea of fatherland and conveying a readiness to be violent but noted that it was popular both with far right youth and with foreigners (*Ausländer*), or more specifically, he notes, with "Nazis or also with Turks."

Others raised the use of the upside-down Alpha logo as they described friends, acquaintances, or others they had seen with the logo in "V" formation, or as they asserted that they would not wear the logo that way. As soon as he noted that he owned an Alpha jacket, for example, Klaus immediately added, "but not the one with the upside-down logo on it, which means ready to riot or fight or something. . . . I mean we just wore it because back then, well, you didn't have your own taste, and [there was] peer pressure." Dennis explained that the Alpha bomber jacket becomes a "provocative jacket" when the logo is turned around, because then the jacket means "ready to fight." Youth also noted its popularity because of marketing text for the brand that labeled it a worldwide *führende* (leading) brand—using an adjective that shares the same root word as Adolf Hitler's title (*Führer*) (see plates 15 and 16).[41] When twenty-one-year-old concrete layer apprentice Hayri got an Alpha jacket, his friends gave him a hard time. "Ey, since when [do you wear] Alpha, and well Alpha is y'know 'Führer' and like that. I mean it was all in fun; it's not like anybody said, hey why are you wearing an Alpha jacket?" All the same, he said, since he knew that if one wears the logo turned one way it represents the right wing and if one wears it turned the other way it means "Vaterland," "I don't want anything to do with either one, so pow! I took it off, left it at home."

Microvariations in meaning exist across local spaces, too. Dennis explains how the interpretation of Alpha jackets' meaning depends on the neighborhood one is in: "in some neighborhoods it's seen as a right-wing jacket, and in other neighborhoods now not at all. In [my neighborhood] for example it's not a right-wing brand at all. Because no one wears it anymore; [they] only wear Thor Steinar now; that's actually the main thing that they wear." This is true for other brands as well. Lukas explains how after he got a Lonsdale jacket in fifth or sixth grade, his family moved from a diverse neighborhood in former west Berlin to Lichtenberg, a suburb in the former east Berlin. In his first neighborhood, Lukas says, where most of his friends were "Turks," it was totally normal for him to run around the neighborhood with his Lonsdale jacket. But once he moved to Lichtenberg, he was "labeled a Nazi."

There are several other ways in which historical symbols are deployed — some of which merit their own chapter-length analyses in the remainder of this book. Fantastical and mythical symbols like Thor's Hammer are common, in use for their Nordic connotations as well as for how they convey a sense of resistance against a perceived oppressor. Staecker explains that Thor's Hammer was a "symbol of pagan reaction against Christianity."[42] Youth in interviews repeatedly identified images of Thor's Hammer — on the back of a T-shirt in one image and in a necklace on a marcher at a protest in another image — as reflecting far right ideology. Oliver, a twenty-three-year-old scaffold builder, described a right-wing demonstration near his house not long ago, where they "all looked the same, probably with Thor Steinar, well, obvious clothing. Black, mostly dark clothing, whatever kind of hammer symbols or out-in-the-open swastikas, I don't think there are big differences from years ago."

Despite their relatively broad knowledge about the far right youth subcultural scene and its brands, however, there was wide variation in how youth interpreted the coded symbols. During their perusal of thirty-four images that included some Nazi-era codes and references, over 90 percent of youth did not understand the historical references embedded in the iconographical text "Sweet Home Madagascar," "Good Morning Angola," "Expedition Tibet," the name "Rudolf," or the Swedish word "svastika." Far greater percentages of youth correctly volunteered the Nazi-era reference in the Wolfsangel runic symbol (44 percent), the code 88 (70 percent), the code 18 (44 percent), a *U-Boot/Wehrmacht* image (35 percent), and the code "Desert Fox" (22 percent). Table 3 details youth interpretations of a sampling of eleven Nazi-era codes.

There was also quite a bit of variation in youth interpretation of nonhistorical images, which youth often recognized as far right in general, but sometimes described in alternative ways, such as as "racist," "aggressive," or "provocative." Table 4 details youth interpretations of a sampling of twelve of the nonhistorical codes. Most frequently, youth either did not know the

Table 3. Youth Interpretation of Sample of Nazi-Era Codes in Commercial Products*

	UNDERSTAND HISTORICAL REFERENCE	DO NOT UNDERSTAND HISTORICAL REFERENCE
Wüstenfuchs/Desert Fox	11 (22%)	40 (78%)
Sweet home Madagascar	3 (6%)	48 (94%)
Good morning Angola	2 (4%)	49 (96%)
Svastika	4 (8%)	47 (92%)
Expedition Tibet‡	4 (8%)	47 (92%)
18†	22 (44%)	28 (56%)
88†	35 (70%)	15 (30%)
Jeans "Rudolf" †§	1 (2%)	49 (98%)
Runic alphabet†	11 (22%)	39 (78%)
U-boot/Wehrmacht image	18 (35%)	33 (65%)
Wolfsangel rune**†	22 (44%)	28 (56%)
TOTAL	133	423

*Data in this table is drawn from specific images where these codes were visible; each row reports on the understandings as reported in youth reflections on one particular image. The only exception is the "runic alphabet" row. Because runes were present in several images, this row reports on whether youth understood the Nazi-era reference in the runic alphabet/symbols across their interview. The runic symbols youth reflected on are primarily the Sig, Tyr, and Wolfsangel runes, which were Nazi symbols, as well as runic symbols in the Thor Steinar brand. Youth do not generally see the entire runic alphabet as far right or make Nazi-era connections to the entire alphabet (although they do connect the runes to Nordic symbols, which they in turn associate with the far right), but some connect specific runes to the Nazi era.

†Total number of youth responses to this code as seen in an image is fifty instead of fifty-one, owing to partial missing data from one interview; a small portion in the middle of an audio file for one interview was corrupted, which included discussion of these five codes.

‡ This total includes one respondent who made an educated guess about this code based on contextual clues such as the old German script and the use of the word "expedition." In fact, in addition to the four respondents who knew the Nazi-era reference in "Expedition Tibet," many additional youth (thirteen) identified this image as right-wing based on the model's appearance (six) and contextual clues such as the old German script (seven) without actually understanding the Nazi-era reference specifically.

§ The low number of respondents who understood the code "Rudolf" may be due to the fact that Rudolf was the product name, rather than in the iconography of the product itself. The image was a screenshot of the product, and many youth focused primarily on the jeans and the brand logo without noting the product name. The other historical codes were all embedded in the clothing or tattoo design or iconography.

** Only two interviewees knew the actual Wolfsangel runic symbol and the name for it; an additional two knew it was a Nazi-era symbol but could not identify the meaning or name. Many recognized it as an SS symbol (six), a modified swastika (eight), or a possible reference to either (four).

Table 4. Youth Interpretation of Sample Multivocal/Other Codes in Commercial Products

	FAR RIGHT	"PROVOKANT," AGGRESSIVE, VIOLENT	RACIST/ XENOPHOBIC/ OFFENSIVE	OTHER INTERPRE- TATION	NORMAL/ DON'T KNOW
My favorite color is white	9	4	25	9	12
Keep your country clean‡	7	5	7	9	27
The white continent**	20***	5	12	7	14
Killer Döner‡	20	4	21	12	3
Twin towers‡	6	7	5	46	3
Kategorie C§	22	13	1	26	3
168:1‡	14	1	3	16	20
14****	7	0	2	7	36
Hilf uns Thor!!! (Help us Thor)	16	4	4	15	14
Ach Sie suchen Streit? †	10	20	1	14	10
Dancing in the air/ ACAB‡	17	10	6	16	13
Sport Frei! *	9	5	1	8	31
TOTAL	157	78	88	185	186

Note: some respondents offered multiple interpretations; totals therefore exceed number of interviewees. Interpretations were often based not only on the code itself but on the context in the rest of the image.

‡ See chapter 4 for further discussion of death images. For the "Killer Döner" shirt, twelve of the twenty students who interpreted this T-shirt as "far right" also specifically noted its reference to the terrorist right-wing extremist cell (National Socialist Underground, or NSU). "Killer Döner" appears in grey script above a modified skull-and-crossbones, in which the crossbones are made of cooking skewers. "Dancing in the Air" appears in white block script on a black T-shirt above a white silhouette dangling from a noose off a tree branch; the man wearing the shirt has A.C.A.B. tattooed on his neck. The Twin Towers shirt depicts a plane flying into the World Trade Center towers, surrounded by the words "Take a flight to the World Trade's, to visit the J . . . nited States." Twelve of the forty-six "other interpretation" for this image saw it as anti-American, eighteen interpreted it as representing Islamist terrorism, and six interpreted it

as terrorism more generally. The "score" 168:1 appears in large red numbers on a black T-shirt under the phrase McVeigh vs. Government. The code 168:1 was not understood by anyone, but students speculated on its meaning based on the rest of the image (closely cropped hair, a polo shirt in the background with red, white, and black colors, etc.).

† "Ach Sie suchen Streit" is written across the back of a T-shirt (Translation: "Oh, you're looking for a fight?"). This phrase is set in red typeface above an image of a muscular, bearded Viking in a helmet wielding a Nordic hammer. See plate 10.

§ Kategorie C appears in white, old-Germanic script across the back of a black sweatshirt over the words "hungry wolves." Fifteen of the twenty-six "other interpretations" correctly identified the phrase as the name of a rock band.

* Text appears across the front of a light-blue zipped hoodie (also shown in red on same screenshot), under the word STEINAR. Some of the students who identified the hoodie as far right did so based on the brand name rather than (or in addition to) the textual phrase "Sport Frei."

** Text appears in red print on the back of a white hoodie under the words "T. Steinar Expedition Antarctica" and over iconography depicting a snowy expedition with the Norwegian flag.

*** This total includes five youth who did not specify far right with words but said it was "totally clear" what the sweatshirt meant, especially because of Thor Steinar's reputation as a brand, thereby evoking the far right.

**** Only three interviewees correctly understood "14" to refer to the pan-Aryan code 14 Words (see table 1), but several identified it as far right based on the number 88, which was in the same image (the image was of the numbers 14 and 88—as large, Styrofoam figures—being held up by soccer spectators in a stadium).

code in question or thought the product (typically a T-shirt) was just a normal item of clothing. Some products were more likely to be identified as far right (such as the "Killer Döner" T-shirt and a Thor Steinar sweatshirt depicting an expedition to Antarctica with the phrase "the white continent"). In other cases, the code itself was uninterpretable to the students (such as 168:1), but some identified it as a far right code based on other contextual clues in the image.

Trying on Extremism

Most often, youth who own the clothing acquired it during early-to-mid adolescence, typically because their friends owned similar brands, sometimes receiving the brands as birthday gifts from their parents or siblings. Twenty-three-year-old Joachim explains that when he was younger—in what he labels a "fourteen-year-old phase," he listened to right-wing radical music and wore an Alpha jacket, which he received as a birthday present from his parents. He wore the jacket because everybody else did, and wearing it gave him a sense of belonging (*dazugehörig*): "everybody had it; it was a trend."

Benjamin, a twenty-two-year-old technical assistant apprentice, describes how he came to own a Lonsdale pullover. He bought it when he was fourteen at a store called Jawbreaker—a memory he has retained because his family did not have much money and it was a brand name sweatshirt at a time when brands were important. When kids in his class pointed out the brand's meaning to the far right scene, "I wore it less, because I didn't want the confrontation." Georg, who was part of the far right for a few years in early adolescence (from about age twelve to fifteen), explains that he got involved with far right youth culture through its clothing style: "actually all of my friends, we've known each other forever, y'know? Since we were kids and we simply grew up together. We always did things together and . . . yeah, the first one showed up with an Alpha [Industries] jacket and then the second one showed up with an Alpha jacket, that's how it began. Yeah, then one gets embroiled into the scene, y'know? I took a look at what it was about, but then I distanced myself from it, y'know?"

INTERVIEWER. What scene do you mean?
GEORG. Yeah, of course, the right-wing extreme one.

Across the interviews, it was overwhelmingly clear that the clothing and brands are a significant part of the broader far right wing scene. Style is clearly important to far right youth. Martin, a sixteen-year-old masonry apprentice, self-identifies as far right. In response to the first interview question about how he would describe his own style, Martin explains, "When I go out in my free time I [dress] as a right-wing extremist. . . . I'm a nationalist, and I embody that in my style . . . [along] with other people who [dress] just the same, so for me the clothes are an orientation point." After school, at home, he changes into combat boots and tends to wear a bomber jacket with a polo shirt. At school, he explains, "there are mostly teachers there" and so he notes that he tones down his style at school. He also describes how the clothing can lead to violent interactions, describing a time when he and a friend went to a demonstration and exited "on the wrong side of the train station," and when they tried to cross under a bridge to get back, "just because we were wearing Thor Steinar, we were attacked by six men; there were only two of us."

Hans, a twenty-seven-year-old scaffold builder trainee, unequivocally states that Lonsdale and Thor Steinar "belong to the right-wing scene," contrasting today's far right with "when I was younger, you could recognize them by combat boots, shaved heads, bomber jackets. . . . Now they have New Balance for example; it's a brand of shoe that is [part of the far right]." Markus, a twenty-one year-old technical assistant apprentice, described a "gang" of youth he used to know in his neighborhood who wore Alpha

Plate 1. May 1, 2009, demonstration in Mainz.
Photo: Attenzione / Sascha Rheker.

Plate 2. May 1, 2008, demonstration in Nürnberg. Translation: Black is the night in which we get you; White are the men who are victorious for Germany; Red is the blood on the asphalt.
Photo: Attenzione / Sascha Rheker.

Plate 3. May 1, 2007, demonstration in Rauheim.
Photo: Attenzione / Sascha Rheker.

Plate 4. Right-wing demonstration in Fulda, 2008. Translation: Eager/happy (to be in contact) and adventurous.
Photo: Attenzione / Sascha Rheker.

Plate 5. Cologne protest against new mosque, 2007.
Photo: Attenzione / Roland Geisheimer.

Plate 6. Stolberg, neo-Nazi demonstration, 2011.
Photo: Attenzione / Roland Geisheimer.

Plate 7. Demonstration in Friedrichshafen, 2005.

Photo: Attenzione / Roland Geisheimer.

Plate 8. Right-wing demonstration in Dortmund, 2011. Translation: Stop USrael; annihilate imperialism.

Photo: Attenzione / Roland Geisheimer.

Plate 9. Saarlois, July 2007.
Photo: Markus Mandalka.

Plate 10. Berlin, October 2006. Translation: Oh, you're looking for a fight?
Photo: Markus Mandalka.

Plate 11. September 2007, Goeppingen.
Photo: Markus Mandalka.

Plate 12. Lampertheim, October 2005.
Photo: Markus Mandalka.

Plate 13. May 1, 2009, Berlin.
Photo: Markus Mandalka.

Plate 14. Dresden, February 2010.
Photo: Markus Mandalka.

ALPHA INDUSTRIES INC.
KNOXVILLE, TENNESSEE, U.S.A.

Plate 15. Alpha Industries logo on T-shirt.

Photo: Kate Oczypok.

Plate 16. Postcard of SA Group School in Westfalen, Fredeburg. SA Civil Badge shown in Glass window, Reichsadler on wall.

Image: Postcard "SA-Gruppenschule Westfalen, Fredeburg, Ehrenhalle," in LOT 2747 (F), Folder "German press photographs, 1935–1944." Prints & Photographs Division, Third Reich Collection, U.S. Library of Congress. Photograph by Jos. Grobbel, Photogr. Kunstanstak, Ansichskarten-Verlag, Fredeburg i. Westf.

Plate 17. 1933 SS recruitment poster.

Image: Poster encouraging youth to enlist in the Waffen SS at the end of their 17th year. Illustration shows a helmeted SS soldier before a black SS flag. United States Holocaust Memorial Museum Photo Archives #32630. Courtesy of Galerie Prospect. Artifact Photographer: Arnold Kramer. Copyright: United States Holocaust Memorial Museum.

ᚠᚢᚦᚨᚱᚲᚷᚹ ᚺᚾᛁᛖᛃᛈᛇᛉ ᛏᛒᛖᛗᛚᛜᛞᛟ
f u th a r k g w   h n i j p e n s   t b e m l ng d o

Den äldre runraden.

ᚠᚢᚦᚨᚱᚴᛅᚼᚾᛁᛆᛌ ᛏᛒᛘᛚᛦ
f u th a r k   h n i a s   t b m l R

Den svensk-norska runraden.

ᚠᚢᚦᚨᚱᚴ:ᚼᚾᛁᛆᛌ:ᛏᛒᚤᛚᛦ
f u th a r k   h n i a s   t b m l R

Den danska (oftast kallad: den vanliga) runraden.

Plate 18. Runic symbols.
Image: Runic symbols. Image 0068016. Courtesy of The Granger Collection, New York.

Plate 19. Totenkopf, Iron Cross, Reichsadler on Nazi uniform.
Image: Totenkopf, Iron Cross, Reichsadler on Nazi uniform. Image 0525738 OTTO BAUM. First published by Scherl - Suddeutsche Zeitung. Courtesy of The Granger Collection, New York.

Plate 20. Hitler Youth propaganda film still about North Germany as "Holy Land." Translation: "Where is our holy land? North-Germany. The original *Heimat* of the Germanic tribes is our holy land."

Image: 7th Nazi propaganda slide for a Hitler Youth educational presentation entitled "5000 years of German Culture." United States Holocaust Memorial Museum Photo Archives #93633. Courtesy of Stephen Glick. Copyright: United States Holocaust Memorial Museum.

Plate 21. Hitler Youth propaganda film still connecting Germanic tribes and Vikings. Translation: "The Germanic tribes are the oldest sailors. They built the first ships. Vikings discovered Iceland, Greenland, and America."

Image: 30th Nazi propaganda slide for a Hitler Youth educational presentation entitled "5000 years of German Culture." United States Holocaust Memorial Museum Photo Archives #93656. Courtesy of Stephen Glick. Copyright: United States Holocaust Memorial Museum.

Plate 22. 1943, Nazi Germany boarding school students building Viking ship model.
Image: NPEA Schulpforta, Werkunterricht. Courtesy of Deutsches Historisches Museum GmbH, Berlin, Germany. Inv.-Nr: Orgel-Köhne 10009/10. Photo Credit: Liselotte Orgel-Köhne. Copyright: Exclusively with Deutsches Historisches Museum GmbH.

Plate 23. "Imperial Eagle" for the Reichsadler for chancellery fireplace.
Image: "Adler für Kamin (Reichskanzlei)" in LOT 8580 (F), Folder "Sculptured eagles designed for buildings and monuments, 1933–1936." Prints & Photographs Division, Third Reich Collection, U.S. Library of Congress.

Plate 24. Düsseldorf bathroom stall sticker advertising an antifascist protest in Essen. Translation: Say "Goodbye" to your Nazi wear! Antifascist demonstration against Thor Steinar and the right-wing lifestyle. *Photo: Cynthia Miller-Idriss.*

Plate 25. Poster in protest against Thor Steinar store Trømso in Berlin. *Photo: Cynthia Miller-Idriss.*

Plate 26. Thor Steiner name spelled on sweatshirt in runic symbols. *Photo: Cynthia Miller-Idriss, apabiz archives.*

Plate 27. Thor Steinar "Sport Frei" shirt. *Photo: Cynthia Miller-Idriss, apabiz archives.*

Plate 28. Dortmund neo-Nazi march, June 4, 2016.
Photo: Felix Huesmann.

Industries jackets "because they wanted to seem cooler." Klaus talked at length about his consumption of brands popular with the far right, like Alpha Industries and Consdaple, in early adolescence, from about thirteen to fifteen years old. Although he does not come straight out and identify himself as a former right-wing extremist, Klaus positions himself as part of a right-wing peer group by describing his own style and the style of his friends with clear right-wing descriptors. He attributes his clothing choices at that time to group pressure and not having developed his own taste, and describes the intended message of the clothing as "aggressive." He stopped wearing the clothing because he "grew out of it" (*rausgewachsen*), which carries a double meaning: he likely literally grew out of the clothing's size, and also the far right scene of which it was a part. His former friendship group still wears such brands, but he described himself as having grown apart from them (*auseinanderentwickelt*), noting that even though "they still wear the clothing, they are also totally nice people . . . not really ones who would be violent, just totally normal." Felix, a nineteen-year-old technical conservation apprentice, talked about the right-wing extremist peer group of one of his friends, explaining that they are identifiable Nazis because of their "typical" Nazi appearance: "they have the typical Nazi appearance . . . short-cut hair . . . these typical clothes, like Alpha Industries, Consdaple and things." Tobias argued that "most people who I have seen with Alpha Industries or Thor Steinar clothing, especially the male people, from their external appearance appear as if they are trying to represent something. And I think if they simply see each other, there's a kind of sympathy there."

Although youth typically identified particular brands with the far right scene, they were also clear to point out — particularly when they or their friends owned these brands — that wearing styles associated with the far right does not automatically convey far right ideology. Manfred, a twenty-two-year-old scaffold builder apprentice from Hellersdorf — an area well known for its high proportion of right-wing youth, describes "lots" of people who run around the neighborhood with Alpha jackets but notes that they can't all be right wing: "surely there are also totally normal people." He suspects that many people who wear Alpha jackets "feel a little bit cool" because they are expensive, and "they think they are something." Students repeatedly noted that although they owned some of the banned brands, they did not identify as far right. Tobias, for example, does not describe himself as far right but owns several of the clothing brands associated with the far right and notes that his best friend wears only Thor Steinar clothing but is not herself far right. He argues there is a difference between products within the brands that deploy aggressive iconography — like a T-shirt with a set of eagle's "wings from Hitler back then," and "totally normal" fashion produced by the same brands. Consumers differentiate within the brands, he argues, noting for example that the T-shirt with the eagle's wings would only be worn by *"Glatzköpfe* [bald heads, or skinheads]. You wouldn't see anybody with hair [wearing it]." Tim, a twenty-two-year-old masonry apprentice, argued that unless someone is yelling [racist or neo-Nazi] slogans or spraying [racist graffiti] someplace, people can wear whatever they want. "Just because someone wears a Thor Steinar sweater and has a shaved head, doesn't mean he's a Nazi."

One of the clearest examples of the varied contextual clues needed to interpret brand usage's meaning came during an interview with Lukas, a twenty-two-year-old carpentry apprentice. Lukas describes his father as "leaning towards the right wing," noting that his father regularly wears Thor Steinar at home and to work as a ventilation mechanic. He explains that his father wears the clothing because it reflects his political views but also to be provocative, because "he's sick of it, this whole integration thing and blah and it's a little more because of frustration and less tolerance than I have." But Lukas's own consumption of far right brands is more complicated. He once owned a Lonsdale jacket but doesn't have it anymore. His father bought him his first Thor Steinar clothing in midadolescence, and Lukas talked at length about how when he was sixteen to seventeen years old, he wore Thor Steinar clothing in combination with a long Mohawk (*Iro*), which would typically signify left-wing identity, as part of an effort to be confrontational and "more radical than the others." This combination confused everyone, he explained: "[one group] labeled me a Nazi, and then the Nazis labeled me a punk, and I always thought it was so funny, because . . . in the end you just get shoved into a little box." But later, when he cut off his Mohawk, he found he couldn't wear his Thor Steinar clothes anymore without being stamped as a neo-Nazi, and it became too stressful to constantly be defending himself against accusations that he was far right. "Now I don't have this Mohawk, and when you only have this other extreme, then it's also crap; if you have relatively short hair, blond, blue eyes, and then suddenly run through the neighborhood in a Thor Steinar sweater then you are . . . it's not cool." In other words, once Lukas cut off his (leftist) Mohawk, he lost a major contextual clue that disrupted the significance of the Thor Steinar clothing, and he became too clearly stamped as right-wing. Therefore, he stopped wearing Thor Steinar, because "then there wasn't anything left to discuss; I just had to keep defending myself and saying that's not the way it is, and I don't need that. Why? And anyway, at some point the clothes also got too small [laughs]."

Sometimes, it was only during the course of the interview conversation that youth started to disentangle the complicated nature of far right signifiers. Hans initially quickly dismissed the idea that people who wear brands associated with the far right are not far right themselves. He argued, "people who wear [these brands] always say 'eh, y'know it's a sporty brand' and blah blah blah this typical twaddle, but that's crap, because the brands are a part of [the far right scene] . . . I mean . . . they are primarily worn by the people who [are right-wing]." But as he started to reflect on his observations of people who wear the brands, he quickly acknowledged that the brand usage is complicated. "Well, OK, Fred Perry for example, OK, they also have polo shirts, and normal people wear them too, but everything else . . . well OK Alpha Industries, OK, maybe that's not absolutely a part of the far right scene . . . Pit Bull, I don't know for sure, but in any case Alpha Industries doesn't belong [to the right] . . . I know that because it's also . . . [worn by a lot of] . . . how can I say it best, migrants, or something like that." Near the end of the interview, however, Hans returns to his original assertion, arguing that "anyone who is a little bit informed knows that these brands belong [to the far right]. And anyone who says, it's just a sporty brand, that it's not [right wing], he's simply lying in my opinion, because it's totally obvious that that's not the case."

Other students argued that there is a difference between Thor Steinar and other brands that have been appropriated by the far right. Justin explained that "lots of right-wing extremists" wear the brands, and the ones banned at school are "the brands that they wear the most. I mean, Thor Steinar embodies the right-wing extremists a little; if you see someone [wearing Thor Steinar] on the street, then you of course automatically think of a Nazi." But his friends, who he says are not far right wing, wear brands like Lonsdale, Fred Perry, New Balance, and Alpha Industries.

Christoph, a twenty-one-year-old scaffold builder apprentice from Leipzig, talked at length about brands he owned like Lonsdale and Fred Perry, arguing that they are "totally normal clothing that doesn't say anything." But then he immediately follows up with a comparison to Thor Steinar, noting that "I find Lonsdale or Fred Perry don't make as strong a statement as, for example, Thor Steinar." By implication, Christoph suggests that Lonsdale and Fred Perry do make some sort of statement, although they are not as clear or strong in their expression as the brand Thor Steinar. He then links this difference directly to Thor Steinar's use of symbols: "Thor Steinar uses these symbol-ladened arguments, I'd say, and Lonsdale or Fred Perry, I've never noticed that there are any symbols in play with [those brands]." He notes that he has friends and acquaintances who wear Lonsdale, Fred Perry, Thor

Steinar, and Alpha Industries but explains that "some of them [wear the brands] for political reasons and others because they just like [the clothing]." Later, however, he explains that the brand Thor Steinar is a clear and definite right-wing signifier, identifying anyone who wears it as part of the far right scene: "until now I've only seen or known people who are in the right-wing scene who wear Thor Steinar, no one from the left-wing scene, and in Leipzig . . . the left-wing demonstrated against the Thor Steinar shop so that it would close." When the interviewer asked how he knows that Thor Steinar is a brand associated with the far right, he responds: "you just know it, that Thor Steinar belongs to the right-wing scene, but now they also have banned runes, old runes as an imprint, or have modified, for example a black sun. . . . Either you inform yourself about it, what kind of rune that is, or you ask someone who has an idea and then you know it too."

Other youth handily dismiss the idea that consumers are ignorant of the brands' meaning. Timo, a twenty-two-year-old scaffold builder apprentice who has several friends who wear Thor Steinar, New Balance, and other brands, argued that people who buy the brands overwhelmingly are aware of what they are doing. "Maybe out of one hundred people there are one or two ignorant [ones] who buy something like that." Still, consumers apparently sometimes purchase the brand without the intent of deploying it as a far right symbol. Bernd, for example, described how he bought a Thor Steinar jacket despite his concern about what the logo might suggest to observers. His mother told him that the jacket looked great despite its association with the far right and offered to simply replace the logo with another emblem. "So she sewed something else on it so there was no brand name."

Finally, it's important to note that the quality and design of the brands marketing to the far right are often quite appealing to youth, even when they disavow the coded messages. Youth repeatedly used the word "cool" when perusing the images, commenting on the appeal of the products' design, iconography, or coded messaging. Various youth were attracted to Nordic symbols, to military or marine references, and to products' deliberate ambivalence, clever coding, jokes, and indirect threats of violence. Klaus looked at a shirt and said, "OK. This is actually totally cool," explaining that he likes the dark and slightly secretive appearance of the T-shirt. Lukas looked at the T-shirt referencing the Tibet expedition described above and said, "actually at first glance the T-shirt looks totally cool . . . but when you look closer it's, well . . . yeah, not so cool at all," explaining that the motif and its message make the shirt's right-wing connotations clear. Ingo, an eighteen-year-old masonry apprentice, noted how distasteful he found an Erik and Sons T-shirt that, to him, evoked the notion of the Aryan race — but he had praise for the T-shirt itself and its design: "yeah, but in and of itself, just the design, to be honest, I find the T-shirt totally . . . appealing. Good." Justin looked at a photo of a Thor Steinar T-shirt and said, "well, I really like it, the military helicopter. . . . If the [Thor Steinar] logo wasn't there, I would probably wear it." Gerhard, a twenty-two-year-old scaffold builder apprentice from Saxony, reflected on how good the far right brands look on a classmate: "it really has style, the clothing looks really good." Daniel, a twenty-year-old carpentry apprentice, looked at a T-shirt and noted it is so normal it could be in a mainstream store: "That T-shirt could be hanging up at H&M."

Youth are also quick to judge the quality of the products when they do not measure up to their standards. When Hayri looked at a 2008 photo of a young man wearing a black sweatshirt with "Kategorie C" printed in old Germanic script across the back, he dismissed it as "not my style." He continued, "I don't want to sound mean, but [it looks] homemade and cheap."

The Evolution of Extremist Style

As the previous sections have detailed, across the interviews, a clear narrative emerged about the evolution of brands both within and beyond the far right scene. At the tail end of the skinhead era, in the late 1990s and early 2000s, youth appropriated mainstream brands like Lonsdale, Alpha Industries, Fred Perry, Pitbull, and New Balance for their coincidental symbolic resonance with the far right. These existing brands had logos that evoked Nazi symbols or could be interpreted as symbols for the far right, as youth let the "N" in the New Balance shoe stand for "Nazi," for example. In regions and neighborhoods where the far right youth scene was particularly dominant, in the early 2000s, young adolescents latched onto the same brands, combining them with steel-tipped combat boots, bomber jackets, and shaved heads as they imitated their older brothers and peers. At just about the same time, in the early 2000s, the sudden emergence of the Autonomous Nationalist movement radically transformed right-wing protest and demonstration tactics as well as far right group aesthetics by co-opting styles and strategies traditionally associated with the left.[43] This development set a precedent for the adaptation of far right style and opened the door to what ultimately became a more fragmented and mainstream set of subcultural styles.

By 2007 or 2008, when most of the youth I interviewed were in early adolescence, many of them describe a situation where "everyone" they knew had an Alpha jacket, and many also wore other brands popular within the far right scene. For some of these youth, the clothing was an entry point to the scene, which they identified with at this time. But others appear to have worn the clothing without really fully understanding or acknowledging its broader symbolic significance. In the meantime, right around the time that "everyone" started to wear an Alpha jacket, the brand Consdaple produced a T-shirt with an intentionally embedded symbol—the letters NSDAP—within the brand's name. Youth who wore their bomber jackets zipped halfway up over the shirt could thus display the letters of the Nazi party but could just as easily unzip their jacket to avoid the attention of police or other authorities. Thor Steinar and other brands quickly leapt into the market at this point, offering clothing that was as high in quality as brands like Lonsdale and Alpha Industries, but was now deliberately coded with clever, far right ideological references and iconography. As far right youth shifted toward these brands, the co-opted mainstream brands became less central to the far right subcultural scene—but by this point, those brands were broadly embedded within youth cultures across neighborhoods and regions with stronger far right youth representation. Some brands—like Alpha Industries—evolved to take on broader, less ideological symbolism around violence, aggression, and a willingness to fight, which retained an appeal for far right youth but was also adopted by rappers and youth from migrant backgrounds. Other brands—like Lonsdale—launched antiracist campaigns to try to counteract the far right image that they had never intended to create, and some leftist activists started wearing Lonsdale in order to support a company they perceived as fighting the good fight against the far right. The multivocality of particular symbols thus increased, and the style of the far right scene fragmented further. Today, some youth continue to imitate the all-black, leftist style popularized by the Autonomous Nationalists, as twenty-one-year-old carpentry apprentice Max described, noting that the far right has adopted an antifascist style, with "classical black things, sunglasses, Palestinian scarves, and partly copying the symbols." Other youth adopt the sportier, clean-cut look marketed by brands like Thor Steinar and Erik and Sons. Still other brands present as more alternative styles, using models with piercings or tattoos and deploying more aggressive iconography. Ingo noted that many far right youth today have piercings or the ear-stretching plugs called "tunnels," or might wear Nike sneakers instead of combat boots. As eighteen-year-old Thomas simply described during a discussion of transformations in far right style, "they don't really wear these . . . combat boots anymore, but instead blend in to the mainstream population, in order to not attract as much attention. They've also changed the design of their T-shirts so that you have to look longer at them in order to see what . . . to whom [the wearer] belongs, or what this symbol is supposed to express."

This is part of what contributes to the multivocality of the brand usage: while the brands clearly convey far right ideologies, they are not exclusively consumed by far right youth. Some brands have developed broader markets by acquiring a less specific reputation representing violence and aggression, while others have expanded their consumer base with targeted advertising campaigns that denounce the far right. And because some of the brands deliberately market to crossover and multiple markets—capitalizing on the Nordic appeal to rockers and bikers, or on the appeal of fighting messages to martial arts aficionados—youth repeatedly emphasized the importance of using multiple contextual clues—hairstyle, musculature, and more—to interpret whether any given brand reflects far right identity or ideology.

This is where identifying and banning the symbols gets particularly complicated. A number of organizations—local police bureaus, antifascist NGOs, teacher training organizations, and federal and state agencies—regularly produce brochures, pamphlets, and reports that identify and explain right-wing extremist symbols. Both the co-opted mainstream brands (such as Lonsdale or New Balance) as well as the newer brands (such as Thor Steinar, Ansgar Aryan, Erik and Sons, or Label 23/Boxing Connection) are consistently identified in such reports, their logos depicted in color appendices and glossy brochure pages alongside brief textual explanations of their symbolic value to the far right. Schools, stadiums, universities, and other entities then use these reports to make decisions about dress codes, bans, and policies around clothing and symbol deployment. Combined with legal bans on a variety of extremist symbols and expressions, the practice of banning brands and symbols, in turn, has become one of the most significant drivers of the far right game-playing phenomenon. I return to these issues—of how bans are circumvented and subverted, and how school bans in particular are interpreted and reacted to by youth—in chapter 5.

Conclusion: Symbols and Meaning Making

Symbols are popular within the new far right youth subculture in Germany not only because they circumvent bans, of course. They are also—perhaps primarily—ways of conveying insider and outsider status, of forging belonging and connection to a group and of expressing anger and resistance against mainstream society. Despite the cautions I raised about the difference between "real" or hard-core right-wing extremists and far right subcultural style in chapter 1, there is clear evidence that the brands and subcultural style more generally act as a gateway to the far right scene. They help strengthen identity, facilitate access to other like-minded individuals, and provide legitimacy and credibility within the scene. But using a T-shirt to communicate with observers requires that the observer accurately interpret the intended message. And as the youth interviewed here made clear, the coding process doesn't always work: not all consumers or observers understand all the codes; activists deliberately try to disrupt coded references by reclaiming codes; disagreements emerge within the scene about the deployment and interpretation of global codes like Che Guevara or Palestinian scarves (see chapter 5).

Even when they fail, however, the mere existence of coded symbols in the far right scene and their impact on youth's sense of identity and belonging challenges mainstream sociology's way of thinking about the power and role of economic objects. Economic objects—long understood to have exploitative power and contribute to social inequality—turn out to have constitutive power for identity as well. As I argued in chapter 1, the new brands in the far right youth scene not only transmit meaning for the German far right but also constitute it, helping youth construct their identities rather than only express them. While scholars have argued that consumption is a constitutive act, there has been little theoretical articulation about how symbols—including but not limited to logos or consumer products—play a role in such identity construction. In the case of far right economic objects and consumer goods, their constitutive power appears to work through their embeddedness in shared contexts and meaning systems.

Importantly, those shared contexts rest not only on shared knowledge, but also on interpretations of physical context. Youth utilized several different kinds of contextual clues as they interpreted images. First, they studied the consumers and models' bodies: their musculature, haircuts, phenotypical appearances, skin, hair, eye color, tattoos, and facial expressions. A shirt worn by a blue-eyed, muscular man with a shaved head is interpreted differently than the same shirt worn by a person of color or someone who looks bookish or "nerdy," to use one youth's phrase. Lukas, for example, explained that a T-shirt depicting a man being hung with the phrase "Dancing in the Air" doesn't signify violence on its own to him, but in the context of the person wearing the T-shirt in the image, "of course it does. Shaved head, ACAB on his neck . . . but . . . if another person was wearing it" he would interpret it differently. Benjamin had a similar comment about the same shirt: "I think it's actually OK. Well, without the guy who is in it, I think it's OK. It's totally funny." Second, they analyzed not only the wearer's physical appearance but also his or her environment. Youth regularly interpreted and discussed various symbols in the context of what other people look like in the immediate environment, for example, or what the consumer is doing. A T-shirt worn by a consumer at an apparent protest march, in the company of other individuals dressed similarly, may have a different reception from one in a product catalog. Similarly, product names, logos, and brands all contributed to youth interpretations of particular iconographic symbols and messages. This means that the meaning of a given symbol or consumer good does not rest in the symbol alone; rather, it is in the interplay between the symbol and its context—both of which must be interpreted within a set of shared knowledge and meanings.

Finally, as the manipulation and playfulness with symbols described in this chapter shows, symbols are not static entities—they are responsive both to the contemporary social and legal context as well as to the historical context. The broader social context around legal and private bans on particular symbols, combined with social taboos surrounding Nazi-era symbols, has created a playful set of meaning-making processes both within and across the brands. This case identifies a need for further study of the emergence and modification of symbols over time and in different national and cultural contexts in order to more rigorously consider the stability of symbols and cultural meanings and the ways in which cultural meanings, repertoires, and strategies are shaped by historical and contemporary contexts within and across nations and regions. I elaborate on this point in this volume's conclusion. Before I get there, however, in the next chapter, I turn to a more in-depth analysis of how Nordic symbols in particular have been appropriated by the far right, and what they mean for our understanding of the relationship between nationalism, myth, and symbols.

3 HISTORICAL FANTASIES, FANTASTICAL MYTHS
Sacred Origin Narratives

Brands are symbols. . . . We operate in a symbolic economy.
It's one where crass products and their meaningless material
benefits can be transformed into living vessels of meaning.
—Douglas Atkin, brand strategist

From the vantage point of late modernity, myth is often relegated to the distant past, to the fabled and superstitious accounts of premodern societies who found order, comfort, and meaning in systems of Greek gods, ritual sacrifices, and nature worship.[1] But mythic traces have long lived on in the everyday lives of "modern" humans; we encounter "countless mythical motifs," for example, in novels, plays, or films that depict fights between paradigmatic heroes and villains, wayward sons, dueling brothers, distraught maidens, avenging fathers, or paradisal geographies and landscapes.[2] Few concepts have inspired as much cross disciplinary reflection as the notion of myth, animating the scholarly and artistic production of psychologists like Freud as well as musicians like Wagner, of linguists like de Saussure and philosophers like Nietzsche. There is a tremendous variety of forms and expressions of these modern myths — traces are found in the cockfights and wrestling matches Barthes analyzed as well as in Wagner's operatic treatment of the *Nibelungen* saga.

In the following chapter, I focus on symbols and visual representations that reflect a fantasy of Nordic heritage and their relationship to far right youth culture. Through a careful analysis of commercial iconography and accompanying slogans and textual references in T-shirts and other products, I show how these fantastical myths and symbols are used to directly depict or evoke sacred geographies as well as a sense of loss or of a particular way of life "slipping away." By analyzing these symbols in light of theoretical work on fascism's relationship to postmodernity and its roots in mythic and palingenetic nationalism, I suggest that the deployment of symbols evoking national myths help to crystallize a kind of "magical thinking" and evoke fantasy expression of a nation that never existed but that is nonetheless aspired to.[3] The chapter ultimately argues that the fantasy of Nordic heritage may appeal to youth as a strategy for handling the uncertainty and loss of stability in the global, postmodern era. The potential power of mythic fantasies for the appeal of extremist ideologies has been an underexplored area in research on youth radicalization. Instead, far right youth's actions tend to be explained as motivated by economic uncertainty and social change, racism and xenophobia, peer pressure or parental upbringing, or simple ignorance. As this chapter argues, youth yearning for an imagined, pure, and prior form of the collective also explains the allure of extremist movements.

One of the reasons why myths endure is because they have dual purposes, as Roland Barthes pointed out more than half a century ago; they help us to understand something, and they impose that understanding on us at the same time.[4] In the case of national myths—which are a particular subset of myth that shape and reflect national imaginaries and tell foundational stories about core national values, principles, and beliefs—this means that myth simultaneously helps us interpret the nation and helps to constitute or enact it.[5] Myths play a powerful role in shaping the national imaginary. They convey sacred narratives, stories, and messages about a nation's history, foundational principles, ethnic origins, and peoples—thereby mediating the collective past. They filter and reconstruct cultural memory and invoke nostalgia for an imagined past while helping the collective imagine a shared future.[6] They do all this while inhabiting a space somewhere between historical fact and pure fantasy: national myths are, in other words, neither historical accounts nor fictional ones.

Part of why national myths cannot be understood as completely constructed despite the fact that they are at least partly fictionalized is because of the way they integrate factual elements into imagined pasts, as Geneviève Zubrzycki argues. They "present themselves as natural and uncontested" and are understood to be real and true by people within any given nation.[7] In other words, myths differ from pure fantasies, fables, folklore, legends, or literature primarily because of the ways in which they are held to be true, sacred narratives; they blend abstract pasts and stories with elements of the real, even when they are at "crass variance with reality."[8] Myths thus act as filters of reality, purporting "to give a true account of a set of past, present, or predicted political events" that a given social group accepts.[9] They present an idealized version of the nation or its values, principles, and actions. In this way, national myths hold a promise of an alternative existence to which a nation can, or should, aspire. They offer the collective a means to believe in something bigger and better, more noble and illustrious than their present state of being. The myths that the Brothers Grimm wove into their fairy tales, for example, as Brian Attebery points out, were reclaimed narratives of "a kingdom—the German nation that had never existed and yet could be imaginatively reconstructed once its mythology was reclaimed."[10] In this way, national myths work to mediate not only the imagined past but also an imagined—and idealized—future, integrating sacred collective memory with aspirational future glory.[11]

Part of what makes myths so effective is the wide variety of historical and fantastical legends, heroes, stories, and oral accounts to draw on in myth creation. As Roland Barthes argues, myths work by expressing what linguists call the "signified" (like a notion of Aryan-ness) through a "signifier" (like an image of a Nordic place). Barthes suggests that part of myths' power rests on the fact that there are many different kinds of signifiers that express the same signified: "This repetition of the concept through different forms is precious to the mythologist, it allows him to decipher the myth: it is the insistence of a kind of behaviour which reveals its intention."[12]

But national myths do more than mediate imagined pasts and imagined futures. They also hold powerful sway over the present, as Nietzsche pointed out nearly 150 years ago, arguing that myth "frees all the powers of the imagination" in ways that help people transcend the depression of ordinary life.[13] For Eliade, myths and other sacred manifestations are "primordial" experiences that provide an orientation point to help reign in the chaos of the modern world, in which secular rationality has erased the certainty that religious devotion once offered.[14] In this light, a broadly secular nation like Germany may create conditions under which myths and mythic thinking are particularly appealing.[15] National myths offer a salve to the anomie and isolation of secular modernity, in which individuals are increasingly detached from extended family units and unmoored from religious narratives that offered a sense of purpose and meaning. Nietzsche passionately argued for the rebirth of tragic myth, contending that myth was a useful "aesthetic illusion" that masked the pessimism and despair of existence."[16] Greek tragedies offered a "healing potion" to warriors engaged in battle, Nietzsche argued, and more generally, he believed that myth provides a promise of something greater lurking beneath the surface of "this restlessly palpitating civilized life," describing the hope that "there is concealed a glorious, intrinsically healthy, primitive power, which, to be sure, stirs vigorously only at intervals in stupendous moments, and then continues to dream of future awakening."[17] For Nietzsche, myth delivers observers and readers alike from the "primordial suffering of the world."[18]

National myths' effectiveness is bolstered by their ubiquity; they are evoked in rituals and enacted in performances from presidential speeches to national sporting events. They are embodied in visual and material culture like national symbols, slogans, images, flags, anthems, monuments, memorials, and marches. Material embodiments of national myths engage individuals in a variety of ways—as observers, as producers, as consumers, as interpreters, and as performers. Various actors experience national myths through such banal activities as wearing a brooch depicting a crown of thorns or singing a national anthem at a baseball game.[19]

Myths and mythic ideas are thus thought to help individuals navigate the uncertainty and unpredictability of modern, industrialized life. They do this in part by demarcating clear lines between good and evil, providing a sense of clarity and certainty in the face of increasingly complex life choices. But they also help evoke and naturalize a wide range of emotive signifiers and traits to which one might aspire, such as heroism, valor, nobility, purity, loyalty, integrity, strength, victory, or independence. Such mythical attributes serve the nation well, particularly in unsettled or uncertain epochs, but also help to motivate and mobilize potential nationalists even during more stable periods, in part by conveying normative expectations, visions, and values for the collective.[20]

One of the ways that national myths work to override rational thought is through the use of fantasy and magical thinking. Fantasy "uses symbols to tell the truths that the conscious mind cannot grasp or fears to face," explains Attebery, and it does so while pretending "to be a mere game. . . . It is free to speak forbidden truths because no one pays it any mind."[21] Mythical content is often detectable because of this element of fantasy, what we might think of as the "contrast between image and reality."[22] Through the use of fantasy, myths help to build—and to express—a collectivity's shared conscious and unconscious assumptions through a complex blend of imagination and expectations.[23] In the German national origin myth I describe below, for example, modern-day Germans are seen as the descendants of Nordic tribes whose origins were Aryan. This fantasy enables an expression of whiteness, evoking a sense of racial superiority without being overtly racist, and contributes to collective unconscious assumptions about the nature of German-ness and who belongs in the nation.

Mythic and magical thinking thus not only is the domain of fantasy gamers or *Lord of the Rings* fans but is something in which many—perhaps most—human beings indulge in from time to time. "Every human being," writes Eliade, "is made up at once of his conscious activity and his irrational experiences."[24] Ernest Becker similarly argued that all human beings have a fundamental need for heroic myths.[25] Fantasy thinking and magical consciousness—in which emotions are the "primary mode" of communication and dominate actions—are thus "very much a part of contemporary awareness," as Charlton McIlwain put it.[26] Magical and fantasy "forms of imagining," are, as McIlwain contends, expressions of "inner feeling" that can help individuals make sense of particular phenomena.

Fantastical thinking elevates individuals above the tedium of their ordinary existence, allowing them to exist—whether in the brief span of the cinematic performance or in a major life commitment to ISIS—in epic and righteous quests, eternal and apocalyptic battles. The German case is clear on this point. Mythic and heroic figures—typically hypermasculine, strong males—"embodied the values of medieval society resurrected by German romanticism: honor, loyalty, obedience, piety," as Anna von der Goltz contends.[27] Such ideals appear to be tremendously attractive to youth, particularly those who are disenfranchised or disaffected from mainstream expectations for success. There is historical evidence about the appeal of myths for the German far right; the Nazi party's "extensive use of myth" and "mythically charged language," argues Roger Griffin, was "calculated to whip up irrational emotions in the masses, making its followers fully identify with the regenerated *Volksgemeinschaft*."[28] Anna von der Goltz explains that the Nazi party's deployment of myths led national myth to be understood as a "hazardous" propaganda weapon that possessed "dangerous emotional connotations, causing people to depart from rational behaviour."[29]

Scholars have paid some attention to national myths, but most of this work looks at historical cases,[30] with less work focused on how national myths mobilize contemporary citizens and peoples, and still less attention to the ways in which myths and fantasies might appeal to disenfranchised and radical youth more specifically. There is almost no current scholarship on how myth is deployed by contemporary nationalists and radical extremists who yearn for an imagined, prior form of the collective—whether in the Third Reich's efforts to purge the nation of those deemed not to belong or in the contemporary ISIS move to reestablish an Islamic caliphate.[31] And there is even less work on how images, symbols, and material artifacts are appropriated in such deployments or why they are so effective at rousing nationalist and extremist sentiments. In this chapter, I argue that myth holds a powerful sway for contemporary youth, particularly those who may feel disenfranchised from mainstream society, and I analyze how visual and material embodiments of national myth—particularly one form of national myth popular with far right youth—have been marketed in Germany in ways that may help recruit and radicalize susceptible youth.

Envisioning the Nation

In his thoughtful reflection on the notion of national heritage, Stuart Hall argues that the nation is "an on-going project, under constant reconstruction. We come to know its meaning partly *through* the objects and artefacts which have been made to stand for and symbolise its essential values."[32] I take issue with Hall's pronoun choice ("it"), which implies a singular collective meaning rather than multiple and competing ones. But his assertion that objects and artifacts play a key role in conveying meaning is indisputable.

Visual expressions of national myths—such as symbols, images, and other material objects—play a particularly key role in mediating the relationship between emotion and imagination. They help mediate fantastical and imaginary domains, in part by concretizing and actualizing particular national myths. Material objects and symbols can act like thresholds or gateways for the passage from the profane world to the sacred one[33] and can serve, as Zubrzycki contends, "as conduits through which subjects become ideologically and affectively invested in the nation."[34] In this way, "images are agents of socialization," influencing "thought and behavior."[35] Images and material objects can even evoke national myths in visual depictions without explicitly embodying them, subtly shaping observers' understandings of the nation through hinted references and connotations.

Advertisers have done this for decades, of course, as have political campaigns and propaganda. The introduction of visual elements in consumer advertising in Germany in the 1920s meant that "advertisers no longer had to rely on appealing to consumers' rational choice but could appeal to their emotions on a connotative level," argues von der Goltz, explaining that German specialists used "familiar codes and a culturally established visual language" to appeal to consumers' emotional fears and desires.[36] Iconography that deployed Paul Von Hindenburg's image in pre–World War II Germany—meant to represent masculinity, strength, and determination—was thus used by advertisers to sell an array of products, from cars and sausages to brandy.[37] Similarly, companies that market commercial clothing and products to the far right, as I will describe below, rely on the fantasy of Nordic/Aryan descent in their use of Nordic spelling, symbols, landscapes, and other iconography.

Even when implicit and coded, images and symbols of national myths are not arbitrary but rather still have intentional signification, as Barthes argues, noting that there is "no myth without motivated form."[38] Whether used explicitly or implicitly, through coded references or overt representations, symbols, icons, images, and material elements help connect visual and sensory experiences with emotional attachments.[39] Images and symbols are thus a key part of how national myths both reflect and shape understandings of the nation.[40]

Finally, it is important to note that myths can be powerful even in forms that are less than full-fledged narratives: the mythical motifs that Eliade identified, for example, may be present in hints, partial images, or suggestions that are evoked or alluded to indirectly in phrases, symbols, or text.[41] Landscapes are a good example—even when evoked as partial motifs, the natural spaces in which we live act on us emotionally and cognitively.[42] Moreover, not everyone who observes a particular symbol will react in the same way. National myths evoke stronger emotions for some than for others. Zubrzycki notes that there are two primary reactions to what she calls nationalist mythologies, or collections of myths about the nation: namely, one regards such mythologies either as sacred, or as profane.[43] People who experience national myths, symbols, and images as sacred find such images "a metonymic extension of something deeply real and fundamentally solid—though potentially threatened and hence in need of ardent defense."[44] Those who find them to be profane, Zubrzycki argues, maintain a "certain critical distance" that enables a more playful, ironic deployment of national myths and symbols.[45]

The literature has offered few clues about how mythical symbols and images have been used in the contemporary era, particularly among extremists and nationalists in Germany or elsewhere. There is a fairly robust body of scholarship on historical nationalist symbols, particularly those used by the Nazis and on Germanic legends and mythology.[46] These works have been key to my efforts to decode far right images and products, such as the brand Thor Steinar's T-shirts with the word "Asgard," which in Norse mythology is the name of a capital city ruled by Odin. Literature on Germanic and Norse legends is similarly key to understanding the ubiquitous use of images of Vikings and Viking warfare and of other symbols drawn from Norse mythology, such as Walhalla, the hall of the dead. There is a small literature on the use of "folk esoteric," paganism, and Greek mythology by right-wing extremists,[47] but there has been little analysis of how such images have been used over time.[48] Scholars have looked at myths and national identity in tourist sites in former Soviet states and in nationalism more generally.[49] But there is little known about how extreme forms of nationalism and far right extremism rely on myths to recruit, radicalize, or socialize youth.

Sacred Origin Myths

In this chapter, I explore one particular type of national myth: what I call a *myth of sacred origin*. Sacred origin narratives are a type of national myth that helps to convey the core beliefs of a nation,[50] using some combination of the following elements:

1. focus on *ethnic origins* or *blood-based* biological connections in the national population;[51]

2. designation of *hallowed, revered, or consecrated territory*, places, geography, or spaces that belong to the nation or its designated people; these may be thought of as ancestral homelands, ethnoscapes, habitats and as the nation's birthplace or the "resting place" of heroes;[52]

3. use of *magical* thinking (about gods, fantastical legends, revered symbols, rituals, heroes' superhuman capacity, chosen peoples, etc.);[53]

4. reverence for the dead or for *sacrifice through death*; fealty for the "glorious dead";[54] promise of personal redemption, national regeneration, resurrection, or immortality through mortal sacrifice;[55]

5. *designation of a golden age:* an exalted period in which the community's status was triumphant, victorious, positioned at the apex of all civilizations, tribes, or nations;

6. presence of *admirable population traits and virtues* during the golden age or era, such as honesty, purity, piety, loyalty, simplicity, integrity, strength, etc.;

7. expression of *loss of an entire way of life* as the result of the decline of this golden age or because of threats posed by the modern, industrialized, secularized world;[56] the current era is described in terms of loss, of a dying out of a way of life, or as a threatened civilization;

8. *oppositional framing of an epic, enduring, and righteous struggle* with other groups, tribes, or nations,[57] potentially in apocalyptic terms;

9. belief in an *imminent and virtuous restoration to a past utopia*[58] and to a natural state of glory and supremacy, often expressed in terms of "salvation dramas," in which a golden age will be restored, resulting in collective exaltation, renewal, and transcendence;[59]

10. *valorization of violence* and revered weapons consistent with the golden age (spears, swords, axes, etc.) or deployment of violence for a cause;

11. characterization of the entire narrative or myth as *sacred*, to be defended and protected from insult, opponents, infidels, non-believers, or traitors.[60]

Sacred Origin Narratives and the German Far Right

Myth's powerful sway over the historical and contemporary national imaginary — as deployed in sacred origin narratives — is well illustrated by the German case. The German sacred origin narrative blends two sets of mythical sagas: a myth of Aryan racial "stock" and a myth of Nordic descent.[61] Dunlap traces the Aryan myth's origins to a group of German philologists and linguists who discovered the affinities of several languages (including Greek, Celtic, French, and Germanic) with Sanskrit and then superimposed the notion of common ancestry onto the language relationship.[62] Before long, other scholars had expanded the Aryan racial myth by infusing it with racist genetic thinking, attributing superiority to "Aryans whose blood was least degraded by mixture with inferior stocks."[63]

Importantly, the myth took on elements of the classic good-and-evil polarity, as scholars warned of a scenario in which "purer" races could be "overrun" by lesser blood. The French scholar Arthur de Gobineau was perhaps the most influential thinker in this regard; his mid-nineteenth-century treatise (*Essay on the Inequality of Human Races*) described "a world where superior 'Aryans' were nonetheless in danger of being overrun by masses of inferiors."[64] Although the main philologist responsible for this extension of the term "Aryan" from a linguistic designation to a genetic one (F. Max Müller) issued an emphatic retraction more than twenty-five years after his prominent lectures on the subject, asserting in 1888 "that language affinities are not evidence for racial relationships," the intervening decades had done irreversible damage.[65] By the turn of the century, the Aryan myth not only had become deeply embedded with notions of racial purity but was also infused with a sense of foreboding about the potential loss of an entire "race." Racist propaganda in the late nineteenth century used imagery that conjured up this sense of threat, depicting "fortresses and dams, protective walls, 'outposts and pioneers,' all presenting a value of order set against threatening chaos."[66] These ideals reflect classic elements of sacred origin narratives more generally, such as a focus on blood-based origins and a sense of collective loss of identity or way of life.

The Aryan myth became layered onto a prior sacred origin narrative that expressed a belief that Germanic tribes were of Nordic descent. While there are some historical accounts connecting the "blond-haired, blue-eyed" Nordic peoples[67] to the Germans, evidence for Nordic origins of Germanic tribes is thin—even "dubious," as Vejas Gabriel Liulevicius contends.[68] But even if the historical account of a link between Nordic and Germanic groups is factual, the resulting myth—in which modern-day Germans are taken to be descendants of Nordic tribes—conflates "ancient Germanic tribes with the Germans of the present day"[69] in ways that firmly place the sacred origin narrative in the realm of national myth.

There are some clues that point to how the myth of Nordic descent might have developed, and how it became intertwined with the myth of Aryan racial stock. In the late nineteenth and early twentieth centuries, a growing number of antimodern, Germanic, religious groups rooted in ancient Germanic and pagan mythology, along with *völkish* political and youth movement groups, began to explicitly link Nordic, Aryan, and Germanic groups in a blended form of nationalism and spirituality. They did this in part by defining Germanic religion and spirituality as an innate, racial inheritance that was "a living counterpart of the homeland, one's blood, feeling and thinking."[70] Such *völkish* movements—aiming to reclaim the nation from the dislocation and anomie of capitalist industrialism—positioned the Aryan race as locked in an epic struggle with "non-Germans" and "Semites" who were forcing the nation away from its true, Nordic, natural roots; only a "regeneration" of the German nation would offer possible salvation and an eventual future utopia.[71]

Some of the early nationalists relied on the Roman senator and historian Tacitus's manuscript, *The Germania*, which described the Germanic tribes as biologically distinct from the Romans and other tribes; instead, Germans were said to have descended from the Nordic tribes.[72] Shortly before the Reformation, as Martin Bernal explains, the *Germania* was rediscovered, and its "laudatory and idyllic picture of their ancestors . . . encouraged Germans to see themselves as poorer but more virtuous than the degenerate peoples to the south."[73] The fact that the *Germania* was later "celebrated as an accurate reflection of authentic German people" has to be understood, as Krebs argues, in light of the fact that the manuscript "was written by a Roman in Rome for Romans. It was only later that this snapshot of a particular cultural period would be turned into the German people's own national profile."[74]

By the late nineteenth century, as German nationalism began to rise, the Tacitean myth began to be used "to testify to the purity not only of the mores and the language but also and increasingly of the racial constitution of the Germanic ancestors as members of the Caucasian, then Aryan, and finally Nordic race."[75] The Nordic myth in particular held a powerful place in German arts and culture during this period, as George Williamson notes in his description of "scholars and amateurs alike" who, in the early 1800s, "scoured through medieval verse, church libraries, and peasant villages for evidence of forgotten Germanic deities or lost knightly epics."[76] Christopher Krebs documents writers as early as 1505 for whom "the mythical *Germanen* had become the exemplary Germans: pure and noble; long limbed, fair, and flaxen haired."[77] Over the coming centuries, German poets and authors began to turn away from classical and Greek mythology and rely more heavily on Nordic myths and legends, depicting Nordic roots as "original" to Germans.[78] Goethe and Schiller's poems, fairy tales from the Brothers Grimm, and the epic sagas in Wagner's operas have all drawn on mythical fables, allegorical folktales, and heroic legends from Germanic, Nordic, and Aryan lore. Friedrich Nietzsche's late nineteenth-century treatise on Greek tragedy was as much a critique of the decline of the Nordic myth in an increasingly rational German society as it was an analysis of Dionysian heroes. As he concludes *The Birth of Tragedy*, Nietzsche references the Nordic myth and calls for its reawakening in the German spirit:

there have been some indications that nevertheless in some inaccessible abyss the German spirit still rests and dreams, undestroyed, in glorious health, profundity, and Dionysian strength, like a knight sunk in slumber. . . . Let no one believe that the German spirit has forever lost its mythical home. . . . Some day it will find itself awake in all the morning freshness following a deep sleep: then it will slay the dragons, destroy the malignant dwarfs, waken Brünnhilde—and Wotan's spear itself will be unable to obstruct its course![79]

The two myths might have remained fringe narratives, however, were it not for the consequential intervention of Alfred Rosenberg, the director of ideology and education for the Nazi party who was executed for Nazi war crimes in 1946. Rosenberg is credited with having the greatest intellectual influence on the ideological expansion of these two myths into a broader worldview—the Nazi *Weltanschauung*.[80] Among other elements, Rosenberg's development of the Nordic myth definitively linked blood to German-ness in the concept of the "race-soul" (*Rassenseele*), which linked a set of values he identified as Nordic with a genetic and biological definition of German-ness—effectively writing a "history of the Aryan people as he imagined it."[81] The "Nordic soul," also referred to as the "Aryan" race or the "Nordic spirit," embodied values like honor and freedom and expressed "life, vitality and cultural generation," as Amit Varshizky has detailed. Importantly, the Nordic soul was to be contrasted with the Roman

race, which represented cultural degeneration and chaos.[82] This opposition
— between a pure, vital, Nordic or Aryan race and degenerate, polluted elements outside of it — would come to permeate Nazi thinking and far right
extremist ideology up until the present day. Ultimately, Rosenberg posited
that the Nordic soul would free itself from the shackles of a degenerate society and that its diluted racial stock would move the "Nordic man" from
"'darkness into light,'" from "earthly bonds into an eternal unknown."[83] In
so doing, Hitler and his Nazi party would enable a "rebirth and return to
real and imagined past glories."[84]

Thus, it is clear that the myth of Aryan racial "stock" and the myth of
Nordic ethnic origins gradually became inseparable in the years leading
up to the First World War.[85] Eventually they became core tenets of Nazi
ideology. By the time the National Socialists came into power, Aryans were
depicted as the descendants of Germanic tribes whose origins were Nordic.
This intertwined set of Aryan and Nordic myths became the sacred origin
myth of German far right nationalists and extremists. It became a foundational element of right-wing extremist and nationalist goals, culminating in
the Third Reich, when the Nazi party emblazoned its divisions with symbols drawn from runic letters (most famously, the Sig or "S" rune for the
SS troops) (see plates 17 and 18) and used propaganda that was "driven by
genuine and fanatical belief in the imminence of Germany's rebirth . . . [and
in] the utopia of a new order, a racially purified and regenerated state."[86]

Myth turned out to be an ideal tool for National Socialist objectives,
offering "a way of thinking about art, religion, and the nation," Williamson
argues, "that was particularly suited to the political fantasies of Hitler and
the racist policies of the Nazi state."[87] Mythical fantasies rooted in eternal
Nordic and Germanic struggles with outside "races" evoked a sense of rebirth and rejuvenation, and their symbols and images offered Germans the
prospect of a meaningful life, "which would overcome the fragmentation
and dislocation" of the current era.[88] Although he later renamed it, an early
version of the first volume of Hitler's *Mein Kampf* used the title "Germanic
Revolution."[89] The Nazi party used the swastika, variably known as an ancient Viking sun symbol, a Nordic representation of Thor's Hammer, and a
sacred Germanic sign of salvation,[90] as its main political symbol.[91]

Influential intellectual works of this period — like Alfred Rosenberg's *Der
Mythus des zwanzigsten Jahrhunderts* (1930) — positioned the world as in conflict between the Nordic and the Semitic races, framing Aryan and Nordic
as interchangeable.[92] Youth propaganda films taught young Germans the
virtues of their Germanic forefathers, linking the Germanic tribes to the
Vikings. One Hitler Youth propaganda film slide explains, in text next to a

Viking ship: "The Germanic (tribes) are the oldest sailors. They built the first ships. Vikings discovered Iceland, Greenland and America" (see plate 21).[93] Heinrich Himmler, the *Reichsführer* of the SS, was famously obsessed with Germany's Nordic and Germanic origins, cofounding a research group to study spiritual prehistory (*Geistesurgeschichte*) and (re)discover Germany's true ancestral heritage, folk traditions, myths, songs, and pagan symbols.[94] This research group later became a subdivision of the SS, known as the *Ahnenerbe* (ancestral heritage), which among other tasks, was charged with tracking down and confiscating an original copy of Tacitus's *Germania* manuscript in order to use it as a basis for the "re-nordification" and racial selection of Nordic attributes among Germans.[95]

By the time Himmler started his quest for an original copy of the *Germania*, the extent to which Germanic myths were rooted in any potential real past was essentially meaningless. Fantasies of a prior, pure era to which Germany could be returned came to dominate the ideology of the Nazi era. Ultimately, like the mythophiles of the nineteenth century that Williamson describes, extreme nationalists ended up caught "swaying between memory of a past that never was and anticipation of a future that would never be."[96] For Nazis in the Third Reich as well as contemporary right-wing extremists today, Germanic and Nordic legends are not myths but rather a "timeless utopia" where bloodlines and character were pure and ancient Germans were loyal, courageous, honest heroes.[97]

Selling the Nordic Myth

The mythical and fantastical past thus has long roots in German nationalism, as German nationalists throughout the centuries drew on Germanic legends, myths, and symbols to try to align German-ness with Nordic and Aryan attributes—so successfully, in fact, that National Socialists ultimately used the terms "Germanic," "Nordic," and "Aryan" interchangeably.[98] The Nordic obsession of the German far right was comparatively quiet in the early postwar era, and it didn't emerge as part of far right youth subculture in any significant way until after the turn of the century. In the first few decades after World War II, right-wing extremists tended to be older, elite men who had previously been part of the Nazi party.[99] For the first two decades after far right youth culture developed in the 1980s, the subculture was dominated by the influence of British racist skinhead style, with legions of young men shaving their heads and donning leather bomber jackets and high black combat boots. The Nordic fascination did not disappear during this time, but its influence was more muted than under the Nazis. It was most evident in the lyrics and band names of right-wing rock music groups, who began touring throughout Europe in the 1980s and helped create a global, pan-Aryan movement. Early commercial product companies emerged at this time also, selling a limited number of products like pendants, key chains, patches, flags, and buttons through mail-order flyers and brochures. Nordic references, iconography, and symbols are peppered in a fairly limited way throughout this early commercialization, from the straightforward "Nordic" emblazoned across one T-shirt to the very name of an early mail-order company, Asgard-Versand, which translates as "Asgard shipping" and refers to Asgard, a mythical fenced-in world of the Gods, the Æsin, in Nordic mythology.[100]

By the mid-2000s, however, when the first major commercial brands began to produce high-quality clothing for the far right in Germany, Nordic style had become a marketing strategy in its own right, with iconographical designs, motifs, and even product and store names utilizing Nordic references. Right-wing commercial entities rely heavily on nationalist history and historical mythology in brands and logos like Nordland, Viking Company, and Nordmark.[101] Commercial entities appropriate symbols from the mythical past (such as Viking gods, runic letters, and Celtic symbols)[102] as well as symbols associated with Nordic pagan religions—particularly the symbols of the runic alphabet and the Norse gods (like Wotan)[103] in high-quality, expensive, mainstream-style clothing lines.

Today, Thor Steinar, the largest and most successful commercial brand that has a consumer base within the far right, designs much of its clothing with Nordic references[104] (see plates 12 and 13). Its product lines are rife with names like the "Nordvendt" jacket and the "Fjord" cardigan; its store names (Tønsberg, Trømso, Larvik, Oseberg, Haugesund, and most recently, Brevik) are the names of Scandinavian towns; catalog images show blond, athletic men and women in a variety of settings that evoke or make direct Nordic references—sailboats, bridges, snowy ski slopes, glaciers, and boatyards. Landscapes evoke Scandinavian seasides and shorelines; websites position products against backdrops of Nordic coastal architecture, glaciers, and geographies; and Vikings are referenced frequently. The Thor Steinar "Walhall" long-sleeved T-shirt references "Valhalla," which in Norse and Scandinavian mythology is a hall for slain battle heroes.[105]

Another popular brand, Erik and Sons, uses the Nordic spelling of Erik and uses the tagline "Viking Brand" on its website and product catalogs, and it also relies heavily on images of classic sailboats and coastal scenes in its catalogs. Erik and Sons sells T-shirts with the Danish flag and the words "Nordland," along with a range of other Viking, Norse, and Germanic mythological references. Other brands draw heavily on Nordic references and mythology, depicting Viking warfare or ships, Nordic symbols and art, or depictions of the battles such as the legend of Hyperborea (see plates 13 and 14). Ingo, an eighteen-year-old masonry apprentice, looked at a catalog image of a sweatshirt with the text "Expedition Antarctica" and "The White Continent" and discussed the potential dual meanings of the product, teasing out connections to Nazi expeditions and myths before he sums up the overall product's appeal. "Yeah, again it is actually graphically very good," he acknowledges; "you can't really tell it's . . . it's fashion, yes. But it's fashion with a specific background."

Nordic imagery is intertwined with symbols of violence throughout the product catalogs in ways that valorize violent quests and honorable deaths or prominently feature weapons consistent with the Viking period or ancient Norse culture: axes, swords, and spears. One Erik and Sons T-shirt, called the "Rage Rider," uses the tagline "Viking Storm" with printed text: "The wind howls like hungry wolves. Wotan and his wild army pass over forest and meadows. So the hunters' chase wreaks havoc—the rage riders' will knows the way." Such imagery fosters youth fantasies of being fierce warriors or fighters, while naming and identifying their anger or rage at mainstream society.

Nordic Means "Aryan"

According to the construction apprentices I interviewed, Nordic symbols in general are linked to two major subcultural scenes: the far right and the heavy metal scenes. As they explained the appeal of Nordic iconography and symbols, youth repeatedly emphasized that it's not possible to immediately understand how a given Nordic symbol is being deployed unless one considers additional contextual clues, including the brand of the clothing, tattoos, and musculature, or the setting. Young people frequently explained that they knew many "rockers" and youth in the metal scene who use Nordic symbols or who wear Thor Steinar clothing. But they were equally clear that when used by far right youth, Nordic symbols send a clear message about whiteness, while Viking symbols in particular additionally convey a willingness to be violent (*Gewaltbereitschaft*).

Youth had consistent explanations for why Nordic and Viking iconography is appealing to the far right—namely, that Nordic is used as a placeholder for "Aryan," allowing users to evoke whiteness without explicitly referring to race. Kevin, who was from Braunschweig and at thirty-nine was the oldest student we interviewed, explained the connection most clearly: "Vikings are often used as a symbol for Nordic, which is associated with

Aryan." Max, a twenty-one-year-old carpentry apprentice from Berlin, explained that Nordic symbols are appealing to the far right because of "the Aryan thing, the *Überrasse*, who lived a little further north and then the blond, tall guy was held up as an ideal. An ideal human being." Niel, a twenty-year-old construction mechanic trainee, equated the Vikings with the "original race [*Urrasse*], the Germanic tribes" but explained that it depends on the style and context in terms of whether one can interpret the symbol as right wing. Tim, a twenty-two-year-old Berliner masonry apprentice, noted that Nordic symbols aligned with Nazi "racial understandings of how the perfect German should look, tall, blond, and that's simply how the Nordics looked and so on and strong and I'd guess that's why they said, [Germans] should also look like that, and that's why they're so turned on by [those symbols], today's Nazis and the earlier ones." Gerhard, a twenty-one-year-old scaffold builder apprentice from Leipzig, described Viking T-shirts as "very widespread in the right-wing scene" owing to their connection with the "Aryan race" and because Vikings convey a sense of willingness to be violent.

Some young people appear to use the terms "Nordic" and "Aryan" interchangeably. Fabian, a seventeen-year-old roofing apprentice, used the term Nordic-Aryan (*Nord-arische*) to refer to Nordic motifs and symbols, while Mahmut, a twenty-one-year-old technical preservation apprentice, explained the phrase "Nordic lifestyle" conveys the notion that "the further you come toward the north, the whiter the people are." Thomas, an eighteen-year-old building energy design apprentice, looked at an image of a Thor Steinar T-shirt that referenced the *Nordiscke Livsstil* and noted that the T-shirt seemed "national socialist. . . . It must be Swedish or something, right? I could imagine that that's supposed to mean that one should live this Nordic or Aryan lifestyle . . . blond, blue eyes." Ingo looked at an Erik and Sons T-shirt that depicts a Viking sailor and described the man as a "very Aryan . . . person with long hair and a Viking ship, and [this is] supposed to evoke these old traditions." A few minutes later, analyzing another T-shirt from the same brand that overlays the word *Nordlander* in old Germanic script over an image of a Viking warrior with an ax, Ingo says, "the only thing disturbing about this T-shirt is [the word] *Nordlander*, because *Nordlander* . . . means . . . that one belongs to this *Nordic, Aryan* race, to the Celts" (emphasis added). By linking the terms "Nordic" and "Aryan," in such moments youth revealed how intertwined the two concepts are even in their own thinking and explanations of the appeal of Nordic iconography for far right youth. Still later in the interview, while examining a Thor Steinar T-shirt, Ingo notices that the iconography of spread wings evokes the *Reichsadler*, and he notes the T-shirt's use of "a Celtic kind of script." This brings him to reflect on the relevance of the Nordic mythology for Germany. "Some people interpret it that, earlier the people said, yeah, the gods chose us and we are the only true race." Several youth noted that Viking symbols in particular evoked strength, aggressiveness, and a readiness to be violent (*Gewaltbereitschaft*) — a topic that I take up in greater depth in chapter 6. For example, as he perused an image of a T-shirt depicting a Viking with an ax, shield, and helmet overlaid on a historical Viking ship with the word *Nordlander*, Timo, a twenty-two-year-old scaffold builder apprentice, initially connected the T-shirt to the right-wing scene but then corrected himself that Vikings and Viking ships might not be "directly right wing" but rather connected to "soccer fans." He elaborated: "because of the Viking . . . this readiness to attack [*Angriffs-bereitschaft*], well aggressiveness and strength, again because of the Viking and the old Germanic script and then again this *Nordlander*." Kevin, who made the clear connection between Aryans and Vikings above, also explained that Vikings symbolize strength and fighters. Georg, a twenty-one-year-old scaffold builder, described the appeal of a Nordic god with the phrase "oh, you're looking for a fight" in a T-shirt as resting on the gods' reputation for strength: "Because in history, also in films, [Nordic gods] were always the most powerful, they were honored, so this 'Oh, you're looking for a fight' is a proclamation, if someone wants a fight with us he can have it, but he'll lose. And that's why these Nordic gods are applied. If they put an Aphrodite on it, then everybody would say what kind of crap is that?"

Some youth argued that the concept of "Nordic" has been unfairly ap-propriated by or "stamped" as right wing. Thor's Hammer, explains Bernd, a twenty-two-year-old concrete layer apprentice from Berlin, doesn't imply racism, but rather "an honoring of Nordic gods although it sometimes un-fortunately is mistakenly interpreted as racist. . . . 'Nordic' is frequently misinterpreted as racist through the use of the runes, because the Nazis used [them]." Michael, a thirty-four-year-old carpentry apprentice, described the same T-shirt that Timo looked at (depicting a Viking warrior and ship with the word *Nordlander* as reflecting a little "honoring of heritage," which he then elaborates on as a cultish honoring of heritage (*Ahnenkultverehrung*). Others pointed out that not everyone is thoughtful in their choice of cloth-ing, particularly during adolescence. Hans, a twenty-seven-year-old scaffold builder apprentice, argued that "many right-wing [youth] only wear it be-cause the others are all wearing it. . . . I think there are a lot of *Mitläufer* [those who run along with the crowd]." But it is also clear that the producers of this clothing rely heavily on the multivocal nature of the symbols and the ways in which they can be interpreted differently by various observers. Kevin put this best during a discussion of Viking symbols as he simply described their use as falling into a "gray zone," noting that "one can read a little more into it or a little less, y'know?"

Finally, it is also worth noting that although youth frequently described the Nordic imagery as appealing to both rockers and far right youth, the "rocker" scene that the youth refer to is actually a spectrum of scenes ranging from the black metal scene to Hell's Angels bikers, and some of these scenes may overlap with far right youth as well. Benjamin, a twenty-two-year-old technical assistant apprentice, argues that there are significant differences among rocker groups. Some, like the Hell's Angels or rockers with "motorcycles and Easy Rider," he describes as "pretty right-wing extreme"—an impression he says they give because they are "broadly built" and use "many Aryan symbols" and because "before, foreigners, well of Turkish background, and blacks in America weren't allowed to join." But other rockers, in the "Metallica vein," he said, "I don't think they are necessarily right-wing extreme. They're really just in a band." Biker or "rocker" styles were also evident in the photographers' shots of far right and right-wing extremist protest marches, commemorations, and demonstrations.

Sacred Origin Narratives, Postmodern Uncertainty, and Disenfranchised Youth

The current era—an age some characterize as postmodern—is characterized by many things: increasing mobility, transformation in family structures, an acceleration in the pace of globalization and internationalization, and a deterritorialization of space and work environments.[106] Collectivist models of community life have been replaced by individualist models, in which each person is responsible for his or her own welfare, success, or failure. There has been a rise in secular rationalism and an accompanying loss in the certainty of religious guidelines. People are more likely to live alone,[107] far from the places where they grew up, and removed from family networks. "People in the West," writes Philip Sheldrake, "are increasingly an exiled and uprooted people" who have "de-emphasized place for the sake of values such as mobility, centralization or economic rationalization."[108]

These shifts—increasing isolation, secular rationalism, individual autonomy, and a loss of certainty—affect people differently. Many individuals have thrived in this environment, of course. But for millions of others, the postmodern age has been accompanied by rising levels of anxiety, disillusionment, and loneliness. Roger Griffin's theory of "gnostic activism" suggests that extremist radicalization and ideologies are particularly appealing to individuals who are unable to cope in the era of postmodern uncertainty.[109]

Griffin argues that some people's reaction to the existential problem of modern anomie is a drive for "grandiose schemes," "visions of new futures," or "big narratives" that act as a kind of "sacred canopy"[110] to help shield individuals from the absurdity of finite lives and modern anomie or disorientation. Zygmunt Bauman makes a similar argument when he suggests that utopian thinking reflects the desire for a reliability and security in a world we can trust in the face of an "overwhelming . . . feeling that the world was not functioning properly and was unlikely to be set right without a thorough overhaul."[111]

Griffin sees the rise of far right ideologies—or other radical and extremist youth movements—as a response to anomie or as a quest for meaning. Far right ideologies offer clear guidelines and set normative expectations, Griffin argues, offering a larger vision about what is right and wrong and sacralizing a nation, people, or racial group. They offer youth a chance to engage heroically in the struggle against a "decadent" world, thereby restoring meaning by purging the world or nation of everything that has gone wrong. Such engagement is what Griffin calls a response to a "sense-making crisis." Hate crime thus becomes a performative act, according to Griffin, that helps to enact a particular vision of the world.

Varshizky offers a strikingly similar reflection about why disenfranchised or disenchanted people might have been so vulnerable to Nazism:

> The Nazi *Weltanschauung*, as formulated by Rosenberg, offered an appealing mixture of political and spiritual salvation that provided many with consolation and hope in a general climate of uncertainty and despair. . . . This dichotomy between absolute good and evil enabled the purgation of the German nation while blaming the Jews and the Church for the harsh times Germany suffered. This was accompanied by a rejection of the existing political and social order, and the demand for a total revolution of life, starting with the spiritual amendment of reconnecting the German nation with its inner racial-soul.[112]

Disenfranchised, disaffected, or marginalized youth, who have failed to meet normative societal expectations or who are unlikely to fit within traditional markers and narratives of success, are likely particularly susceptible to appeals and quests for meaning and connection that Griffin and Varshizky describe. Moreover, the kinds of deterritorialization and high levels of mobility described above may lead some individuals to more strongly desire a sense of roots and of place; this, in turn, may explain the appeal of the sacred origin narratives that consecrate Nordic-ness. This is particularly the case because of the ways in which space is blended with mythic narrative. "Narrative is a critical key to our identity," writes Sheldrake, "for we all need a story to live by in order to make sense of the otherwise unrelated events of life and to find a sense of dignity."[113] And when the available public narratives privilege elite perspectives that devalue traditional desires for local rootedness or national identity,[114] sacred origin narratives may become more appealing. Such mythic narratives, in other words, are likely to be more powerful and more appealing for disenfranchised youth, for whom alternative narratives promising success in the fragmented, modern, rational, globalized economy seem either false or impossible. Instead, utopian thinking—which "expresses a world of imagination and desire"[115]—enables anticipation of an alternative future world or of a desired past one.

The construction trainee youth interviewed for this book were not all experiencing disenfranchisement from mainstream expectations for economic or social success. But many of them describe lives marked by hardness or challenges: time in prison, friends in prison, prior drug overdoses, failed first apprenticeships, bullying, dropping out of or being expelled from prior schools, classmates who died, colleagues who are alcoholics, or difficult childhoods. Twenty-one-year-old Justus described having participated as a bully in the "extreme bullying" at his previous school, where kids were tied to trees and locked in stairwells—he now regrets having been a bully. Georg, who was a part of the far right for three years in early adolescence, explained that he had to grow up fast as an adolescent because he moved around so often in his life and had to raise his four brothers and sisters—now aged ten to sixteen—mostly by himself. In describing a work colleague who wears a lot of the brand Thor Steinar, twenty-two-year-old scaffold builder apprentice Manfred casually mentioned that "he's been in a prison a lot more times than me. Luckily I only went once; I learned from that." Others describe perceptions of social class discrimination or being looked down on by others for their occupations in manual labor or construction. In this context, as previous scholars have suggested, youth may find far right ideology more appealing. One of the images youth examined in interviews depicts a raised fist with a Thor's Hammer over the words "Help us Thor!!!" Ingo explained that this phrase is meant to call on the god Thor to "pull the whites . . . out of [their] imprisonment by the lesser races." Georg described it as a "cry of help, that maybe he would send down a lightning bolt to Germany so that everyone would wake up, because the conditions in Germany are not exactly great."

To understand the power that the notion of civilization for the far right wing holds, I suggest we need to return to scholarship on what some refer to as "magical" thinking—to a premodern way of thinking about the world that is rooted in myth rather than reality. Scholars such as Julia Hell have traced such kinds of magical (or fantasy) thinking in analyzing postfascist fantasies in east Germany,[116] and Charlton McIlwain uses it in his work on death rituals among white and black communities in the United States. Other scholarship has looked at related issues of invented traditions and the desire for an imagined, idealized past.

What is "magical" about the far right's fantasy construction of Nordic origins, following Charlton McIlwain's linkage of magical thinking to racial understandings, is the ideological link to a notion of common blood and ancestry. McIlwain suggests that although scholars have tended to discuss "magical" thinking as something belonging to prehistorical civilizations, "the magical impulse is very much a part of contemporary awareness" and is evidenced through "forms of imagining" that include images and representations that "are not rational, but rather an expression of inner feeling or one's way of making sense of a given phenomenon." Indeed, emotions are the "primary mode" of communication in magical consciousness, which allows emotional forms and impulses to dominate actions.[117] Thus, I would argue that the fantasy of a blood-based sense of belonging—an Aryan-ness that is directly descended from Nordic tribes and the Vikings—is a powerful manifestation of such magical thinking for far right youth. It has an emotional pull that helps youth make sense of a disorienting world.

I suggest the combined German sacred origin myth—in which modern-day Germans are Aryan descendants of Germanic tribes whose origins were Nordic—works in three primary ways to appeal to youth born three or four generations after the Third Reich's mainstreaming of the sacred origin narrative. First, the sacred origin myth provides youth with a *sense of purpose*. It positions the contemporary era as one of decline and degradation that is nonetheless destined for a return to a past utopia. Fantastical myths and symbols are used to directly depict or evoke a sense of loss, of a particular way of life "slipping away," or of a sense of urgency around a need for preservation, survival, resurrection, or rebirth of a particular kind of nation. They help to crystallize a kind of "magical thinking" about the death (or potential death) of a blood-based ancestral group. Ansgar Aryan's 2010 website and clothing collection featured the Hyperborea, for example, a mythic ancient "lost" civilization that was supposedly home to the Aryans after they migrated from Atlantis; Hyperborea was thus the original Aryan ancestral homeland in the north.[118] Ansgar Aryan sold T-shirts, jackets, and hoodie sweatshirts with "Hyperborea" screen-printed or embroidered in detail, often in combination with swords and crests. Text on the catalog and website pages, or printed on T-shirts, evokes qualities assigned to Hyperboreans or advises consumers on their relationship to mainstream society: one tagline reads "the roots of honour," for example, while another reads "Warriors of the Light," and a third notes "don't believe in the lies of our society."

The website itself prominently featured the Hyperborean legend in text as well as in product design. "Hyperborea's daughters and sons were the bringers and influencers of countless distinguished high cultures of the earth," the text explains, identifying the Germanic tribes as one of those high cultures (along with the Atlantics, Greeks, and Mayans). It continues: "Hyperborea is the educational origin of our art, culture and religion," and it labels the Hyperboreans as the "sun people" whose "opposing pole" is the "southerners." At this point, the website text introduces the notion of continuity between the Hyperborean era and the contemporary one and identifies the conflict as a racial one:

> So began the conflict between the bringers of light (Hyperborean) and the dark men, which has lasted until today. Hyperborea will bring us to a new high culture and this will be true, realistic and worth living for and will emerge through the purity, clarity, and beauty of the light of the sun. Just as every bacteria avoids the sun, so the good in us, in our blood, turns toward the north, toward Hyperborea, to the midnight mountain!* *The midnight mountain is the mountain of the congregation. Here is where the knowledgeable, the good and righteous gather, who will not allow themselves to be hidden anymore.

Ansgar Aryan's clothing line—and others that also sell the Nordic myth —appeal to youth by offering them a role in an epic, righteous quest that will restore Germans to their true nature and to the golden, utopian age of their origins. Such a narrative provides an escape from daily failures or confusion about life's purpose; youth are offered a secure, predictable future and a reason to continue on.

Second, I suggest that the German sacred origin narrative appeals to some youth because it provides them with a strong *sense of identity*. The narrative offers clear emotive signifiers and clarity around their place in the world and the community with which they should orient themselves. Other scholars have noted that symbols are visual devices that denote "identity, recognition, ownership or affiliation."[119] The fantastical nationalist elements of the sacred origin narrative likely offer a sense of identification and belonging during a time of significant demographic change in Germany. Unification, the ongoing expansion and centrality of the European Union, and recent changes in German citizenship law have radically diversified who is eligible to "be" German.[120] The recent PEGIDA protests against the "Islamization of the Occident"—while xenophobic and Islamophobic—were rooted in factual trends that are shifting the demographic landscape of the country. Over one-fifth of Germany's population in 2013 had a migrant background.[121] Religious diversity is also rapidly changing; although the national numbers are still relatively small, with approximately 5 percent of Germans estimated to be Muslim,[122] regional concentrations of immigrants and Germans with migrant background mean that the percentage of Muslim residents is much higher in some cities and regions. Schools in some states have introduced Islamic instruction as an option alongside the traditional Protestant or Catholic choices for required religious classes. Overall, Germany has rapidly shifted from a country whose chancellor vehemently denied being a "country of immigration" less than two decades ago to one whose citizens and residents are increasingly coming to terms with broad demographic diversity. Symbols drawing on a mythical fantasy of a pure, undisturbed nation may, in this context, be especially salient to youth who are negotiating the transformed demographic landscape of a new multicultural Germany. Nordic and Germanic legends and myths would thus appeal as a kind of fatherland for "forlorn patriots,"[123] for whom the reality of a multicultural Germany can be replaced by fantasies of a pure, unblemished past, represented by Nordic places and peoples. Nordic spaces and places become sacred, hallowed geography that is deeply intertwined with individuals' own identity.

Moreover, the fantasy of Nordic heritage—and all the positive traits associated to be a part of that heritage—including loyalty, purity, beauty, integrity, and honesty—help youth establish a sense of identity and who they aspire to be. It offers a sense of identification and belonging with a particular place—labeled as hallowed, sacred territory—and with a people deemed to belong to that territory. One of the Ansgar Aryan Hyperborean products has the text "Hyperborea Elite" on the back of the hooded sweatshirt, suggesting to youth that they are part of a small, privileged group. Such symbols help strengthen group bonds and act as a powerful mechanism of belonging and identification for far right youth. These fantasies are also intertwined with the use of weapons and violent quests in ways that valorize warriors, fighting, death, and violence more generally.

Such fantasies have proven to be compelling in other extremist settings. In the wake of the racist shooting of nine African Americans in a South Carolina church in June 2015, former white supremacist Arno Michealis wrote an essay for the *Washington Post* tracing how he had become a member—and later a leader—of a major U.S. hate group, the Northern Hammerskins.

Growing up in an alcoholic family, Michealis was filled with anger and hate as an adolescent. He writes of his early fascination with being a warrior and described sitting in the library "poring over books of Greek and Norse myths, gravitating to the parts about monsters and violence . . . fancying myself as an unstoppable fighter who made his own rules."[124] Hate group recruiters preyed on people who were isolated, lonely, or vulnerable, he explains, noting that "they know well enough to look for people who are hurting. Simply put, it feels good for a person to feel a sense of belonging, purpose and value, especially if they lack love in their lives."[125]

Finally, the Nordic/Aryan sacred origin narrative is undoubtedly *attractive to youth who already hold racist beliefs*, particularly those who are enamored with violence. The violent nature of many of the Norse myths[126] may appeal to youth who are angry at mainstream society and seek expressions through which they can rebel and lash out. Meanwhile, the Nordic myth enables racist thinking to be couched in softer form, by using the notion of Nordic-ness to evoke whiteness without mentioning race. The deployment of commercialized symbols that imply or reference whiteness reveals the longing of some consumers for a different kind of nation—a nation that is racially pure and returns to an imagined sense of origin. The heavy reliance on Germanic and Norse history and historical mythology in brands and logos[127] reflects the extent to which such symbols are salient to youth who yearn for an imagined prior, pure form of the nation.

In sum, then, Nordic allegories in far right and right-wing extremist iconography facilitate what I call "aspirational nationhood"—in other words, fantasy expressions of a nation that never existed but that is nonetheless aspired to. I call these nationalist symbols *aspirational* because they represent a not-currently-existing nation, as opposed to what I would call *contemporary* (currently-existing) nationhood symbols. Contemporary symbols of German nationhood such as the current German flag, for example, do not appear in the repertoire of symbols deployed by German far right and extremist youth. Aspirational nationhood appears to be a powerful mechanism of belonging and identification for far right youth, for whom bonding with others in the group is already known to be a central aspect of recruitment and radicalization.

Conclusion

This chapter uses a careful analysis of commercial iconography and accompanying slogans and textual references in T-shirts and other products in order to show how fantastical myths and symbols are used to directly depict

or evoke a sense of loss or of a particular way of life "slipping away." I analyzed these symbols in light of theoretical work on fascism's relationship
to postmodernity and its roots in mythic and palingenetic nationalism.[128]
Ultimately, this chapter argues that the deployment of symbols evoking national myths help to crystallize a kind of "magical thinking" and evoke
fantasy expression of a nation that is aspired to, even though it never existed.
The fantasy of Nordic heritage may appeal to far right youth in particular
as a strategy for handling the uncertainty and loss of stability in the global,
postmodern era.

This fantasy narrative not only reflects existing racism, of course, but also
constitutes, reinforces, and socializes racist thinking by identifying those
who do not belong and by setting whiteness as a normative goal or an aspirational national characteristic. For the German far right wing, racial purity is implied in the aspirational Nordic fantasy.[129] Again, we can see here
how cultural symbols and economic objects can have constitutive power,
potentially shaping the identities and extremist engagements of consumers.
In the next chapter, I extend this analysis of myth as I turn to another case
of symbol deployment. Chapter 4 examines how death symbols enable far
right youth to break social taboos, advance racist and xenophobic visions of
the nation, and strengthen fantasy identities linked to the death of a way of
life and a return to a nation that never was.

4 DYING FOR A CAUSE, CAUSING DEATH

The Threat of Violence

For the first time in my life I tasted death, and death tasted bitter,
for death is birth, is fear and dread of some terrible renewal.
  —Hermann Hesse

Death is a strange concept, empirically speaking.[1] Along with love, death is
the central theme for much of the arts, as generations of playwrights, poets,
musicians, filmmakers, and novelists have grappled with themes of grief and
mourning, murder and suicide, tragedies and terminal illness. With a few
notable exceptions, however, social scientists have paid death comparatively
little heed.[2] In this regard, I was just as guilty as anyone else. Although I had
been captivated from the beginning with the Nordic symbols and alphanumeric codes deployed by the new far right subcultural styles, when I began
this project, I mostly looked right past symbols of death in the iconography
and tattoos, even as they stared me, quite literally, in the face.

In part, this is because symbols of death deployed by the far right are
often combined with historical or mythological references in ways that led
me to read iconography and codes that invoked or evoked death through
those lenses instead of analyzing them in their own right. But it is also because scholarship on nationalism, extremism, or the far right has not devoted
much time to death—or its representations—as a potential explanatory
factor for the appeal of radical or extremist engagements. This may be partly
because theories of nationalism in general have paid more attention to the
political motivations of nationalism and not enough to the cultural manifestations of its extremist fringe. But the gaps on death are more specific still.
There is very little attention to themes of death and dying within the small
body of scholarship that focuses on far right and right-wing extremist symbols, in Germany or elsewhere. The robust body of scholarship on German
nationalist symbols, Germanic legends and mythology, and Nazi symbols
have not attended at all to themes of death and dying. Literature on Germanic and Norse fables and sagas were key to understanding the ubiquitous

use of images of Viking warfare and legends that evoke or directly reference death, such as Walhalla, the hall of the dead, but this literature has been thinly connected to the far right, mostly through limited scholarship on the use of "folk esoteric," paganism, and Greek mythology by the far right.[3] Despite the centrality of themes of death and dying within these myths, there has been no analysis of how such images have been used within historical or contemporary National Socialist and far right movements. In fact, to the best of my knowledge, there has been no focus on images of death across any of the literatures examining the far right in contemporary or historical Germany. Yet death symbols turn out to be one of the more ubiquitous symbols deployed by the new commercial brands in and around the far right scene.

For artists, death's appeal likely rests on its deep and immediate connection to intense emotions, such as sadness and grief, nostalgia and regret. So perhaps it should come as no surprise that death appeals to extremist groups for the same reasons. Whether mediated through a tattoo, a T-shirt, or a terrorist attack, symbols of death provoke a sweeping range of emotions in observers. But when deployed by extremists and integrated into a broader ideology of violence, I realized, symbols of death do not only evoke grief or sadness among observers but also elicit feelings of revulsion, distress, anger, anxiety, and fear. Death is the penultimate celebration and valorization of violence that is so central to far right identity and ideology.[4] For those who stage these performances—or display such symbols—still other emotions come into play, as symbols of death mobilize and radicalize new recruits by invoking fantasies of martyrdom and rebirth. Symbols of death help youth enact the performances of strength, machismo, and bravado that are so deeply embedded in far right youth subcultures. Volunteering as a martyr—even if only on a T-shirt—positions youth as mercenaries for justice, as heroes who are unafraid and willing to die for a cause. And symbols of death socialize participants and observers alike by threatening individuals and groups deemed not to belong to the nation and by deploying humor, jokes, and clever codes that help dehumanize victims.

Death, as I ultimately came to understand, signifies many things to the far right. This chapter analyzes three categories of death symbols that I suggest represent different "kinds" of deaths to far right youth and rightwing extremists who deploy these symbols. I first review my classification and interpretation of these three categories before turning to an analysis of youths' reactions to images of death symbols during interviews, and I then present an argument for how I suggest these symbols might challenge existing theories of nationalism and extremist engagement. Ultimately, I use symbols of death as a case that illuminates how nationalist and extremist allegories within contemporary right-wing coded symbols and brands are one of many powerful mechanisms of belonging and protest that may shape young people's engagement with the far right. On the one hand, symbols of death act as straightforward threats of violence and physical harm, evoking both a general and unspecified fear as well as a more specific threat against ethnic, religious, or racial minorities. But I also argue that the use of nationalist allegories in conjunction with death symbols helps facilitate what I call "aspirational nationhood," a concept I introduced in chapter 3. Aspirational conceptions of nationhood are fantasy expressions of a nation that never existed but that is, nonetheless, aspired to.

In my analysis of contemporary and historical right-wing iconography, I find that symbols refer to at least three different kinds of death: *abstract death* (Death personified), *specific death* (the death of an individual), and *collective death* (the death of a way of life or imagined civilization). The following sections analyze each of these categories in turn, focused on the iconographic representations of death used in commercial, coded far right products and symbols. I then turn to the interview data, examining how youth's reactions to a subset of these images explain the appeal of death symbols for far right youth.

Abstract Death (or Death Personified)

Abstract death refers to Death with a capital D—it is an abstract representation of death, typically personified in the "death's head," also known as the skull-and-crossbones symbol or *Totenkopf*. I include in this category not only the traditional death's head but also modified death's heads, which are even more common than the straightforward death's head. The skull, as Panofsky notes, "now, was and is the accepted symbol of Death personified, as is borne out by the very fact that the English language refers to it, not as a 'dead man's head,' but as a 'death's head' "[5] (see plates 1, 8, 13, and 19). Importantly, one specific iconographical representation of the death's head—the form used by the SS-Totenkopf division—is illegal in Germany because of its clear connection to the SS.[6] This particular, historical iconographic form is not found in the iconography of the mainstream commercial brands, but in some cases, the use of other death's heads are evocative of the historical symbol.

The death's head is the most straightforward and direct death symbol in far right wing and right-wing extremist iconography. It is widely used in the graphic designs of several different brands whose consumer base is far right, and is peppered throughout the iconography of commercial products like hats and T-shirts as well as on banners and posters at right-wing marches or concerts. In its simplest form, the death's head iconography is not particularly original. Death in an abstract sense is used to evoke fear and produce anxiety among viewers. Because death is, as Panofsky suggests, one of the "two fundamental tragedies of human existence" (the other is "frustrated love"),[7] the loss of both one's own life and of those one loves is deeply feared in cultures where right-wing extremism tends to exist (predominantly western and developed countries in the global north). As Seale argues, we are taught to simultaneously fear, accept, and avoid death.[8] The death's head image is a reminder of mortality, of our "most ephemeral" nature, in the words of Rilke's "Ninth Elegy"—because, as Rilke writes, "being here is so much" and we are here only "once" (*Ein Mal*).[9] Life, in other words, is fleeting, and its eventual loss (whether of our own or of our loved ones) is guaranteed.

Western societies have developed elaborate rituals to help manage the anxiety, grief, and fear associated with death,[10] which are part of accepted normative strategies for confronting death. Because of this strong cultural desire to avoid death—a prevailing normative expectation of death avoidance—death symbols therefore breach societal taboos and evoke fear and an unsettling anxiety. Images of death serve as an unavoidable reminder of the ephemeral nature of life, the eventual death of all of us. Images of a skull convey a "warning" to remember one's own end.[11] To the extent that death symbols evoke the banned form of the *Totenkopf* used by the SS-Totenkopf division—who among other duties served as concentration camp guards—they also convey the extreme brutality, discipline, and violence associated with the Holocaust and the concentration camps more specifically.[12] In this light, it is also notable that youth frequently described particular brands, logos, and symbols associated with the far right as reflecting a sense that the individual is *gewaltbereit*—a word that translates as "ready to be violent" and communicates a willingness to fight (see chapter 2 for additional discussion).

So on the one hand, using the death's head iconography can be understood as a straightforward, aggressive display intended to provoke fear, anxiety, and horror. Death symbols subtly threaten or even terrify viewers. But displaying death symbols can also be understood as a countercultural move because of the ways in which they break prevailing societal and cultural norms and taboos that suggest that death should be entirely private[13] or even, as Aries describes it, "shameful and forbidden."[14] As Geoffrey Gorer describes, death is (in the United States) the only remaining "unmentionable" thing—it is associated with denial and fear.[15] Freud argued that avoidance of death is a strategy for dealing with the lack of control and sense of powerlessness in the face of death's eventual certainty.[16] In this context, the brazen display of death symbols might provide a sense of power and strength to those displaying it, either by asserting fearlessness or simply refusing to adhere to social norms that render death silent and invisible. Perhaps by embracing the unknown, youth are able to "front," to pose as if unafraid, to represent themselves as strong and fearless. This is particularly evident in modified death's head or skull-and-crossbones images that replace crossbones with weapons such as guns or axes.

This interpretation supports the contention I made in chapter 1 and that I will revisit in chapter 6 regarding the relationship between coded, commercialized symbols and youth resistance to societal expectations.[17] Manipulating and coding symbols—particularly ones that provoke adults or would be consciously or unconsciously abhorred by the general public—may provide agency for youth who feel constrained or let down by the adult world. Death symbols are clearly deployable by far right youth—as well as other subcultural groups—as a source of resistance, protest, and cultural subversion against perceived hegemonic authorities.[18] Such an interpretation also supports Van der Valk and Wagenaar's findings that the extreme right is "a place of excitement, provocation and violence" for youth.[19] The fact that death's head symbols are also popular in other youth subcultures—such as the heavy metal scene or punk scenes—would also support this interpretation.[20] Indeed, youth were aware that the death's head symbol is multivocal and reflects potential affiliation with a variety of youth subcultures. Hayri, a twenty-one-year-old concrete layer apprentice, looked at a screenshot displaying T-shirts with a skull and a Viking helmet and noted that he would tend to think shirt signals the "rocker" or "far right" scene "because of the *Totenkopf*."

This thesis—that displaying the death's head is a way of asserting fearlessness and expressing a sense of countercultural protest—might also explain the recent pop cultural fascination with the death's head and the popularity of the death's head in consumer goods such as designer scarves retailing for hundreds of dollars and even children's clothing. Johann, a seventeen-year-old building energy design apprentice, looked at the same screenshot as Hayri did and saw the iconography as both appealing and mainstream: "with *Totenköpfen* somehow . . . these days everybody wears something similar, somehow dark like that, and I like it." Perhaps for mainstream consumers, displaying a death's head image merely reflects a sense of vague countercultural and norm-breaking values, because one embraces death instead of adhering to social norms that would silence it. A similar impulse might partially explain the widespread use of the death's head among far right and right-wing extremist youth or for youth in other subcultural scenes.

These two explanations for the use of the death's head (as a strategy to express threats and produce fear and as a way of asserting power and fear-lessness through breaking taboos) are likely intrinsically linked—a point I return to below in a discussion of how theories on protest and resistance might shed light on the use of death symbols more generally among right-wing youth. But before I turn to the next category of death symbols, it is worth noting that there are two other—more specific—usages of the death's head iconography that combine the death's head image with other visual cues in order to evoke or make more direct political statements. The first is the use of the death's head to replace the head in the Statue of Liberty. In this case, far right youth (and graphic designers for commercial entities that market to the far right) are using the death's head to make a specific political statement—either anti-American or anticapitalist (see plate 8). Replacing the image of Liberty with one of Death is an allegorical strategy that has multiple connotations. Here, I would suggest that this image is intended less to provoke fear or convey a specific threat than it is to send a message about the impact of capitalism or of American policies and to provoke a sense of nationalism or anti-Americanism among viewers.

The second is the combination of the death's head symbol with a modified form of eagle's wings or Nordic imagery (see plates 1 and 23). The eagle's wings evoke the *Reichsadler* (imperial eagle) used in the Third Reich and are a very common symbol in commercial products popular with the far right, as chapter 2 explained. The combination of eagle's wings and death's head evokes a very specific sense of "death in the name of the Nation"—and in-deed, in the name of a particular version of the Nation—the one pursued by the Third Reich. The fact that a specific form of the death's head was also used as a symbol of the SS-Totenkopf division (and is therefore illegal under the German criminal code) is also a key issue here.[21] There are other examples of this connection between death symbols, the historical far right, and Nordic imagery; we see the death's head and the skeleton in satirical cartoon depictions of the Nazis in the 1940s, for example.[22] And the text "Rosengarten" underneath the skull in a Thor Steinar T-shirt likely refers to the Rosengarten at Worms, a reference from the Nibelungen saga from Norse mythology that became, through Richard Wagner's *Ring* cycle, a beloved Nazi performance.[23] The combination of Nordic imagery with the death's head also has nationalist implications, as I will elaborate on later in this chapter. Moreover, because of the appeal of Nordic imagery not only for the far right but also for the rocker/biker subculture, as chapter 3 explained, the combination of Nordic imagery with death symbols—such as the use of a skull with a Viking helmet in an Erik and Sons brand T-shirt—may further contribute to the blurriness of certain symbolic meanings across youth subcultures. I discuss nationalist and Nordic imagery later in this chapter but highlight these examples here to signal the ways in which there are multiple layers of complexity in these images, due both to the appeal of particular symbols across subcultural groups and to the efforts of commercial producers to broaden their market share beyond single subcultural groups.

Specific Death (or Death of an Individual)

The second category of death symbols that I analyze are symbols, images, and codes that go beyond abstract depictions or basic personifications of death to more specifically reference or threaten the death of an individual as a person or as a member of a particular group. There are two subcategories here: specific representations of or threats that evoke the death of individuals as persons or as members of particular groups, and specific representations of the death of collectives or groups of people through past atrocities.

Often death is not directly represented or conveyed but is rather hinted at through depictions of weapons that can cause death (guns, axes, swords, but also nooses and guillotines), illustrations or references to blood, war, physical fighting or confrontation, or violence. I have limited myself in this particular analysis to symbols that I interpret to directly or indirectly depict or threaten an individual's death, as opposed to (mere) physical harm. These are codes, symbols, and images not that reference death in the abstract but rather that refer to dying or to death in specific and particular ways. Such symbols not only depict but also celebrate violence, which must be understood in light of broader far right ideological views that distinguish members of the strong, valued, cherished Aryan race from individuals and groups deemed to be weak, diluted, unworthy, or somehow threatening to the purity of the "dominant" race.[24] In right-wing ideology, Daniel Köhler argues, violence not only is a means to an end but is in fact a "core essence," deeply connected to right-wing identity and to ideals about being warriors, being political soldiers, or fighting in a "struggle for existence of the Aryan race." Violence has a "spiritual and timeless value" for the extreme right, acting in a cathartic way to establish or resurrect a natural order.[25] Symbols that directly reference or evoke the death of specific individuals and groups are thus very much in line with core far right ideologies and the far right's valorization of violence.

Sometimes these symbols are very straightforward, such as a tattoo with the words "Born to Kill" in Germanic script, while at other times they are more complex. Straightforward death images in this category, for example, depict lynching through an image of an empty noose, refer to a "shooting club" with an image of an automatic gun, or directly mention the death of racial and ethnic minorities or people of color, as in one sweatshirt with the words "Born yellow, born red, born black, born dead." Text along the sweatshirt's sleeve reads "White Aryan Pride" (see plate 7). But there are also subtler images that evoke death, such as an image of robed Ku Klux Klan figures. And there are very complex combinations of images, as in an Ansgar Aryan T-shirt that depicts a version of the murderer Jason from the Hollywood horror film "Halloween" in a hockey mask with a chainsaw under the words "Hunting Season"; the number 88 (representing the eighth letter of the alphabet, H, with 88 meaning HH for Heil Hitler) is etched on the chainsaw blade, over the text "Teutonic Brand." The same brand features a T-shirt with a similar mask depicted over two bloody cleavers under the words "Hate Crew" with text on the back that says "We know where you work, we know where you live, you're not that hard to find." The complexity in these images are a form of bricolage—a complex way of linking together often disparate and sometimes contradictory cultural symbols and fragments in order to convey a broader allegorical message: in this case, to threaten and evoke the potential death of those deemed not to belong. The use of the phrase "Teutonic Brand," the number 88, and indeed the very brand name "Ansgar Aryan"—itself a bricolage of Nordic and Third Reich references—make it clear just who the potential victims of such violence are meant to be.

Another example of a combination of aggressive death symbol and complex coded reference is in a 2014 Ansgar Aryan T-shirt with the text "All pigs must die." The symbols of death on the T-shirt are unequivocally clear—a noose, a guillotine, and the phrase "all pigs must die." But it is not entirely clear exactly who the "pigs" in question are. This may be an antipolice remark, but it could also be an Islamophobic or an anti-Semitic one (in English language slang, "pigs" is a derogatory reference to the police, while the word may also be interpreted as an epithet for Jews or Muslims). The phrase "all pigs must die" is therefore open to multiple interpretations. The phrase "finishing business" and the word "finisher" both evoke past attacks or atrocities, but which specific groups or attacks these phrases refer to is an open question. Indeed, the designers appear to have left this deliberately open, as the descriptive text to the right of the product image states, noting that "with this T-shirt, one's imagination has no bounds." But regardless of who the particular target is, the open call to violence and the threat to whomever is understood to be a "pig" is crystal clear.

Often these references are linked in some way to the nation—or an aspirational version of the nation promoted by the extreme right wing. One T-shirt, for example, uses the historical German black, white, and red flag colors with the text "black is the night in which we will get you; white are the men who will be victorious for Germany; red is the color of blood on the asphalt"; above the text is an image of a large machine gun. In another product, the iconography on a baseball hat depicts an ax above the words "keep your country clean." By linking symbols of violence and death to a particular vision of the nation, youth evoke death and violence in the name of the nation, while making coded or oblique references to contemporary immigration and diversity in ways that indirectly or directly threaten members of minority and nonwhite groups. Such symbols clearly reflect right-wing ideological goals that valorize violence as a core part of right-wing identity.[26]

It is not only symbols referencing the death of individuals that appear in the iconography of far right products, but also symbols and images that depict the death of a collective or a group of people, especially in the past. In these instances, far right symbols reference past atrocities as a way both of evoking past horrors that were enacted against particular groups and in some cases simultaneously conveying a sense of threat against those groups. We see here symbols that reference deaths through terrorist attacks such as 9/11 and the 1995 right-wing extremist attack in Oklahoma City in the United States as well as references to the 2011 atrocity in Norway, the Ku Klux Klan, the Holocaust, the Christian Crusades, and historical pogroms against Jews and Muslims.

The code 168:1, as chapter 2 explained, is one example; it refers to the number of people killed in Oklahoma City versus the U.S. government's execution of the right-wing extremist bomber Timothy McVeigh. Another contemporary right-wing symbol depicts the "hangman's stand" with a noose and a figure, a potential reference to Ku Klux Klan lynchings of blacks in the United States. Another T-shirt shows an image of a plane flying into the World Trade Center towers with the phrase "take a flight to the World Trade's, to visit the J . . . nited States" (which is meant to be read "Jew-nited States"). By combining an image of a terrorist attack that killed three thousand people with a play on words that implies that the United States is a "Jewish" place, and in a tone that suggests lighthearted travel ("take a flight . . . to visit"), these symbols act as a direct affront or threat to Jews.

Other examples are illustrative as well. One recent T-shirt references the deaths of Turkish immigrants at the hands of the German neo-Nazi (NSU) extremist cell that was discovered in 2011 with iconography of a stylized skull-and-crossbones symbol in which *Döner* skewers replace the crossbones (with the *Döner* meat itself shaped into a modified, screaming skull), underneath the words "Killer Döner." The "Killer Döner" T-shirt appeared not long after the right-wing extremist National Socialist Underground (NSU) terrorist cell was found to be responsible for the so-called *Döner* murders—the murders of nine people with an immigrant background.[27] Importantly, the company that produced the "Killer Döner" T-shirt is called Reconquista, which is itself a reference to a pogrom against Muslims in Andalusia in the Middle Ages. In another example, the brand Thor Steinar opened a store in Chemnitz in 2012 named Brevik, a slightly different spelling of Anders Breivik's name, not long after Breivik killed seventy-seven people—most of them young people at a summer camp—in a right-wing terrorist attack in Norway in 2011. Following public outcry, Thor Steinar changed the Chemnitz store name to Tønsberg—but as of January 2014, the Thor Steinar website still listed the store with both names.[28]

I include such references and codes in my analysis of death symbols because they either directly depict (as in the 9/11 images) or evoke deaths, pogroms, and atrocities against members of groups. Like the use of specific death symbols against individuals, the use of death symbols that reference collective or group deaths have the effect of making particular individuals (especially those that are members of the targeted groups) feel afraid and unwelcome. Such symbols evoke fear, terrorize, or threaten individuals and groups, much as the symbols about specific individual deaths do. But they also simultaneously present a particular political extremist and nationalist platform in which Jews, Muslims, immigrants, racial and ethnic minorities, or even (in the Norwegian example) "multiculturalists" are unwelcome. They establish and identify the nation as a place with particular kinds of ethnic, racial, religious, linguistic, or cultural boundaries. Signs at right-wing extremist marches that say "spätzle not Döner" (*spätzle* is a traditional pasta specific to the Baden-Württemberg region of Germany, while *Döner* is a popular Turkish roasted meat dish often eaten as a pita sandwich), for example, make this especially clear.[29] But more subtly coded symbols also clearly present an image of the nation as one that is either Christian or pagan (but definitely not Jewish and not Muslim), where the nuclear family is made up of a blond, masculine father and a devoted, adoring mother and where Aryan-ness is something to be preserved through cultural traditions, foods, and ethnic heritage. Of course, one of the many ironies and contradictions of these symbols is that many of the textual references are in English—calling into question the value of the German language within the larger context of cultural preservation that the far right often references.

In the case of death symbols that reference specific deaths of groups and individuals, then, death symbols are used not only to provoke a general sense of anxiety and fear among observers, but rather to produce fear and anxiety among particular groups who might be targets of such violence. Such images also produce particular revulsion among observers who are not themselves members of the "targeted" groups, but who are reminded by the images of past horrors, which may evoke either guilt and shame for past national atrocities (such as the Holocaust) or a reminder of vulnerability and loss (such as 9/11). Using these kinds of death symbols is thus not only a countercultural move, but also a terroristic one. Such symbols can "terrorize" members of mainstream society, especially by evoking past horrors, by making light of them, and by threatening future harm. Death symbols are therefore not only an expression of resistance but also a performative message to outsiders, conveying a specific sense of threat.[30]

Collective Death, or the Death of a Way of Life or Imagined Civilization

The third and final category I will analyze here are death symbols that refer to or evoke the death of an entire way of life—of what some might refer to as a civilization. Here, we see symbols that either utilize a metaphor of death or draw on a kind of magical or fantasy thinking in which an actual blood-based ancestral group is "dying out." As in the second category of death described above, violence is celebrated as a strategy to achieve a particular outcome—in this case, however, the end goal is the restoration of a dying civilization.

This category of death symbols draws heavily on Nordic and Viking imagery—which are a core part of the fantastical and mythical past laced through so many of the products and brands associated with the far right, as I explained in chapter 3. I extend the previous chapter's analysis here to focus primarily on the framing of that fantastical and mythical past in terms that evoke a sense of loss, of a particular way of life "slipping away," or of a need for preservation, survival, resurrection, or rebirth. This is the least direct and least clear category of death symbols. By and large, what we see in this category are not direct depictions of death (whether general or specific) but rather images that are suggestive of a kind of death without directly stating it. These images evoke meanings through visual cues, helping crystallize an image of the death of a civilization or blood-based ancestral group but rarely stating this very directly.

As chapter 3 detailed in greater depth, far right iconography today —particularly as seen in commercial products—is rife with references to Nordic mythology, legends, and myths. Some of these myths and legends utilize death symbols or suggest that a way of life has been lost, or else needs to be preserved and protected, and it is this subset of images that is the focus of this section of this chapter. "In this dishonorable period in which old values don't exist anymore," asserts an Ansgar Aryan catalog, "Ansgar Aryan stands for true friends, old heroes, Germanic gods and real ideals." Thus we see T-shirts that mention Nordic souls (of the dead) or call for "survival" of the strongest. This latter notion, of course, draws on a sport metaphor, but in the larger context of the brand and the other T-shirts and products it sells, "survival" also draws on a broader right-wing political discourse. The NPD for example has used comparisons with Native Americans in the United States, suggesting that increasing immigration to Germany means that "native Germans" will end up like Native Americans, restricted to reservations.[31] There are also much more subtle references to survival, like the Erik and Sons sweatshirt "Viking Attack," which in smaller print underneath lists the date "793 A.D." and the word "Lindisfarne," a direct reference to the violent Viking attack in the year 793 on an island monastery in the British Isles thought to be the start of the Viking raids of western Europe (see plate 14).[32] Such references evoke past atrocities in a way that hints at an ongoing epic battle to be led by the descendants of the Vikings, using legends like Hyperborea—a mythic, "lost" civilization said to be home to the Aryans—to mobilize and motivate the quest for restoration (see longer discussion in chapter 3).

The notion of survival of a people or a civilization is key to the numeric code 14, which is a global, pan-Aryan code peppered throughout right-wing extremist iconography that refers to the number of words in a sentence by the late American right-wing extremist David Lane, "We must secure the existence of our people and a future for white children." The number 14 became a kind of mantra for global right-wing extremists, and we see it blended with other iconographical elements such as the old Germanic script. The code 14 hints at the potential for the death of a "race" or a "people" if something is not done to "protect the future." Indeed, as chapter 3 explained, sacred origin narratives and national myths rely heavily on reverence for the dead, sacrifice through death, or the promise of personal redemption and national regeneration through mortal sacrifice.[33] Such national myths not only suggest that an entire way of life is threatened but also call individuals to join the fight to help restore the golden era and defend it from opponents and enemies. Perhaps the clearest example of this in the commercial brands is from a recent T-shirt on the Phalanx Europa website—a brand described by antifascist activists as "hip and modern"[34]—called *Stirb und Werde* in reference to a poem by Goethe that references dying and transformation. The T-shirt itself displays the poem, with *Stirb und Werde!* in larger lettering. But the text in the product description is much more instructive, telling potential consumers, "Because it's only from the gaze of the mainstream that being ready to die looks like a desire for death. Because a life lived in search of destiny only looks like a failed existence through the eyes of our parents. Because our dangerous thinking only looks like extremism from the eyes of mediocrity [*Kleingeister*]. . . . Therefore we are not merely guests on this earth but rather live according to Goethe's words: die and be transformed."[35]

Finally, across the brands and products associated with the far right, there are frequent references to Walhalla (Valhall), which is the "hall of the dead" or the "hall of slain warriors," as well as the residence of the god Odin, in Norse mythology. The myth of Walhalla says that those slain in battle will live in Odin's hall, the hall of the dead, until they are called to fight in a great battle on the side of the gods against "the mighty powers of chaos."[36] Occasionally a product extends the stand-alone reference to Walhalla by deploying the phrase "see you in Walhalla," which hints not only at the wearer's own death but also at the death of the observer.

The notion of civilization—and of its potential loss and need for heroic restoration—is a powerful trope for the far right wing, as chapter 3 elaborated in greater depth. There, I argued that the fantasy of Nordic heritage is appealing to far right youth because the sacred origin myth itself helps facilitate a sense of belonging and purpose for youth. In this chapter, I extend this argument by suggesting that the ways in which that fantasy is intertwined with the valorization of violence and key far right ideological values and norms around life and death—such as the idea of survival of the fittest—deserves closer attention.[37]

Why Death Appeals to Far Right Youth

Several of the thirty-four images of commercial products, symbols, and styles that youth analyzed during interviews contained death symbols and weapons that reference death or that can cause death: modified skull-and-crossbones symbols, axes, a person dangling from a noose off of a tree branch, an image of planes crashing into the World Trade Center towers in New York, the coded symbol 168:1, and more. As youth discussed the images, it became clear that there were consistent reasons why symbols that evoke, reference, depict, or threaten death might be particularly popular among far right youth. In the following sections, I draw on German youth's discussions of far right iconography and symbols, particularly those that evoke or invoke death, in order to examine reasons why death symbols in general may be appealing to far right youth. The interview data maps well onto the categories analyzed above, suggesting that death symbols appeal to far right youth for three reasons that are similar to the categories of symbols I analyzed from the image database. First, death symbols are a strategy to provoke and terrify observers, both by evoking past tragedies and by breaking cultural taboos about death. Second, death symbols are used to advance racist, xenophobic, and exclusionary ideological and political platforms and visions of the nation, by threatening immigrants, Muslims, Jews, and others deemed not to belong to an ideal nation that is white and Aryan. Third and finally, death symbols help bond insiders in these groups to one another, in part by helping to create or strengthen fantasy identities linked to the notion of a "dying" way of life or civilization and a return to a nation that never was. I examine each of these categories in turn below through an analysis of the interview data.

First, death symbols are clearly an efficient strategy to express threats, produce fear, and terrorize observers, by evoking and making light of past pogroms and tragedies and by breaking societal taboos and cultural norms that render death invisible and silent. Youth express resistance to mainstream society by embracing and brazenly displaying symbols that horrify, disgust, and frighten viewers. Such symbols offer opportunities for youth to perform or "front" a sense of fearlessness, strength, masculinity, and power. Interviews with young Germans in and around far right scenes revealed that being "provocative" was a large part of the appeal of far right symbols and codes.

In interviews, as chapter 2 explained in some detail, young Germans repeatedly identified far right clothing brands, symbols and iconography as *provokant*, meaning that they are intended to provoke a reaction in observers. Lukas explained that his right-wing-leaning father's choice to wear Thor Steinar clothes was based both on his political views and on a desire to be provocative, and he linked his father's consumption of far right clothing to a performative display of anti-immigrant or anti-multicultural sentiment. Georg, a twenty-one-year-old scaffold builder apprentice who repeatedly discussed his deliberate choice of clothing he called "provocative," said, "these days, either you go the way of society, or you go the way of provocation." Although he had previously worn clothing from Thor Steinar and Label 23/ Boxing Connection, he has now shifted to primarily wearing clothes from the brand Yakuza, which sells high-quality clothing that has some far right iconography and symbols but is not exclusively far right, as it is also laced with a variety of racist, misogynistic, and other taboo-breaking iconography. He describes his own style as extremely important, both in terms of distinguishing himself from his friends and provoking mainstream society. In the interview excerpt below, he describes how being provocative is extremely important to him, using an example of death iconography to illustrate:

GEORG. Of course, one draws a kind of provocative attention to one-self, when you see the crass motifs from Yakuza, they provoke in a certain way. . . . I like the crass expressions. . . . I have almost only Yakuza things in my closet. . . . [It] gets the attention of people, and that's exactly why people want to wear it, because they want to show, "whoa, look at that motif, totally crass" . . . when they see that on the street. That's why it's been my style for years. . . . It's also in the USA, there are even crasser motifs there, which would of course be banned in Germany.

INTERVIEWER. When you say "crass motifs," can you describe a little, because I don't know [the brand Yakuza].

GEORG. Well there was, for example a motif in Germany, in the early days [of the brand when] they used the slogan, "The Yakuza Deathfinisher," or they had a girl kneeling near somebody in Ku Klux Klan robes holding a shotgun to her head, and so, that was the beginning, y'know?

Throughout the interview, Georg referenced other examples of what he called "provocative" iconography in the brand Yakuza. He recalled an entire catalog in which "they were in a slaughterhouse, with guns, axes, chopped-off heads, and things like that. . . . Provocative." And he described a T-shirt with a machine gun and bullets over the shoulders and text that tells consumers, "you can shop here without bad consequences." Other youth also referred to the allure of provoking the mainstream. For example, Dennis, a nineteen-year-old training to be a civil engineering technician, explained that he had owned an Alpha Industries jacket when he was younger "because it was the style in the neighborhood . . . it was provocative. . . . One probably wanted to show somehow strength, I'd say. To provoke and see if anyone else reacts to that."

Death symbols are not only strategies to provoke mainstream society in general; they also convey specific content that directly or indirectly threatens and targets particular individuals and groups of individuals. Thus, the second reason why death symbols are useful to far right youth is because they allow youth in and around far right scenes to advance a particular political platform and vision of the nation, both threatening nonwhite groups and firmly establishing an idea of "German-ness" that is white and Aryan. Importantly, racial purity is often implied without being directly stated within this iconography — it is evoked, in other words, without being explicitly invoked. Reference to Nordic-ness and Aryan-ness implies whiteness in the name of a national culture. Thus it is not only Death in general (or death personified) that is represented, but the specific and particular deaths of certain individuals and groups of people either in the past or in the future: of immigrants, of religious, racial and ethnic minorities, of nonwhites, or of non-Aryans. By linking death symbols to allegorical images of the nation (or by using particular national cues, such as the historical black, white, and red flag colors or logos, that evoke a swastika), death and violence are evoked in the name of an exclusionary vision of the nation.

One of the images that youth perused during the interviews was of a T-shirt whose iconography depicted an old passenger transport ship and the words "Sweet Home Madagascar," which as chapter 2 explained is a reference to an early Nazi "final solution" for the Jewish population, who, it was proposed, would be deported and resettled in Madagascar. Only a few students understood the historical reference to Madagascar (see table 3). Felix explained that he once had to do an oral report on the Wannsee Conference, and so he knew that among other things there had been "a decision to send all the Jews to Madagascar." Michael connected the T-shirt more clearly to contemporary right-wing extremism, pointing out "Holocaust deniers . . . cite that Jews weren't supposed to be exterminated but were to be resettled in Madagascar." And Ingo told the interviewer she should show the image to someone who has an interest in history, noting that Hitler "didn't only want to kill all the Jewish citizens but rather also send [them] to Madagascar."

But even youth who didn't catch the historical connotation sometimes got the general meaning of the shirt. Martin took a look at this image and said, "of course one can interpret this as "go back home . . . that one of course could send the immigrants back home." Shortly after Steffen, a twenty-four-year-old carpentry apprentice, expressed his opinion that headscarves should be banned in school—because "I'm not allowed to enter a bank with a motorcycle helmet . . . so why are they allowed to run around here with a headscarf?"—he examined an image of the Madagascar T-shirt. Although he clearly did not know the historical significance of the image when he examined the image, he understood its implication, suggesting that it means "Well, have a good trip away, eh?" and then linking it to a controversial 2011 political advertisement by the NPD, a far right political party in Germany. The NPD poster depicts a "flying carpet" with three figures on it—including a woman in a headscarf, and a man in a turban, under the words "Have a good trip home."[38] "Yeah, I would wear it," says Steffen, after examining the T-shirt for a bit, "Why not? Of course." Steffen made it clear that he wouldn't wear all the T-shirts he saw in the images—some statements, like the phrase "my favorite color is white," seemed "too hard," even though he found the

T-shirt itself "cool," describing it as a "cool phrase." Rather, as he explains, he wears only T-shirts that he can stand behind, noting, "we are flooded with people who don't belong here. I have no problem with foreigners, and, absolutely not, it sounds stupid in this context, but I really like to travel, I'm often in other countries, I like to experience other cultures, but then I return alone back here. And I don't stay there."

Steffen then qualifies his argument a bit, noting that the social system is abused in Germany and that he has "no problem" if foreigners are coming to work because Germany is "too dumb" to have its own well-qualified people and "have to get the Chinese man who could already play the piano at age four. . . . I have no problem with him working here and paying taxes, but I have a problem when they come here and open a pseudo-*Döner* shop . . . but then mommy, daddy, pappi, and company also come here, because our German state still has these war debts. . . . I can't do anything about the fact that we lost the war and started it and what we did." A few minutes later, he looks at the Reconquista T-shirt with the phrase "Killer Döner" described above and says, "yes, I'd wear that immediately. Definitely. Because it's cool. It's cool. . . . It again has this double-meaning, . . . or maybe it doesn't have a double-meaning, no idea. I'm going to have to really think about [what it means], but in any case it's anti-Turkish. And for that reason I would wear it. Definitely yes." Several other youth also perceived anti-Turkish messaging in this particular T-shirt. Niel, a twenty-year-old construction mechanic apprentice, interpreted this T-shirt as saying "that one wants to make the Turks disappear. It doesn't matter how." Ingo noticed the skull-and-crossbones imagery on this shirt and said "that's the *Totenkopf*, and it's probably supposed to bring death." He interprets the image to mean that people want to expel foreigners from the German federal state of Thüringen (which is referenced on the T-shirt), or more specifically as a threat against owners of *Döner* stands. "Yeah, I'd say it's also in the direction of Turks and everything that comes from the Orient and so sells *Döners*, eh?"

Other iconography using weaponry or death symbols was interpreted as similarly antiforeigner. Justus, a twenty-one-year-old concrete layer apprentice, looked at a photo of a T-shirt with a fist holding a large Thor's Hammer over the phrase "Help us Thor!!!" and noted that it conveys a sense that "someone should come and help kick the foreigners out." Most youth did not see any particular meaning in an image of an Erik and Sons baseball cap with an ax and the phrase "Keep your Country Clean" — in part because the print underneath the ax was not only in English, but was also quite small; twenty-nine of the fifty-one youth interviewed did not observe anything noteworthy about the cap. Some of the remaining youth saw the ax as "aggressive" or "brutal," or they noted its Viking symbolism. But ten of the youth who read the English phrase and understood it, however, described the cap as "racist," "right-wing," or "xenophobic," interpreting it as indicating support for, as Felix succinctly described, "racial separation." Klaus suggested the cap is meant to say "one should make sure . . . no foreigners, they should be driven out, that's what it means," while Ingo said it means "everything should be slaughtered that doesn't belong in our country, and build it new again."

Finally, death symbols are not only meant for outside observers; they also help bond insiders in these groups to one another, in part by helping to create or strengthen fantasy identities linked to the notion of a "dying" way of life or civilization. This is the third reason why death symbols are useful to far right youth. They directly depict or evoke a sense of urgency around a need for preservation, survival, resurrection, or rebirth of a particular kind of nation. They help to crystallize a kind of "magical thinking" about the death (or potential death) of a blood-based ancestral group. Benjamin interpreted the Erik and Sons cap whose text declares "keep your country clean" as "xenophobic" but then elaborates: "it seems Scandinavian, Nordic, Aryan . . . keep your country clean tralala, on top of that, have blue eyes, be tall, blond."

Vikings in particular are beloved by many far right youth (as well as youth from other subcultural scenes, such as the metal and biker scenes, as chapter 3 explained). Youth repeatedly connected Viking symbolism with expressions of power, strength, and a willingness to be violent. But youth also admire Vikings for their reputed ingenuity and craftsmanship and their accomplishments as sailors and shipbuilders. Simon, a twenty-year-old studying for his technical high school degree, talked at length about his admiration for the Vikings, for their innovations in ship construction and for how they established trade routes. "They had a degree of commerce that couldn't have existed today. The Vikings . . . had specific systems that wouldn't have been possible today. Or they would be possible if people would behave more sensibly. . . . They weren't only warriors . . . they also had extreme capabilities in craftsmanship, like goldsmiths." He describes at length the kinds of accomplishments Vikings made without modern methods and technology, noting that he doesn't think humans today would be capable of the same achievements. And, notably, he singles out Viking symbols as especially laudable: they made "cool things, and they have awesome symbols. The symbols from back then are really beautiful." Later, Simon praises Viking tools, including weapons: "in order to build their Viking ships, they had thirteen different types of axes, that's totally tough." And a few minutes later, he looks at a screenshot of an Erik and Sons T-shirt with a *Totenkopf* wearing a Viking helmet, noting, "cool, cool, chic T-shirts, I have to Google that right away when I get home." When the interviewer asks if he would wear it, he says, "Um, privately, yes," signaling that he knows the shirts would not be socially acceptable or permitted at school, but that he likes them nonetheless. Carpentry apprentice Michael looked at a T-shirt depicting a Viking warrior with a Nordic ax and said, "it's all a little bit ancestor worship, the cult of ancestor worship." Ingo examined an image of a Viking on a black T-shirt and said it means "that I'm showing what I am and I'm proud of what I am . . . and I have my culture and I won't let myself be suppressed . . . it's provocative."

Such symbols help strengthen group bonds and act as a powerful mechanism of belonging and identification for right-wing youth. But the allegorical images around Nordic and Germanic mythological references do more than strengthen subcultural group bonding—they contribute to what I call "aspirational nationhood"—imagined fantasies and aspirations about a nation that never was. And because they are deeply intertwined with symbols evoking, depicting, celebrating, and valorizing violence, such images also help naturalize and normalize linkages between fantasies of national regeneration with ideas about justifiable violence. This intersection—national restoration, justifiable violence, and racial purity—are at the core of right-wing ideology and extremist action.[39]

Death and Its Contexts: Humor and the Limits of Acceptability

Death symbols produced more laughter among the interviews than I had expected, although other scholars have pointed out the use of humor by the far right.[40] The image that consistently produced some of the most laughter from youth was one that I found personally hardest to look at, because I read the symbol within the context of the history of the lynching of African Americans in the United States. The black T-shirt uses white iconography and script depicting an individual with a noose around his neck, dangling from a tree branch and grabbing onto the rope with a hand as if to try to save himself, under the phrase "Dancing in the Air" (see plate 9). The person wearing the T-shirt in the image—who is facing away from the camera—has a shaved head and a tattoo across the back of his neck reading "A.C.A.B." (All Cops Are Bastards). The T-shirt was, as one of the youth interviewed pointed out, likely designed in reaction to an antiracist music concert by the same name (Dancing in the Air) held in March 2012 in Rostock, in the northeast of Germany.[41]

Nineteen of the fifty-one youth interviewed saw humor in this image, although not all nineteen found the image funny themselves. Several pointed out that the iconography was intended as black humor or as a prank about death, and others explained it was intended as funny but was not. But several other youth laughed at the image. "It's funny," says Lukas, because "before somebody is hung they might twitch again, well, if someone is hung slowly, otherwise the neck would break, I'd think. . . . I also have a T-shirt where there's a guy with a gun stuck in his mouth, and it says "Bam" on it; it's funny somehow." Mahmut first looked at the image and didn't understand it. But as he looked more deeply, he noted, "ah . . . OK, now I get it [laughs]. It's funny. It's a guy who is being hung . . . great . . . and he's fidgeting around."

Markus explains that this T-shirt is meant to communicate to "the blacks, the foreigners, and so on . . . it's a logo for, 'look at me, I'm a Nazi and want you all to get out.'" A person who wears such a T-shirt, he argues, would either hate foreigners or belong to an organization where hatred is part and parcel of the normal routine. "Well, hatred of foreigners . . . that only Germans should live in Germany and we are supposed to be the best country and so on." Karl, an eighteen-year-old who found the T-shirt "totally tasteless," interprets it as being about the "persecution of Jews, I don't know if they were also hung, but it's not good at all."

The fact that death symbols produce laughter reinforces the notion that interpretation of extremist iconography is only possible in the broader context of an image's performance or deployment as well as its reception, including the attitudes and ideology of the observer. The youth I interviewed did not find death images that they perceived to be deployed by Islamist terrorists to be funny, for example, as I discuss below. In the case of youth in and around the far right scene, their own experiences in racist environments is relevant to the broader context and lenses through which they interpret coded symbols. Several of the youth described right-wing or racist environments in their lives outside of school — family members, friends, and coworkers who they described as far right, neo-Nazi, or racist. Martin, who self-identifies as far right, said that he's often heard he should not shop at H&M because "it's the brand of a Jew, everyone has to decide for themselves [if they want to buy there]," although he says, "that doesn't matter to me." There were repeated instances across the interviews when youth made statements criticizing Germany's increasingly multicultural nature. Most of their ire was directed toward Muslims, but there were also occasional anti-Semitic remarks or more general anti-immigrant sentiments and critiques of religious and cultural practices like the headscarf.

Artur, a twenty-two-year-old concrete layer apprentice, described his experience in a previous apprenticeship, where he had studied to be a painter.

One of his coworkers at his work placement was "really a . . . he was definitely a little bit racist, in any case. He even said to me, when I had let my hair grow out a little and hadn't been to the barber in a long time, 'go get a German haircut' and so on, well, I thought, whoa." Such instances illustrate how youth are taught and learn what it means to be "German" in a context where normative expectations for German-ness can be narrowly defined around ethnic origins and phenotypical appearance. Some of the youth quoted in this book live in contexts in which xenophobia is normative and expected.[42] Michael, who at thirty-four was the second-oldest interviewee, spoke at length about coming of age around the time of German unification, when all the youth he knew became right wing. "Very few were really convinced. . . . I think it was more a kind of sport. They run around like that, so I will too. And scream 'Heil Hitler,' even though one doesn't have any idea why." At that time, he noted, "50–60 percent of all people called themselves Nazis or right-wing radicals." When he was twelve years old, he explains, "in the schoolyard everyone was a little bit bigger and a little bit older, and all the bigger teenagers [laughs], they wore bomber jackets and combat boots. It was rare [to see] someone normal in the middle of that."

The scaffold builders in particular describe work environments marked by xenophobia and racism. While discussing the text on a T-shirt, twenty-seven-year-old scaffold builder apprentice Hans explains that it seems to him to reflect a right-wing attitude and then links this to his occupation: "Maybe not necessarily extremism . . . but in any case definitely the [right-wing] attitude a little. Just like a lot [of people] have in scaffold building." Oliver, a twenty-three-year-old scaffold builder trainee, spontaneously mentioned that there are a "relatively high" number of right-wing radicals in the occupation. When the interviewer asks how he knows, he explains that while political opinions aren't directly a topic at work, it becomes clear by the ways in which his colleagues talk about foreigners: "They don't say they are right-wing radical, but they occasionally make xenophobic remarks . . . and then it's totally obvious, then there's no need to ask about the political attitudes."

Thus, for many of the youth we interviewed, racism, Islamophobia, xenophobia, nationalism, or anti-Semitism have been part of the context of their lives, through peer groups, families, and work environments that normalize, validate, and encourage such attitudes. Even youth who were not vocally far right sometimes expressed views that were xenophobic, anti-Semitic, or Islamophobic. While Artur found the experience of being told to get a German haircut a little over the top, for example, earlier in the interview, as he looked at an image of a T-shirt depicting a plane flying into the World Trade

Center towers, he revealed his own anti-Semitic beliefs. "For me, the media are somehow the biggest . . . the second terrorist, I'd say. . . . Look for example at the *Bild Zeitung*, who does the *Bild* belong to; it's all Jews, the biggest powers of the media and the Jews are together with America. Germany only helps because we—through the Hitler period, everything was ruined for us."

Most anger at "others" in Germany is directed not toward Jews, however, but toward Muslims and newer immigrants. Benjamin even makes this distinction clear in his interpretation of a T-shirt with the English phrase "Old School Racist" on it, arguing that this phrase refers to being a racist "according to the old school," which for him means "an anti-Semite." Anti-Semitism is thus perceived as an older form of racism; by implication, newer expressions do not focus on Jews as the primary target.

There were limits, however, to how acceptable youth found symbols and images of death, and the context in which the image was deployed (or youth's interpretation of that context) was particularly important in this regard. This was especially true of one image in particular—the image of a plane crashing into the World Trade Center towers, which in the photograph shown to youth was worn by a young man with a Palestinian scarf around his neck. Although the photograph was captured by a professional photographer at a right-wing extremist street scene, youth did not have this context available to them when they observed the image. Youth were overwhelmingly uncertain about who the wearer of the shirt is supposed to be: they variably interpreted the wearer of the shirt as an "Arab," "the Taliban," an "Islamist," "al Qaeda," a "Salafist," or a "Muslim," while others saw the T-shirt as simply anti-American, and a few students described it as belonging to the far right scene. A few connected it to conspiracy theories about U.S. involvement in 9/11, and several saw the shirt as anti-Semitic, although no one caught the specific anti-Semitic reference within this image (in which the words "United States" were replaced with "J . . . nited States" to signify "Jew-nited States"). Hayri contends that the shirt would appeal to "Jew-haters and other idiots who are happy [about 9/11] . . . and American-haters too." Mahmut noticed the strangely-written "U" but couldn't interpret it. "To visit the United States, I think it says, but it's strange, the 'U' is not really written out. In any case, it references September 11. . . . It's probably supposed to represent a terrorist." Michael first described the shirt as likely worn by people who come from "Islamic" countries, but then notes "it could just as likely be some Nazis wearing it," because "the enemy of my enemy is my best friend." He explains that Muslims generally don't speak well of Jews and then notes that the two towers are symbols "of high finance" (which he thus implies is related to being Jewish) and so "would be for a Nazi totally unproblematic to wear it." Although most youth did not see this particular T-shirt as far right wing, noting for example that "right-wing radicals wouldn't wear something like that" (Erdinc), they sometimes connected far right ideology to the anti-American sentiment of the shirt (Joachim). Steffen, a twenty-four-year-old carpentry apprentice who described the shirt as vicious, anti-American, and "Islamic," angrily reflected that the wearer of a shirt would not be sanctioned at school if they were a Muslim rather than a far right wing youth. "And guaranteed," he complained, "no one would say anything if Achmed Abdula ran around here with such a T-shirt, no one would say anything." Artur, who expressed anti-Semitic views during the interview, also expressed strong anti-American ideas, noting that he's "a little bit behind" the T-shirt politically because "a lot of hypocritical stuff happens in America. . . . I think it's a rigged game; I think there are a lot of lies behind it that we don't get. I think a lot is censored." As he continues, he admits, "To be honest, I wanted to have a T-shirt made like this one, with Osama bin Laden," and then he uses U.S. support for Israel as an example of what he does not support.

Regardless of what they felt it meant, though, youth expressed far more revulsion for this image than for any other, describing the T-shirt as "brutal," "provocative," and "crass." More than racist or nationalist T-shirts referencing historical pogroms like the Holocaust or contemporary murders against Turks, this T-shirt was offensive to the youth I interviewed. There are likely several explanations for why this is the case, but I would suggest the most likely is that their interpretation of the T-shirt's consumer as a terrorist or a "Muslim" makes them feel more threatened in comparison to shirts referencing violence against migrants, ethnic and religious minorities, or non-Germans. In this case, extremist symbolism becomes too provocative, because it is received as threatening.

Conclusion

I suggest that a close examination of nationalist and extremist allegories within contemporary right-wing coded symbols and brands can shed important light on powerful mechanisms of belonging and protest that may shape young people's recruitment to, engagement with, and radicalization within the far right. The case of death symbols illustrates how youth use social taboos to provoke and horrify mainstream society while simultaneously sending political and ideological messages about the kind of nation they aspire to. These findings ought to refine theories of nationalism and extremist engagement, which have been more centrally concerned with political motivations than with cultural ones. I take up this point in greater depth in this volume's conclusion, but first, I turn to two remaining empirical cases from the commercialization of far right ideology: the use of global and transnational iconography, and the embodiment of masculinity in far right iconography and commercial products.

5 GLOBAL SYMBOLS, LOCAL BANS
Transnational Nationalist Symbols

One of the most obvious and terrifying responses to tendencies
of cultural merging is the upsurge of fundamentalism.
—Marcelo Gleiser

The 2016 collection from Erik and Sons features a T-shirt depicting two guns
raised in the air over the text *"Mi Casa is not your fucking Casa."*[1] The combination of English and Spanish evokes Mexican and Latin/Central/South
American immigration to the United States, but in this case, is likely a statement against immigrant groups in the German or European context. The
traditional Spanish phrase referring to one's personal home thus becomes a
metaphor for national belonging and *Heimat* (homeland) in a different terri-
torial space. The use of global codes and references like this one shows how
far right ideologies have broadened, in the global era, beyond (mere) national
borders. This development is consistent with the well-documented spread
of popular culture through globalization, and in some ways it is therefore
unsurprising. But for policy makers, educators, and other authorities who
seek to reduce and restrict the use of extremist signification, the use of global
codes and references poses significant challenges.

Over the past several decades, the German response to right-wing extremism has evolved into what is now the broadest and most comprehensive strategy to combat the far right globally.[2] This includes monitoring by
federal, state, and local authorities; formal school and community-based
interventions; dedicated research centers and divisions of government agencies that specialize in the far right; scores of nonprofit and nongovernmental
organizations, and an extensive community network of "mobile far right ad-
visors" who intervene in cities, small towns, and neighborhoods throughout
the country. There are organizations that identify youth who are at risk of
engaging in the far right, and other organizations to help youth "exit" violent
far right groups. There are educational outreach programs that bring former
neo-Nazis to speak in schools to try to disrupt radicalization and youth
violence, and programs that educate teachers on how best to recognize and
respond effectively to far right youth in their classrooms.[3]

Part of the success of these interventions rests on the ability of government authorities, watchdog organizations, and educators to accurately identify youth who are at risk for or already engaged in far right groups and movements.[4] There are a range of efforts to improve the knowledge of educators and the public. Legal authorities and agencies, local police, and nongovernmental organizations run workshops and publish information pamphlets for educators and the public that detail trends and symbols within far right youth scenes. There are guidelines for local departments of motor vehicles informing staff of specialized combinations of codes and numbers that are not permitted on vanity license plates (like 88 or 18). There are civic education centers at the federal level as well as in each state that organize events, workshops, and conferences and distribute free or heavily subsidized curricular materials, books, and information about a range of political topics, including on the far right wing and extremism more generally.[5]

Legal guidelines help educators and local police officers understand what constitutes criminal right-wing extremist activity, such as reciting the Heil Hitler or displaying a swastika. But authorities monitor and track not only right-wing extremism (criminal actions that are hostile to or against the constitution) but also right-wing radicalism (actions that are part of the legitimate spectrum of democratic political opinion). Legal interventions and criminal charges can apply only to activities or symbols deemed extremist or that directly reference extremist organizations, but schools, stadiums, or other organizations can establish broader dress codes or policies. One of the growing challenges in recognizing, interpreting, and addressing far right symbols, however, rests on the extent to which much of the discourse and some of the specific subcultural elements within the far right draw explicitly (and perhaps increasingly) on global references and codes. Such global references can help circumvent bans (by changing the language of an illegal phrase, for example) but also confuse interpretations, pushing products further into "gray areas" where it is difficult to interpret intent.

As German authorities navigate the use of non-German language phrases and texts, global pan-Aryan codes, brands produced in other countries, and product advertisement and sale across national borders, there is a need for sustained attention to these transnational nationalist and global far right symbols. There has been little systematic study of how subcultural scenes and social movements with explicitly nationalist goals appropriate, reinterpret, and deploy a variety of global symbols and images in ways that are sometimes quite distant from their original meanings.[6] Drawing on an analysis of images of global symbols and iconography and of young people's interpretation of "global" symbols, this chapter examines the phenomenon of what I call "transnational nationalism" and its implications for public and private bans of ideological symbols, brands, and iconography. Following an analysis of global and transnational symbols and their impact on legal bans, I turn to the question of local bans in schools, examining youth reactions to school bans of particular symbols and codes as well as the enforcement of those bans. Ultimately, I argue that banning policies tend to backfire, further contributing to the game-playing aspect of code modification that make the symbols appealing in the first place.

Local, National, Global

Far right extremist subcultures and movements have long been analyzed through national lenses, and for good reason: such movements have primarily been organized around national themes, politics, and identities. Far right politicians regularly appeal to themes of national restoration and rejuvenation; nationalist myths and legends rely on narratives, legacies, and fantasies specific to particular nations and tribes; contemporary debates about belonging reference immigrant groups that are largely specific to local migration patterns. The previous three chapters have highlighted how particular national(ist) legacies show up in the coded symbols deployed in brands marketed to the far right in Germany. From the numeric code "88" (signifying HH, or Heil Hitler) and Nazi references to the use of Viking, Germanic, and Norse mythology, much of the iconography in German far right subcultural style distinctly relates to German nationhood.

Because of the decisively national frame of far right political movements, most research on the far right similarly studies national contexts. Scholars have analyzed fascism in Italy, the far right in Hungary and the United States, or contemporary parties like the U.K. Independence Party (UKIP) and the British National Party (BNP), to name just a few examples.[7] Research that has gone beyond individual country analyses has tended to focus on cross-national comparisons by contrasting far right political rhetoric, xenophobia, strategies and repertoires, and voting patterns across groups of countries or regions.[8] But in fact, many of these nationalist movements have distinctly and strikingly global aspects.

Deterritorialization and Global Pan-Aryanism

One of the most dramatic consequences of the acceleration of globalization over the past few decades has been the rapid transformation in communication and knowledge sharing across national boundaries, a phenomenon

Jan Scholte and others have referred to as deterritorialization: the extent to which one's physical location has become less consequential in everyday life compared to previous generations.[9] Employees can telecommute or participate in meetings via videoconference; ATM machines communicate with banks globally so that travelers can withdraw local currencies as needed; supermarkets supply produce from varied climates year-round, edging consumers away from local and seasonal eating patterns. Most notably, the ability to communicate with individuals who are widely dispersed in time and space—via text, e-mail, chatrooms, blogs, or social media—helps forge faster and broader connections and means of sharing information across local and national boundaries. The increasing global use of English further facilitates communication between populations previously more restricted by national languages.

For social movement groups—including extremist organizations and subcultures—these developments enable recruitment, radicalization, and communication across boundaries that have historically been less porous. New social media platforms, for example, create means for rapidly sharing news about protests, marches, manifestos, events, arrests, opinions, music, and more. The rapid mobilization of youth during the Arab Spring demonstrations and the well-documented recruitment and radicalization of youth outside the Middle East by ISIS are just two examples. As Michael Casey explains in his analysis of the globalization of Che Guevara's image, global countercultural movements—whether terrorist or not—are enabled by new communication technologies and the "computers, cell phones, cameras, servers, fiber-optic cables, transmitters, and satellites" that help them "disseminate their messages widely."[10]

Thus, Benedict Anderson's astute observation about how the introduction of national newspapers and printing presses facilitated communication and identity building within nations[11] has a parallel today in how Internet-based communication platforms facilitate collaboration and identity building across groups and individuals regardless of national boundaries.[12] This is no less true for extremist movements than for other groups of people; globalized communication platforms and possibilities have made it easier for white nationalists and other extremists to align, cooperate, communicate, and support each other across national contexts.

For example, the U.S.-based right-wing extremist web forum Stormfront is peppered with discussions about support for WN (White Nationalist) companies, suggesting that white supremacists and right-wing extremists express solidarity and support for each others' movements and efforts across national borders and boundaries. Racist theories, antigovernment rhetoric, and extremist ideologies circulate globally as individuals post on chat rooms from varied national contexts, although the common language is typically English. Social media and Internet-based communication platforms thus facilitate and help align like-minded extremists across the globe. Right-wing musicians' global concert tours and music festivals similarly unite youth subcultures across national boundaries.[13]

Some of the global alignment across far right movements can be traced to pan-Aryan and white supremacist goals that see the preservation of whiteness and racial separation as more important than (merely) national goals. As one poster explained on a Stormfront discussion, "Remember we are not a 'hate group' but a cultural and racial preservation group. In fact we are the true 'Multiculturalists' and genuine believers of cultural and racial diversity. By keeping the different races and people separate the world can enjoy the diversity of the human species."[14] Stormfront's very motto is "White Pride World Wide," indicating they view themselves as a global platform for white supremacy. In addition to specialized discussion forums on topics ranging from financial planning to children's education, Stormfront hosts fifteen international forums across Europe, the Baltics, Russia, South Africa, and Australia. Thus, pan-Aryan and white nationalist groups express solidarity and support for right-wing extremists in other countries.

For many white supremacists, then, alignment with other whites worldwide is part of their objective, and the ease and speed of communication technology in the global era has only aided these goals. But globalization's impact on communication does not fully explain why global symbols are so widely in play within the far right scene. I refer to the deployment of non-national symbols and codes in the name of nationalist goals as "transnational nationalism." Below, I examine three categories of explanations for why far right movements and subcultures in Germany have so broadly made the use of global iconography, symbols, codes, and references so popular—even ubiquitous—in some of the brands. These three categories—global circulation and traveling images, the role of global markets, and the role of legal and private bans—are explored in the following sections.

Global Circulation and Traveling Images

The first explanation rests on the concept of "traveling" or "circulating" images, which become iconic through repeated appropriation and deployment in contexts often wholly removed from their origin.[15] David Morgan, for example, analyzes several categories of such imagery—including exported, appropriated, and imported imagery—in an examination of religious images that migrate during missionary work.[16] Traveling images are, generally speaking, images that are produced at a particular moment in a specific political, national, or cultural context, but that then acquire a circulatory afterlife as iconic symbols, becoming part of what artist Hito Steyerl calls a "labyrinth of traveling images."[17] They are visual representations of "the circulation of meanings and the instability of iconography as images cross the boundaries of one culture and become the property of another."[18]

Che Guevara's image is perhaps the best example of a traveling image, deployed on patches, T-shirts, banners, stickers, and billboards by people across the globe who see Che's image as an expression of their willingness to resort to extreme measures to fight perceived injustice.[19] Thus decontextualized, an image of a specific revolutionary fighter from a particular national context in a particular historical era emerges as a timeless symbol of freedom fighters and anti-imperialists across political spectrums and national contexts, uniting right-wing and antigovernment resistance groups, leftist social movements, and self-styled rebels across the globe. The iconic image itself becomes ideologically empty, emerging instead as a symbol of generalized resistance, deployed to legitimize local protests and resistance movements by linking them to a "global narrative of revolution and rebellion."[20]

Lina Khatib's analysis of images in Middle East politics uses the related term "floating images" to refer to images that are appropriated and redeployed in ways that are often wholly unrelated to their original context and meaning.[21] In the German far right, traveling or floating images show up in the shared codes of the pan-Aryan movement but also in the appropriation and deployment of iconic images and symbols from revolutionary struggles and resistance movements historically and globally.

Symbols in text form can also travel globally; iconic words attributed to Gandhi, for example — "First they ignore you. Then they laugh at you. Then they fight you. Then you win." — are translated into German (*Erst ignorieren sie Dich, Dann verlachen sie Dich, Dann bekämpfen sie Dich, und Dann gewinnst Du*) and adorn the back of a T-shirt captured in a street scene by a professional photographer. Across the top of the T-shirt is the phrase www .widerstand-weiden.de, the website of a right-wing social movement group in the town of Weiden. The T-shirt attributes the quote to Mahatma Gandhi; however, there is no evidence that Gandhi actually said this,[22] showing how traveling symbols may be appropriated and authorship attributed to other (iconic) global sources even if there is no evidence of the original source or context.

It is not only iconic images of revolutionaries like Che Guevara or words attributed to Gandhi that travel from their original usage. Within the far right scene, a plethora of symbols, images, icons, and slogans have "traveled" quite far from their origins, taking on nonnational, pan-national, or global meanings and statuses. The global pan-Aryan code "14 Words," as chapter 2 explained, represents the number of words in a sentence spoken by the late American neo-Nazi David Lane: "We must secure the existence of our people and a future for white children." The number 14 appears throughout the German (and global) far right scene in vanity license plates, tattoos, T-shirts, requested telephone numbers, and more. In one photo captured at a Berlin right-wing gathering in May 2005, a young man with closely cropped hair faces away from the camera, sporting a backpack made of military-style green canvas with the misspelled, handwritten words "I BELIVE [*sic*] IN 14 WORDS." Symbols and codes like "14 Words" thus became part of a global mantra for the pan-Aryan movement, symbolizing shared objectives that supersede national boundaries, evidence of what George Michael refers to as "a new pan-Aryan identity based on race and civilization that transcends national borders."[23] The fact that far right wing groups and individuals across the globe draw on shared codes like "14 Words" speaks to the transnational dimensions of meaning systems. Shared national(ist) meanings cross boundaries and borders and emerge as global meanings — a process that we might expect to increase in the face of globalization's ongoing acceleration.

While "14 Words" is a symbol created by and for white nationalists, there are other examples of "traveling images" that originated in one context but have been appropriated in a fully different way by the German far right scene, or a subset of it. Palestinian scarves wrap around the necks and shoulders of far right youth who claim them as a visual symbol of freedom fighters (see plate 12). Nordic imagery abounds, as discussed in chapter 3, although the "transnational" origins of Nordic imagery are claimed as "national" by German extremists who believe they are descendants of Nordic tribes. Brands marketing to the far right draw on historical Nordic imagery and symbols as well as more contemporary iconography, including Scandinavian flags and spelling and the names of Scandinavian towns.

One of the most common uses of global images and symbols is to express political commentary on contemporary geopolitical issues; iconic American symbols like the U.S. flag and the Statue of Liberty circulate as symbols of capitalism or imperialism, for example. Sometimes these symbols are modified or combined with other symbols popular with the far right, as chapter 4 highlighted with the example of the Statue of Liberty's head being replaced with a *Totenkopf*, or skull, while her raised torch is replaced by a pistol or a dollar sign.

Global U.S. political conflicts and relationships are also referenced. The close U.S.-Israeli relationship is the subject of a banner held up during a

2011 street march in Dortmund (see plate 8), for example, that depicted the Statue of Liberty with a skull replacing the face, holding up a raised pistol; the banner's text reads "STOP USRAEL: END IMPERIALISM," (USRAEL STOPPEN: IMPERIALISMUS VERNICHTEN). U.S.-Iranian relations also merit iconographical reference; a poster sold by Ansgar Aryan features a drawing of Iranian president Mahmoud Ahmadinejad wearing mirrored sunglasses and pointing at the observer. The sunglasses reflect twin images of the Statue of Liberty's crown resting atop a skull, while text across the top of the poster reads "Ansgar Aryan & Friends."

Iconography, symbols, and codes deployed by the German far right also travel transnationally when they co-opt historical and contemporary symbols celebrating, claiming, or representing other nations' white nationalist attacks or events. References to U.S. atrocities or the American context are particularly popular, such as the symbolic code 168:1 discussed in chapters 2 and 4, in which German youth claim a victory of an American right-wing extremist bombing, using the deaths of the victims versus the death by execution of the bomber as the soccer-style score. Youth also wear T-shirts with images of the planes crashing into the World Trade Center towers.

The Ku Klux Klan is referenced in several different iconographical representations; one T-shirt depicts the "hangman's stand" with a noose and a figure, while a shirt made by Erik and Sons shows a group of figures clad in Klan garb standing in a circle under the words "team player." A more complex combination of global symbols and pop culture iconography is depicted in a T-shirt in Ansgar Aryan's 2016 collection, which depicts a hooded Ku Klux Klan figure, holding a machine gun, above graphic text imitating the Star Wars lettering that reads "Join the Empire." Text at the top of the T-shirt reads "We want you to enlist today." A large "blood drop cross"—a known Ku Klux Klan symbol that depicts a circle around a cross with a drop of blood in the center—sits in the background of the T-shirt.[24]

Atrocities and attacks from outside of the United States also figure prominently in iconography and symbols. The brand name Reconquista references a European pogrom against Muslims. A 2016 Ansgar Aryan T-shirt depicts images of Mao, Lenin, and Stalin under the words "The Truth about Communism" and over figures reporting numbers of deaths: "13 million killed" under Lenin's face, "around 70 million deaths" under Mao's face, "42.5 million killed" under Stalin's face. Across the back of the T-shirt is large print reading "130 million deaths." Alongside the T-shirt, the product marketing text describes the quality of the cotton material and its sizing before concluding, "With this motif, we pull Lenin, Mao and Stalin back into focus. 'The truth about communism' is hardly found in history textbooks."

Finally, the "traveling images" phenomenon also extends to the co-optation and borrowing of brand names across national contexts. Symbols, logos, and icons that circulate globally through marketing and consumption patterns are appropriated for new uses because of the coincidental symbolic resonance of particular logos or symbols on the brands. Such "traveling images" are also facilitated through and by globalization and its circulation of images, logos, slogans, and brand names. Thus British brands like Lonsdale and American brands like New Balance become part of German far right subculture because of the ways in which their logos can be appropriated and redeployed with new meanings, as chapter 2 detailed.

The first far right commercial brand in Germany, Consdaple, was started by Frank Glasauer, a member of the right-wing political party NPD, in reaction to a multicultural campaign Lonsdale undertook to try to dissuade far right consumers.[25] Consdaple imitates the graphic of the Lonsdale logo, but by adding the letter "p," a half-zipped jacket can reveal the full five letters of the National Socialist party (NSDAP). Shortly after Consdaple T-shirts emerged in the early 1990s, a series of other T-shirt brands, including Masterrace and Troublemaker, came onto the scene. These brands imitated the same arched logo of the Lonsdale and Consdaple shirts, thus creating a national(ist) brand while evoking a nonnational one.

Using global symbols helps confuse the interpretation of far right iconography in ways that can be appealing to consumers who want to circumvent bans or social stigma on the far right, as I discuss in greater depth below. But the deployment of symbols far removed from local or national contexts also increases the odds that consumers themselves won't understand the meaning of the iconography. Traveling images are not always recognized or understood in their intended context, in other words. The following section details the muddled reception of the global symbols among the youth interviewed for this book.

Global Symbols, Muddled Reception

In interviews, youth often were confused by codes and symbols drawn from global contexts, particularly when they appeared in photographed scenes from demonstrations and marches where more straightforward far right symbols were evident. None of the fifty-one youth interviewed was able to decode the T-shirt with 168:1, although several noted it seemed to reflect a score or soccer score of some kind. In another image, two young men wearing sunglasses and Che Guevara T-shirts—one with a Palestinian scarf around his neck and the other with a Mohawk haircut—walk within a crowd where several typical far right symbols and styles are evident. Behind the two youth, a woman with bleached blond hair sports a small *Reichsadler* (the imperial eagle, a common Nazi symbol)[26] on her shirt; on the right-hand side of the photo, a young man wears a Thor's Hammer necklace and has a haircut, facial hair, and leather suspenders that youth pointed to as signaling the far right. This image was confusing for youth, many of whom see Che Guevara and Palestinian scarves as clear leftist symbols. Most youth interpreted the Che Guevara image as representing "freedom fighters" or "revolutionaries" but saw it as a symbol primarily deployed by the left or by "normal" people. As they detected far right signals in other parts of the photo, though, they found the Che Guevara icon difficult to interpret. Daniel, a twenty-year-old carpentry apprentice, had trouble figuring out what was going on in the image. He noted that "in this picture, I don't exactly know, for me it's neither fish nor flesh [a German idiom meaning "neither one thing nor the other"] . . . because the man on the right here doesn't exactly look as if he is necessarily left-wing. I'd characterize him as having a *völkisch*[27] stance, from his clothing style, his haircut, from the necklace. . . . It's a puzzle . . . well, I wouldn't exactly connect Che Guevara with the nationalist frame." Daniel detected what he thought were both right-wing and left-wing signifiers in the image, which left him uncertain as to its meaning. Others thought the image was a good example of the multivocality of particular symbols and icons, as Kevin noted, explaining that "symbols are taken over these days. . . . The right wing is stealing the symbols of the left-wing scene." Seventeen-year-old Jan describes what he knows about Che Guevara, describing him as someone who he thinks helped people, and that the far right might be just as interested in wearing an image of him as anyone else. "Of course [Nazis] can wear it. Of course, they could buy this exact T-shirt. . . . I don't think that Nazis only have Nazi things at home. I think they also have H&M [clothes] and not [just] Thor Steinar. I mean there are also Nazis that don't have so much money, and I think Thor Steinar is more expensive than H&M."

Other global symbols were more easily recognizable. The Palestinian scarf frequently drew notice as youth perused the images, although its meaning was not consistently clear. Some youth talked about the scarves as merely fashionable, while others noted they are perceived as left wing, and still others described different patterns on the scarves that convey varied meanings. Shortly after Kevin noted how the far right is "stealing" the left wing's symbols, he explained that the Palestinian scarf might indicate "Nazis" because of the "parallels [in the] fight against Jews." The abbreviation ACAB (for All Cops Are Bastards, co-opted from the United States) was widely noticed and accurately decoded. And not all youth were receptive to the idea of global codes being deployed for nationalist aims. Georg, a twenty-one-year-old scaffold builder apprentice, scanned a list of frequently banned brands and logos, discussing which ones he owns, and stopped when he got to the brand Pit Bull, noting that its iconography is for American audiences, not for German ones. "I don't have Pit Bull anymore either. . . . I used to, a long time ago. It's Pit Bull West Coast, to be exact, right? . . . West Coast is in America. There are no right-wing radicals there. There's only gang members. For me . . . a brand like that wouldn't make any sense."

Globalization—and the concomitant global circulation and cooptation of images across national borders—is only part of the story of how far right national movements deploy and appropriate symbols drawn from other nationalist movements, foreign brands, and even events and social movements that have little or nothing to do with nationalist goals. Producers have also made concerted efforts to build global markets for their products. Below, I turn to the second explanation for transnational nationalist symbols: profit-driven incentives and the quest for global extremist markets and consumers, before returning in the second half of this chapter to a closer examination of the interpretation and impact of banning policies on youth in and around the far right scene.

Global Markets

In the summer of 2010, as I was launching my fieldwork for this project, I spoke with an antifascist activist who related her experience with the Thor Steinar shop that was then on the chic Rosa Luxemburg street, alongside major brand-name stores and elite boutiques selling Italian shoes and handbags. The activist spotted three young tourists exiting the store carrying bags and speaking French. A common mainstream and antifascist concern about the presence of high-end physical stores for the Thor Steinar brand has been that tourists would inadvertently stumble into stores and purchase the clothing, thereby supporting a brand that by that point had been identified as a known brand within far right extremist youth subculture. Assuming the youth had gone to the store inadvertently, the activist approached them to warn them about the brand's reputation. To her surprise, she related, they reported that they knew the brand well and had intentionally traveled to Berlin from France in order to purchase some clothing there, because of its far right connotations. The physical store, in other words, had contributed to a sort of far right youth consumer tourism.

This anecdote illustrates the potential for coded nationalist and far right extremist messages to appeal to transnational audiences—a potential that several major brands have begun to exploit. Thus, the second major reason why companies that market to the far right draw so heavily on transnational symbols, global iconography and the English language, as I discuss below, has to do with the large brands' traditional profit orientation and the emerging competition for global consumer markets. While German consumers remain a primary consumer base, brands are eager to stake additional claim outside of Germany—particularly Thor Steinar, which has aggressively sought outside markets and has moved away from more explicit far right coding as it has done so.[28]

There are dozens of brands—small and large—marketing to far right youth, whether they have direct connections to far right scenes or not. In addition to the larger, high-quality brands—Thor Steinar, Ansgar Aryan, and Erik and Sons—smaller brands like Masterrace Europe, Reconquista, and Troublemaker Germany compete for market shares and niches within far right youth subcultures in Germany.[29] Other large brands, like Yakuza, offer high-quality clothing with a wide range of offensive and provocative iconography, including racist and misogynistic images as well as symbols related to the far right.

The big firms have been joined by look-alike firms overseas like the Polish brand Doberman's Aggressive, whose T-shirts sport aesthetic design nearly indistinguishable from Thor Steinar motifs.[30] A much larger number of websites exist globally that act as distributors of a variety of clothing brands that deploy coded or overt racist and far right messages. These include the United States' White Trash Rebel and Dirty Tees (which carries Aryan Wear clothing) and the white nationalist site Tightrope (whose website's header features a hand raising a noose, a hypermasculine male figure with crossed arms, and the phrase "It's not illegal to be white . . . yet!"). These latter websites, however, bear no similarities to the sophisticated, large, mainstream-style brands that have won such success in the German and European market.

The ease and availability of goods through the Internet is the primary driver of this trend, but it is not only Internet sales that enhance global markets for the clothing. Brands deploying far right symbols and marketing to the far right scene are also sold in physical stores—some of which are linked exclusively to particular brands. Thor Steinar currently operates eleven physical stores in Germany and thirty-five stores in Finland, Italy, Croatia, Russia, Slovakia, the Czech Republic, Ukraine, and the U.K.; there are thirteen stores in Moscow alone. International representatives sell the clothing in several other countries, including France, the Netherlands, Denmark, Sweden, and the United States. In the United States, for example, where Thor Steinar has registered a U.S. trademark but does not currently have physical stores, clothing and products are sold through Dortrix, Inc., which the website lists as the representative of "Thor Steinar Mediatex GmbH in the United

States."[31] A representative of Thor Steinar's parent company, Mediatex, told a journalist that the company plans to "expand worldwide."[32] The brand's financial success was thrust into sharp relief when MediaTex GmbH, which represents the brand, was bought in November 2008 by a conglomerate based in Dubai, International Brands General Trading (IBGT).[33] In 2010, the company put a Swiss CEO—Marco Wäspe—at the helm.[34]

Keeping physical stores open is not always easy, however. The opening of Thor Steinar stores has consistently been met with organized protests from the left (see plates 24 and 25). When existing store owners in the central Berlin shopping mall Europacenter began to sell Thor Steinar clothing, the mall owners protested, and the clothing was removed. Days later, however, the store's entire inventory was swapped out with Erik and Sons clothing. A neighborhood group formed to protest the store (Bündnis gegen Rechts Charlottenburg-Wilmersdorf), handing out flyers protesting the store and informing mall shoppers about the brand. Within three months, the store closed, and the mall authorities noted that future lease contracts would be changed in order to prohibit "the sale of products with extremist content."[35]

The heart of corporate efforts to create global markets rests in the virtual world, however. The brands' websites offer translation into multiple languages, ship goods globally, and point global consumers to officially certified resellers in other countries. Internet-based blogs and chatrooms provide space for consumers to communicate about product availability in various countries. For example, before the U.K. Thor Steinar store opened, a Stormfront member in the U.K. posted a question in 2012 about whether there was a U.K. stock list for Thor Steinar items. The growing use of English also plays a role; as the current de facto global lingua franca, English text is more likely to appeal to global consumers than German text and thus helps build global markets for national(ist) products. English is also appealing for other reasons, however, perhaps most notably because the use of foreign languages in far right iconography and symbols helps manufacturers circumvent legal bans on German-language symbols and signs. In the following sections, I explore the issue of legal and private bans on symbols associated with the extreme right wing in greater depth, as a third explanation for how global iconography, symbols, images, and codes have grown particularly popular in Germany.

Global Meanings, National Bans

German youth in and around the far right scene are keenly aware of how brands and symbols associated with the far right are received by the broader public. They understand that some symbols are illegal and that others, including brands, are banned in particular places where they spend time, such as schools or stadiums. As they examined a variety of images of coded symbols, logos, iconography, and commercial products, youth frequently labeled them "racist," referenced bans on particular symbols or brands, or explained that peer pressure, social stigma, or reactions from others would prevent someone from wearing such symbols in ordinary contexts. Georg explained how the brand Yakuza produces clothing that's "all on a provocative line between the legal and the illegal. And that's how [the owner] makes his money, because there's a lot of people who think like that. Because if you say what you think about Germany these days, you're [labeled] a right-wing extremist, an NPD member or a neo-Nazi. If you're wearing a T-shirt like that, other people see it, might have exactly the same thoughts, but won't say it, simply keep it inside. Because it's always in the frame of the legal and illegal. Always exactly on the zero line."

In some cases, youth seemed to be self-monitoring, expressing distaste for particular far right symbols not so much because of their own dislike for them as for the ways in which such symbols might incite anger or violence against them. As he examined a lavender Erik and Sons T-shirt with the phrase "MY FAVORITE COLOR IS WHITE" in block letters, Tim, a twenty-two-year-old masonry apprentice, noted that such a shirt has a double meaning. "Of course, you could say this is [your] favorite color . . . but then you'd also definitely have to hear stupid phrases if you wear it into the U-Bahn or walk around out in public, and a foreign co-citizen is standing there and he reads it, then of course he'd feel attacked."

Youth do not only self-monitor their own consumption and performance of far right brands and symbols. There are a variety of ways in which they are externally monitored and constrained from deploying extremist symbols and brands. As I explained in the introduction, as soon as brands are created, if producers try to trademark their new brand, their applications are reviewed to ensure they do not contain extremist messaging prior to being granted. The trademark review committee does not always catch the complex coding in brand names, however. As a colleague explained to me, the first explicitly far right brand, Consdaple, was initially approved by the German trademark commission until they caught the reference to NSDAP imbedded in the brand; a few weeks after the initial trademark approval, the brand's trademark was revoked. However, this does not mean that producing or wearing the T-shirt is illegal, only that the brand itself is not protected through trademark.

There are other ways that authorities try to prevent youth from deploying particular kinds of symbols. Legal bans on particular symbols in Germany have historically been restricted to cases where the symbol could be clearly linked to an illegal organization. In some cases, this is fairly straightforward; the swastika, for example, is banned because it was an official symbol of the Nazi party. Commercial entities work around the legal restriction on the use of the swastika by writing the term in foreign languages (see discussion below) or by altering the iconography of the symbol or the spelling of the word just enough to escape legal trouble. As chapter 2 detailed, in early June 2016, youth at a Dortmund neo-Nazi march were spotted wearing T-shirts with the letters HKNKRZ (*Hakenkreuz*—the German word for swastika—with its vowels removed) (see plate 28). The police and other legal authorities did not intervene; the Dortmund police media representative noted that although the shirt is outlandish, it is not illegal. "Its aim is to provoke and test legal boundaries."[36] But other legal scholars argued that because the shirt was worn in the context of a neo-Nazi demonstration, it should have been interpreted as clearly illegal. There are other cases where the courts have had to develop elaborate semiotic interpretations of symbols and their contemporary usage, as in the case of the Thor Steinar logo. In that case, state courts overturned earlier rulings banning the brand's logo because they deemed the combination of two banned runes had created a new symbol that no longer referenced the banned Nazi party. The entire process took several years, during which Thor Steinar used a new logo: an X with two dots, which had no apparent far right connotations.

In fact, in recent years, German courts have made a number of decisions that are shifting the clear linkage between symbols and organizations in terms of banning based on article 86a in the constitution. A 2008 federal court of justice (Bundesgerichtshof) case related to the Celtic cross, for example—a symbol in widespread use by the global white power/pro-Aryan movement—aimed to ban the Celtic cross as a youth cultural symbol absent its formal connection to a banned organization.[37] The Bundesgerichtshof faced a similar semiotic challenge when it ruled in 2009 on a case about the legality of the English phrase "blood and honour," which is a translation of the German Hitler Youth slogan *Blut und Ehre*. The case dated to the 2005 arrest of a man who was arrested with a car full of T-shirts with the phrase "Blood and Honour/C18," along with an image of a hand holding a gun. Across the back of the T-shirt was the phrase (in English) "Blood and Honour is our voice, Combat 18 is our choice."[38] The code C18 refers to Combat 18, referencing the potential for violent warfare and the first and eighth letters of the alphabet (AH) for Adolf Hitler. On its own C18 is not legally punishable, but because the phrase "Blood and Honour" was considered to be against the constitution (Verfassungswidrig), a lower court found the defendant guilty and he was fined €4,200.

The Bundesgerichtshof overturned the lower court's decision, arguing that symbols and signs should no longer be illegal if they are in a language other than German.[39] In a statement, the court explained that right-wing slogans only referenced the Nazi party if they were in German, noting that "a national socialist parole is inseparable from the use of the German language." They acknowledged that this ruling created new opportunities for playfulness for the far right,[40] a situation that appears to have borne out in the usage of English in brands and products marketed to the far right scene.

English text is peppered throughout the clothing of the far right scene, particularly through textual reference on T-shirts and sweatshirts, but also in product names, descriptions, and ordering instructions. Phrases and text that would be illegal if in the German language—like the German word for swastika, *Hakenkreuz*, are legal if they are depicted in a language other than German. Brands marketing to the far right made quick use of this opening; Ansgar Aryan, for example, sells a jacket with the Swedish word *svastika* spelled in large letters across the back of the shoulders. Along with information on sizing and a description of the quality of the cotton and the zippered pockets, the text to the right of the product image on the website informs the customer that the product is "perfectly legal" (*gesetzlich unbedenklich*)—a distinction they clearly think is important for consumers to know. Lukas, whose father wears Thor Steinar clothing, explains that this phrase helps consumers know they are on solid legal footing. "If you had [something] from the old Thor Steinar collection that is really banned, you're not allowed to wear it, you can get a [legal] citation, but if you wear this [jacket] then you're allowed to wear it and no police can stop you." He suggests, further, that this phrase reveals the brand's far right connection: "that's what I mean, the people who buy that are people who already could be connected with [the far right]."

Other English text is ubiquitous in the brand's clothing, in phrases like "Fortress Europe," "Send 'Em Back," "Illegals go Home," "Truth," "Finisher," "Our Day," "Hate Club," "The World is Ours," "Legion of Doom," "Streetfight," and "Patriotic Ink." Erik and Sons sells a T-shirt depicting three silhouetted figures holding baseball bats or clubs over the English phrase "ULTRA INTOLERANT," while others use phrases like "Fight Club" or "team player." The winter 2011–12 Erik and Sons collection, for example, sold both the "MY FAVORITE COLOR IS WHITE" T-shirt described above (in lilac or black) as well as a women's T-shirt (available in three colors) whose text reads "Erik and Sons/ For Viking Girls," with the two phrases separated by a pair of bright blue wolf eyes. Thor Steinar carries T-shirts, sweatshirts, and jackets that proclaim a variety of English phrases, including "100 % Viking Blood, "You'll Never Walk Alone," "Nordic Brewed," "Rebellion," and "Brotherhood."

English is appealing for multiple reasons. On the one hand, as I described above, English language symbols and text are less likely to cause legal problems than German language text. Combined with the use of the Internet—which as Laura Klostermann Kidd notes, has created space for clothing designers and manufacturers to circumvent various national bans on white power and white nationalist clothing—English language products are a safer choice for producers.[41] The growing use of English, meanwhile, makes it more difficult for educators and other adult authorities to interpret various T-shirts, symbols, or signs that far right youth deploy. This is true of other global symbols as well, as Michael explains during a discussion of school bans on particular brands of clothing, explaining that the far right practice of copying global symbols or leftist style makes the banning of particular brands useless. "There are enough Nazis who wear Palestinian scarves or copy the clothing style of the left-wing subculture, [so such a ban on brands would be] invalid."

Youth's reception of codes and symbols in languages other than German was variable. On the one hand, the ambiguity and dual meanings in coded iconography may be especially appealing when they are in a language other than German, which makes them even harder to interpret. Steffen, a twenty-four-year-old carpentry apprentice, looked at a sweatshirt with a grainy image of explorers under the English words "Expedition Antarctica: The White Continent 1910" and laughed. "Yeah, I'd wear it," he said. "Because it's very good . . . well, again, they really used their heads with the double meaning, sort of. . . . It must [refer to the] discovery of the North Pole by Amundsen, right? . . . I'd wear it. But only because for once it's an intelligent Thor Steinar advertisement."[42]

On the other hand, youth often missed the meanings of foreign language words. Hardly anyone correctly interpreted the Swedish word "svastika" written in large, red block letters across the upper back of a sporty Ansgar Aryan jacket. When they examined an image of this jacket, young people consistently did not recognize the word "svastika" as the word *Hakenkreuz*. Julian, who is from Rostock and at twenty-eight is studying to get his technical high school degree, looked at the image, read the word "svastika" out loud, and noted, "it sounds Scandinavian, but I can't think of any other meaning." This was true even when young people interpreted the meaning of the phrase "European Brotherhood," which was written underneath the word "svastika" on the jacket, as far right. Benjamin noticed the word "svastika" in the image of the jacket as well as the phrase European Brotherhood. The latter phrase suggests to him that the jacket could be a symbol of "European right-wing extremism," but he explains that such symbols are multivocal and depend on the physical appearance of the consumer. "If it was a skinny nerd with horn-rimmed glasses, I wouldn't think it was somebody right-wing, but [this guy is] such a huge beast. . . . So it looks more like European right-wing extremism." But then as Benjamin looks a bit more deeply, the phrase "svastika" throws him off. "But I would tend to think more that it comes from Scandinavia." When the interviewer asks why, he replies, "I don't know, this 'svastika' sounds so Scandinavian for me. Or is it Dutch? It doesn't say. But it sure is expensive." "What's written there?" asked Hayri. "Svastika, svastika? What kind of brand is that, if I may ask? But the jacket's not bad at all, it looks good. Well . . . I'd wear it, but I don't know what's written there, so I'd probably hold back, because if I don't know what it says, I'd rather not wear it." Only four of the fifty-one apprentices understood "svastika" to mean *Hakenkreuz*. One thought it was the name of a (music) band, while another suggested it might be a brand name. Several noted it sounded like a different language, suggesting it might be in Polish, Russian, or Dutch, or describing it as sounding "Scandinavian." They were much more likely to understand the smaller block print under "svastika," however, which read "European Brotherhood." Although some youth read this as a neutral symbol of group membership, several connected it to the U.S. prison gang Aryan Brotherhood.

In contrast, thirty-one of the fifty-one youth interviewed understood the double meaning behind the "MY FAVORITE COLOR IS WHITE" T-shirt produced by Erik and Sons, describing the shirt as racist, xenophobic, or right wing. They typically noted the shirt's play on words, noticing that the T-shirt itself was purple and that this juxtaposition itself might be the joke (e.g., my favorite color is white, but I'm wearing a purple T-shirt). The English text in this particular shirt was clearly understood by a majority of those interviewed. There were other examples where youth did not understand English language text, though. Christian, an eighteen-year-old carpentry apprentice, looked at a T-shirt with the number 18 and the phrase "Old School Racist" and could not interpret what it might mean: "Yeah, what does 'racist' mean? 'Race' means running or car race [*Rennen*]. 'Racist,' I don't know what . . . race . . . racism, old school racism maybe? No, I don't know what 'racist' means. . . . If someone could translate it, they would probably think something different than me right now."[43]

Circumventing and Subverting Private Bans

Private bans are more flexible than official legal bans or laws prohibiting the display of particular symbols, and some schools, stadiums, and employers have taken advantage of their ability to establish dress codes and institutional rules to implement bans on symbols, brands, and styles with extremist ideological content. Schools were thus an ideal site for me to investigate as I sought to understand how young people interpret the new far right coded symbols and whether and how they are affected by bans on the brands and symbols. There is a long history across the globe of schools monitoring and controlling student dress, style, and use of symbols through dress codes; as Dianne Gereluk concisely contends, "virtually without exception, schools have minimum dress codes in place: rules about what cannot be worn at school."[44] What becomes more controversial, she explains, is whether and how schools can police the display of symbolic clothing. Uniforms and dress codes are variably defended as means to reduce visible signs of social class inequality, reduce school violence and improve safety, create school identity, and improve student achievement and behavior.[45]

As the introduction and methodological appendix detail, the Flusser school has implemented a comprehensive policy banning the display of all right-wing extremist symbols, brands, and codes (along with other ideological symbols). At the Erker school across town, there is no banning policy; students can freely display right-wing extremist brands and symbols unless they are legally banned, like the swastika. At both schools, these policies are intentionally aimed to affect the student population in particular ways. While at the Flusser school the ban is intended to make a clear statement against racism, xenophobia, and violence—as well as other forms of ideological extremism—teachers at the Erker school have argued against a ban in favor of democratic expression and in order to facilitate lines of communication with far right youth who would presumably be more identifiable without a ban.[46]

Youth who attend the Flusser school must sign an agreement to adhere to the school rules (*Hausordnung*). The school rules in effect during my fieldwork included an explicit section detailing the banning of symbols that express left- or right-wing ideology. This includes "the use of all political and pseudo-religious (including Germanic and Nordic gods, heroes and runes) representations, symbols, marks, paroles, and number-codes which conceal nationalist, racist, xenophobic or military content and willingness to be violent or openly illustrate, propagate or demonstrate." Students are also banned from wearing "combat boots and brands of clothing which in the extreme (youth) scene have a symbolic or recognizable character or which are banned." A "current but incomplete" set of examples is in an appendix to the school rules, which shows a list of brand name logos, including Alpha Industries, Consdaple, Lonsdale, Pit Bull, and Thor Steinar, alongside brief explanations for the reason for the ban.

In the Flusser school, youth interpret the rationale for the ban in a wide variety of ways—most frequently arguing that bans exist because the symbols were right-wing or because they improved the school climate and helped prevent conflict. Five students opined that the bans were meant to show that Germany is no longer right wing or to establish the school's reputation as a tolerant, non-right-wing place. Several students noted that the bans existed because such symbols were provocative, racist, or anti-Semitic, and one student suggested that the bans were intended to avoid insulting or hurting foreigners.

At the Erker school, where symbols were not banned, students spoke with greater passion and anger about the banning of particular brands. Fourteen of the twenty-six youth interviewed from this school were against bans entirely, while another nine students argued for limited bans on clear extremist symbols. Only three students at this school were in favor of bans. Students who were against the bans most commonly argued that banning doesn't change opinions or what's in people's heads, additionally noting that everyone should be able to wear what they want. "You can only help [a right-wing person]," explained Hayri, "if I am able to enlighten him." Youth who were in favor of the ban, on the other hand, argued that brands with far right associations should be banned because they provoke youth at the school who have a migration background and could lead to conflict, fighting, or violence at school.

Twenty-five apprentices at the Flusser school who were studying to be carpenters, roofers, concrete layers, masons, and related construction fields participated in interviews. All but two were familiar with the school ban on ideological symbols and brands, and most explained that they knew about the bans because they had had to sign an agreement when they started their training program that they would adhere to the ban and all other school rules. They had varying opinions about the ban and its efficacy, however. Of the twenty-three students who knew about the bans, ten stated outright that they disapproved of the ban, either because it was unfair and infringed on individual freedom or because it was useless, pointless, or ineffective. Klaus, a twenty-one-year-old roofing apprentice at the school with the bans, described a classmate who always wears "anti-antifa" (anti-antifascist) T-shirts, which refers to being against the antifascists. "Anti-antifa" refers to a specific subset of the extreme right that intentionally copies left-wing, antifascist strategies and techniques, such as intelligence gathering on purported enemies.[47] No one has challenged the student, he explained, in part because no one pays attention to the writing on the T-shirt. But he also argued that the T-shirt should be allowed: "as long as he doesn't somehow yell or act out with it or make some kind of [extremist or racist] statement, it's actually OK. He should [be allowed to] wear it in my opinion. Well, I don't have anything against it." Thomas, an eighteen-year-old building energy design apprentice, also felt

Table 5. Youth Interpretation of School Bans

	AGAINST BANS	SUPPORT BANS	SUPPORT LIMITED BANS	NO OPINION
The Flusser school (has existing ban)*	10	6	4	3
The Erker school (no existing ban)	14	3	9	0
TOTAL	24	9	13	3

*Two students in the Flusser school were unaware of the banning policy and are not included here.

that only extreme symbols should be banned: "well, indirect messages are perhaps still allowed in school. But if there's a swastika or something visible on it, something strong. A strong symbol that expresses a lot, I'd rather ban that too." Mahmut, a twenty-one-year-old technical preservation apprentice, argued there would have to be a "brand police" (*Markenpolizei*) in the hallways if the bans were to really be enforced. Gabriel, a twenty-five-year-old historic preservation apprentice, scoffed at the idea that school authorities can keep up with the rapid changes in youth subcultures: "in the meantime [those brands] are actually not, I'd say, [the ones] with which people from the scene identify. There are already other [brands]."

Across both schools, young people who opposed the ban frequently pointed out that bans on clothing would not change how people think or that it was impossible for teachers to really see the logos and interpret the symbols systematically. Michael, a thirty-four-year-old carpentry apprentice at the school without the bans, put this succinctly when he simply explained, "It doesn't solve the problem. If you don't wear the clothing, it doesn't mean that anything has changed in your head. . . . And school-based bans are especially ridiculous, because that's exactly where it's really important that people start to learn to self-regulate their individuality." Lukas, a twenty-two-year-old carpentry apprentice at the school with the bans, was opposed to it, explaining, "OK, if there's a two-meter-tall skinhead in front of me, or five of them in a bar wearing Thor Steinar clothes and then you think as a little Asian, then you'd be a little afraid. But I think you'd be just as [afraid] if you saw a two-meter-tall skinhead [without the clothes] so . . . I don't know. No idea, they'd have to ban hairstyles too." But earlier in the interview, Lukas noted that he approves of a similar ban at workplaces: "at the same time I can also understand, that at a construction site . . . the reputation [of the firm] is damaged through that. Because as a Turkish employer I wouldn't want to hire workers who were running around the neighborhood in Thor Steinar sweatshirts, so I can understand it." He generally adheres to the ban at the workplace, not wearing his own Thor Steinar sweatshirt there, but primarily so he can avoid conflict. "Because it's not allowed and why should I seek out this problematic conversation . . . nah, I just simply pull another sweatshirt on."

Others pointed out that bans could actually backfire by reinforcing a sense that adult authorities are suppressing youth or by making the symbols and brands more appealing. Jan, a seventeen-year-old masonry apprentice at the school without the bans, was one of many youth who did not understand the Swedish word "svastika" across the back of a jacket in an image. But he did catch the reference in the product description to the fact that the jacket is "perfectly legal" and found the in-your-face nature of the marketing appealing. "I find that pretty funny, 'perfectly legal.' . . . I don't know [laughs]. It's good that they write it like that . . . [because] well, there are a lot of things that are banned." He laughs twice more as he notes that regardless of whether this product is actually banned, he thinks it's good that the producers tell the consumers "it's OK for you to wear it in any case." Other youth expressed a strong sense of frustration or anger about the bans. Paul, a twenty-four-year-old construction mechanic apprentice, for example, talked at length about the injustice of his school ban, arguing that he should not be prevented from wearing his Alpha jacket and that youth experience the bans as oppressive:

> Because I find these bans also have the effect that people who wear banned things feel a little justified, that's my opinion. . . . [And] if it wouldn't be banned, then maybe people wouldn't find it so awesome . . . because I also wear a jacket that's banned. The Alpha Industry [logo] is written there . . . but it doesn't say anything in the constitution. . . . In the constitution only the swastika is banned. [And] if it's not in the constitution, why should some school get to make its own law that can stand above [the constitution]? And I don't wear it upside-down. That's . . . when it's worn upside-down, the Alpha Industry [logo] here, then it would be bad, because then [it turns into a] V and Vaterland and that's for Nazi.

Across the interviews, only nine students supported school-based bans—six students at the school with the ban and three at the school without it

—either because they felt right-wing symbols were unacceptable or because they thought it led to a better school climate with less conflict. Bans could prevent cliques or bullying or fighting, explained Tobias, a twenty-one-year-old civil engineering apprentice. Hans, a twenty-seven-year-old scaffold builder apprentice training in the school that does not have bans, suggests that school bans would prevent the brands from marketing to youth at school, noting that schools "can't do anything against the actual opinions, but they can help prevent [the right wing] from advertising themselves with [these brands]. [Because] there are a lot [of students] who are in their younger years, who aren't so far along and who don't know what that is and I don't know, would find it great, would go get it and don't realize that as a result they could be stamped [right wing]." Four students were conflicted, arguing that some things should be banned (such as swastikas) but others (such as the brand Lonsdale) should not be banned. The remaining three students had no opinion, couldn't articulate a clear view, or didn't care one way or the other about the bans.

It was often unclear to students whether particular brands were banned and if so, why. Georg, whose case is discussed at length below, complained that no one really knows what is banned and what isn't: "It was always unclear. Some people said [Thor Steinar is] banned, some people said it's not banned, others said it's only the old logo that's banned." Martin, a sixteen-year-old masonry apprentice who self-identifies as far right, describes varied experiences with teachers' attention to his attire. At one point in the interview, he notes he wore a Thor Steinar T-shirt yesterday but kept it under his jacket and no one noticed. But he also relates a recent episode in the construction teaching yard (*Lehrbauhof*) when the weather was warm and he was working and removed his jacket to cool off. "A half hour later the master trainer [*Meister*] came along and talked to me. I had to turn it inside out. . . . It wasn't a Thor Steinar shirt; it was from an online shop and had an eagle that used to be on the army [*Wehrmacht*] helmet and underneath in old German script it said 'Deutschland.' "

Ingo, an eighteen-year-old masonry apprentice, related an anecdote from when he was in tenth grade and his teacher was standing behind him in class, and noticed "Thor Steinar" written in large print across the back of his shirt. "And she said to me 'based on your clothing it's clear what [kind of person] you are.' And I'm not making that up, that really happened to me. And so I asked myself, OK, well, in Lonsdale there's the NSDA . . . that's related to National Socialism, to fascism, that makes complete sense that someone would react that way. But it's my opinion that as long as the brand doesn't preach hatred on its T-shirts . . . then [it should be OK] to wear the

clothes. I don't think it's bad. . . . And Thor Steinar . . . I got a T-shirt, where
there were some kind of stones on it. Showed some kind of Nordic landscape and maybe this was supposed to represent this Aryan image, but . . .
hey, there was no swastika, no Iron Cross, no *Reichsadler* [imperial eagle]
on it . . . and so I don't think it's right. Everyone can wear what they want
and — if someone is, alone based on my story, shoved into a shoebox . . . that
happens a lot." But when the interview turned to the question of whether
brands or symbols should be banned at school at all, Ingo clearly stated that
there should be some limits. "There shouldn't be any T-shirts — whether they
are self-printed or from whatever brands, I'd say — that aren't legal, and there
shouldn't be any right-wing extremist expressions, what's against democracy
and so on." Extreme propaganda should be banned, he notes, but then qualifies his response further, noting that as long as political opinions are within
the constitution and no one is getting hurt, then people should be allowed
to wear what they want.

While several students mentioned that style and clothing appear to play a
role in recruitment and socialization within the far right scene, Ingo offered
the most thoughtful analysis of how this happens. "We live in this democratic state here and something like that just doesn't belong here. . . . People
try to infect youth with these thoughts, so that these brands get a broader
market or so that something develops like 'look, all of you, if we all wear
these jackets, then they know . . . the Kanaken,[48] Turks, we won't let you
provoke us, this is always still our country' and this extreme national pride."
He explained how things could escalate from there, describing that many
people could get angry at Germany because "they are too tolerant and let
everything and everybody into the country," and "then it develops further
[into more far right ideology], and then [other] people would say 'we have to
try something, we have to kick [the far right] out of the school.'" In the end,
he argues, the clothing creates a risk of radicalization and is banned by some
schools "so that it doesn't happen that, let's say I start wearing something
like that in the eighth grade, that then I show up in the tenth grade with
a shaved head (*Glatze*) and a lot of angry tattoos and drop out of school or
something."

Georg offered an impassioned diatribe, in strong east Berlin/east German
dialect and slang, against the banning of brands like Thor Steinar. Georg
argues that people who "flip out right away" about brands like Thor Steinar
are "dumb people, I can't talk to them. They are just afraid of whatever's
next, y'know? And to . . . ban clothing, 'cause they don't like it . . . I could
just as well say I don't like all of the headscarves. We're here in Germany,
they should adapt to us. Of course that makes me a right-wing extremist

again. I wear Thor Steinar, I'm a right-wing extremist. And . . . to ban Thor Steinar? Only because the right-wing scene co-opted it?" He then encourages the interviewer to look at the Thor Steinar website after the interview, even providing the website, so that she can see how normal the clothing is, just "a normal sweater, where there's nothing on it, where two people are on a mountain, where Nordland Expedition is written and Thor Steinar . . . yeah what about that is right-wing radical, what about that's right-wing extreme? Someone should tell me what's right-wing about that. That's so crazy." He broadens his diatribe to include Lonsdale, noting that it's a brand "a colored boxer created" and that it's seen everywhere. "No pig says anything but at school it's supposed to be banned? Because of racist hatred or what do I know?"

At this point in the interview, Georg gets increasingly frustrated with what he perceives to be unequal treatment of symbolic clothing for Muslim students. He makes a vague reference to what "they in the other room" (i.e., students who are presumably of a migrant background) "think about us Germans" and complains that "even in gym they're allowed to wear head-scarves," even though it's a "huge risk of injury" if the headscarf got caught on something. "But it's all OK with them," he laments; "no one here cares. I heard they got sport headscarves." Georg then turns to a story about his own experience with school bans, explaining that in his previous school he ended up in court to force the school to allow him to wear Thor Steinar brand clothing:

> I should — I was wearing a Thor Steinar T-shirt, it simply said "Thor Steinar" on the back, and there was a lion, and I was supposed to take it off. I said, "What?" What's wrong with it?" "It's banned at this school" [they said]. I said there ain't nothin' in the *Hausordnung* [school rules]. . . . I said, you can't do nothin' to me. I said and what's banned about this T-shirt? What do you want to tell me? So then, at my secondary school [*Oberschule*], where I was, I had to go before the school court [*Schulgericht*]. . . . I was at the school court, I said, what's wrong? My T-shirt was hanging on a clothes hanger. I said, what's wrong with that T-shirt, there are mountain climbers on it . . . it wasn't anything forbidden. . . . I won the thing, I got to wear Thor Steinar at school, it didn't matter to me. Like I said, I don't think anything about stuff like that, not at all, because it was just crap and stupidity.

But despite his anger and passion about the banning of brands like Lonsdale and Thor Steinar, when the interview turned to the question of whether schools should ban particular clothing or symbols or logos, Georg also expressed much more support for a limited kind of ban. "Yes, of course, if they're really right-wing extremist people . . . swastika sweaters and crap like that, I'd ban all of that. Also from the other people, from the Turks and the Muslim whatever there is, I'd also say, that's not allowed. If they had brands like that."

Twenty-two of the fifty-one youth interviewed supported either a total (N=9) or limited (N=13) ban on brands or symbols at school. Students who supported limited bans felt there should be clear bans on illegal symbols or on obvious or clear expressions of extremist ideology. Timo, a twenty-two-year-old scaffold builder apprentice, described how he had seen a couple of students wearing Consdaple sweatshirts at school, which made him wonder, "why doesn't anyone recognize that? Why isn't that confronted? And I find that really terrible, y'know? That something like that is tolerated here. Especially because there are also a lot of people here with a migration background." Youth who supported limited bans often mentioned the swastika as a symbol that should clearly be banned from clothing worn at school. But here is where the question of coded symbols gets complicated, since—as described above—few of the youth interviewed recognized the Swedish word "svastika" as the word *Hakenkreuz*, since they did not know the Swedish word or the English word swastika. In practical terms, in other words, enforcing a limited ban on particular symbols or banning only when political intent is behind apparel or brands is nearly impossible. In the context of the playful, game-playing culture of commercialized brands marketing far right ideology, schools and other authorities face an increasingly complicated set of decisions about whether to ban symbols and brands or not.

Enforcing the Bans?

Youth clearly find multiple ways to circumvent bans, relying on the producers' use of non-German text and phrases, manipulating codes so they are difficult to interpret, and deploying codes that are deliberately ambivalent. They also physically manipulate codes and symbols, using a half-zipped jacket to reveal a block of letters inside the brand Lonsdale, as chapter 2 explained, or utilizing the Velcro-removable Alpha Industries to turn the logo upside down. Erdinc explains that the upside-down Alpha Industries logo is a deliberate effort to disrupt bans, noting that if one turns the logo around "then it's not banned. So it's not banned then on the street or in the schools either."

Enforcement of the bans by adult authorities appears to be mixed. Although many youth gave examples from their observations of teachers and training "masters" (*Meister*) reacting to far right clothing or symbols, enforcement appears uneven at best. Schools are not the only places where youth encounter bans; they are also aware of dress codes and restrictions at soccer stadiums, cafés or restaurants, or governmental buildings like the *Bundestag*. Georg explained how he navigates bans on particular brands of clothing at clubs with his friends, noting that there are rumors that clubs won't let in people wearing Yakuza, which he attributes to "this race thinking, y'know?" He acknowledges that although Yakuza has some simple things that wouldn't pose a problem, there are other articles of clothing where you "couldn't get in everywhere [wearing it]." He owns some of these T-shirts and notes that "the clubs don't like to see them, but when I go partying with my buddies, we know the club owners and mostly it's not a problem. . . . We have our clubs, where we go, where we are known, where we have our peace and quiet and where one can go have a real party . . . because the [bouncers] at the front door wear the stuff too."

While youth can target particular clubs where they know bouncers will look the other way at the door, school is a different story when there are official bans on the books. However, of the twenty-five students interviewed at the Flusser school, which has a ban in place, only eight noted that they thought the bans were enforced or followed, or had seen a teacher telling a student to remove a piece of clothing. But even among these eight students, the issue of enforcement was not entirely clear. One of the eight youth—Dennis, a nineteen-year-old civil engineering technician apprentice—contends the bans are enforced about 80 percent of the time, while two other students observed that the bans are enforced for some brands (like Thor Steinar) but not for others (like Alpha Industries). Eleven students felt the bans were not enforced, either because teachers looked the other way or because they were unable to interpret and recognize the symbols and brands when they did see them. "I wouldn't know which teacher really knows the brands well enough to recognize them," explained nineteen-year-old Felix, a civil engineering technician apprentice. And six students noted that they did not know, or had not noticed, if the bans were enforced or not.

Teacher interviews in the Flusser school, which has the ban in place, were illuminating on this point, although the small number of teachers interviewed means the data is only illustrative. Some teachers actively oppose the bans on philosophical or logistical grounds, arguing that the bans do not address the core issues, are an unfair restriction on students' rights or personal freedom, or create too much work. Teachers look the other way, complained one teacher, on cell phone bans, on smoking bans, and on the clothing bans. "Of the 160 colleagues here," he argued, "for sure every tenth one would walk right through a group [of smokers in a non-smoking area outside] and say nothing. It's the same thing with the clothing; not all of the colleagues react appropriately." But he noted that enough of the teachers do enforce the bans that they appear to work, noting that banned clothing is hardly ever visible at the school. Another teacher describes the enforcement as mixed: some colleagues don't pay attention to the bans, but there are others "who were really hunters. . . . In a [crowd of] a hundred people they were able to see the one who was wearing a T-shirt or a sweater that was banned."

Those who do try to enforce the bans readily admit that it's impossible to fully monitor ever-evolving bans. Not all the teachers understood the far right references in the images they perused during the interviews. "Sometimes I have the feeling that I don't get a lot of the things [that go on]," explained one teacher. "I just don't have an eye for it." A teacher in the Erker school related an instance on the subway when he noticed the "pretty blue color" of the T-shirt of the young man sitting across from him. As he looked closer at the T-shirt, he gradually disentangled the iconography and realized it contained a historical reference to the Nazi era. "And then I saw somewhere, totally small, Thor Steinar, and then it was clear to me," he laughed; "again it was a totally encrypted message. If you didn't know the historical background, you'd never get that, not even in a dream." One of his colleagues described the new coded style as "wolves in sheep's clothing."

But when teachers do catch abuses, there are consequential punishments. Students are asked to turn T-shirts or jackets inside out, are sent to the principal, or are sent home. The same teacher who complained about the lack of enforcement on the part of others recounted with amusement a situation a few years ago when he was the department head and a new student showed up at school wearing a banned brand jacket. He told her she had to remove it, but then underneath the jacket she was wearing a Thor Steinar T-shirt. So he sent her to the bathroom to turn the shirt inside out, but it was stitched through and still visible from the other side. Ultimately, he explained, he let the infraction slide for that day but was clear that from the next day forward she had to adhere to the school policy. In the same passage, he also noted that it is more difficult to enforce the ban in winter, when students come to school with winter jackets with "not-removable symbols stitched into them." This is when complaints come in from parents, who argue that "he only has the one winter jacket." In summer this is less of a problem.

The bans appear to be a largely accepted part of school policy, but not all teachers are fans of the policy, and there are occasions when the faculty have had to debate their enforcement. For example, the principal at the Flusser school described at length an incident when a team of students was slated to participate in a concrete boat competition[49] when teachers found out that they were planning to wear clothing displaying far right symbols. An emergency school-wide faculty meeting convened to discuss whether the students should be allowed to compete. "We discovered it at the last minute and banned . . . them from participating," described the principal. "Only when they guaranteed that 'we will race in neutral clothing' did we then permit it again." Meanwhile, however, the other construction school in Berlin (the Erker school, in this study) sent a team to the competition that raced with the same kinds of symbols on display. "I went there and saw it myself; it was actually shocking," the principal recounts.

Teachers at the Erker school, which does not have bans as part of school policy, had varied thoughts on the efficacy of banning. One clear view was that engaging youth directly in conversation about the clothing or ideology is a more effective strategy than banning symbols or brands. As one teacher explained:

> I think that banning clothing alone doesn't do much; of course it also has to be paired with other strategies so that you engage the problem openly. . . . To act openly against racism and take up the problem and discuss it, talk with the students. . . . Personally, I already pay attention to that and if I notice something, I raise it directly. And I think that's perhaps more likely to be successful than saying, 'you have to take that T-shirt off now.' To talk about it. What propaganda it is conveying, which attitudes it transmits, or which impression it gives to students; to discuss that . . . I think that's more sensible than . . . a ban or a . . . coercive action.

Another teacher argued that the school's obligation is to enforce the laws of the state, but that schools should not add additional restrictions. "It's my opinion that if I can buy it and it's not illegal, then he should [be able to] wear it." Another teacher in the Erker school pointed out that despite discussions in the school around whether to implement a ban, it was difficult to know where to draw the line. "Yeah, where are the lines drawn now, where should they be drawn next year? Y'know? Eh, Thor Steinar is a relatively clear story, but there are constantly new brands coming out that are known first in the scene and that have clear impacts, which, let's say, are not at all apparent at first to outsiders." But like the Flusser school teachers, there was not full agreement on these issues at the Erker school: another teacher, for example, argued that bans make sense, noting that "school must be a place of neutrality."

It is also worth noting that attention to the first wave of mainstream brands may have hastened the subculture's move into new and different brands. Ingo mentioned in an aside that Thor Steinar is out of fashion and has been "talked to death" by teachers. He expressed his shock that when he came home from a trip to Poland with a Thor Steinar T-shirt he had purchased there, he was surprised to discover that his parents were familiar with the brand and told him he couldn't wear the shirt to school. "Even my parents, when I brought these T-shirts back . . . my parents, my grandparents, my parents said you can't wear Thor Steinar clothes, or else you are . . . well, I was shocked, how did my parents know about that. . . . But Thor Steinar has simply been talked to death. Yeah. That's totally true." When even the parental generation has become aware of the subcultural scene's codes, symbols, and brands, Ingo argues, the scene has already moved on. Change in the subcultural scene is a constant. Thomas argued that observable changes in far right style came about because "a lot of things are banned politically, and then they can't wear these exact T-shirts anymore or their jackets and so this way they still know who belongs together, but through indirect phrases on the T-shirts or through some kind of new symbols that have been modified."

Conclusion: How Global Multivocality Challenges Local Practice

The use of iconography within the German far right scene that is drawn from other national contexts highlights the multivocality of far right symbols that are simultaneously nationalist and global. This multivocality is further amplified by the ironies of far right youth deployment of non-German symbols such as Palestinian scarves and—for a brief time, Che Guevara T-shirts—to signify a view of themselves as "freedom fighters," while simultaneously adhering to anti-immigrant sentiments or enacting violence against ethnic and racial minorities in the name of the German nation.[50] The Palestinian scarf is deployed not only as an expression of solidarity with the Palestinian cause—as it is for many leftist activists, for example—but rather as a decontextualized, traveling, or floating image that has taken on new symbolic meaning. Removed from its context, the scarf becomes a symbol of resistance, (re)appropriated for a local nationalist movement in a wholly different context from its original symbolism.

These actions echo the kind of bricolage discussed in chapter 2—in which youth use or modify historical symbols of anti-Semitism, for example, to express animosity against new immigrant groups. But here, bricolage is taken a step further, as youth draw on global icons and symbols and reappropriate them for contemporary uses. It is likely that there are parallels for how other geographically dispersed extremist ideologies—from Islamist extremism to ecoterrorism—might mobilize followers across national and linguistic boundaries.

The question of whether to implement school-based bans is a complicated one. Ultimately, despite the good intentions of teachers and school leaders who implement such bans in an effort to clearly signal that the school is a place of tolerance and diversity, there is little evidence that bans are effective. At best, their enforcement is uneven. At worst, they contribute to the appeal of the game-playing coding, as producers and youth work around bans by removing or turning around logos, using foreign languages, and deploying coded messages that themselves add to the appeal of the iconography and products for some youth.

In the final empirical chapter, I turn to the role that masculinity, the quest for male comradeship, and the valorization of rebellious violence play in the appeal of the coded, far right brands, symbols, and style.

6 SOLDIER, SAILOR, REBEL, RULE BREAKER

Embodying Extremism

> The new right-wing radical clothing . . . [requires] the creation
> of a pure and exclusively masculine, powerful body, as has
> characterized all fascist movements.
> —Barbara Vinken

In order for T-shirts to function as performative screens, they require a
physical body that can act as a billboard, displaying and communicating
ideological messages through iconography and text.[1] In this way, youth who
wear commercialized products conveying far right ideology literally embody
extremism. The gendered nature of the products means that this embodiment, in turn, both draws on and helps to construct idealized notions of
physical maleness. Tobias looked at the jacket described in chapter 5 with
"svastika" written across the back, for example and, after laughing that the
model looks like a friend of his, noted that he couldn't wear it because his
back isn't broad enough. "The text is broad, and one needs a broad back so it
can be displayed," he explained. Indeed, a quick glance at any of the catalogs
or websites shows that broad backs that stretch the upper portion of T-shirts
and biceps straining armholes are common features of the models who display the clothing. It is not only the (idealized) physical features of male-ness
that are appropriated within the new far right subculture, however, but also
key emotional aspects that highlight and reinforce desired aspects of traditional masculinity.

In this chapter, I focus on the embodiment of extremism both by showing
how the (male) body is deployed to perform extremism and by analyzing
how the emotional appeal of the styles help to articulate a hegemonic masculinity of the far right. I argue that far right style links masculinity and
nationalism by articulating shared aspirations for ideal national traits and
ideal masculine ones, clearly identifying what it means to be a "real man" in
any given nation.[2] It does so by idealizing male strength and physicality and
by playing on two emotional impulses that appeal to marginalized men in

particular: the desire for male comradeship and belonging, and the urge to express anger and frustration at mainstream society. The first articulation relies on iconographic and textual tropes of the male soldier/sailor/warrior to valorize traits like conformity, belonging, trust, loyalty, solidarity, comradeship, courage, and heroism, while the second draws on the rebel / rule breaker trope to celebrate attributes like transgression, challenge, rebellion, hatred, anger, and violence. There are also shared qualities across both expressions, such as strength, power, and bravado. Each articulation enables the far right to mobilize young men around a core set of virtues and values that are framed as what good nationalists believe and do. Together, they help construct a hegemonic far right masculinity in which the male body is a key site for inscribing, articulating, and performing far right wing ideology. The emotional appeal of subcultural style as a place to reinforce a sense of identity and group belonging and as expressions of resistance against mainstream society can thus be understood as a key mechanism through which nationalism and masculinity become mutually self-reinforcing. This mechanism represents a key contribution to a burgeoning literature on nationalism that has clearly identified masculinity's link to the nation, but has not adequately explained *how* masculinity and nationalism work together.

Masculinity and the Embodiment of Nationalism

Much of the scholarship on the intersections among masculinity, youth, and violence can be traced to R. W. Connell's seminal conceptualization of hegemonic masculinity and its many subsequent elaborations.[3] Connell's framing argues that specific constructions of masculinity become culturally ideal, or "hegemonic," during particular historical eras, while subsequent scholars have extended this work to show that multiple hegemonic and marginalized masculinities can coexist and interact across various social settings and milieus.[4] Thus, we can speak of the hegemonic masculinity of the German far right, for example, while recognizing that youths' lives are likely to also be embedded in competing, subordinated, marginalized, or oppositional masculinities within the broader social contexts of their lives—such as school, work, home, and broader peer groups.

A number of scholars have traced how modern masculinity and modern nationalism emerged in parallel and intertwined ways throughout the Western world during the nineteenth and twentieth centuries.[5] Colonialist, imperialist, and militaristic projects positioned "civilized white men" against "inferior savage men of colour," establishing a chauvinistic nationalism in which racist patriotism and manhood were inextricably linked,[6] in part as men negotiated dual anxieties about the nation and about masculinity. In the case of Hindu nationalism in India, for example, Dibyesh Anand argues that an "anxious masculinity lies at the heart of right-wing nationalism."[7] Similar notions of manhood were key to Zulu nationalism in apartheid South Africa[8] and to national identity in interwar France. For example, Joan Tumblety finds that normative ideas about muscular manhood in interwar France were "bound up with the expression of public anxieties about French national strength" but also with ideas about racial supremacy and degeneration.[9] Public attention to athletics, toned physique, and muscular power during this period in France, Tumblety argues, shared a "conviction that each man owed to himself, to his nation, and to his 'race' to develop . . . physical and moral virtues" like strength, willpower, decisiveness, and courage.[10] Taken together, such scholars have demonstrated that modern understandings of masculinity and recent expressions of nationalism are inextricably intertwined.[11]

In the German case, early nationalist expressions clearly identified masculinity as a key part of national dominance, alongside the emerging ideal of a masculine master Aryan race.[12] By the end of the eighteenth century, the physically and mentally strong German man had become the bourgeois ideal, identifying a physically fit body as reflective of traits like "strength, willpower, determination, bravery and a readiness to resort to violence."[13] The Nazi party had a well-documented cult of the body—expressed through physical fitness regimes as well as eugenics and an obsession with white skin and the purity of German blood; for the Nazis, the perfect, sculpted male body symbolized the nation's strength, virility and manliness.[14] In fascist Germany, this hegemonic masculinity was reinforced both through everyday cultural practices and through military violence.[15]

The Nazi cult of the body illustrates how important physical bodies are for the expression and articulation of identities; bodies are, as Patterson describes, "means through which we think."[16] Personal style is part of these expressions, in part because clothing "turns bodies into 'readable' signs," as Inés Dussel argues, pointing out that fashion sends messages about social positioning as well as attitudes about compliance and transgression.[17] But there are also significant pressures on how bodies are used to send those messages; individuals are subject to a broad cluster of forces and cues that help define what is normal, what is appropriate, what is expected, and what is idealized for their bodies at any given time point in any particular place.[18] This regulation and its power is part of what explains why the body is so often a site for resistance against mainstream norms, as Richardson and Locks argue, noting that adolescents' initial acts "of rebellion, against parental or school authority, will nearly always be manifested via the body." Hair dye, piercings, or tattoos thus might be regarded as transgressive acts through which young people challenge the establishment's social rules or "boundaries of propriety."[19] Personal style is part of these expressions and rebellions. How youth dress and style their bodies, hair, and clothing, and their views on appropriate style for various contexts (such as for work, sports, school, or social events), as well as how they perceive and judge others' styles or their reactions to their own style, are negotiated in the context of what their parents, teachers, employers, and others mandate and how they react to those conditions. Youth style and bodies are not only reactive and regulated, of course; they are also constituted and enacted by their own and their peer groups' beliefs and practices. Youth style thus serves both as a means of group cohesion and identity and as a reactive expression against mainstream society.[20]

Although research on the body has long recognized the relationship between individuals' bodies and self-expression,[21] most scholarship has focused on the regulatory power of social and cultural norms for girls and women. Academic research as well as media attention has widely attended to the impact of the beauty industry, Barbie dolls, magazine images, plastic surgery, and more on girls' and women's relationships with their bodies, eating disorders, or Botox treatments, to name just a few examples. The field has also suffered from the common assumption that research on "gender" refers to research on women, leaving what Ghannam aptly describes as a "mistaken impression that the male body is not subject to social regulations, meanings, and expectations."[22] But a growing body of work has begun to attend more systematically to male bodies. It is clear that boys and young men feel significant pressure to conform to scripted, idealized images of manhood and manliness and appropriate masculine behavior, and that they are coaxed to "regiment and sculpt their bodies' musculature" in particular ways.[23] Over the past forty years, for example, male action figure toys have featured ever-increasingly large biceps and bulging chest muscles and shoulders.[24] Meanwhile, a broader range of clothing, hair gel, beauty products, lotions, soaps, spa services, and plastic surgeons have all expanded their markets to men.[25] From the time they are young boys, men are constantly reminded of social ideals about manhood and of what they should strive toward in order to be a "real man." Masculinity is even more deeply embedded in extremist expressions of nationalism. Anoop Nayak explains that skinhead style articulates "multiple masculine fantasies of existence related to manual labor, militarism, prison identity and 'hardness.' "[26]

Men who are marginalized from mainstream models of male success — whether through lack of opportunity, economic disenfranchisement, or divergence from heterosexual masculinity — may be even more likely to gravitate toward models of masculinity that celebrate physical strength and working-class style.[27] Of course, it's important to note that male bodies are not only acted on through these social pressures but also help to enact social practices that define, reinforce, and regulate masculinities and their intersections with various other identities, including national ones.[28] Style and fashion can be empowering expressions of identity and bonding with peers or can simply be an act of pleasure.[29] But for the purposes of this chapter, it is clear that ideas about masculinity intersect with ideas about nationhood in ways that help to construct idealized notions of national men—of what it means to be a good man, or a real man, or an ideal man in any particular nation.[30] Bodies are sites through which nations and national identities are constructed and reinforced. Bodily practices—from wearing national costumes to participating in a protest march or performing traditional dances or ceremonies—can thus be understood as physical and emotional embodiments of nationhood. Such practices use the corpus to enact and, in Kristin Surak's words, in-corporate the nation, to embody political action, and to express individual affect and subjectivity.[31] In some cases, understandings of national membership even become intertwined with biological markers like blood.[32] This understanding of the importance of bodily practices to the nation also helps explain why bodies are so often the primary targets for judgment and disdain of practices deemed nonnational (such as wearing headscarves in France) and why bodies are the sites of much violence directed against those deemed not to belong to the nation.

Kristin Surak argues that physical embodiments of nationhood not only are performative but also have a pedagogical quality—cultivation—that "works to transform people into better or idealized members of the nation."[33] After formal schooling, Surak argues, the bodily practices through "which nationhood is in-corporated and enacted" are one of the most powerful means through which the nation is constituted and reconstituted.[34] Clothing, fashion, and style are part of this—not only in the most obvious ways (i.e., traditional national costumes, colors, or distinctly national styles of dress)—but also in symbols woven into clothing. In this chapter, I extend this point by examining how the bodily incorporation of nationhood is inextricably linked to idealized notions of masculinity. The nation is indeed embodied and enacted through physical form—but this happens in gendered ways.[35]

The hypermasculine nature of much of the far right and its idealized notions of manhood and of what a "real man" does for the nation are key to far right and right-wing extremist scenes and groups.[36] There has been relatively little attention, however, to how these idealized notions of national men become articulated in far right youth subcultures. As this chapter demonstrates, masculinity is no less important to the far right wing scene today than it was in the past, but its expressive form has shifted. During the 1980s and 1990s, traditional skinhead style — in Germany as well as elsewhere in Europe, the U.K., and North America — "recreated the model-worker," as Hilary Pilkington suggests, by using "heavy industrial boots" along with work clothes like jeans and suspenders [braces] and shaved heads in order "to articulate a tough masculinism, chauvinism (anti-gay and anti-black), puritanism, and working-class communalism."[37] The stylistic shift away from skinhead style since the early part of the twenty-first century also means, however, that masculinity is performed and enacted in new ways.[38]

Embodying Extremism

The young men who form the predominant base for far right and nationalist groups in Germany (and elsewhere) live much of their lives embedded in social contexts espousing traditional notions of manhood and masculinity. The two schools I studied prepare youth for construction trades — male-dominated occupations like masonry and roofing and concrete laying, many of which rely on physical strength and endurance during daily work tasks. Classrooms are typically all male; crowds of young men gather in the school courtyards during class breaks, smoking and chatting. Workplaces are also likely to be all male, as groups of men work building scaffolds or laying tile and concrete and perform masculinity through banal workplace displays of toughness, virility, and physical prowess, or during smoking breaks punctuated by whistles and catcalls to women walking by.

In interviews, both young men and the two women occasionally made casual remarks that revealed much about the masculine world of school and work in the construction trades. Katrin — who at twenty-one is in her third year at the school in order to obtain a technical high school degree, which opens access to further postsecondary education — was one of only two women interviewed. She describes how the environment affects her own clothing choices, and how she adapts it to minimize her sexuality or femininity at school. Her own style is totally casual, she explains, but she is particular about her choice of clothing at school, "where we have a pretty big majority of male [students]." In the summer, she explains, she has to "think twice" about what she wears, opting for a "long skirt" or clothes that don't show too much skin or emphasize the legs, "because then one would have to run the gauntlet . . . someone would whistle or catcall and so in general one avoids that." Paul, a twenty-four-year-old training to be a construction mechanic, mentioned in an aside that it's common in construction to hear off-color jokes about women. Klaus, a twenty-one-year-old roofing apprentice, talked about girls' clothing having been a problem in his previous school, where "some teachers felt hit on . . . if women or girls wore clothes that were too short or tight" and then notes that such situations don't occur in this school, where it's "only boys."

Young men sometimes talked about their own bodies as they perused the images of clothing and products marketed to the far right. As they examined particular T-shirts or jackets, they would sometimes remark that the design would be better suited to someone with a broader back or shoulders, or that the particular product wouldn't work for their body. Benjamin looked at a T-shirt with Celtic knots on the upper back corners and a Viking face and ship in the center of the back, and described it as a "cool" T-shirt, but one that he wasn't sure he would wear himself. "I don't know. I don't really like the color, and the things [Celtic knots] are a little ugly; I think they are also made for people who are built pretty broad, to give them a sort of shoulder cap."

Youth also clearly pay attention to issues of physical stature and sculpted musculature more generally, frequently commenting, for example, on the physical build of the models or figures wearing T-shirts in photographs and screenshots. As Timo observed while looking at an image of a man wearing a T-shirt, "yeah, 'Help us Thor,' muscle-packed . . . maybe ready to be violent." Eckart, a twenty-one-year-old masonry apprentice, looked at an image of two men facing away from the camera. After discussing the iconography on the men's T-shirts, he looked at the crowd behind the men and commented on the size of one of the men: "they could be security . . . one of them looks like a fridge." Hayri talked about working out all winter long so that one's chest gets broader before wearing shirts a little more open in the summer, showing a little more chest and letting one's body be seen.

The clothing lines that I studied carry overwhelmingly men's product lines. Although some women's lines exist, they are smaller, with a more limited range of products. By and large, this is clothing marketed by and for men; it is worn by men, its messages performed by men. Idealized images of male bodies abound: catalog and website shots of broad-shouldered, young men with bulging biceps and six pack, washboard abs, positioned in catalogs to maximize images of strength and manliness: lifting something in a boatyard, crossing arms across a hypermasculine chest, or hunched over an open fire. But the clothing does more than promote physical ideals of manliness or masculinity; it also markets traditional masculine ideals around belonging and resistance, as I discuss in greater detail below.

Soldier, Warrior, Viking, Sailor: Male Comradeship and Belonging

Fabian Virchow identifies a cluster of factors that are repeatedly manifested in the hegemonic masculinity of the German far right. In particular, the far right idealizes images of soldiers, a sense of service to the nation and its people, valorization of heterosexuality and national reproduction through fatherhood and childrearing, and a set of characteristics including strength, self-sacrifice, heroism, comradeship, loyalty, discipline, order, bravery, toughness, and courage in the face of death.[39] The constant portrayal of soldiers in the organized far right's printed materials helps to construct a hegemonic far right masculinity, Virchow argues, by strengthening the impression that a "strong German nation" exists only with a strong military and brave, male soldiers who engage in the face of "real or imaginary danger."[40] Thus, conceptions of nation are semantically linked to ideals about manliness, power, aggression, and violence. Similar formulations of this hegemonic masculinity appear in far right and neo-Nazi music lyrics as well;[41] even the names of shops that sell clothing popular with far right youth often reference strength or violence. Georg explained that the brand Yakuza not only is for sale in individual Yakuza shops but also can be found in "street wear shops like *Doorbreaker, Body Check*" (emphasis added) — names that directly invoke physical violence.

The soldier-sailor-warrior trope is closely tied to hero fantasies about being a guardian, protector, vanquisher, champion, defender, challenger, or conqueror. Commercial product iconography often plays on these themes, integrating references to immigration or the recent migrant and refugee crisis in Europe by positioning the situation as a defense against an incursion of "others" or protection and rescue of a homeland. A bright-yellow T-shirt from Ansgar Aryan declares in large block letters, "Send 'Em Back," with the phrase repeated on the back of the shirt along the phrases "Fortress Europe" and "Illegals Go Home." Phalanx Europa sells several shirts that draw on these themes, from a black shirt that boldly declares "Islamists Not Welcome" with smaller text declaring "stay back or we'll kick you back," to a shirt depicting an anchor and the phrase "raise the border and batten down the hatches" (*Grenzen Hoch und Schotten Dicht*). The text to the right of this latter T-shirt directly references the recent influx of refugees. When Michael looked at an image of an Ansgar Aryan T-shirt depicting a U-Boot captain, he noted "at first glance it looks a little bit like . . . hero worship."

The militarized man as warrior-hero is not unique to Germany, of course; it is a common trope cross-nationally within far right cultural scenes. Right-wing militias and white supremacist groups in the United States, for example, consistently promote a fantasy about the "real" American manhood that will be violently restored to its former glory.[42] Simi and colleagues note that the hypermasculinity and authoritarian attitudes so central to far right extremist groups are also traditional characteristics of the military.[43] In Germany, military iconography is peppered throughout the commercial clothing of the new German far right youth subcultural scene. Military motifs like camouflage are common, along with references to German colonialism and Nazi military expeditions, or to commanders and leaders like Rudolf Hesse and Erwin Rommel. The "heroes" of the U-Boot fleet are valorized in a T-shirt by Ansgar Aryan, while the Nazi expedition to Tibet led by professor and SS Hauptsturmführer Ernst Schäfer is celebrated in a Thor Steinar T-shirt.[44]

The trope of the soldier-sailor-warrior articulates an ideal male body image that includes physical traits like muscular strength and stamina. But it also conveys a set of nonphysical traits common to the same trope, such as loyalty, integrity, belonging, and male comradeship. Such traits have already been shown to appear with regularity in the printed materials of the far right across national cases; in a comprehensive analysis of right-wing extremist group statements in Italy, Germany, and the United States, Manuela Caiani, Donatella della Porta, and Claudius Wagemann analyze several ways in which identity is built within the far right. In their analyses, the far right presents itself to members as "omnipotent, able to solve every problem," and as an "active and hard-working part of society" reflecting virtues like "honour, nation, and comradeship." The far right positions itself as working to overcome the current system in favor of a "romanticist, utopian ideal of a 'pure,' solidaristic, and co-operative society."[45] This chapter extends Caiani and colleagues' and Virchow's work by showing how such traits are evidenced not only in the printed material of formal and organized far right groups but also in the iconography of far right subcultural style, as depicted in commercial far right products.

Traits like male comradeship, loyalty, and belonging were clearly evident in the far right symbols and commercial products I analyzed. Label 23/Boxing Connection, a "crossover" brand known for appealing to youth across the martial arts, far right, and soccer hooligan subcultures,[46] sells a black T-shirt with a red and white motif whose large text reads "THE UN-BREAKABLE BROTHERHOOD." Ansgar Aryan sells a T-shirt that notes "Volksgemeinschaft statt New World Order" on the front ("The people's community instead of new world order") and on the arm, in smaller print, the words "Loyalty, Respect, Solidarity." Other products also evoke or directly reference trust, togetherness, solidarity, or belonging, such as a T-shirt from Erik and

Sons named "Trust" or a Thor Steinar T-shirt that proclaims in bold text across the back, "You'll Never Walk Alone!"[47] Another strategy is the use of the pronouns "we" and "our" to clearly demarcate belonging to the group. An Ansgar Aryan T-shirt uses the words "Hate Crew" in large print on the front, over an image of a masked face and two bloody cleavers; underneath that image are the words "our day will come." Bold lettering on the back of the T-shirt more clearly identifies the "us" and "them," noting "We know where you work; we know where you live; you're not that hard to find." Georg, who was a part of the far right for a few years in early adolescence, uses the word "us" in a discussion about a Thor Steinar T-shirt that reads "You looking for a fight?" together with an image of a Viking with a raised Thor's Hammer. "I have that shirt in my closet," Georg said, "of course it's provocative," noting that "the Nordic Gods are very strong." The phrase on the T-shirt reads like a proclamation, he explains: if anyone "wants a fight with us, he can have it, but he'll lose" (also see discussion of this excerpt from Georg's interview in chapter 3).

In another example, an Erik and Sons T-shirt depicts a group of figures clad in Ku Klux Klan white hooded gowns, with the phrase "team player" in the middle. Youth frequently explained that consumers wear far right clothing and symbols in order to express affinity with like-minded individuals. Michael suggested that the message of such clothing is first and foremost for the individual and like-minded individuals, "because it symbolizes a feeling of solidarity and replaces the uniform [style] that is banned." But he notes that it also sends a message to outsiders who the wearer wants to impress or intimidate. Justus, a twenty-one-year-old concrete layer apprentice, explained that when someone is in public, such clothing would signal political affinity to other people who "are just as racist but don't show it. So that they know, that's somebody who would help me in need." Katrin, who was quoted above, reflected that a lot of far right youth are not engaged for political reasons, but rather to be a part of a bigger group. "They find it nice to be in a group and to have this sense of cohesion." Eckart explained his sense that far right coded symbols and brands allow consumers to express opinions but also to belong to a group and a community, "to feel somehow strong with several others who wear things like that." The importance of this sense of group belonging and solidarity is consistent with prior research, such as Elena Omel'chenko's analysis of the critical role that fraternal bonds, male friendship, and intimacy play in Russia's skinhead subculture.[48]

In some cases, national solidarity is directly invoked, as in an early mail-order catalog sweater with the words "I am proud to be a German" in large stitching; the catalog text suggests the sweater is a "wonderful Christmas gift" for anyone who wants to "express their patriotism." In other cases, belonging to a group defined by racial purity is implied or directly referenced, as in the Thor Steinar T-shirt with giant letters proclaiming "100% Pure Viking Blood." The most ubiquitous iconographical images in the clothing brands are Nordic symbols and imagery, as I explored in chapter 3. Far right ideology has classically drawn a linear or genetic linkage between Nordic tribes or Vikings and Germanic tribes, arguing that contemporary Germans are the direct descendants of Nordic tribes whose origins were in turn Aryan. The use of Nordic symbols and images—runes, Nordic spelling of words, Scandinavian architecture and seascapes, shipyards, sailboats, compasses, glaciers, snowy ski slopes, and more—evoke or directly reference this lineage. Combined with textual references to race, such as "My favorite color is white," "the white continent," or "welcome to white man's island," to name just three examples, Nordic iconography, spellings, symbols, and images directly link or evoke a sense of belonging to a white community. Viking warriors or weaponry are often depicted on T-shirts or tattoos. One T-shirt shows a raised hand wielding a Nordic hammer over the words (in old Germanic script) "Help us Thor!!!" In addition to evoking the soldier-sailor-warrior trope, Viking sailors, as Michael Kimmel points out, "represent an untrammeled masculinity, an 'armed brotherhood' of heroes and martyrs."[49] Klaus looked at a photo of a man wearing this T-shirt and remarked, "that's sort of a Viking-type . . . what is that trying to symbolize? To be a real guy, or something . . . he looks pretty brawny, y'know?" Georg explained that Vikings symbolize power and hierarchy (*Wikingerherrschaft, Hierarchie*). Justus referred to an image of a Viking as a "soldier." Kevin noted that Vikings "symbolize strength, fighter." As I discussed above, catalog and website models also often reflect hypermasculine features like bulging biceps and are positioned in ways to showcase strength, muscularity, and power.

Such products do much more than market male comradeship and strengthen group belonging, of course. They convey clear xenophobic, racist, nationalistic, and extremist content. But that content is couched in iconographic tropes and images that explicitly aim to forge solidarity, togetherness, unity, trust, and a sense of belonging to a group, packaged within clothing that is marketed explicitly to men. Such performances of masculinity not only reflect the normative practices and beliefs of the far right scene but also help constitute and strengthen individuals' identities and sense of self—including their sense of manhood and masculinity more generally.[50]

The soldier/sailor/warrior trope, and all that it evokes in terms of male comradeship and belonging, is only one of the two dominant tropes I identified that reflect the hegemonic masculinity of the German far right. The rebel / rule breaker trope, which reflects a desire for resistance and cultural subversion, is equally powerful and is discussed in greater detail below.

Rebels and Rule Breakers: Resistance, Power, and Machismo

The 2015 winter collection on the Ansgar Aryan website features a male model staring into the camera, defiantly raising a black-gloved middle finger. Elsewhere among the brand's products are T-shirts that prominently state "Aryan Resistance," a pair of sweatpants with "my life my rules" printed across the seat of the pants and in large print down the outside right pant leg, and another pair of pants with "Fuck your Society" printed along the back of the left leg. The product line's name is H8CORE—shorthand for "hate core." Other brands also play directly on the appeal of resistance and anger toward mainstream society. One Thor Steinar T-shirt features a large gun at the end of an outstretched hand over the words "straight answer," while another shows an image of a Viking yelling and wielding an ax, over the word "Reaction" printed in old Germanic script.

Products like these illustrate the extent to which commercial products that are marketed to or have a consumer base among far right youth do not only forge community and a sense of belonging for male consumers. They also deploy the body as a place to express and perform anger and resistance against mainstream society in direct and indirect ways, all while clearly identifying these activities as part of male nationalists' domain. Tobias examined an image of three men with shaved heads and black shirts, one of which had a symbol of a figure kicking a ball and the phrase "good night left side," surrounded by the words "anti-antifa network"—a phrase that signifies anti-leftist engagement. As he looked at the photograph, Tobias noted, "Yeah, well that says a lot. They're waiting for someone to stupidly talk to them and then they can have their fun and fight." He explains that "everything" about the picture conveys that message: "everything, the tattoos, the way the body is held, of course the hair, the identical appearance." For Tobias, the young men in the photo have embodied a sense of violence and readiness to fight.

Both iconography and text in the far right brands repeatedly emphasize resistance and rebellion. One of the most subtle and complex extremist brands, Reconquista, had a series of taglines flashing across the top of their commercial website, including the phrase "Widerstand ist anziehend," which carries a double meaning. While *widerstand* singularly communicates as "resistance," the word *anziehend* has dual meanings, used to communicate "attractive" and "wearable," from the verb *anziehen*, which means "to put on." Reconquista is thus selling "wearable" resistance that makes one attractive.[51]

By using the notion of resistance itself to market extremist clothing in this way, the brand Reconquista ultimately commodifies the very concept of resistance.

Expressing resistance is key to racist, nationalist, and extremist identities, particularly among young men. Work on oppositional subcultures has shown that boys' rebellion—through things like pranks and vandalism—can be a means to express and validate hegemonic masculine ideals that conflict with the obedience and restraint required of boys by their teachers and other authority figures.[52] Lukas looked at an image of a T-shirt with the phrase "My favorite color is white" and reflected that it would take "a lot of courage" to wear a T-shirt like that. "In the end, it is this feeling that is tempting, like oh, I have something totally wicked and forbidden on my shirt." Previous research also has demonstrated that right-wing extremist radicalization is closely tied to a sense of injustice, being disgruntled and angry at societal institutions that are deemed to have let one down.[53] Subcultural style can be a part of such resentment and rebellion, particularly in light of research showing that style not only strengthens internal group values and belonging but acts to deliberately engage the outside world.[54] In the following discussion, I explain how the rebel / rule breaker trope valorizes key traits like transgression, challenge, rebellion, hatred, anger, and violence in ways that mutually reinforce masculinity and nationalism.

As they perused a selection of thirty-four images of commercial products and symbols, youth used words like "brutal," "tough," "violent," "hard," "aggressive," "fierce," "provocative," "fighter," "solid," "looking for problems," "angry," "not a loser," and "power" to describe the images as well as their intended messages. Michael described one T-shirt as "riot-brother-clothes" (*Krawallbrüderklamotte*). Ingo described the clothing as a strategy to scare people off (*Abschreckmodus*). As they looked at the images, they often referenced models' physical build and stature. "They look like kick boxers or fighters," remarked Cihan, a twenty-three-year-old concrete layer apprentice, as he looked at one image; "they all have a shaved head, well, they want to show this typical testosterone so, 'we are men.'" Large, puffy jackets like those produced by Alpha Industries were repeatedly singled out as appealing because they make the wearer appear more muscular. Klaus simply described them as "bomber jackets that make one look broader."

Youth repeatedly described the "provocative" nature and purpose of such clothing, as chapter 4 analyzed in greater depth, and its usefulness for showing strength or toughness. They also remarked on the clothing models' or consumers' heavy tattoos and musculature. Simon examines an Erik and Sons shirt with the phrase "Mauljucken"—a slang term that conveys a readiness to fight—and remarks, "shaved head, heavily muscled" before commenting on the phrase, explaining that it's essentially asking if the observer wants "a punch in the face." For others, the intended reaction is clearly fear. Martin, who self-identifies as a right-wing nationalist, explained that he was initially attracted to the style of right-wing extremists because it evokes fear in others:

"I always found it . . . somehow fascinating, because in my view there is an embodiment [*Verkörperung*], when you appear dangerous and that's how others view you, then other people receive you with a sort of respect or fear. . . . If one sees three people standing there dressed like [a right-wing extremist], then one normally doesn't get closer."

Justin similarly described the purpose of coded messages in clothing as a way for individuals to "embody [their] political interests." Ingo described a far right wing friend who "embodies this [right-wing] image in the extreme, and . . . unfortunately also has these [right-wing] ideas. . . . He tattoos himself and in any case one can see that he has these ideas and that he dresses that way also." Tim, a twenty-two-year-old masonry apprentice, also argued that the body is used to express political opinions. Shortly after explaining that Alpha bomber jackets appeal to his buddy (*Kumpel*) because it makes him feel a little stronger and broader when he wears it, Tim explained why he thinks people wear far right clothing in general: "[it's] for those who are looking at me, or for whom I feel a certain hatred. If I don't like somebody in another group of people and I wear something like that, then look here, my swollen chest expresses that and . . . don't touch me or else."

It is also clear that the messaging and iconography appeals to youth as a performance of violence and strength more generally, whether or not there are political motives as well. Lukas explained that the brand Yakuza is less politically oriented and more geared toward violence: "Yes, it is generally worn by broad, short-haired people, but it's not automatically right wing. . . . It has a little more style behind it and threats and death and I don't know, and less this right-wing extreme." Twenty-two-year-old Benjamin looked at the T-shirt with the phrase "Mauljucken"—the slang phrase suggesting readiness to fight—and laughed. "Well, that second [T-shirt] is cool, well *Mauljucken*, that T-shirt is wicked [*geil*], I'd wear it. . . . I find it funny somehow, I mean, I wouldn't wear it because I'm saying I will beat someone up, but rather because I hope that then people would see it and think that [I would]."

Rios and Sarabia suggest that marginalized men—who are economically or socially vulnerable—enact "compensatory masculinities" through deviant behavior.[55] Such behavior is, they suggest, a direct act of resistance toward institutions and power structures that exert control over these men's lives. Most notably, the young men they studied often responded to the emasculation brought on through interactions with police or "institutions of control" by "symbolically remasculinizing themselves by subjecting young women to physical and symbolic violence."[56] For Georg, a twenty-one-year-old scaffold builder who was once "taken away" by police for wearing a Thor Steinar jacket in public and allowed to leave with the jacket only after the police, as he describes it, "ripped out the logo before my eyes"—misogynistic iconography is clearly part of Yakuza's appeal, as are iconographic and textual references that threaten violence toward immigrants or those deemed otherwise not to belong to the nation. Such iconography thus simultaneously remasculinizes and asserts racial and ethnic dominance, clearly identifying what it means to be a "real" man in the German nation.

Although further research is needed to explore the question of economic marginalization in greater depth, it is worth pointing out that the young men I interviewed—future masons, roofers, scaffold builders, concrete layers, and those in related occupations—are not a part of what Kimmel refers to as "global hegemonic masculinity."[57] They are predominantly working-class young men who are marginalized from traditional notions of male success in the modern economy. Economically, construction is a declining industry in Berlin; employment in the construction trades has dropped dramatically in the past two decades, from nearly sixty-one thousand employees in 1995 to under twenty thousand in 2011, although the numbers have more or less stabilized since 2004. Employment numbers in construction in Brandenburg (the state surrounding Berlin) have experienced similar decline, dropping by more than half between 1995 and 2011, from 72,607 to 34,333.[58] More generally, the German vocational system has declined somewhat in status and relevance in the face of a labor market that increasingly values knowledge-based skills and flexibility over more predictable and physical manufacturing and craft trades. Once the global standard for non-university-bound careers, the German apprenticeship model has struggled in several ways in recent years.[59] Several of the youth made casual, off-the-cuff references in interviews to challenging aspects of their lives, as chapter 3 discussed in greater depth, referencing prison stints, a drug overdose, or school expulsions, or with vague mentions of hard childhoods. A few talked about their perception that mainstream society looks down on manual labor and construction work.[60] The cost of clothing came up frequently when they talked about particular brands. As chapter 1 discussed, there is evidence showing that far right attitudes or engagements are linked to economic anxiety, particularly through the experience of growing up with parental unemployment. These contexts are important for understanding the appeal of the tropes of resistance and rebellion.

Lukas describes how the object of hatred for far right youth has shifted from foreigners to the influx of wealthy Germans who have moved to (relatively inexpensive) Berlin from other parts of Germany, gentrifying the city and driving up prices. "In the meantime the hate object is not necessarily the foreigner, rather more these Germans who moved [to Berlin], with all their money, and they can afford everything and oh . . . and rents are more expensive and then all at once a big car . . . there's another scapegoat [now]." But then he also explains that as the percentage of foreigners in eastern Germany has increased, xenophobia may also be declining, since "one has to get along."

Scholars have demonstrated that frustration and anger play a key role in extremist group recruitment and radicalization. In research with U.S. rightwing extremists, Pete Simi and his colleagues found that radicalization was most likely to occur when anger about personal experiences—such as involuntary exit from the military—created a sense of personal failure in the face of an uncertain future. Particularly through engagement with others who have had similar experiences or who are already extremists, the process of radicalization ultimately redirects anger at a sense of personal failure toward the government and other groups.[61] Former white supremacist Arno Michaelis recently described his own socialization into a hate group in the United States, explaining how the strong hatred he developed as a teenager—of his family, his teachers, his school, his town, and other kids—found its key expression when he encountered racist skinhead music. He discovered that the swastika "is an effective way of angering others," and that the hatred and anger he "radiated" was in turn reflected back from others, which then "validat[ed] the paranoid ideology that had become my identity."[62]

In Rios and Sarabia's research with urban gang members, boys who were frustrated with few viable employment opportunities or guidance from the adult world easily fell into "the seductive arms of hypermasculinity,"[63] in which exaggerated displays of aggression and strength both express resistance and serve as a "resource for self-affirmation."[64] The performance of these kinds of markers of masculinity are particularly important pull factors for young men who may be disenfranchised from traditional markers of mainstream success—university educations, high-paying or high-status jobs, or a sense of clear future opportunities. Rios and Sarabia explain that traditional elements of masculinity like toughness, dominance, and the willingness to be violent "are central resources for men less able to acquire mainstream masculinity-making resources."[65] Masculinity is thus "utilized as a vehicle for attempting to alleviate forms of social marginalization and subordination"[66] and acts as a key mechanism linking culture and social structure more generally. As James Messerschmidt has argued, cultural ideals about masculinity "encourage specific kinds of gendered action," but it is social structures that "shape the capacities from which gendered strategies of action are constructed over time."[67]

Finally, it is important to note that far right wing products don't only aim to provoke outsiders; they also valorize violence more generally, and they do so in clearly gendered ways. The phrase *Kontaktfreudig und Erlebnisorientiert* —which loosely translates as "eager/happy to be in contact and looking for adventure"—is used by Thor Steinar in both its men's and women's lines, for example, but is paired with very different iconographical images (see plate 4). In men's T-shirts and sport jackets, the phrase is written over an image of red, spattered blood; in the women's T-shirt, the phrase is written over an image of red, puckered, lipstick-covered lips. Men are thus depicted as seekers of violent adventure, whose contact with others will lead to their own or other's blood to splatter. "Contact" for women, on the other hand, is sexualized, reflected in puckered lips ready to be kissed.

The clothing lines also valorize taboo breaking, both through the use of iconography and text that offends social norms as well as by carefully toeing the line between legal and illegal symbol usage. The brands' symbols and iconography—including use of colors, text scripts, phrases, historic references, and more—break cultural taboos while toeing the line of legality—a line that in turn is used directly to market the products to consumers, as chapter 5 detailed. Part of the attractiveness of these clothing brands to youth in and around the scene is that they carefully tread along the line of legality, enabling youth to resist mainstream norms and cultural rules while not getting into official legal trouble. Martin, who self-identifies as a right-wing extremist, for example, explained that his parents don't approve of what he's doing but know that he won't do anything illegal.

In sum, the articulation of a hegemonic far right masculinity through the trope of the rebel / rule breaker has several points of appeal for young men. Most centrally, it is clear that the iconography, symbols, and texts on products and clothing popular in the far right subcultural scene evoke and encourage the performance of strength, power, machismo, bravado, and fearlessness and are intended to provoke a reaction in observers, particularly mainstream society.

Dual Articulations

While many of the traits associated with the hegemonic articulation of far right masculinity I have analyzed here fall into either the soldier/sailor/ warrior or the rebel / rule breaker categories, the division between the two categories is not a completely clear or bounded one. Martin argued, for example, that the main purpose of the brands is to help insiders forge an identity, but that the brands are consistently stamped by the outside world as aggressive and provocative (see chapter 1 for a fuller discussion of Martin's views on this point).[68] Masculine ideals like strength, power, and bravado are celebrated both in the valorization of military soldiers and sailing explorers as well as in rebels who provoke fear in mainstream society. Indeed, the Viking warrior may be so ubiquitous across the brands precisely because it epitomizes many of the ideals in both articulations. For youth in and on the periphery of the far right scene, hypermasculine symbols like the inflated biceps of Viking gods depicted in right-wing tattoos may reflect youth fantasies of a romantic, pure, and untroubled past in ways that help them navigate uncertain labor markets and transitions to their adult lives.[69] More generally, it is important to note that desire to belong to a group and expressions of anger toward outsiders are likely mutually reinforcing emotional expressions. Enacting violence against others as part of a group may make an individual simultaneously feel more powerful and more closely bonded to his fellow aggressors.

Conclusion

I have aimed here to articulate a key mechanism through which a hegemonic articulation of masculinity intersects with nationalistic ideals in ways that mutually reinforce masculinity and nationalism. I argue that far right youth subcultural style in Germany valorizes hegemonic far right masculinity and appeals to marginalized young men's simultaneous desire to belong to a group and to resist mainstream authorities. During stressful economic, political, or social periods in the nation's history, scholars have suggested that images of males and females may become increasingly idealized and romanticized.[70] I would suggest that this is also the case for marginalized subcultural groups who are detached from mainstream notions of success and for whom traditional ideas about male and female roles, or masculinity and femininity, may have particular appeal.

I focused here on two primary ways in which the emotional appeal of the styles are particularly important in articulating a hegemonic masculinity of the far right and linking masculinity with nationalism through the expression of shared ideal traits. First, I showed how the desire for male comradeship and belonging is illustrated in iconographic and textual references to the male soldier/Viking sailor/warrior in ways that emphasize conformity, trust, comradeship, courage, heroism, loyalty, and belonging. Second, I showed how the appeal of expressing anger and frustration at mainstream society is expressed through the rebel / rule breaker trope and its valorization of traits like rebellion, violence, transgression, hatred, and anger. By linking these traits to nationalistic, xenophobic, and racist content, the male body becomes a site for inscribing and performing far right wing ideology and helps articulate what it means to be a "good nationalist man." Subcultural style thus acts not only as a key site for reinforcing identity and belonging to a group and for expressing resistance against mainstream society, but also as a mechanism through which nationalism and masculinity are jointly articulated and reinforced.

These findings clearly demonstrate that clothing and subcultural style have the potential not only to reflect but also to create, cultivate, and strengthen identities, including masculinity and femininity and their intersections with nationalism. Far from being mere "subcultural style," I argue that commercialized extremist products can be a gateway to radicalization and violence by both helping to strengthen racist and nationalist identification and by acting as conduits of resistance to mainstream society. Future work on masculinity and nationalism could extend this finding by focusing on additional mechanisms that help explain *how* masculinity and nationalism work together in ways that might contribute to the appeal of extremist groups.

CONCLUSION
Mainstreaming the Extreme

The headlines about youth recruits to ISIS and the right-wing backlash to the migration crisis in Europe that I referenced in this book's preface have not subsided as I write the conclusion. But they were joined, in the meantime, by media coverage of the United States' own populist right-wing support for Donald Trump. Throughout 2016, Trump protesters and supporters clashed at rallies across the country, sometimes violently, against a backdrop of campaign speeches in which Trump referred to Mexicans as rapists and murderers, called for a ban on Muslim immigration, and advocated building a wall at the Mexican border.[1] As the campaign continued, the Ku Klux Klan (KKK)'s official newspaper endorsed Trump, and their former leader David Duke argued that Trump's policies "show the country is open to a white power message."[2] In March 2016, the Public Broadcasting System (PBS) faced a wave of criticism after its *PBS News Hour* show featured a Trump campaign volunteer on air with visible right-wing extremist and neo-Nazi tattoos, including the Celtic Cross and the number 88.[3] In the wake of the election, white nationalist Richard Spencer's National Policy Institute (NPI) held a celebratory conference in DC, followed by a dinner at a local Italian restaurant, where participants were photographed giving the Sieg Heil salute.[4] Trump's success stunned liberals, moderates, and conservatives across the political spectrum in the United States, much as the previous populist growth of successful electoral parties in France, the U.K., Germany, Austria, and other European countries surprised many in Europe. On both sides of the Atlantic, increasingly, the extreme is becoming more mainstream in ways that academics and policy makers have struggled to fully explain.

In this book, I have focused on one aspect of the mainstreaming of extremist ideology and rhetoric, examining how coded racist, xenophobic, Islamophobic, anti-Semitic, and nationalist ideas become embedded in high-quality mainstream clothing and products. I studied the deployment and reception by youth of these coded symbols, focusing on how such symbols might contribute to the mainstreaming of extremist ideas and the recruitment and radicalization of young people. In the following conclusion, I trace several implications from these findings, suggesting that this analysis of the German case has lessons for how we think about culture, economic objects, emotions, and their role(s) in extremist engagement.

Extremism as Emotional Engagement: Belonging and Resistance

There are important lessons to draw from this work for our understandings of nationalist and extremist engagement, which have paid more attention to the political motivations of nationalism and not enough to the cultural manifestations of its extremist fringe. Nationalism—whether in extremist forms or not—is driven not only by the quest for political autonomy but also by emotional impulses related to collective identity, belonging, resistance, and rebellion. Scholars have been somewhat slow to recognize the importance of these cultural and emotional issues to youth extremist participation, even as case after case of ISIS recruits in Europe or dropouts from right-wing extremist groups, for example, report on the centrality of these factors to youth engagement. Dorle Hellmuth's series of case study vignettes on several of the estimated 790 German nationals who have left Germany for Syria and Iraq since 2012, for example, describes Germany's most prominent foreign fighter (Denis Cuspert) as having wanted to "desperately belong."[5]

The mainstreaming of far right style that I analyzed here—and its related embedding of coded symbols in clothing—is at least partially driven by youth's emotional engagement with extremism. While far right extremism has long been understood to be not only a space for political engagement but also a site for youth aggression and violence through racist skinhead subcultures, there has been little attention to the emotional aspects of youth engagement in the far right.[6] My analysis of far right coded symbols suggests that extremist engagement is not always rational or even politically motivated; on the contrary, sometimes it is the emotional appeal of extremist rhetoric that is the driving force for youth to engage. There is evidence that similar impulses are behind the appeal of foreign fighters who join ISIS. Indeed, the stylized aspects of the appeal of radical jihad to alienated Muslim youth in Europe is captured in the phrase "jihadi cool," a term coined by terrorism expert Marc Sageman and popularized by the media in the wake of the beheading of James Foley, an American photojournalist, by a former British rapper known as "Jihadi John."[7] As Caroline Picart details, ISIS now has its own clothing line that "specializes in ISIS-themed T-shirts and hoodies," sold online via Indonesian websites. Picart attributes the popularity of "jihadi cool" style to the "seductive appeal of being a 'badass.'"[8] Being a badass, as she explains, requires a kind of toughness and amenability to violence that many youth, along with other "symbols of deviance," consider a "good thing."[9]

The youth I interviewed—who were in and on the periphery of the far right scene—clearly saw far right symbols and clothing as a means to forge (male) comradeship as well as a space to express anger, provoke mainstream society, and rebel against authority. This combination of coming together and lashing out—of belonging and resisting—animated the analysis across the empirical chapters in this book. I argued that alphanumeric codes, historical and fantastical references, myths and legends, symbols of death, global icons and "traveling images," and masculine ideals all have the power to mobilize and motivate youth. They appeal to youth as a strategy for handling the uncertainty of the postmodern era, as a space to express anger and rebel against mainstream society, and as a mechanism to facilitate belonging, group cohesion, and relationships with peers. Moreover, the ephemeral nature of clothing means that by its very nature, displaying symbols on clothing requires a relatively small ideological commitment, and one that is easily modified (in comparison to a tattoo or some other form of body modification, for example). Consuming and displaying subtly coded symbols may require even less of a commitment (compared to swastikas or more obvious symbols), allowing youth to experiment with entry to the far right scene, literally "trying on" extremism and participating in more flexible ways in far right subculture than was possible for previous generations.[10] In this sense, coded clothing may resonate particularly well with youth who are playing with various subcultural scenes or who function primarily at the peripheries of youth extremism rather than at the core.

The Constitutive Power of Symbols and Economic Objects

Several of the empirical chapters suggested implications from this work for scholars' understandings of how culture works. First, the empirical analysis shows that symbols matter in a myriad of ways that are often overlooked in work on culture. Most notably, these findings demonstrate that symbols not only are "tools" to social action, but sometimes constitute that very action. Coded, commercialized symbols might be understood as everyday forms of resistance as youth react to perceived societal pressure or the unattainability of their future goals. But while previous scholars have positioned symbols as background tools to everyday resistance,[11] I suggest that symbols and their manipulation may be a form of resistance on their own. Symbols thus should be understood to have autonomous power to motivate human behavior, which directly challenges recent critiques insisting that culture does not have causal power.[12] However, I also suggest that particular social structural contexts help strengthen this power. Youth are more likely to be receptive to the power of extremist symbols when they are disenfranchised or disaffected, or feel excluded from mainstream norms, or face models for success that seem unattainable. These findings thus confirm what Orlando Patterson, among others, has recently argued—that culture and social structure thus work most powerfully in tandem.[13]

Symbols are not only powerful as a means to resist—they also have the power to create meaning and constitute identity. This work thus challenges prevailing notions of economic symbols and their role in meaning making, by asserting that economic objects have the power to shape identities and motivate choices. As Jeffrey Alexander and Dominik Bartmański aptly observe, social scientists have long known that material objects hold symbolic power for a community, as Durkheim's work on totemism showed, but economic objects have been locked into a narrower view through the influence of Karl Marx's understanding of commoditization as exchange.[14] The exchange lens views commodities primarily as the end result of a system in which labor is exchanged for a product. By design, consumer goods produce and reproduce inequality by requiring some people to sell their labor to create products, while others gain the profit from their sale. Economic objects themselves are an essential part of this process, but they are not understood to have causal power on their own; they are merely the end product in a larger exploitative set of labor and production processes. For Marx, commodities hold value only as "expressions or embodiments" of human labor—leaving no possibility for economic objects to hold symbolic value outside of their role as products.[15]

For generations, the exchange lens has trained the sociological gaze on how the production of commodities leads to workers' exploitation and alienation. Scores of sociologists have broadened research on inequality beyond wage laborers to the study of its intersections with social class more generally as well as with race, gender, sexuality, global north/south dynamics, and more. Such issues are understandably front and center for a discipline whose core interests revolve around social structures and inequalities. Even the increasing body of literature that attends to consumption directly primarily has been examined through the lens of inequality, examining how consumer goods play a role in status systems and hierarchies of social inequality. Bourdieu's *Distinction* and a generation of studies that followed, for example, examined how consumption patterns and the purchase and display of particular kinds of objects and goods work to build and convey cultural and social capital.[16]

What I suggest here is that this focus on the role that economic objects play in the production and reproduction of inequality has distracted most social scientists from the potential for these objects to hold symbolic meaning and play a significant role in other aspects of social life. The exchange lens has also led scholars to presume that culture and commoditization are wholly separate phenomena, as Igor Kopytoff has argued, describing culture as a counterweight to commoditization, helping to ensure that some things remain sacred and are "publicly precluded from being commoditized."[17] My contention, on the contrary, is that commodities—economic objects—are also cultural objects that carry emotion, convey meaning, and constitute identities. This latter point has long been obvious to advertisers and marketers, but it has received less attention from social scientists. Douglas Atkin, a brand strategist who wrote *The Culting of Brands*, explained in a 2004 PBS interview that consumers look to brands for "a sense of fulfillment that society and religions used to offer. They want brands to take stands on things. Brands have values. Brands have points of view. Brands have personalities. Brands are whole societies in which they participate."[18] In his book published that same year, he writes *Few stronger emotions exist than the need to belong and make meaning. And brands are poised to exploit that need*" (emphasis in original).[19]

There is a small but growing number of anthropologists, cultural sociologists, and social historians who investigate the symbolic and cultural dimensions of consumption, examining consumer goods not only as a part of economic systems but also as objects that hold and create meaning for consumers.[20] Viviana Zelizer describes this turn as an "increasing concentration on consumption as expressive behavior—this site of mentalities, identities, and culture."[21] Recent efforts have included the study of fashion models and the global VIP party circuit, the ways in which nations package and sell national identity, and how ethnicity itself is marketed and sold.[22] Others have shown that consumption is linked in clear ways to racial and ethnic identities and to green or "eco" identities.[23] But across the growing number of rich analyses of particular cases tracing these relationships, the focus has primarily been on how, in Zelizer's words, "groups use goods to add meaning to their lives" and how consumption shapes social relationships.[24] I aim to extend this work by showing how consumer goods not only reflect and add meaning but also help constitute identity itself as well as potentially motivate political and extremist action.

My analysis of commercial, coded symbols conveying extremist ideology shows they play a key role as conduits of youth's emotional desires to belong and rebel, acting as gateways to the broader far right scene while simultaneously helping mainstream extremist ideas. This means that the production and consumption of economic objects are not only exploitative acts but also constitutive ones; economic objects have the power to shape the identities, sensibilities, attitudes, and political engagements of individual actors and their peers. My findings thus support Harvey Molotch's contention that mundane and everyday consumer goods do "identity work" over time: "identities and consumption constitute one another through routines of daily acquisition and continuous use."[25] They also follow from Roger Griffin's contention that capitalism is more than a set of institutions. Griffin argues that through the use of "brand-names, adverts, and signs, capitalism as a socio-political system weaves its way 'stylistically' into the fabric of everyday life; dying the strands of each individual's experience of normality, conditioning the way people speak and feel."[26]

In this way, economic objects and embodied symbols—consumer goods and products like clothing, but also tattoos and hairstyles—not only add meaning to individuals' and groups' lives but also can inform consumers' life choices, actions, behaviors, beliefs, and identities. Commercial products that dehumanize migrants and make light of historical pogroms, for example, normalize anti-immigrant, anti-Semitic, Islamophobic, and racist attitudes and beliefs. Combined with symbols that overtly and covertly express resistance and rebellion, such symbols position far right beliefs and attitudes as anti-authority and anti-mainstream. Paul Willis and Dick Hebdige made similar claims in the 1970s about the subcultures they studied in the United Kingdom, showing that subcultural groups, in Paul du Gay's words, "use commodities as signifiers in an active process of constructing 'oppositional' identities."[27] Subcultural groups transformed material goods from symbols of "estrangement and price value" into objects that are firmly integrated into their relationships and group identity.[28]

In contrast to Robert Putnam's claim that consumption ultimately privatizes and isolates individuals,[29] I suggest consumption can do just the opposite—consumer goods can forge connections and build identity. This theoretical contention thus aims to refine prevailing theories of culture and challenges mainstream sociologists to take economic objects more seriously not only for their exploitative power, but also for their constitutive possibilities. Economic objects have the potential to constitute identity and shape engagement in social movements or extremist groups in ways that deserve our close attention.

How Symbols Link Cultural Strategies with Cultural Systems of Meaning

The analysis of coded symbols also shows that the two predominant ways that sociologists have thought about culture—as a "tool kit" of tangible strategies and actions that help individuals navigate their daily lives or as an entire system of meaning or way of life—are not as separate as they have been discussed analytically up until now.[30] Coded symbols are an example of a mechanism that links these two ways of thinking of culture. The act of producing or deploying coded symbols laced with racist, xenophobic, and far right wing content is a strategy that might be thought of as part of a broader "tool kit" with which far right youth engage with the broader world and convey their attitudes, emotions, and ideologies. Youth use these objects to express emotional and oppositional resistance and foster a sense of belonging to peers and to something bigger than themselves. However, these coded symbols are not only abstract or independent tools—rather, they are anchored, in Chan's words, in shared meaning systems, interpretable only within the broader context in which they are embedded. They can be decoded in ways that make sense, by insiders or by outsiders, only using a shared web of meaning that includes commonly understood historical references, social taboos, cultural norms, and recognized national myths, legends, heroes, landscapes, and homelands.[31]

In order for them to work, in other words, the coded symbols in commercialized far right clothing must be deployed, received, interpreted, and understood within a network of cultural, social, and historical knowledge that is shared among producers, consumers, and other observers. Producers of coded symbols need to develop extremist codes with an understanding of what is socially taboo, what is legally banned, what atrocities have been committed in the name of the nation, and what kinds of contemporary and historical narratives of migration, exclusion, nationalism, and racism exist. Coded products need to access shared myths, heroes, legends, and nationalist narratives. They play on cultural norms around masculinity and heteronormativity. They embed coded messages within motifs, scripts, colors, and vocabulary that evoke far right histories or ideologies, even when these are not invoked directly.

The fact that consumers don't always understand the coded symbols adds an intriguing layer of complexity to the mechanism; individuals may have elements in their tool kits that are not accessible to them because they lack the shared knowledge or meanings to deploy them. It is also important to consider the key ways in which the broader social and historical context in any given place impacts symbols' usage. Legal and private bans on particular symbols as well as social stigma and taboos, for example, have contributed to the playful set of meaning-making processes evidenced in the profitable and sophisticated commercialized deployment of coded far right symbols.

Combating Youth Extremism

This book does not only aim to shift how we think about culture—it also offers lessons for how we think about youth extremist engagement. At the outset of this book, I argued that it would be a mistake to try to forget the right-wing extremist "bullies and thugs" that Joyce Carol Oates's poem about the Holocaust wishes we could erase. Bullies and thugs, I believe, are made—which means they can be unmade. Our ability to counter extremist violence and deradicalize youth, however, has been hampered by major holes in our understanding of what motivates youth to join extremist movements and engage in extremist violence.

There are potential lessons from this work for educators and policy makers who try to combat extremist engagement, radicalization, or youth gang involvement. First, I argue that symbols themselves are powerful markers and mechanisms of belonging and protest that deserve attention in their own right and that ought to help us better understand the appeal of extremist thinking. Far from being mere "subcultural style," clothing can be a gateway to radicalization and violence. Commercialized extremist products communicate far right ideological positions to youth, informing them of far right views on immigration, race, national identity, and normative expectations for masculine behavior, among others. In this way, such products literally concretize abstract and invisible right-wing ideas into tangible, material objects that youth can consume and display, reinforcing their own identification with and understanding of far right ideology.[32] These products help youth strengthen racist and nationalist identification. But they also provide access to far right scenes and help youth establish legitimacy at key subcultural entry points like concerts or far right demonstrations. They help signal political affiliation and attitudes to others, allowing "like-minded" youth to find each other, and acting as a potential icebreaker for striking up conversations in school, at stadiums, in bars, and at parties. Finally, commercialized extremist products act as conduits of resistance toward—and carriers of extremist ideas into—mainstream society, as youth in and on the margins of the far right display far right codes and symbols in non–far right settings, with peers, classmates, siblings, and friends. In some cases, expensive brands become status symbols, popularized by older siblings, neighbors, and friends who help establish what is "cool" or desired within and across subcultures and scenes and thus helping broaden the ideological reach of the far right.

This means that educators and policy makers ought to take subcultural style more seriously. In addition to the ways in which it is consequential for radicalization to the far right itself, subcultural style can help us understand youth motivations and attitudes toward violence and exclusionary practices more generally. My interviews with young people showed that clothing choices are often centrally important to peer groups, identity, and self-understanding. The coded symbols embedded in the clothing I studied have the potential to desensitize youth to violence, to dehumanize ethnic and religious minorities, and to make light of past atrocities and contemporary expressions of hatred. The degree to which youth found humor in some of the images they reviewed, as chapter 4 detailed, makes this point abundantly clear. Shirts that tell observers that "all pigs must die" or that poke fun at murders of *Döner* shop owners at the hands of neo-Nazi terrorists; iconography that depicts a hung man "dancing" in the air as he dies; symbols that valorize Nazi leaders as heroes; and codes that link early twentieth-century planned expulsions of Jews with contemporary far right rhetoric telling Muslims and other immigrants to "have a good trip home" are just a few examples. While it is tempting to try to shut down or silence the deployment of such symbols, I suggest that we need to do the opposite, working to pedagogically engage youth in discussions about the meaning of these symbols, why youth find them appealing, and what the broader implications are of their usage for democratic coexistence.

Second, cultural and emotional rationales for extremist engagement are powerful and should be taken seriously. The mostly young men interviewed for this study strongly conveyed a sense that part of the appeal of far right and coded extremist clothing and style is to provoke mainstream society. The emotional desire to lash out, to express anger, rebellion, and resistance has not received enough attention from scholars or practitioners who work on extremist youth engagement or deradicalization. Thinking through ways to create spaces for youth to express these emotions—their anger, frustration, exasperation, resentment, outrage, and fury—is critically important. Talking to youth about their anger and listening to what they say—the roots of their hatred, their sense of being let down, their frustration with uncertain futures or economic outlooks—could go a long way toward diffusing their rage and understanding what their emotional and practical needs are. These findings echo work on youth motivations to join radical jihadist movements, as Marc Sagemen's work shows; the members of the global Salafi jihad he studied "sought a cause that would give them emotional relief, social community, spiritual comfort, and cause for self-sacrifice."[33]

Young men also clearly need spaces and mechanisms to help them forge a sense of belonging and male comradeship. The hero fantasy in particular appears to be quite compelling to young men who are attracted to extremist groups' calls to join a movement in which they become defenders, protectors, and vindicators of homelands and sacred territories. Finding ways to engage young men's desire to help reclaim honor, demonstrate loyalty and devotion, engage in honorable quests, or perform heroic rescues could be a critical intervention technique. There are some initiatives that have already embraced this idea; for example, the German federal government has promoted volunteer firefighting brigades as a site for civic engagement for youth at risk for extremist engagement.[34] The digital game Battle for Humanity—currently in beta testing—engages youth in real-life heroic quests and civic engagement in their communities outside the game space.[35] But more work is needed to develop serious prevention, intervention, and deradicalization programming that takes as a starting point the desire of young men to feel needed and to make heroic contributions to a larger cause.[36]

Research has shown that boys have difficulty sustaining male intimacy, connection, and friendship as they grow older.[37] Some find other mechanisms to forge these bonds, such as through sports teams, fraternities, the military, or the fantasy worlds of video gaming. But others flounder in ways that leave them vulnerable to groups who promise they always have their back and they will never be left alone, as far right ideology marketed through the commercial products I studied here does so clearly. Their sense of collective identity—expressed through real or fantastical and aspirational nationalism, for example—may take on greater centrality to their lives for similar reasons, as they struggle to create a secure sense of identity and connection to others. Educators and practitioners would do well to attend in much greater ways to not only the ideological and political motivations for youth extremism, but also the emotional ones.

Finally, the findings analyzed here suggest that policies that ban particular symbols or brands are not an effective strategy to counter extremist ideologies. Despite my strong sympathies for the educators and authorities who pursue banning strategies as a statement against hatred and violence, it is my conclusion that banning, in the end, misses the mark. Bans of particular brands, logos, or symbols fail to address the core appeal of the brands' coded messages or to effectively counter their use. Bans are not well understood by youth in and around the far right scene, many of whom expressed a sense of unfairness or even injustice at the imposition of bans. They are enforced unevenly, in part because it is incredibly difficult for teachers, principals, and other authorities to keep up with the codes and their modification. Principals and teachers were clear that they cannot constantly monitor and decode new signs and symbols as youth deploy them. But bans are not only ineffective—they also have the potential to further fuel the game-playing culture of the clever code modification, as youth and clothing producers find ever-new ways to manipulate symbols. Alphabetic sequences are converted into numbers and mathematical equations; brand logos are removed and reversed with Velcro to convey new meanings; new codes and symbols emerge as commercial entities create them and as youth appropriate, reappropriate, and deploy them.

Rather than aiming to shut down youth expressions of identity, I suggest that pedagogical interventions ought to focus on finding ways to give voice to youth's emotional experiences with identity and to create spaces to express them. As Cherian George argues in his examination of how hate is intentionally manufactured and manipulated by strategic political actors in what he calls "hate spin," hateful words and symbols have the power both to create positive societal counterreactions and to further flame racist or religious violence. "Provocative expression," he argues, "has both creative and destructive potential, and laws must somehow find a way to facilitate the former while limiting the latter."[38] There have been occasional intervention efforts in Germany to deploy the clever coding of the far right in efforts to combat it. The initiative Endstation Rechts (which loosely translates as "final stop for the far right"), for example, runs a well-known project called Stork Heiner (Storch Heinar), which originated as a parody of the brand Thor Steinar and uses humor—and a stork mascot—to challenge the far right. Stork Heiner products for sale on the website include umbrellas, T-shirts, buttons, pins, bags, and more, all adorned with the stork logo.[39] Another example is a 2011 "Trojan T-shirt" project run by the deradicalization group EXIT-Germany, in which free T-shirts designed with far right iconography and messaging were given to far right youth at concerts and festivals, but once washed, the T-shirts revealed a message and telephone number to help people exit right-wing extremism.[40]

More initiatives like this that aim to engage the far right and its subcultural style rather than silence it would be a welcome start. But these findings also suggest that educators and adult authorities need to acknowledge the many ways in which identities can be multiple, complex, and contradictory. Youth may experiment with various subcultural scenes or move in and out of extremist engagements over time, as I explained in the introduction. Pedagogical efforts should thus not be focused on particular identities or on achieving an outcome of the recognition and acceptance of identities (as traditional multicultural curricula has done, for example), but rather on creating tools to negotiate difference. Interventions focused on *process* rather than *outcome* are particularly key; the aim here would be to equip individuals with the skills to continually work toward coexistence across their lives, as identity-based conflicts may surge and retreat or be marked by diverse kinds of tensions and fractures over time.[41]

What Comes Next?

This project employed several aspects of research methods that were unconventional and that have lessons that may inform future research projects. First, we need more studies of extremist engagement with not only youth who are in the "core" of extremist and radical right-wing movements, but also those who are on the "periphery" or in interstitial spaces, moving in and out of far right scenes throughout their adolescence and young adulthood. Developing a better understanding of youth who are "at risk" for far right radical and extremist engagement would be extremely useful. What makes some youth more vulnerable to recruitment, mobilization, and radicalization at any particular moment, compared with their peers? Studying those on the periphery might also help shed light on how radical and extremist actions, attitudes, and beliefs engage youth who are not entirely marginalized from the mainstream. Youth in, around, and on the periphery of extremist scenes may be just as informative—or even more informative—as youth who were or are actively engaged in extremism.

Second, we need more research attending to the embodiment of extremist and nationalist beliefs and behaviors. Political ideologies are not only held intellectually, particularly for youth; they are inscribed on bodies in youth choices about clothing, hair style, tattoos, musculature, body image, and violence enacted against other bodies.[42] There may be ways in which the bodily incorporation of nationalism and extremism—its physical enactments and performances, its intersections with masculinities and sexualities, its cultivation of physical prowess and the reproduction of future citizens—proves particularly appealing for young men who are disenfranchised from traditional markers of economic and career success. Relatedly, visual and material culture—including iconography and symbols—are critical empirical domains for understanding the appeal of extremist thinking. I argue that a close examination of nationalist and extremist references within contemporary far right coded symbols and brands can shed important light on powerful mechanisms of belonging and protest that may shape young people's engagement with the far right. Similar approaches could be taken in the analysis of urban graffiti, the iconography and symbols of protest march signs and banners, or ISIS recruitment videos, to name just a few examples.

Third, I would call for more research that explicitly aims to disentangle the varied ways in which structural and cultural factors work together to motivate and radicalize youth. This would likely mean pursuing more mixed-methods studies, since structural explanations have tended to be based on large-scale, quantitative surveys and regression analyses, while cultural explanations have tended to be based on small-scale, qualitative ethnographies of youth. Additional work on institutional environments like schools would also be extremely useful, particularly when those settings are places where youth encounter mainstream authorities or norms.

It important to note that the analyses included here do not represent the sum total of far right subculture, in Germany or elsewhere. There are additional chapters that could be written, and additional ways of looking at and understanding the data. There are whole categories of youth subculture in the far right scene(s) in Germany that I do not address here — such as the Autonomous Nationalist movement and its stylistic expressions, although they are detectable in the images — in part because they have been well analyzed elsewhere.[43] The rapid commercialization of right-wing ideology in sophisticated brands and products has been a startling development in Germany, and because the phenomenon is so new, there has been little scholarly attention to the phenomenon. This work has only scratched the surface.

METHODOLOGICAL APPENDIX
Narrative Account of Research Methods

The data collection for this project took place in two major phases: the assembly and analysis of the image archive in 2011–12 and the qualitative fieldwork in two vocational schools in 2013–14. Each of these phases involved multiple preparatory fieldwork and archival visits, and the addition and analysis of images is ongoing as new brands and new collections within the brands appear. I continue to decode, disentangle, and understand new layers of historical references and coded symbols as I analyze interviews and learn from youth's accounts of subcultural style in and around the far right scene. Thus, I have come to think of the research methods "phase" of this project as encompassing the entire time period between my initial visit to the Anti-fascist Press Archive and Educational Center in Berlin in February 2009 and the writing of this narrative account in January 2017, with two more intense periods during the primary image and interview phases.

Phase I: Image Collection and Archive Assembly

The digital archive enabled me to track the explosion, fragmentation, and commercialization of symbols among far right youth over time. The initial assembly of the image archive pulled together thousands of images drawn from a variety of sources, which I describe below by their era (historical, more recent historical, and contemporary). I use the term "we" in places where data collection was done in conjunction with a field-based research assistant in Berlin.

Historical images from the 1930s–40s. Historical images from the 1930s–40s were drawn from three sources. First, I gathered images from the special collections of prints, photographs, and Nazi propaganda at the John W. Kluge Center at the U.S. Library of Congress in Washington, DC. These were primarily images confiscated by U.S. military intelligence authorities in 1945–46, but captured scenes and settings from the early 1930s onward. These images included photos of official Nazi symbols and logos, drawings, souvenirs and early commercial products, parades, Hitler Youth events, and more. Second, historical images from the 1930s–40s are drawn from the digitized collections housed at the U.S. Holocaust Memorial Museum in Washington, DC. These collections include photographs of insignia of various Nazi groups, digitized slides from Hitler Youth propaganda films, and images of a wide variety of Nazi symbols on display at various events, such as an image of a Harvest Festival maypole decorated with Nazi symbols. On site at both locations, I sorted through hundreds of photographs and digitized images that contained clear examples of symbols and codes. I was especially interested in tracing contemporary symbol usage backward to the Nazi era in order to see whether and how similar symbols have been deployed by historical and contemporary right-wing extremists in Germany, and whether and how those symbols have been modified or redeployed in different ways. Finally, I also sorted through the digitized historical images at the Granger Archive, although owing to more restrictive policies and fees for research usage at this private archive, only a few images were ultimately included in the final archive.

Historical images from the 1980s–90s. More recent historical images from the 1980s and 1990s, as well as contemporary images from the past decade, came from the collections at the Anti-fascist Press Archive and Educational Center (apabiz) in Berlin. This archive has an extensive historical archive and repository of far right extremist artifacts and material objects, including product catalogs, flyers, stationary, political brochures, and other material objects on which logos and symbols are visible. On site at the archive in the fall of 2011, I digitized hard-copy product catalogs back to brand creation, took digital photographs of clothing and products held in the archive, and digitized additional brochures, flyers, early mail-order catalogs, and more. During the summer of 2010 and fall of 2011, I also spent time talking with the apabiz archivists and researchers about the brand trademarking process, the ways in which the archive monitors and collects information about far right youth culture, and the collection of material objects. During the same period, I spoke with antifascist activists, academics, lawyers, and government officials at the Verfassungsschutz Brandenburg (the Office for the Protection of the Constitution) to try to understand how legal and private bans of brands and symbols work as well as how antifascist resistance to the physical stores and brand emergence over time. These conversations were critical in helping me contextualize the images and the symbol deployment over time.

Contemporary images from the 1990s to the present. The largest subset of images in the digital archive are the thousands of contemporary images from the digitized collections of three professional German photographers who specialize in photographing far right youth, right-wing extremists, and neo-Nazi groups. The German photographers track the extreme far right throughout Germany in settings such as neo-Nazi rallies and protest marches, as well as in everyday life settings (such as on license plates, at soccer games, and on storefronts) and gave me generous access to their full, searchable archives. The size and scope of this set of data required the support of my field-based research coordinator in Berlin, Katharina Börner. Using a variety of search terms like right-wing, Nazi, extremist, rechts, thor, steinar, neonazi, demo, and right, we identified images in the photographers' databases with far right content and then did a second sort to pull out images that contained symbols, iconography, brand names, representations of subcultural style, codes, and historical references. Finally, the digital archive also includes screen shots of the websites of several commercial brands that sell far right extremist clothing and products, and digital images I captured on the street in Berlin and other German cities. Such images included stickers, posters, graffiti, buttons, patches, banners, flags, clothing, and other products I observed in places like an antifascist rally, subways, bus stops, train stations, bathroom stall doors, sidewalks, stairwells, and commercial stores.

All told, we initially assembled 4,221 images, and then deleted 1,297 duplicate or irrelevant images (e.g., where a photographer had taken multiple images of the same scene or symbol from different angles). Many of the images then had to be "cleaned" and resized before they could be uploaded into Atlas.ti for coding. The final, original digital archive comprised 2,924 images. We coded both inductively and deductively, using a predetermined codebook but adding new codes as they emerged. Table 6 offers a list of sample codes and their frequencies to illustrate the scope of the digital image coding.

I use the word "initially" here to refer to the assembly of the digital images archive, because as it turned out, the archive did not ever become a finite entity. Over the years I continued to take additional screenshots and photographs as new brands, product lines, symbols, and coded references appeared. Moreover, at least a few dozen of the original 2,924 images were essentially duplicate images that we retained because I had photographed some clothing items or catalog images from multiple angles in order to show the larger context of the catalog page or frame. And some products could be associated with as many as three or four single images, because I had digitized separate codes, iconography, symbols, or text on a shirt sleeve, front, back, pocket, and so on, or had "zoomed in" on particular symbols in order to make text legible or parts of a symbol more visible. For this reason, quantitative descriptors for the archive turn out not to be very useful except to illustrate its scale and scope.

Table 6. Sample Codebook, Digital Image Coding

CODE	FREQUENCY	DEFINITION
Brands	695	Brands of clothing
Nazieraref	534	Reference to the Nazi era, such as images of Nazi soldiers, reference to Hitler, etc.; may overlap with USEDBYNAZIS
Usedbynazis	429	Symbols used by Nazi party directly, e.g., runic symbols, swastika, flag colors, etc.
Resistance	317	Reference to resistance to mainstream society/ societal norms
Auton-Nationalist	306	Autonomous Nationalists/ far right and right-wing extremist style imitating radical left style (all black etc.)
Nationalpride	295	Refer to or aim to evoke pride; including national flags, national colors, the word "Stolz," etc.
Useofenglish	238	Codes and symbols, slogans in English
Coopted-brands	234	Co-opted brands (New Balance, Lonsdale, etc.) or brands modeled off those logos (Masterrace etc.)
Germanic	234	Reference to Germanic myths, old Germanic script, etc.; may be double-coded with OTHER HISTORICAL
Otherhistorical	203	Reference to other historical moments or eras that are not reflected in other codes, such as pre–Third Reich flag color, pre–WWII history, etc.
Militaryref	194	Direct or indirect military reference; imitate current or historical military uniforms, colors, patterns (camouflage etc.)
Othernations	189	Reference to other nations' extremist movements or legacies; symbols that reference other (real or perceived) liberation movements; gang culture from overseas, etc.
Oldskinhead	143	Old skinhead style of black boots, shaved heads, etc.
Othernordic	125	Nordic symbols that don't seem to fit in other categories

CODE	FREQUENCY	DEFINITION
Panaryan	95	Reference to the global pan-Aryan movement, white power, etc.
Nordicmyth	75	Nordic/Norse mythology references, such as Nordic gods (THOR), mythological places (VALHALLA), etc.
Nordicviking	78	Viking references
Nordicimagery	70	Images evoking "Nordic," e.g., sailboats, icebergs, Scandinavian flags and town names, runic letters, Vikings
Alphanumeric	62	Codes that are sequences of letters or numbers
Masculinity	60	Instances of idealized images of males or females (i.e., inflated biceps of Vikings, broad-shouldered sailors, references to manliness or femininity in catalogs, etc.)
Totenkopf	53	Use of the "death's head" skull and crossbones
Colonialref	51	Reference to colonial era, German colonialism, countries formerly German colonies, to a "bigger Germany," etc.
Antiimmigrant	49	Symbols that are anti-immigrant, Islamophobic, xenophobic, etc.
Antisemitic	25	Anti-Semitic references
Bricolage	21	When two or more cultural references or symbols are combined; stitching together of disparate elements into a new symbols; layering of symbols

Image Analysis

The analysis of the image archive took place in several phases, starting with a year of coding and analysis during a research sabbatical in 2011–12. First, all images in the initial archive were coded in Atlas.ti, which essentially entailed assigning a "tag" to a portion of an image to enable them to be sorted and analyzed at a later date. Images were kept whole unless they had been digitized in parts (e.g., to zoom in on a sleeve, or a logo), in which case there were multiple images for one clothing item, for example. Any given image might thus have multiple "tags" or codes associated with it, depending on the complexity of the references within the image. While this first round of coding has some quantitative value in terms of illustrating the scale and scope of the project, its primary utility was in helping break the digital archive down into manageable, sortable categories. This enabled me to then study groups of images by code, so that I could examine the hundreds of images with Nordic references, or all fifty-three of the images that contained a *Totenkopf* (death's head) as a single group.

Following this initial coding in Atlas.ti, I analyzed images according to groups of codes. I did not analyze every image within each group but rather spent much more time with individual images and clusters of images from each category, focused this time on how the symbols were being used, what the codes meant, and what groups of codes as a unit—such as "Nordic symbols"—might mean for our understanding of the appeal of far right symbols more generally.

This slow process required me to broaden my methodological skills considerably. I had the tremendous stroke of luck to be nominated during this period to spend a year in residence as a fellow at the Morphomata Center for Advanced Studies in the Humanities at the University of Köln during the three-year cycle in which Morphomata's global fellows were studying images of death in contexts across various eras and geographies. This second dedicated year for this project away from my teaching and administrative responsibilities in the United States was, of course, extraordinarily valuable for my analysis and writing. But my year with a group of art historians and literary scholars who were also studying what Morphomata called "figurations"—images, symbols, and other visual and material representations—was more helpful methodologically than I could have anticipated. As I listened to the group of mostly humanities scholars present their work and observed their use of images in their own analyses, my use of images in my own work began to evolve. I found myself considering the images as more than just data points—more than a collection of thousands of visual representations of symbols. Instead, I found myself slowing down, spending more time considering individual symbols in context. My colleagues' feedback on my work encouraged me to look at symbols in the context of the entire photograph, for example. This included taking notice of the setting in which the symbol was present—such as a protest march—as well as the position, facial expressions, and activities of other youth, counterprotesters, and police around the individual wearing the clothing. For catalog and website products, I paid increasing attention to the model's musculature and tattoos, their haircuts and facial expressions, the background imagery, the colors and form of the script, and the framing. This same point—that context mattered—would later be echoed in interviews when youth insisted that the meaning of a symbol couldn't be interpreted absent its context. It was not enough, I learned, to analyze an image of a T-shirt on its own—each product needed to be understood within the contextual clues provided in a catalog photo (with model, background etc.), the context of the person wearing the product, or its surrounding environment.

The decoding process was also slow and deliberate. I already knew the meaning of some symbols—like 88 and 18—but had to spend considerable time disentangling the meanings of others. I spent significant time consulting historical sources and speaking with antifascist experts and scholars in the field. My native German research assistants were also very helpful throughout the decoding process. Methodologically, I drew on literature on iconography and iconology in my efforts to understand the symbol usage, particularly for the work on myths and fantastical aspirations of nationhood. As I described in the introduction, I found especially insightful Panofsky's work on the meaning of images and how they can be interpreted, such as his assertion that images' meaning is linked to stories and allegories that convey some broader idea or notion, such as Faith, Luxury, or Wisdom—or, in the case of my work, Nation.[1] Allegorical images have what Ernst Cassirer calls "symbolical values," meaning that the image is a "symptom of something else."[2] The discovery of this "something else"—of the "symbolical values" (which Panofsky suggests may be unknown even to the artist—or in my case the graphic designer) is the object of iconology—the method of interpreting images.[3] Thus, images that convey allegories about the Nation use particular iconographical and compositional forms that actually say "something else"—they hold other symbolic values that must be detected, decoded, and interpreted.

Despite these efforts, there are no guarantees as to the "correctness" of my interpretations, as I explain in the introduction. Symbols are multivocal, and the coded products deliberately convey multiple meanings in order to avoid legal problems and social stigma. In some cases, interpretation of a given symbol or product is fairly straightforward, as in the case of widely recognized brands that market to the far right, have a strong consumer base in the far right, or have a history of far right engagement. But in other cases—in the use of the historical flag colors red, black, and white, for example, or of photographs of youth in public settings, for example, I understand images or symbols to reflect right-wing or nationalist allegories and ideologies only when there is supporting evidence through multiple symbolic codes or cues (e.g., symbol is in a brand known for its association with the far right or worn by someone with multiple tattoos and images conveying far right ideology).[4] Even here, interpretation must be done cautiously because some of these symbols are also adopted and co-opted by left-wing groups, who may be in attendance at similar events in protest and could therefore be captured in a photo that I analyze, for example. I opted to steer a very conservative path in terms of image selection, using only symbols where I felt confident that multiple contextual clues indicate a clear link to right-wing extremist and far right ideology.

Phase II: Interviews and Fieldwork in German Vocational Schools

Although I had originally planned to write this book based on the digital archive alone, I quickly found I was dissatisfied with my inability to answer a number of questions about the commercialization phenomenon. I knew little about the production process or how designers selected and embedded coded messaging into the clothing. I knew even less about how consumers interpreted the coded symbols, whether they understood them and how they deployed them. I only had anecdotal evidence of whether ordinary Germans understood the brands' significance, based on my conversations with German colleagues and friends. And there was little evidence to say whether public policy interventions—including but not limited to public and private bans on brands and symbols—were effective deterrents against the phenomenon, or if they might be spurring it on. I wondered whether youth might wear the clothing to school and cover it up, whether they took notice of bans, and how school principals and teachers felt about them. While I analyzed the image archive, I gradually began to think about conducting fieldwork to address some of those questions.

All fieldwork has limits, and I knew that—given that I had a full-time teaching job and a family back in New York—I would not be able to do the kind of full ethnographic study that I would ordinarily design. I also knew I had to put some boundaries around the kinds of questions I could focus on now and set aside the questions I had to leave for other projects and other researchers. Ultimately, I narrowed the project to a focus on the reception side of the phenomenon, because my primary interest is in the youth/consumers themselves. I decided to base the fieldwork in vocational schools because I knew they were a site where educators were consciously thinking about how to reach youth who were engaged in various dimensions of antidemocratic, xenophobic, and extremist behaviors. With funding from the Spencer Foundation, I thus launched a second phase to the study that involved fieldwork and interviews in two schools.

Table 7. Interviewees' Apprenticeship
Occupations

OCCUPATION NAME	NUMBER OF APPRENTICES INTERVIEWED
Scaffold builder	9
Concrete layer	7
Masonry	7
Interior carpentry/ furniture builder (Tischler)*	5
Technical high school degree (Fachabi Bauwesen)	4
Technical conservation assistant (Denkmal Technischer Assistant)	3
Roofer	3
Construction mechanic	2
Building energy design	2
Civil engineering technician (Tiefbaufacharbeiter)	2
Exterior carpentry (Zimmerer)*	2
Technical assistant (Technischer Assistant, TA)	2
Conservation (Denkmalschutz)	1
Electrician	1
Systems mechanic (Anlagemechaniker)	1
TOTAL	51

*For the purposes of this book, I refer to both Tischler
and Zimmerer as "carpenters."

Table 8. Interviewee Information

PSEUDONYM	AGE	FIRST SCHOOL DEGREE	BORN IN	OCCUPATION
Thomas	18	Middle (Realschule)	Berlin-Wedding	Building energy design
Johann	17	Middle (MSA)*	Berlin	Building energy design
Gabriel	25	No degree named	Berlin	Conservation
Felix	19	Middle (MSA)	Berlin	Technical conservation
Rainer	18	Middle (MSA) (KSSF)	Berlin-Wilmersdorf	Technical conservation
Katrin	21	Middle (Realschule)	Berlin	Technical high school degree
Paul	24	Middle (Realschule)	Berlin-Spandau	Construction mechanic
Mahmut	21	Middle (Realschule)	Berlin	Technical conservation
Finn	18	Middle (MSA)	Berlin-Chab	Electrician
Fabian	17	Expanded lower (Erw. Hauptschule)	Berlin	Roofer
Klaus	21	Middle (Realschule)	Berlin	Roofer
Tobias	21	Expanded lower (Erw. Hauptschule)	Königs Wuster-hausen	Civil engineering technician
Dennis	19	Expanded lower (Erw. Hauptschule)	Berlin-Neukölln	Civil engineering technician
Daniel	20	Technical University (Fachhoch-schulreife)	Neumünster	Carpentry (Tischler)
Lukas	22	Middle (Realschule)	Berlin	Carpentry (Tischler)

PSEUDONYM	AGE	FIRST SCHOOL DEGREE	BORN IN	OCCUPATION
Niel	20	Higher (Abitur)	Bernau	Construction mechanic
Max	21	Technical University (Fachhoch-schule)	Berlin	Carpentry (Tischler)
Christian	18	Middle (MSA)	Berlin-Spandau	Carpentry (Tischler)
Leonardo	19	Expanded lower (Erw. Hauptschule)	Berlin	Roofer
Artur	22	Expanded lower (Erw. Hauptschule)	Berlin-Reinickendorf	Concrete layer
Cihan	23	Expanded lower (Erw. Hauptschule)	Berlin-Chab	Concrete layer
Heike	22	Middle (MSA)	Siegburg NRW	Concrete layer
Gregory	17	Expanded lower (Erw. Hauptschule)	Berlin-Wedding	Systems mechanic
Justin	17	Middle (MSA)	Berlin	Carpentry (Tischler)
Tim	22	Expanded lower (Erw. Hauptschule)	Berlin	Masonry
Bernd	22	Middle (Realschule)	Berlin	Concrete layer
Kevin	39	Dropped out of Abitur	Braunschweig	Technical high school degree
Gerhard	22	Lower (Hauptschule)	Leisnick, Sachsen	Scaffold builder
Christoph	21	Lower (Hauptschule)	Leipzig	Scaffold builder

Table 8. Continued

PSEUDONYM	AGE	FIRST SCHOOL DEGREE	BORN IN	OCCUPATION
Hans	27	Expanded lower (Erw. Hauptschule)	Bergen, Rügen	Scaffold builder
Markus	21	Middle (MSA)	Dschabel, Kazakhstan	Technical assistant (TA)
Julian	28	Middle (Realschule)	Rostock	Technical high school degree
Simon	20	Middle (Realschule)	Berlin-Pankow	Technical high school degree
Erdinc	21	Expanded lower (Erw. Hauptschule)	Berlin	Concrete layer
Benjamin	22	Middle (Realschule)	Berlin	Technical assistant (TA)
Manfred	22	n/a	Berlin-Lichtenberg	Scaffold builder
Karl	18	Middle (Realschule)	Berlin Chb	Scaffold builder
Timo	22	Lower (Hauptschule)	Braunschweig	Scaffold builder
Micheal	34	Higher (Abitur)	Altentreptow	Carpentry (Zimmerer)
Steffen	24	Expanded middle (Erw. Realschule)	Berlin	Carpentry (Zimmerer)
Joachim	23	Expanded lower (Erw. Hauptschule)	Berlin	Masonry
Ingo	18	Expanded lower (Erw. Hauptschule)	Berlin	Masonry
Holger	25	Higher (Abitur)	Berlin-Reinickendorf	Scaffold builder

PSEUDONYM	AGE	FIRST SCHOOL DEGREE	BORN IN	OCCUPATION
Georg	21	Middle (MSA)	Heningdorf	Scaffold builder
Oliver	23	Expanded lower (Erw. Hauptschule)	Borken NRW	Scaffold builder
Justus	21	Lower (Hauptschule)	Berlin	Concrete layer
Ulrich	17	Lower (Hauptschule)	Polen	Masonry
Eckart	21	11th grade	Strausberg	Masonry
Jan	17	Middle (MSA)	Berlin	Masonry
Hayri	21	Expanded lower (Erw. Hauptschule)	Berlin-Spandau	Concrete layer
Martin	16	Lower (Hauptschule)	Berlin	Masonry

*Both Realschule and MSA are the "middle" degree; "erw." is short for the word "expanded."

Case Selection and Access

Construction trade vocational schools were of particular interest because I knew from my previous book that the construction trades have relatively high far right youth participation, and I would thus be able to gain access to a population of youth who were high risk for far right and extremist participation or who had spent much of their lives around other youth who were part of those scenes.[5] As I explained in the introduction, a lucky coincidence helped my research design when I discovered that the two vocational schools for construction trades in Berlin had inadvertently set up a natural experiment, since one had implemented a comprehensive ban on ideological and extremist symbols, while the other had not. I refer to these two schools by pseudonyms—the Flusser school and the Erker school. The Flusser school has implemented a comprehensive policy banning the display of all extremist symbols, brands, logos, and codes, including but not limited to those reflecting right-wing extremism. At the Erker school, there is no banning policy; students can freely display brands and symbols unless they are legally banned, like the swastika. The schools' student populations are quite similar, drawing largely from the same region and youth backgrounds, and students do not directly choose the schools—they are assigned based on their selection of occupation. The similarities in the student bodies and the variation in policy decisions thus set up a naturally occurring, quasi-experimental design, providing the opportunity to examine whether and how the bans affect the use of coded symbols among youth and the participation of youth in the right wing more generally.

Because these two schools are the only construction trade schools in Berlin, all youth from Berlin and much of the surrounding state of Brandenburg who want to train in a construction field become students at one of these two schools. Additionally, Berlin is one of only a few locations where young people can train to become scaffold builders. Scaffold builder apprentices travel to Berlin for residential sessions of several weeks at a time, staying in a dorm and attending theoretical training in school intensively before they return to their home cities for further practical training, meaning that I was able to interview young people from other cities throughout eastern Germany. Moreover, I knew from my previous research at the same school that scaffold builder classrooms were likely to have higher numbers of far right youth.

I took several trips to Berlin—ranging from a few days to six weeks—to establish my relationships with the two schools, gain access and permission, develop preliminary instruments, and present my research plans to teachers and principals in adherence with Berlin School Senate rules (which require that the faculty at each school approve the research). Research procedures and instruments were reviewed and approved by a human subject study panel (Institutional Review Board) of my home university as well as by the Berlin School Senate. Data collection began in January 2013. Interviews were conducted from January 2013 through March 2014.

We recruited youth to participate in the interviews by soliciting volunteers through brief classroom announcements. We oversampled the occupational field that I knew from previous research to have historically high far right wing participation and attitudes (scaffold builders) as a strategy to ensure that we had some students in our sample who were actively or formerly engaged in the far right scene. But we also intentionally recruited from other classrooms and interviewed students who were not far right. Because all these students are in career fields with a reputation for far right engagement and in schools with histories of far right youth presence, I describe the youth we interviewed as youth who are in and around the far right scene. This is an important, and deliberate, sampling choice—I wanted to interview both youth who identified as far right wing as well as youth who were "at risk" for far right participation and/or who had rejected the far right even though much of their lives were embedded in neighborhoods, schools, and workplaces where their fellow youth, employers, bosses, and colleagues were far right.

In so doing, I hoped to avoid what Mabel Berezin has described as a key methodological problem for scholars of far right movements—namely, that researchers who study the right tend to sample on the dependent variable, forgetting that the far right exists as part of an entire spectrum.[6] On the contrary, the approach I followed here aims to study not only youth who are already far right but those who are in and around the scene. This includes youth who dabble in far right scenes, going to right wing concerts and festivals but not engaging in violence; youth who live in neighborhoods and are educated in classrooms with far right peers; and youth who may be very opposed to the far right but for whom far right youth subcultures are a daily experience in some way. These varied youth turned out to be excellent informants of what the coded symbols mean to youth, why they wear brands associated with the far right, and what school and legal bans mean to them and to far right youth in their social networks.

Ultimately, with the help of my field coordinator and research assistant based in Berlin, I conducted sixty-two interviews in 2013–14[7] with youth (N=51) and their teachers (N=11), which focused on how young people interpret the brands and symbols and the effect of school bans on the game-playing nature of coded extremist symbols.

We conducted interviews with fifty-one youth aged sixteen to thirty-nine, with an average age of twenty-one. All but two of the youth interviewed were born in Germany, though the two born elsewhere (in Poland and in Kazakhstan) grew up in Berlin. Four of the youth (who were born in Germany) had names that are traditionally Turkish in origin, indicating at least partial Turkish heritage. Two of the fifty-one youth were female, which is consistent with male-dominated fields in construction. Although some of the brands have limited women's product lines, there are far fewer options, and the iconography tends to contain fewer coded symbols, compared with the men's clothing (see chapter 6 for further discussion), and so the study intentionally focused on young men as the primary target group. Although I did not officially restrict the sample to men, we knew we were likely to have primarily male volunteers in construction trades, since many of the classrooms do not have any women in the cohort. The two young women in the study happened to be in classrooms where we recruited volunteers, and each volunteered to participate in an interview.

The average length of the interview was fifty minutes, although they ranged from about a half hour to an hour and a half, depending on how much any given youth elaborated on the interview questions and their interpretation of images. In order to ensure continuity and standardize the interview process as much as possible, given the fact that I had to travel back and forth to Berlin from New York or Cologne during data collection, my native German field coordinator was present for every interview, even when I was the lead interviewer. All interviews were conducted in German.

Scaffold builders (N=9), who we had deliberately oversampled, made up nearly 20 percent of the fifty-one interviewees. Concrete layer (N=7) and masonry (N=6) apprentices interviews comprised an additional 25 percent of the final sample, with the remaining interviewees spread across a variety of construction fields, from roofing and carpentry to more specific fields related to historic preservation, building energy design, and street construction (see table 7 and table 8). We also conducted interviews with eleven teachers and school principals in order to examine their experience with coded and commercial right-wing extremist symbols in the school, their schools' policies on banning, and whether they enforce those bans, but there was insufficient space in this manuscript to include the teacher data in any great depth. Chapter 5 draws in a limited way on the teacher interviews as supplemental information on the issue of whether and how school bans are enforced.

Youth interviews aimed to understand whether young people own or wear any of the banned clothing, how they define their own sense of style and its meaning to them, how they feel about school bans of symbols or clothing brands, and how they interpret a series of images depicting far right symbols in clothing. Using a semistructured interview instrument, we asked youth to describe their own personal style and its evolution over time, and to talk about how important their style was to them. We asked what brands of clothing they like, how similar or different their own personal style is to that of their closest friends, and whether their style changes depending on where they are (school, work, home, parties, etc.). We asked their opinions about school bans of clothing, why they think such bans exist, how they became aware of the bans, and whether they had seen them enforced. In the second half of the interview, we asked specifically about brands of clothing known within the far right scene. We talked about whether they or people they knew owned any of the brands, how they acquired it, and why they own it. They talked about how the clothing makes them feel and what kind of message they think it sends to people who see them wearing it.

Finally, perhaps the most important data to emerge from the interviews came from the portion of the interview when we showed them a notebook with thirty-four images of clothing, tattoos, and other subcultural styles and asked them to tell us what they saw in each of the images—the symbols, iconography, and styles. We asked what they thought about the clothing and what kind of message, if any, they think the clothing, symbols, or styles might be trying to send. The images included professional photographers' shots of youth as well as screenshots and digital photos I captured of products sold by brands popular with the far right. The photographer's images were of youth deploying symbols in normal situations—at soccer matches, protests, outdoor gatherings, and so on. The codes in the images included alphanumeric codes like 14, 18, 168:1, and 88, historical codes like desert fox, Madagascar, and Expedition Tibet, as well as contemporary codes valorizing violence or antipolice messages like Kategorie C and ACAB. They included xenophobic iconography like "Killer Döner," antileftist symbols like anti-antifa, transnational codes like a jacket with the Swedish word *svastika*, Palestinian scarves, and products with English phrases. The images contained a wide variety of Nordic imagery, including landscapes, Viking warriors, runic letters, and references to Thor (see table 2 for a sample list of codes and their meaning). Following the image analysis, we asked directly about the far right youth scene for the first time in the interview, specifically asking youth to talk about their knowledge of the scene and whether they had observed any stylistic changes in recent years.

The interviews helped to refine what by then had emerged as two working explanations for why coded symbols might be attractive to youth—on the one hand, because they strengthen their sense of connection and self-identification with peers, while on the other hand, because they are a source of resistance and protest against the mainstream. I had also anticipated that institutional bans on symbols and clothing brands would produce resistance in the form of further manipulation of symbols and coding.

The project also included a limited—but not systematic—amount of ethnographic observation. Both my research assistant and I kept field notes and wrote reflective memos, observing academic and nonacademic school spaces and the surrounding neighborhoods (bus and tram stops, cafés, parks, etc.). We noted whether and how we observed if coded far right symbols were displayed or hidden by youth, and I took photographs of far right and antifascist symbols, iconography, posters, stickers, and logos whenever I encountered them, on subways, graffiti, posters, bathroom stalls, patches and pins on backpacks, or on the outside of buildings.

Analysis

The overall project—including the digital archive and the fieldwork—is guided by the tenets of grounded theory, which has as a primary aim the generation of explanatory theories rather than the testing of theory.[8] The multiple phases of research and data collection were essential to this process. Based on the analysis of the digital archive, I generated preliminary conceptual frameworks that were then elaborated on through continued data gathering and analysis during the fieldwork. Observational notes were typed up as notes and memos. All interviews were fully transcribed in German. All the student interviews were coded and analyzed in a qualitative software program (Atlas.ti) using the constant comparative analysis method, in which observational moments and transcript incidents, codes, and categories of codes are constantly compared with one another in order to generate theoretical categories and frameworks.[9] I translated all quotes used in the manuscript into English, and the accuracy and style of all translations were cross-checked by a native German research assistant in Berlin. Teacher interviews were fully transcribed but were not coded; rather, I read transcripts in toto, in order to gain an understanding of the history of teacher discussions about the bans, their understandings of the symbols, and whether and how the bans are enforced. Selected quotes from teacher and principal interviews are used here illustratively, particularly around the issue of the enforcement of school bans (see chapter 5).

Note on the Use of Antifascist Sources

Some of the background and descriptive detail in this manuscript relies on articles or source material published on websites or from organizations with a clear antifascist ideological stance. There is a wide range of antifascist research sources on the far right in Germany—including some, like apabiz, that operate as physical libraries and archives and are among the most comprehensive and largest collections of far right material and primary data on the far right in Germany. Others use web-based platforms to publish articles and information about the far right. These web-based articles were important sources for illustrating antifascist reactions to far right commercial activity, such as store openings or brand expansions, and as sources to describe far right commercialization itself—such as the reported connections between the brands and the organized far right or far right bands that I describe in the introduction. The use of antifascist sources is a valid and justifiable empirical decision; antifascist sources are widely used in Germany as primary data—by journalists, researchers, politicians, and even the intelligence and police services—for their highly accurate and expert information on the far right wing. But the use of antifascist sources raises some ethical issues that should not be ignored, because the methods used by antifascist groups to obtain information are not always clear. Moreover, some antifascist organizations have anti-democratic aims or support the use of violence to achieve their goals. I cite the website indymedia, for example, twice in this book as a source of information on the meaning of right-wing codes and about the reaction to a store selling the brand Erik & Sons in a Berlin shopping mall. Indymedia was shut down by the German government in August 2017—well after I had used the site as a source—in the wake of the violent protests at the Group of 20 summit meeting in Hamburg. It is important to emphasize that my limited use of antifascist sources relies on information their activists communicate in published form on their websites. Whenever possible, I cross-checked this factual information with other sources, citing more traditional source citations in addition to the antifascist sources. I share this note in the interest of research transparency, particularly for researchers who may be newly entering this field and confronting such ethical and research dilemmas for the first time.

Conclusion

Two methodological innovations in this manuscript may be of particular interest to future researchers. First, visual and material culture—captured in historical and contemporary photographs, artifacts, clothing items, posters, banners, stickers, license plates, and more—proved to be a critical empirical domain for understanding the appeal of extremist thinking. But it is the combination of visual data and qualitative interviews that proved most critical for this project. Without the digital archive, I would have overlooked dozens of coded symbols, key images, and right-wing clothing and products that youth display and wear. The archive on its own would also have been inadequate, however, because the images alone cannot tell us why youth are utilizing these symbols or whether and how public policy decisions—like school bans—have an impact on their consumption of those symbols. The qualitative interviews with youth in and around the far right scene were invaluable to my understanding of the brands, the symbols, and their meanings. In particular, youth's analysis of the selection of thirty-four images was especially critical to my understanding of how the symbols and codes are received and interpreted.

Second, my deliberate sample of youth who are "in and around" the far right scene proved to be a particularly useful set of informants. Future researchers ought to consider studying not only youth who are in the "core" of extremist and radical right-wing movements, but also those who are on the "periphery" or in interstitial spaces, moving in and out of far right or extremist scenes throughout their adolescence and young adulthood. In my research, youth on the periphery of the far right proved to be just as—and in some ways, more—informative compared to youth who were or are actively engaged in the far right.

NOTES

Preface and Acknowledgments

1. Stevens, Mitchell, Cynthia Miller-Idriss, and Seteney Shami. Forthcoming. *Seeing the World: How Universities Make Knowledge in a Global Era*. Princeton, NJ: Princeton University Press.

Introduction. Selling the Right Wing

1. The Billy Bragg phrase used as an epigraph for this chapter was quoted in Casey, Michael. 2009. *Che's Afterlife: The Legacy of an Image*. New York: Vintage, p. 298. The phrase comes from the lyrics of Bragg's 1988 single "Waiting For the Great Leap Forwards." See the Billy Bragg website for the full song lyrics, http://www.billybragg.co.uk/music/singles.php?singleID=36&songID=47, accessed May 24, 2017.

2. Rogers, Thomas. 2014. "Heil Hipster: The Young Neo-Nazis Trying to Put a Stylish Face on Hate." *Rolling Stone Magazine*. June 24, http://www.rollingstone.com/culture/news/heil-hipster-the-young-neo-nazis-trying-to-put-a-stylish-face-on-hate-20140623, accessed May 2, 2017; Rogers, Thomas. 2015. "Authoritarian Outfitters." *New Republic*. March 4, https://newrepublic.com/article/121199/germanys-thor-steinar-neo-nazis-favorite-clothing-brand, accessed May 1, 2017.

3. U.S. Library of Congress, folder "Kitsch," LOT 9856 (G) and folder "Souvenirs decorated with Nazi symbols," LOT 5212 (F).

4. Article from *Der Feuerreiter Köln*, handwritten date 1.6.1933 and article from *Berliner Illustrierter Zeitung*, May 28, 1933, in U.S. Library of Congress, folder "Kitsch," LOT 9856 (G).

5. Also see the literature on propaganda and the Third Reich, particularly Nicholas O'Shaugnessy's 2016 book *Selling Hitler: Propaganda and the Nazi Brand*. London: C. Hurst.

6. Beirich, Heidi. "Essay: Racist Music," SPLC Intelligence Files, retrieved December 26, 2010, http: //www.splcenter.org/get-informed/intelligence-files/ideology/racist-music/racist-music; Miller-Idriss, Cynthia, and Elizabeth Knauer. Forthcoming. "Buying into the Far Right: Material Culture and Right-Wing Consumption." In *The Cultural Dimensions of Far Right Politics*, edited by Fabian Virchow and Cynthia Miller-Idriss. Wiesbaden: VS Verlag; Simi, Pete, and Robert Futrell. 2010. *American Swastika: Inside the White Power Movement's Hidden Spaces of Hate*. New York: Rowman and Littlefield.

7. Paul, Gerhard. 1995. "Rechtsextremismus im vereinten Deutschland." Pp. 33–46 in *Gewalt unter Jugendlichen, Rechtsextremismus und Fremdenfeindlichkeit*.

Erfurt: Friedrich Ebert Stiftung. Steinmetz, George. 1997. "Social Class and the Reemergence of the Radical Right in Contemporary Germany." Pp. 335–68 in *Reworking Class*, edited by John Hall. Ithaca, NY: Cornell University Press.

8. Stylistic and aesthetic changes in far right German youth culture can be traced to the emergence of the Autonomous Nationalist movement in the early 2000s, which has been well-documented by German scholars (see especially, e.g., Schedler, Jan, and Alexander Häusler, eds. 2011. *Autonome Nationalisten: Neonazismus in Bewegung*. Wiesbaden: VS Verlag). The commercialization and coding I analyze in this book began shortly after the Autonomous Nationalist movement changed the aesthetics of far right youth protest by co-opting the style and strategies of far left activists. See chapter 2 for a brief discussion; also see Peters, Jürgen, and Christoph Schulze, eds. 2009. *Autonome Nationalisten: Die Modernisierung neofaschistischer Jugendkultur*. Munich: Unrast Verlag.

9. Nolan, Rachel. 2008b. "Wearing Identity on Its Sleeve, German Far Right Gets a Makeover." Forward.com. May 8, http://forward.com/news/13346/wearing-iden tity-on-its-sleeve-german-far-right-g-01822/, accessed May 1, 2017; Staud, Toralf. 2005. *Moderne Nazis: Die neuen Rechten und der Aufstieg der NPD*. Köln: Verlag Kiepenheuer & Witsch; also see Nolan, Rachel. 2008a. "Neo-Nazi Fashion: Thor Steinar and the Changing Look of the German Far Right." In *Spiegel Online*. November 20, http://www.spiegel.de/international/germany/neo-nazi-fashion -thor-steinar-and-the-changing-look-of-the-german-far-right-a-587746.html, accessed May 1, 2017.

10. Rogers (2015).

11. Osuch, Florian, and Moritz Eluek. 2016. " 'Thor Steinar' mit Millionenumsatz." *Antifa Infoblatt*. January 25, https://www.antifainfoblatt.de/artikel/%E 2%80%9Ethor-steinar%E2%80%9C-mit-millionenumsatz, accessed May 1, 2017; Wedekamp, Johannes. 2008. "Tønsberg macht zu, Tønsberg macht auf." *Zeit Online blog Störungsmelder*. February 4, http://blog.zeit.de/stoerung smelder/2008/02/04/t%C3%B8nsberg-macht-zu-t%C3%B8nsberg-macht -auf_223, accessed May 1, 2017.

12. Osuch and Eluek (2016).

13. Hammerbacher, Michael, ed. 2015. *Kennzeichen und Symbole der rechtsextremen Szene: Bausteine der Prävention von Rechtsextremismus und Gruppenbezogener Menschenfeindlichkeit in der beruflichen Bildung Nr. 6. Eine Handreichung für Demokratie und Vielfalt*. Edited by OSZ für Demokratie und Vielfalt. Berlin: DEVI e.V. Verein für Demokratie und Vielfalt in Schule und beruflicher Bildung.

14. See discussion in the Amadeu Antonio Foundation's digital platform *Belltower News*: Garrel, Théo. 2015. "Phalanx Europa: Kleidung von Identitären für Identitäre." *Belltower News: Netz für digitale Zivilgesellschaft*. January 26, http://www.belltower.news/artikel/phalanx-europa-kleidung-von-iden tit%C3%A4ren-f%C3%BCr-identit%C3%A4re-10007, accessed May 18, 2017.

15. All names are pseudonyms. See tables 7 and 8 for information about interviewees, as well as discussion in the methodological appendix.

16. The conglomerate, International Brands General Trading (IBGT), listed their managing director as Mohammed Aweidah. See Osuch and Eluek 2016; also see Berliner Morgenpost. 2009. "Arabischer Investor kauft Thor Steinar," March 20,

http: //www.morgenpost.de/berlin/article1058671/Arabischer_Investor_kauft_
Thor_Steinar.html, accessed January 11, 2011.

17. Rogers (2015).
18. Osuch and Eluek (2016).
19. linksunten. 2010. "Erik & Sons weiter im Berlin Europacenter." linksunten.
    indymedia.org. December 29, https://linksunten.indymedia.org/de/node/31207,
    accessed May 2, 2017; Osuch and Eluek (2016).
20. Also see Kidd, Laura Klosterman. 2015. "The Nazi Aesthetic in Fashion." In *Berg
    Encyclopedia of World Dress and Fashion*. Berg Fashion Library. New York: Berg.
21. "Phalanx-Klamotten in deiner Clique, deiner Schule, beim Fortgehen oder
    beim Sport zu tragen positioniert dich klar. Es ist eine Aussage, eine ästhetisch-
    politische Tat: Gegen das Multikulti-Empire, gegen tatenlose Spießer und
    visionslose Pessimisten. Nein zur Überflutung Europas, Nein zu dump-
    fem Konsum—ja zum Heroismus." http: //www.identitaere-generation.info/
    phalanx-europa-ein-identitaeres-label/, accessed January 16, 2017. As of May 21,
    2017, the link to this pro-Identitäre website is broken; a message tells visitors
    the website will be accessible again soon.
22. Miller-Idriss and Knauer (Forthcoming).
23. All cited figures from the 2014 elections are from Mudde, Cas. 2014. "The Far
    Right in the 2014 European Elections: Of Earthquakes, Cartels and Designer
    Fascists." In *Washington Post*. May 30, https://www.washingtonpost.com/news/
    monkey-cage/wp/2014/05/30/the-far-right-in-the-2014-european-elections-of
    -earthquakes-cartels-and-designer-fascists/?utm_term=.e1b6d55f05e6, accessed
    May 2, 2017. Mudde points out that despite these numbers, it is important not
    to overly sensationalize the overall rise in the far right, particularly because far
    right parties lost seats in seven countries in 2014 and because five far right par-
    ties also lost their representatives in Brussels in the 2014 elections. For a more
    detailed analysis, see Mudde (2014); also see media coverage at, e.g., Higgins,
    Andrew, and James Kanter. 2014. "Fringe Groups Gain in European Voting." In
    New York Times. May 25, https://www.nytimes.com/2014/05/26/world/europe/
    turnout-in-european-parliament-election-hits-record-low.html?_r=0, accessed
    May 2, 2017; Traynor, Ian. 2015. "Europe's Far Right Gets the Attention, but the
    Left Is Making the Political Running." *Guardian*. January 17, https://www.the
    guardian.com/world/2015/jan/18/europe-greece-far-right-anti-austerity-left-pow
    er-syriza-podemos, accessed May 2, 2017.
24. See *Spiegel Online*. 2016. "Die Ergebnisse der Landtagswahlen im Überblick."
    March 14, http: //www.spiegel.de/politik/deutschland/wahlen-2016-die-ergeb
    nisse-der-landtagswahlen-im-ueberblick-a-1082093.html, accessed February 6,
    2017. For a comprehensive overview, see Mudde, Cas, ed. 2017. *The Populist
    Radical Right: A Reader*. New York: Routledge. Also see Marcks, Holger. 2016.
    "Don't Call Me Right! The Strategy of Normalization in German Right-Wing
    Extremism." Pp. 65–72 in *Trouble on the Far Right: Contemporary Right-Wing
    Strategies and Practices in Europe*, edited by Maik Fielitz and Laura Laloire.
    Bielefeld: Transcript Verlag; and Saal, Oliver. 2016. "On Patrol with the New
    German Vigilantes." Pp. 73–78 *Trouble on the Far Right: Contemporary Right-
    Wing Strategies and Practices in Europe*, edited by Maik Fielitz and Laura Laloire.
    Bielefeld: Transcript Verlag.

25. For media coverage on these events, see, e.g., Margaronis, Maria. 2012. "Fear and Loathing in Athens: The Rise of Golden Dawn and The Far Right." October 26, http: //www.theguardian.com/world/2012/oct/26/golden-dawn-greece-far-right; and BBC News. 2016. "German Far-Right Pegida Founder Bachmann in Race Trial." April 19, http: //www.bbc.com/news/world-europe-36079533, accessed April 19, 2016.

26. Bonikowski, Bart. 2016. "Nationalism in Settled Times." *Annual Review of Sociology* 42: 427–49.

27. As detailed in the Swiss OSCE Chairmanship conclusions to a November 2014 OSCE Conference on Anti-Semitism, http: //www.osce.org/odihr/126710?down load=true, accessed November 15, 2014.

28. See the Pew Research Center Global Attitudes and Trends Report at http: // www.pewglobal.org/2014/05/12/a-fragile-rebound-for-eu-image-on-eve-of-eu ropean-parliament-elections/pg-2014-05-12-eu-0-09/, accessed November 15, 2014. For other recent historical data on the far right, see the 2015 Verfassungsschutzbericht, available at https: //www.verfassungsschutz.de/de/oef fentlichkeitsarbeit/publikationen/verfassungsschutzberichte/vsbericht-2015; Braun, Stephan, Alexander Geisler, and Martin Gerster. 2009. "Die extreme Rechte: Einleitende Betrachtungen." Pp. 9–20 in *Strategien der extremen Rechten: Hintergründe, Analysen, Antworten*, edited by V. S. Verlag für Sozialwissenschaften. Wiesbaden: VS Verlag für Sozialwissenschaften; and Agentur für soziale Perspektiven e.V., Hg. 2009. *Versteckspiel: Lifestyle, Symbole und Codes von neonazistischen und extrem rechten Gruppen*. Antifaschistisches Pressearchiv und Bildungszentrum Berlin.

29. Compared with 43 percent in 2014. Of the respondents in 2016, 41.4 percent said that Muslims should be banned from immigrating to Germany (compared with 36.6 percent in 2014). See Decker, Oliver, Johannes Kiess, Eva Eggers, and Elmar Brähler. 2016. "Die 'Mitte' Studie 2016: Ergebnisse und Langzeitverlauf." Pp. 23–66 in *Die enthemmte Mitte: Autoritäre und rechtsextreme Einstellung in Deutschland*, edited by Oliver Decker, Johannes Kiess, and Elmar Brähler. Giessen: Psychosozial Verlag, p. 50.

30. The Verfassungsschutzbericht is an annual report issued by the Federal Office for the Protection of the Constitution (Bundesamt für Verfassungsschutz) and is available at https: //www.verfassungsschutz.de/de/oeffentlichkeitsarbeit/publika tionen/verfassungsschutzberichte/vsbericht-2015, accessed February 7, 2017. For further discussion of trends in right-wing violence, see Köhler, Daniel. 2017a. *Right-Wing Terrorism in the 21st Century: The "National Socialist Underground" and the History of Terror from the Far Right in Germany*. New York: Routledge.

31. Altman, Anna. 2014. "Radical Chic." *New York Times*. July 2, https://op-talk .blogs.nytimes.com/2014/07/02/radical-chic/, accessed May 2, 2017.

32. Office for the Protection of the Constitution (Bundesamt für Verfassungsschutz), http: //www.verfassungsschutz.brandenburg.de/cms/detail.php/bb2 .c.423435.de, accessed September 23, 2011.

33. Hammerbacher (2015).

34. See text of article 86a in English at http: //germanlawarchive.iuscomp.org/?s =86a&submit=, or in German at http: //www.strafgesetzbuch-stgb.de/stgb/86a .html. For a deeper comparative analysis of banning policies in Europe and the

United States, see Bleich, Erik. 2011. *The Freedom to Be Racist? How the United States and Europe Struggle to Preserve Freedom and Combat Racism.* New York: Oxford University Press.

35. See Thor Steinar's old logo, plates 11 and 12 and new logo, plate 3 for a comparison. While the old logo's iconography — in a red-and-white shield-like shape under the phrase "Ultimate Thule" on a hooded sweatshirt in plate 11, for example — combines two runes into a symbol that bears some resemblance to a swastika, the new logo, visible in plate 3 under the brand name Thor Steinar on the back of a T-shirt, is a simple "x" with two dots. The old logo is now back in use.

36. Pientka, Claudia, and Martin Knobbe. 2008. "Die Klamotte der Neonazis." *Stern.* December 21, http://www.stern.de/panorama/gesellschaft/thor-stein ar-die-klamotte-der-neonazis-3747124.html, accessed May 2, 2017.

37. For more information on this process, see the website of the German Patent and Brand Office and its discussion of brand protections at https://www.dpma .de/marke/markenschutz/, accessed May 2, 2017.

38. Radke, Johannes. 2008. "Hausverbot im Bundestag." *Der Tagesspiegel.* March 16, http://www.tagesspiegel.de/berlin/hausverbot-im-bundestag/1189634.html, accessed May 2, 2017. DieWeltOnline. 2010. "Universität verbietet 'Thor Steinar'-Kleidung." *Welt Online.* September 10, https://www.welt.de/vermischtes/arti cle9521785/Universitaet-verbietet-Thor-Steinar-Kleidung.html, accessed May 2, 2017.

39. The Trømso store closed in 2013, while the Tønsberg store — having already relocated after a previous lease ended — reopened under police protection, with dozens of protesters outside — in a new location in the east Berlin neighborhood of Weissensee. http: //www.morgenpost.de/berlin-aktuell/arti cle105209982/Thor-Steinar-Laden-eroeffnet-unter-Polizeischutz.html, accessed April 22, 2016.

40. Sherwin, Adam. 2014. "Outrage as Far-Right's Favourite Outfitter 'Thor Steinar' Opens Shop in Heart of London's Jewish Community." *Independent.* April 16, http://www.independent.co.uk/news/uk/home-news/outrage-as-far-rights-fa vourite-outfitter-thor-steinar-opens-shop-in-heart-of-londons-jewish-9265311 .html, accessed May 2, 2017.

41. Connolly, Kate. 2012. "Anger after German Shop Allegedly Namechecks Norwegian Mass Murderer." *Guardian.* March 6, https://www.theguardian.com/ world/2012/mar/06/germany-far-right, accessed May 2, 2017; *Spiegel Online.* 2012b. "Neo-Nazi Fashion: Thor Steinar Names New Store after Norwegian Killer." March 6, http://www.spiegel.de/international/germany/neo-nazi-fashion -thor-steinar-names-new-store-after-norwegian-killer-a-819611.html, accessed May 2, 2017.

42. Eliade, Mircea. 1957. *The Sacred and the Profane: The Nature of Religion.* San Diego: Harvest/HBJ. See also Attebery, Brian. 2014. *Stories about Stories: Fantasy and the Remaking of Myth.* New York: Oxford University Press, p. 37.

43. Davies, Douglas. 1988. "The Evocative Symbolism of Trees." Pp. 32–42 in *The Iconography of Landscape: Essays on the Symbolic Representation, Design, and Use of Past Environments,* edited by Stephen Daniels and Denis Cosgrove. New York: Cambridge University Press, p. 33.

44. Davies (1988: 33).
45. Patterson, Orlando. 2014. "Making Sense of Culture." *Annual Review of Sociology* 40: 1–30.
46. Miller-Idriss, Cynthia, and Bess Rothenberg. 2012. "Ambivalence, Pride, and Shame: Conceptualizations of German Nationhood." *Nations and Nationalism* 18(1): 132–55.
47. See, for example, Vozella, Laura, and Jenna Portnoy. 2015. "Virginia's McAuliffe Plans to Phase Out Confederate Flag License Plate." *Washington Post.* June 23, http: //www.washingtonpost.com/local/virginia-politics/virginias-mcauliffe -plans-to-phase-out-confederate-flag-license-plate/2015/06/23/bb8a1738-19b0- 11e5-93b7-5eddc056ad8a_story.html, accessed June 23, 2015.
48. Panofsky, Erwin. 1955. *Meaning in the Visual Arts.* Chicago: University of Chicago Press, pp. 31–35.
49. Panofsky (1955: 35).
50. Panofsky (1955: 38).
51. I am indebted to Arunima Gopinath for this concept, particularly as articulated during her 2013 lecture at the Morphomata Center for Advanced Studies, University of Cologne.
52. Miller-Idriss, Cynthia. 2009. *Blood and Culture: Youth, Right-Wing Extremism, and National Belonging in Contemporary Germany.* Durham, NC: Duke University Press.
53. See, e.g., Polletta, Francesca. 2001. "Collective Identity and Social Movements." *Annual Review of Sociology* 2001(27): 283–305; Polletta, Francesca. 1999. " 'Free Spaces' in Collective Action." *Theory and Society* 28: 1–38; Leach, Darcy K., and Sebastian Haunss. 2009. "Scenes and Social Movements." In *Culture, Social Movements, and Protest,* edited by Hank Johnston. Burlington, VT: Ashgate.
54. Bovier, Elke, and Klaus Boehnke. 1999. "Do Liberal Teachers Produce Violent and Xenophobic Students? An Empirical Study of German Ninth Graders and Their Teachers." *Teaching and Teacher Education* 15: 815–27.
55. Bacher, Johann. 2001. "In welchen Lebensbereichen lernen Jugendliche Ausländerfeindlichkeit? Ergebnisse einer Befragung bei Berufsschülerinnen und Berufsschülern." *Kölner Zeitschrift für Soziologie und Sozialpsychologie* 53: 334–49; Miller-Idriss, Cynthia. 2005. "Citizenship Education and Political Extremism in Germany: An Ethnographic Account." Pp. 101–22 in *Political and Citizenship Education: International Perspectives,* edited by Stephanie Wilde. Wallingford, U.K.: Symposium; Miller-Idriss (2009); Schnabel, K., and D. Goldschmidt. 1997. "Ausländerfeindlichkeit bei Auszubildenden-ein Handlungsfeld für Berufsschullehrer?" *Zeitschrift für Berufs- und Wirtschaftspädagogik* 93: 607–29; Schnabel, Kai U. 1993. "Ausländerfeindlichkeit bei Jugendlichen in Deutschland: Eine Synopse empirischer Befunde seit 1990." *Zeitschrift Für Pädagogik* 39: 799–822.
56. See, e.g., Brown, Timothy. 2004. "Subcultures, Pop Music and Politics: Skinheads and "Nazi Rock" in England and Germany." *Journal of Social History* 38: 157–78.
57. See Bovier and Boehnke (1999); Hagan, John, Hans Merkens, and Klaus Boehnke. 1995. "Delinquency and Disdain: Social Capital and the Control of Right-Wing Extremism among East and West Berlin Youth." *American Journal of Sociology* 100: 1028–52; Hagan, John, Susanne Rippl, Klaus Boehnke, and

Hans Merkens. 1999. "The Interest in Evil: Hierarchic Self-Interest and Right-Wing Extremism among East and West German Youth." *Social Science Research* 28: 162–83; Heitmeyer, Wilhelm. 1999. "Sozialräumliche Machtversuche des Ostdeutschen Rechtsextremismus." Pp. 47–79 in *Rechtsextremistische Jugendliche — Was Tun?*, edited by Karin Sitte, Peter E. Kalb, and Christian Petry. Weinheim: Beltz Verlag; Möller, Kurt. 2000. *Rechte Kids: Eine Langzeitstudie über Auf- und Abbau rechtsextremistischer Orientierungen bei 13- bis 15jährigen.* Weinheim: Juventa Verlag; Rippl, Susanne, and Dirk Baier. 2005. "Das Deprivationskonzept in der Rechtsextremismusforschung." *KZfSS Kölner Zeitschrift für Soziologie und Sozialpsychologie* 57(4): 644–66; Schubarth, Wilfried, and Richard Stöss, eds. 2001. *Rechtsextremismus in der Bundesrepublik Deutschland: Eine Bilanz.* Opladen: Leske und Budrich; Watts, Meredith W. 2001. "Aggressive Youth Cultures and Hate Crime: Skinheads and Xenophobic Youth in Germany." *American Behavioral Scientist* 45: 600–15.

58. Miller-Idriss (2009).

59. One interview was conducted in spring 2012, prior to the full data collection, owing to an impending retirement.

60. Two of the apprentices were in their thirties, but the vast majority were in their late teens and early twenties.

61. Baier, Dirk, Christian Pfeiffer, and Susann Rabold. 2009. "Jugendgewalt in Deutschland: Befunde aus Hell- und Dunkelfelduntersuchungen unter besonderer Berücksichtigung von Geschlechterunterschieden." *Kriminalistik* 6: 323–33.

62. Dinas, Elias. 2013. "Opening 'Openness to Change': Political Events and the Increased Sensitivity of Young Adults." *Political Research Quarterly* 66(4): 868–82.

63. See Hall, Stuart, Dorothy Hobson, Andrew Lowe, and Paul Willis, eds. 1991 [1980]. *Culture, Media, Language: Working Papers in Cultural Studies, 1972–79.* London: Routledge; Muggleton, David. 2000. *Inside Subculture: The Postmodern Meaning of Style.* New York: Berg.

64. Nayak, Anoop. 2003. *Race, Place and Globalization: Youth Cultures in a Changing World.* New York: Berg, p. 19.

65. Williams, J. Patrick. 2011. *Subcultural Theory: Traditions and Concepts.* Malden, MA: Polity, p. 10.

66. In the German context, actions that are considered right-wing radical fall within the spectrum of legitimate democratic engagement, but actions deemed right-wing extremist are a specific subset of criminal engagements that threaten the constitutional order. I thank Daniel Köhler for helping me clarify this point.

67. Mudde, Cas. 2005. "Racist Extremism in Central and Eastern Europe." *East European Politics and Societies* 19(2): 161–84; Rydgren, Jens. 2007. "The Sociology of the Radical Right." *Annual Review of Sociology* 33: 241–62.

68. Shafer, Joseph A. 2002. "Spinning the Web of Hate: Web-Based Hate Propagation by Extremist Organizations." *Journal of Criminal Justice and Popular Culture* 9(2): 69–88, p. 84.

69. Appadurai, Arjun. 1990. "Disjuncture and Difference in the Global Cultural Economy." *Theory, Culture and Society* 7(2): 295–310.

70. Benhabib, Seyla. 2002. *The Claims of Culture: Equality and Diversity in the Global Era.* Princeton, NJ: Princeton University Press.

71. See, for example, Worden, Elizabeth Anderson, and Cynthia Miller-Idriss. 2016. "Beyond Multiculturalism: Conflict, Co-existence, and Messy Identities." Pp. 289–311 in *Annual Review of Comparative and International Education 2016: International Perspectives on Education and Society*, vol. 30, edited by Alexander Wiseman. Bingley, UK: Emerald Group.

72. See Worden and Miller-Idriss (2016), especially pp. 298–99.

73. Alexander, Jeffrey C., Dominik Bartmański, and Bernhard Giesen, eds. 2012. *Iconic Power: Materiality and Meaning in Social Life*. New York: Palgrave Macmillan.

74. See Bartmański, Dominik, and Jeffrey C. Alexander. 2012. "Materiality and Meaning in Social Life: Toward an Iconic Turn in Cultural Sociology." Pp. 1–12 in *Iconic Power: Materiality and Meaning in Social Life*, edited by Jeffrey C. Alexander, Dominik Bartmański, and Bernhard Giesen. New York: Palgrave Macmillan.

75. Griffin, Roger. 2014. "Fixing Solutions: Fascist Temporalities as Remedies for Liquid Modernity." *European Journal of Modern History* 13(1): 5–23.

76. Pascoe, C. J. 2007. *Dude, You're a Fag: Masculinity and Sexuality in High School*. Berkeley: University of California Press; Way, Niobe. 2011. *Deep Secrets: Boys' Friendships and the Crisis of Connection*. Cambridge, MA: Harvard University Press.

77. Also see Claus, Robert, Esther Lehnert, and Yves Müller. 2010. *"Was ein rechter Mann ist . . .": Männlichkeiten im Rechtsextremismus*. Berlin: Karl Dietz Verlag; Virchow, Fabian. 2010. "Tapfer, stolz, opferbereit—Überlegungen zum extrem rechten Verständnis 'idealer Männlichkeit.'" Pp. 39–52 in *"Was ein rechter Mann ist . . .": Männlichkeit im Rechtsextremismus*, edited by Robert Claus, Esther Lehnert, and Yves Müller. Berlin: Karl Dietz Verlag.

Chapter 1. Trying on Extremism: Material Culture and Far Right Youth

1. Fuchs, Thorsten. "Der Neonazi neben mir." *Hannoversche Allgemeine*. September 16, 2016, http: //www.haz.de/Sonntag/Top-Thema/Der-Neonazi-neben-mir-Was-tun-mit-Rechtsextremen, accessed January 5, 2017. Original German: "Der Kampf gegen den Rechtsextremismus ist immer auch ein Streit um Symbole. Um Kleidung, Zeichen, Sätze oder Worte, die unwidersprochen stehen bleiben und irgendwann als normal gelten."

2. For example, see Alexander, Bartmański, and Giesen (2012); Aronczyk, Melissa. 2013. *Branding the Nation: The Global Business of National Identity*. New York: Oxford University Press; Aronczyk, Melissa, and Devon Powers. 2010. "Introduction: Blowing Up the Brand." Pp. 1–28 in *Blowing Up the Brand: Critical Perspectives on Promotional Culture*, edited by Melissa Aronczyk and Devon Powers New York: Peter Lang; Bowler, Wendy. 2012. "Seeing Tragedy in the News Images of September 11." Pp. 85–99 in *Iconic Power: Materiality and Meaning in Social Life*, edited by Jeffrey C. Alexander, Dominik Bartmański, and Bernhard Giesen. New York: Palgrave Macmillan; Zubrzycki, Geneviève. 2011. "History and the National Sensorium: Making Sense of Polish Mythology." *Qualitative Sociology* 34(1): 21–57; Miller, Daniel. 2010. *Stuff*. Boston: Polity; Richey, Lisa

Ann, and Stefano Ponte. 2011. *Brand Aid: Shopping Well to Save the World*. Minneapolis: University of Minnesota Press; Zubrzycki, Geneviève. 2013. "Aesthetic Revolt and the Remaking of National Identity in Québec, 1960–1969." *Theory and Society* 42(5): 423–75; Rauer, Valentin. 2012. "The Visualization of Uncertainty: HIV Statistics in Public Media." Pp. 139–54 in *Iconic Power: Materiality and Meaning in Social Life*, edited by Jeffrey C. Alexander, Dominik Bartmański, and Bernhard Giesen. New York: Palgrave Macmillan.

 3. See, e.g., Berezin, Mabel. 1997. *Making the Fascist Self: The Political Culture of Interwar Italy*. Ithaca, NY: Cornell University Press; Mock, Steven. 2014. *Symbols of Defeat in the Construction of National Identity*. Cambridge: Cambridge University Press; Molnár, Virág. 2016. "Civil Society, Radicalism and the Rediscovery of Mythic Nationalism." *Nations and Nationalism* 22(1): 165–85; Zubrzycki, Geneviève. 2006. *The Crosses of Auschwitz: Nationalism and Religion in Post-Communist Poland*. Chicago: University of Chicago Press; Zubrzycki, Geneviève. 2016. *Beheading the Saint: Nationalism, Religion and Secularism in Quebec*. Chicago: University of Chicago Press.

 4. See, e.g., Rommelspacher, Birgit. 2006. *"Der Hass hat uns geeint": Junge Rechtsextreme und ihr Ausstieg aus der Szene*. Frankfurt: Campus Verlag; Shoshan, Nitzan. 2016. *The Management of Hate: Nation, Affect, and the Governance of Right-Wing Extremism in Germany*. Princeton, NJ: Princeton University Press.

 5. See, e.g., Khatib, Lina. 2012. *Image Politics in the Middle East: The Role of the Visual in Political Struggle*. New York: I. B. Tauris; Agentur für soziale Perspektiven e.V. (2009); and Beifuss, Artur, and Francesco Trivini Vellini. 2013. *Branding Terror: The Logotypes and Iconography of Insurgent Groups and Terrorist Organizations*. London: Merrell.

 6. Some scholars refer to this as the "ethnic competition" thesis, in which far right wing anger stems from a sense of competition for scarce resources, jobs, or marital partners. See Rydgren (2007) for a critical analysis.

 7. See, Betz, Hans-Georg. 1993. "The New Politics of Resentment: Radical Right-Wing Populist Parties in Western Europe." *Comparative Politics* 25(4): 413–27; Katsourides, Yiannos. 2013. "Determinants of Extreme Right Reappearance in Cyprus: The National Popular Front (ELAM), Golden Dawn's Sister Party." *South European Society and Politics* 18(4): 567–89, p. 569. Also see Fuchs, Marek. 2003. "Right-Wing Attitudes among Adolescents: Testing the Explanatory Power of Theoretical Concepts." *Kölner Zeitschrift für Soziologie und Sozialpsychologie* 55(4): 654–78.

 8. See for example the UKIP rhetoric during the "leave" campaign leading up to the 2016 Brexit referendum as discussed in Cooper, Marta. N.d. "The 'Romantic' and 'Distorted' Language of Campaigners Who Want Britain to Leave the EU. https://qz.com/703078/language-experts-say-the-rhetoric-of-campaigners-who-want-britain-to-leave-the-eu-is-romantic-and-distorted/, accessed February 3, 2017.

 9. See McLaren, Lauren M. 1999. "Explaining Right-Wing Violence in Germany: A Time-Series Analysis." *Social Science Quarterly* 80: 166–80.

10. See Siedler, Thomas. 2011. "Parental Unemployment and Young People's Extreme Right-Wing Party Affinity: Evidence from Panel Data." *Journal of the Royal Statistical Society: Series A (Statistics in Society)* 174: 737–58, p. 754.

11. See, e.g., Lucassen, Geertje, and Marcel Lubbers. 2012. "Who Fears What? Explaining Far-Right-Wing Preference in Europe by Distinguishing Perceived Cultural and Economic Ethnic Threats." *Comparative Political Studies* 45(5): 547–74.

12. Bay and Bleksaune's cross-national analysis of the effects of being unemployed on young people's political marginalization found that in general, both employed and unemployed youth were not very interested in politics at all, and that unemployed youth were "less interested than the little-interested employed youth." Bay, Ann-Helen, and Morten Bleksaune. 2014. "Youth, Unemployment and Political Marginalization." Pp. 21–35 in *Youth and the Extreme Right*, edited by Cas Mudde. New York: IDebate, p. 32. More recently, Siedler (2011)'s research on the German case found that youth's own unemployment is not related to their identification with a far right party—rather, it is the experience of growing up with an unemployed parent that matters. The effect is stronger among sons than daughters and is especially strong for youth living in east, rather than west, Germany. The relationship even has a negative effect for youth in west Germany, where youth who are unemployed are less likely to support far right parties (Siedler 2011: 754).

13. In part, this is because—as Geertjie Lucassen and Marcel Lubbers (2012) argue—variation across individual countries is significant enough that the selection of cases in cross-national comparisons affects the findings in ways that may produce contradictory evidence from study to study. But it is also because differentiation within groups in any given country is significant. Stacia Gilliard-Matthews's recent work on white supremacist groups in the United States found, for example, that economic factors are related to increases in Ku Klux Klan (KKK) participation rates but not to neo-Nazi group rates—the latter were affected only by political rather than economic or social factors. Gilliard-Matthews, Stacia. 2011. "The Impact of the Economic Downturn, Immigrants, and Political Representation on White Supremacist Group Organization in the United States." *Sociological Focus* 44(3): 255–79.

14. See Griffin, Roger. 2008a. "Fascism's New Faces (and New Facelessness) in the 'Post-fascist' Epoch." Pp. 181–202 in *A Fascist Century: Essays by Roger Griffin*, edited by Matthew Feldman. New York: Palgrave Macmillan, p. 181; also see Miller-Idriss, Cynthia. Forthcoming. "Youth and the Radical Right." In *The Oxford Handbook of the Radical Right*, edited by Jens Rydgren. Oxford University Press.

15. Durso, Rachel M., and David Jacobs. 2013. "The Determinants of the Number of White Supremacist Groups: A Pooled Time-Series Analysis." *Social Problems* 60(1): 128–44, p. 140.

16. See Potok, Mark. 2010. "Rage on the Right." *Intelligence Report*. Southern Poverty Law Center. March 2, https://www.splcenter.org/fighting-hate/intelligence-report/2010/rage-right, accessed May 3, 2017; and Potok, Mark. 2013. "The Antigovernment 'Patriot' Movement Expands for the Fourth Year in a Row as Hate Groups Remain at Near-Historic Highs." *Intelligence Report*. Southern Poverty Law Center. March 4, https://www.splcenter.org/fighting-hate/intelligence-report/2013/year-hate-and-extremism, accessed May 3, 2017.

17. See Semyonov, Moshe, Rebeca Raijman, and Anastasia Gorodzeisky. 2006. "The Rise of Anti-foreigner Sentiment in European Societies, 1988–2000." *American Sociological Review* 71(3): 426–49; Wilkes, Rima, Neil Guppy, and Lily Farris. 2007. "Comment on Semyonov, Raijman, and Gorodzeisky, ASR, June 2006:

Right-Wing Parties and Anti-foreigner Sentiment in Europe." *American Sociological Review* 72(5): 831–40. Wilkes et al. argue that classically racist views (such as those espoused by the British National Party, or BNP) are more likely to be dismissed as fringe and are not taken seriously by the majority of the population. But extreme right wing parties that espouse "culturally" racist views (such as France's Le Pen) have a significant impact on prejudice within the national population as those culturally racist views "become part of the normal political landscape" (p. 836).

18. On the issue of gender and the far right, see Pilkington, Hilary, and Cynthia Miller-Idriss, eds. 2017. "Gender and the Radical and Extreme Right: Mechanisms of Transmission and the Role of Educational Interventions." Special issue, *Gender and Education* 29(2); also see Blee, Kathleen. 2003. *Inside Organized Racism: Women in the Hate Movement.* Berkeley: University of California Press; and Gigengil, Elisabeth, Matthew Henniger, Andre Blais, and Neil Nevitte. 2005. "Explaining the Gender Gap in Support for the New Right: The Case of Canada." *Comparative Political Studies* 38(10): 1171–95. Individual personality traits and characteristics are also key factors, but not always in the ways that scholars assume. For example, while popular explanations for adolescent male violence often suggest that anomie and isolation drive young men to lash out, at least for far right youth, this explanation has largely fallen out of favor in the face of strong evidence that far right activity is strongest in socially strong communities and that far right wing party members are not particularly isolated or asocial. See Rydgren (2007: 247).

19. See Gigengil et al. (2005: 1183).

20. See, e.g., Simi, Pete, Bryan F. Bubolz, and Ann Hardman. 2013. "Military Experience, Identity Discrepancies, and Far Right Terrorism: An Exploratory Analysis." *Studies in Conflict and Terrorism* 36(8): 654–71.

21. See Siedler (2011: 756).

22. Siedler (2011: 756).

23. See, for example, especially Heitmeyer, Wilhelm. 1988. *Rechtsextremistische Orientierungen bei Jugendlichen.* 2nd ed. Weinheim: Juventa; and Heitmeyer, Wilhelm, Heike Buhse, Joachim Liebe-Freund, Kurt Möller, Joachim Müller, Helmut Ritz, Gertrud Siller, and Johannes Vossen. 1992. *Die Bielefelder Rechtsextremismus-Studie: Erste Langzeituntersuchung zur Politischen Sozialisation männlicher Jugendlicher.* Munich: Juventa Verlag.

24. Gabriel, Thomas. 2014. "Parenting and Right-Wing Extremism: An Analysis of the Biographical Genesis of Racism among Young People." Pp. 36–47 in *Youth and the Extreme Right*, edited by Cas Mudde. New York: IDebate, p. 44.

25. There is a related body of work on moving from radicalization to extremism, although most of this work focuses on radicalization to Islamist movements and has not focused on far right extremism. Daniel Köhler's thorough review identifies four schools of research on radicalization, which he labels sociological, social movement, empirical, and psychological. Köhler (2017a). Several of the findings across these schools of thought identify issues related to identity, emotion, peer groups, and belonging as important for radicalization. More work is needed to show whether and how these models apply to the far right, but the findings I present here indicate there is significant overlap. I thank Daniel Köhler for bringing this connection to my attention.

26. Simi, Pete. Forthcoming. "The Culture of Violent Talk: An Interpretive Approach." In *Cultural Dimensions of Far Right Politics*, edited by Fabian Virchow and Cynthia Miller-Idriss. Wiesbaden: VS Verlag; Köhler, Daniel, and Chilja Speransky. Forthcoming. "Humour and the Extreme Right." In *Cultural Dimensions of Far Right Politics*, edited by Fabian Virchow and Cynthia Miller-Idriss. Wiesbaden: VS Verlag; Rydgren (2007).

27. Griffin, Roger. 2008b. "Fatal Attraction: Why Nazism Appealed to Voters." Pp. 71–82 in *A Fascist Century: Essays by Roger Griffin*, edited by Matthew Feldman. New York: Palgrave Macmillan, p. 75.

28. Schuppener, Georg. 2007. *Spuren germanischer Mythologie in der deutschen Sprache: Namen, Phraseologismen und aktueller Rechtsextremismus*. Leipzig: Edition Hamouda, Wissenschaftsverlag, p. 97.

29. Watts (2001).

30. Griffin (2008b).

31. Griffin (2008b: 78–80).

32. Futrell, Robert, and Pete Simi. 2004. "Free Spaces, Collective Identity, and the Persistence of U.S. White Power Activism." *Social Problems* 51: 16–42; Goodwin, Jeff, and James Jasper. 2004. "Rethinking Social Movements: Structure, Meaning, and Emotion." Rowman and Littlefield; Leach and Haunss (2009); Polletta (2001); Willis, Paul. 1981. *Learning to Labor: How Working-Class Kids Get Working-Class Jobs*. New York: Columbia University Press.

33. Simi, Bubolz, and Hardman (2013: 657).

34. See Simi, Bubolz, and Hardman (2013: 660).

35. Simi, Bubolz, and Hardman (2013: 664).

36. Simi, Bubolz, and Hardman (2013: 662).

37. Alexander, Bartmański, and Giesen (2012).

38. See Durkheim, Emile. 1995 [1915]. *The Elementary Forms of Religious Life*. New York: Free Press; Bartmański, Dominik, and Jeffrey C. Alexander (2012: 4).

39. On religious symbols, see especially Zubrzycki (2006, 2016); also see Billig, Michael. 1995a. *Banal Nationalism*. Thousand Oaks, CA: Sage; Fox, Jon, and Cynthia Miller-Idriss. 2008. "Everyday Nationhood." *Ethnicities* 8: 536–62.

40. Bartmański and Alexander (2012: 3). Also see Alexander, Jeffrey. 2012. "Iconic Power and Performance: The Role of the Critic." Pp. 25–35 in *Iconic Power: Materiality and Meaning in Social Life*, edited by Jeffrey C. Alexander, Dominik Bartmański, and Bernhard Giesen. New York: Palgrave Macmillan.

41. For exceptions, see Molotch, Harvey. 2005. *Where Stuff Comes From: How Toasters, Toilets, Cars, Computers, and Many Other Things Come to Be as They Are*. New York: Routledge; Zelizer, Viviana A. 2011. *Economic Lives: How Culture Shapes the Economy*. Princeton, NJ: Princeton University Press.

42. See especially Mitchell's scholarship in art history: Mitchell, W.J.T. 2005. *What Do Pictures Want? The Lives and Loves of Images*. Chicago: University of Chicago Press.

43. Daniels, Stephen, and Denis Cosgrove. 1988. "Introduction: Iconography and Landscape." Pp. 1–10 in *The Iconography of Landscape: Essays on the Symbolic Representation, Design, and Use of Past Environments*, edited by Stephen Daniels and Denis Cosgrove. New York: Cambridge University Press, p. 2.

44. Morgan, David. 2005. *The Sacred Gaze: Religious Visual Culture in Theory and Practice*. Berkeley: University of California Press.

45. Panofsky (1955).
46. Khatib (2012: 6–7).
47. Khatib (2012: 8); Wedeen, Lisa. 1999. *Ambiguities of Domination: Politics, Rhetoric, and Symbols in Contemporary Syria*. Chicago: University of Chicago Press.
48. Khatib (2012: 7).
49. Khatib (2012: 11).
50. Surak, Kristin. 2013. *Making Tea, Making Japan: Cultural Nationalism in Practice*. Stanford, CA: Stanford University Press, p. 5; also see, on school uniforms and disciplining the body in Japan, McVeigh, Brian. 2015. "Wearing Ideology: How Uniforms Discipline Minds and Bodies in Japan." *Fashion Theory* 1(2): 189–213.
51. Alexander, Jeffrey C. 1990. "Analytic Debates: Understanding the Relative Autonomy of Culture." Pp. 1–27 in *Culture and Society: Contemporary Debates*, edited by Jeffrey C. Alexander and Steven Seidman. Cambridge: Cambridge University Press; Gans, Herbert J. 2012. "Against Culture versus Structure." *Identities: Global Studies in Culture and Power* 19(2): 125–34.
52. In particular, see Eagleton, Terry. 2000. *The Idea of Culture*. Malden, MA: Blackwell; Gans (2012); Lamont, Michèle. 1994. *Money, Morals, and Manners: The Culture of the French and the American Upper-Middle Class*. Chicago: University of Chicago Press; Lamont, Michèle. 2002. *The Dignity of Working Men: Morality and the Boundaries of Race, Class and Immigration*. Cambridge, MA: Harvard University Press; Patterson (2014); Steinmetz, George. 1999. *State/Culture: State-Formation after the Cultural Turn*. Ithaca, NY: Cornell University Press; Williams, Raymond. 1985. *Keywords: A Vocabulary of Culture and Society*. New York: Oxford University Press.
53. DiMaggio, Paul. 1997. "Culture and Cognition." *Annual Review of Sociology* 23: 263–87; Swidler, Ann. 1986. "Culture in Action: Symbols and Strategies." *American Sociological Review* 51: 273–86.
54. Chan, Cheris Shun-ching. 2012. *Marketing Death: Culture and the Making of a Life Insurance Market in China*. New York: Oxford University Press, p. 175.
55. Swidler (1986).
56. Chan (2012: 175), citing Goffman, Erving. 1967. *Interaction Ritual: Essays in Face to Face Behavior*. Piscataway, NJ: Aldine Transaction, p. 13.
57. DiMaggio (1997).
58. Patterson (2014: 7).
59. Patterson (2014: 20).
60. Patterson (2014: 21).
61. Bourdieu, Pierre. 1984. *Distinction: A Social Critique of the Judgement of Taste*. Cambridge, MA: Harvard University Press.
62. Baudrillard, Jean. 1998. *The Consumer Society: Myths and Structures*. Thousand Oaks, CA: Sage; Bauman, Zygmunt. 2007a. *Consuming Life*. Malden, MA: Polity.
63. Campbell, Colin. 2004. "I Shop Therefore I Know That I Am: The Metaphysical Basis of Modern Consumerism." Pp. 27–44 in *Elusive Consumption*, edited by Karin M. Ekström and Helene Brembeck. New York: Berg.
64. Hebdige, Dick. 1979. *Subculture: The Meaning of Style*. New York: Methuen, p. 18.
65. Fox and Miller-Idriss (2008: 550).
66. Quinn, Malcolm. 1994. *The Swastika: Constructing the Symbol*. New York: Routledge, p. 113. Also see p. 112.
67. Aronczyk and Powers (2010).

68. For work on ethnic identities, see Comaroff, John, and Jean Comaroff. 2009. *Ethnicity, Inc.* Chicago: University of Chicago Press; for a discussion of green consumers, see Todd, Anne Marie. 2004. "Environmental Consumer Ethics of Natural Care Products." *Ethics and the Environment* 9(2): 86–102; on African American consumer identities, see Lamont, Michèle, and Virág Molnár. 2001. "How Blacks Use Consumption to Shape Their Collective Identity." *Journal of Consumer Culture* 1(1): 31–45.

69. Campbell (2004).

70. Lee, Benjamin, and Edward LiPuma. 2002. "Cultures of Circulation: The Imaginations of Modernity." *Public Culture* 14: 191–213, p. 192.

71. Lee and LiPuma (2002); MacInnis, Deborah, C. W. Park, and Joseph Priester, eds. 2009. *Handbook of Brand Relationships.* New York: M. E. Sharpe.

72. MacInnis et al. (2009).

73. Zubrzycki (2011: 52).

74. On the performance of symbols, see Kang, Milaan, and Katherine Jones. 2007. "Why Do People Get Tattoos?" *Contexts* 6(1): 42–47; also see Bauman, Zygmunt. 2000. *Liquid Modernity.* Malden, MA: Polity; and Bauman, Zygmunt. 2007b. *Liquid Times: Living in an Age of Uncertainty.* Malden, MA: Polity; Harris, David. 1996. *A Society of Signs?* New York: Routledge.

75. Bauman (2007a, 2007b).

76. Martin, Andres. 1997. "On Teenagers and Tattoos." *Journal of the American Academy of Child and Adolescent Psychiatry* 36: 860–61; Watts (2001).

77. Miller-Idriss (2009).

78. Comaroff and Comaroff (2009: 9), emphasis in original.

79. Campbell, Colin. 1996. "The Meaning of Objects and the Meaning of Actions." *Journal of Material Culture* 1(1): 93–105.

80. Hebdige (1979: 17).

81. Scott, James C. 1985. *Weapons of the Weak: Everyday Forms of Peasant Resistance.* New Haven, CT: Yale University Press, p. 40.

82. Wallace, Clare, and Sijke Kovacheva. 1996. "Youth Cultures and Consumption in Eastern and Western Europe: An Overview." *Youth and Society* 28: 189–214.

83. Wallace and Kovacheva (1996).

84. See, e.g., Schnabel and Goldschmidt (1997).

85. Scott (1985).

86. Simi, Pete, and Robert Futrell. 2009. "Negotiating White Power Activist Stigma." *Social Problems* 56(1): 89–110.

87. Linden, Annette, and Bert Klandermans. 2006. "Stigmatization and Repression of Extreme-Right Activism in the Netherlands." *Mobilization: An International Journal* 11: 213–28.

88. As documented in my earlier book (Miller-Idriss 2009).

89. Clarke, John. 2007. "Style." Pp. 147–61 in *Resistance through Rituals: Youth Subcultures in Post-war Britain,* 2nd ed., edited by Stuart Hall and Jefferson Tony. New York: Routledge; Hebdige (1979).

90. See, e.g., Barthes, Roland. 1972. "Mythologies." New York: Farrar, Straus, and Giroux; Hall, Stuart. 1973. *Encoding and Decoding in the Television Discourse.* Birmingham: Centre for Contemporary Cultural Studies; Hall, Stuart, and Tony Jefferson, eds. 2007. *Resistance through Rituals: Youth Subcultures in Post-war*

Britain, 2nd ed. New York Routledge; and the work of the Birmingham Centre for Contemporary Cultural Studies/CCCS, closed 2002.

91. Caicedo, Martha Marín, ed. 2012. *Subculture*. New York: Routledge; Soep, Elisabeth. 2012. "Resistance." Pp. 126–30 in *Keywords in Youth Studies: Tracing Affects, Movements, Knowledges*, edited by Nancy Lesko and Susan Talburt. New York: Routledge.

92. Scott (1985: 38).

93. See, for example, Gans (2012).

94. Luschen, Kristen. 2012. "Style." Pp. 268–72 in *Keywords in Youth Studies: Tracing Affects, Movements, Knowledges*, edited by Nancy Lesko and Susan Talburt. New York: Routledge; Pilkington, Hilary. 2010a. "No Longer 'on Parade': Style and the Performance of Skinhead." Pp. 143–65 in *Russia's Skinheads: Exploring and Rethinking Subcultural Lives*, edited by Hilary Pilkington, Elena Omel'chenko, and Al'bina Garifzianova. London: Routledge.

95. Hebdige (1979).

96. Milner, Murray. 2006. *Freaks, Geeks, and Cool Kids: American Teenagers, Schools, and the Culture of Consumption*. New York: Routledge; Hebdige (1979).

97. Nayak (2005).

98. I thank Wolfgang Beilenhoff for his observations of how the body can be used as a screen.

99. Also see Pilkington (2010a).

100. Braun, Geisler, and Gerster (2009).

101. Funke, Hajo. 2011. "Rechtsextreme Ideologien, strategische Orientierungen und Gewalt." Pp. 21–44 in *Strategien der extremen Rechten: Hintergründe — Analysen — Antworten*, edited by Stephan Braun, Alexander Geisler, and Martin Gerster. Wiesbaden: VS Verlag.

102. Decker, Kiess, Eggers, and Brähler (2016: 39). The terms "west" and "east" Germany are deliberately in lowercase in order to reflect the fact that these are distinct regions within unified Germany, not separate states.

103. *Sturmführer* is a rank of officer in the SS; see, for example, http: //www.jewishvirtuallibrary.org/sturmf-uuml-hrer, accessed January 31, 2017, for a more detailed explanation.

104. Köhler, Daniel. 2015. "Contrast Societies: Radical Social Movements and Their Relationships with Their Target Societies; A Theoretical Model." *Behavioral Sciences of Terrorism and Political Aggression* 7(1): 18–34, p. 23.

105. In January 2017, the German Federal Constitutional Court rejected what was the second attempt to ban the NPD. See "German Supreme Court Rejects Bid to Outlaw Far-Right Party," *New York Times*. January 17, 2017. Available at http: //www.nytimes.com/aponline/2017/01/17/world/europe/ap-eu-germany-far-right .html, accessed January 17, 2017.

Chapter 2. Branding Identity: Coded Symbols and Game Playing

1. Nolan (2008a); Nolan (2008b); Staud (2005).

2. In particular, see the analysis of the Autonomous Nationalist movement in Schedler and Häusler (2011); the discussions of right-wing extremism and youth in Langebach, Martin. 2016. "Rechtsextremismus und Jugend." Pp. 375–440 in *Handbuch Rechtsextremismus*, edited by Fabian Virchow, Martin Langebach, and

Alexander Häusler. Wiesbaden: VS Verlag; the analysis of extreme right youth culture in Germany in Langebach, Martin, and Jan Raabe. 2011. "Die Genese einer extrem rechten Jugendkultur." Pp. 154–66 in *Autonome Nationalisten: Neonazismus in Bewegung*, edited by Jan Schedler and Alexander Häusler. Wiesbaden: VS Verlag; Staud's (2005) discussion of modern Nazis and the analysis of the "new right-wing" in Germany in Langebach, Martin, and Jan Raabe. 2016. "Die 'Neue Rechte' in der Bundesrepublik Deutschland." Pp. 561–92 in *Handbuch Rechtsextremismus*, edited by Fabian Virchow, Martin Langebach, and Alexander Häusler. Wiesbaden: VS Verlag.

3. Schedler, Jan. 2011. "Style Matters: Inszenierungspraxen 'Autonomer Nationalisten.'" Pp. 67–89 in *Autonome Nationalisten: Neonazismus in Bewegung*, edited by Jan Schedler and Alexander Häusler. Wiesbaden: VS Verlag; also see Peters and Schulze (2009).

4. See Schedler (2011: 78); see Peters and Schulze (2009: 16) for a discussion of the black bloc strategy's origins. I am indebted to Daniel Köhler for discussion of the Autonomous Nationalists and their role in transformations in far right subcultural style in the early 2000s (personal correspondence).

5. Smith, Anthony. 1991. *The Ethnic Origin of Nations*. Hoboken, NJ: Wiley-Blackwell; Smith, Anthony. 2003. *Chosen Peoples: Sacred Sources of National Identity*. Oxford: Oxford University Press.

6. For discussions of the emergence of nations and nationalism, see especially Calhoun, Craig. 2007. *Nations Matter: Culture, History, and the Cosmopolitan Dream*. New York: Routledge; Greenfeld, Liah. 1992. *Nationalism: Five Roads to Modernity*. Cambridge, MA: Harvard University Press; and Smith, Anthony. 1989. "The Origins of Nations." *Ethnic and Racial Studies* 12(3): 340–67.

7. As detailed in Cerulo, Karen. "Symbols and the World System: National Anthems and Flags." 1993. *Sociological Forum* 8(2): 243–71; and Anderson, Benedict. 1991. *Imagined Communities: Reflections on the Origin and Spread of Nationalism*. New York: Verso.

8. See, for example, Smith, Anthony. 2008. *The Cultural Foundation of Nations: Hierarchy, Covenant, and Republic*. Hoboken, NJ: Wiley-Blackwell.

9. Casey (2009: 340).

10. Barthes (1974: 5).

11. Hebdige (1979: 18).

12. See the regularly published brochure on far right coded symbols published by the Anti-fascist Press Archive and Educational Center (apabiz). For example, Agentur für soziale Perspektiven e.V., Hg. 2009. *Versteckspiel: Lifestyle, Symbole und Codes von neonazistischen und extrem rechten Gruppen*. Antifaschistisches Pressearchiv und Bildungszentrum Berlin.

13. Nolan (2008b).

14. Welt Online (2010).

15. The analysis of specific codes is indebted to the description of codes in several publications produced by NGOs and agencies working to educate teachers and the general public about the far right, including Agentur für soziale Perspektiven e.V. (2009, 2011); Hammerbacher (2015); discussions of the codes and the commercial brands in antifascist scene materials and publications such as those produced by linksunten, https://linksunten.indymedia.org/de, accessed May

18, 2017, and the regularly published Antifaschistisches Infoblatt, https://www
.antifainfoblatt.de/, accessed May 18, 2017; conversations with local experts
on right-wing scene-typical codes; and youth explanations during interviews.

16. Stiehm, Enno. 2012. *Rechtsextreme Jugendliche: Erkennungsmerkmale, Begriffe,
Erklärungsansätze und schulische Handlungsmöglichkeiten.* Hamburg: Diplomica
Verlag.

17. See Michael, George. 2009. "David Lane and the Fourteen Words." *Totalitarian
Movements and Political Religions* 10: 43–61.

18. Kidd (2015).

19. As detailed in Hammerbacher (2015).

20. See Duden's explanation of observieren and abservieren at http: //www.duden
.de/rechtschreibung/abservieren and http: //www.duden.de/rechtschreibung/
observieren. With thanks to Annett Graefe and Daniel Köhler for discussions
on the interpretation of the slang/colloquial and the embedded code.

21. Miklavcic, Alessandra. 2008. "Slogans and Graffiti: Postmemory among Youth
in the Italo-Slovenian Borderland." *American Ethnologist* 35: 440–53.

22. Harris (1996); Hebdige (1979).

23. Herf, Jeffrey. 2006. *The Jewish Enemy: Nazi Propaganda during World War II
and the Holocaust.* Cambridge, MA: Belknap Press of Harvard University Press,
especially pp. 146–47.

24. Reitzenstein, Julian. 2014. *Himmlers Forscher: Wehrwissenschaft und Medizinverbrechen im "Ahnenerbe" der SS.* Paderborn: Ferdinand Schöningh.

25. See Zacharoff, Lucien. 1934. "Angola Again Being Discussed as Possible Haven
for Jewish Exiles." *Jewish Daily Bulletin.* May 6. Jewish Telegraphic Agency, http:
//www.jta.org/1934/05/06/archive/angola-again-being-discussed-as-possible-hav
en-for-jewish-exiles, accessed May 9, 2016.

26. Hannemann, Jana. 2016. "Wie Dortmunder Neonazis das Run-DMC-Logo
missbrauchen." *WAZ- Westdeutsche Allgemeine Zeitung.* June 9, https://www.der
westen.de/politik/wie-dortmunder-neonazis-das-run-dmc-logo-missbrauchen
-id11901373.html, accessed May 4, 2017.

27. Hannemann (2016).

28. Kohlstruck, Michael. 2005. " 'Ich bin stolz, ein Deutscher zu sein': Zur Entstehung und Verbreitung eines politischen Symbols." Pp. 53–76 in *Stolz deutsch
zu sein? Aggressiver Anspruch und selbstverständlicher Patriotismus,* edited by Ute
Benz and Wolfgang Benz. Berlin: Metropol Verlag.

29. Kohlstruck (2005: 58); also see Weißmann, Karlheinz. 1991. *Schwarze Fahnen,
Runenzeichen: Die Entwicklung der politischen Symbolik der deutschen Rechten
zwischen 1890 und 1945.* Duesseldorf: Droste Verlag.

30. Heller, Steven. 2000. *The Swastika: Symbol beyond Redemption?* New York: Allworth, p. 67.

31. Kohlstruck (2005: 58–59).

32. Miller-Idriss (2009).

33. Oschlies, Renate. 2001. "Hinter die, ideologische Kostümierung' schauen." *Berliner Zeitung* 69 (March 22): 6.

34. Cohen, Roger. 2001. "Schroeder Joins Debate, Taking Side of Pride in Germany." *New York Times.* March 20, http://www.nytimes.com/2001/03/20/world/
schroder-joins-debate-taking-side-of-pride-in-germany.html, accessed May 4,

2017; Parade, Heidi. 2001. "Ungebetene Mitstreiter." *Der Tagesspiegel* 17358 (March 23): 5.

35. Miller-Idriss (2009).

36. Andreasch, Robert. "Widerstandsschritte: Die radikale Rechte in der Bundesrepublik, zwei Jahre nach dem ersten PEGIDA-Spaziergang in Dresden: Ein Ein- und Ausblick." *Lernen aus der Geschichte- Magazin* 09/2016. November 23, 2016. Brandenburgische Landeszentrale für politische Bildung, p. 5.

37. Miller-Idriss (2009). See cover photo and back cover.

38. See the regular report "Das Versteckspiel," published by the Anti-fascist Press Archive and Educational Center in Berlin, which details the varied codes of the far right scene, http: //www.dasversteckspiel.de/index.php?id=28&stufe=28&finder =1&artikel=61, accessed April 12, 2016.

39. See the regular report "Das Versteckspiel" for more detail on the codes and symbols of the far right subcultural scene, http: //www.dasversteckspiel.de/index .php?id=28&stufe=28&finder=1&artikel=58, and the Alpha Industries history described at http: //www.alphaindustries.com/history.htm#16, accessed April 12, 2016.

40. See the promotional text on the Alpha Industries website at http: //www.al phaindustries.com/mens-flight-jackets/alpha-industries-cwu-45p-flight-jacket .htm, accessed April 12, 2016.

41. Although the phrase "weltwide führende Marke" (worldwide leading brand) is not on the official Alpha Industries website, it is in wide use in the product descriptions on other websites that sell the brand. See, e.g., an Amazon listing for a jacket: https: //www.amazon.de/Alpha-Industries-Damen-Mantel -gr%C3%BCn/dp/B012ZI3APQ, accessed January 18, 2017.

42. Staecker, Joern. 2003. "The Cross Goes North: Christian Symbols and Scandanavian Women." Pp. 464–82 in *The Cross Goes North: Processes of Conversion in Northern Europe, AD 300–1300*, edited by Martin Carver. York: York Medieval Press, University of York, p. 468.

43. See Schedler and Häusler (2011).

Chapter 3. Historical Fantasies, Fantastical Myths: Sacred Origin Narratives

1. Epigraph: Atkin, Douglas. 2004. *The Culting of Brands: When Consumers Become True Believers*. New York: Portfolio, p. 111.

2. Eliade (1957: 205).

3. See Griffin (2014) on the relationship between postmodernity and fascism.

4. Barthes (1972: 117).

5. Also see Attebery (2014: 19).

6. For more on national imaginaries, see Billig (1995a); and Billig, Michael. 1995b. "Rhetorical Psychology, Ideological Thinking, and Imagining Nationhood." Pp. 64–81 in *Social Movements and Culture*, edited by Hank Johnston and Bert Klandermans. Minneapolis: University of Minnesota Press. On collective pasts, see von der Goltz, Anna. 2009. *Hindenburg: Power, Myth, and the Rise of the Nazis* New York: Oxford University Press, especially p. 4; Eller, Cynthia. 2013.

"Matriarchy and the Volk." *Journal of the American Academy of Religion* 81(1): 188–221, especially p. 212; and Williamson, George S. 2004. *The Longing for Myth in Germany: Religion and Aesthetic Culture from Romanticism to Nietzsche.* Chicago: University of Chicago Press, especially p. 16.

7. Zubrzycki (2011: 22).
8. See Attebery (2014), especially pp. 12 and 20; final quote in sentence is from Kershaw, Ian. 1987. *The "Hitler Myth": Image and Reality in the Third Reich.* New York: Oxford University Press, p. 2.
9. Von der Goltz (2009: 6).
10. Attebery (2014: 15).
11. See Eller (2013).
12. Barthes (1972: 120).
13. Nietzsche, Friedrich. 1995 [1872]. *The Birth of Tragedy.* Mineola, NY: Dover, pp. 85 and 76.
14. Eliade (1957: 21–23).
15. Von der Goltz (2009: 7).
16. Williamson (2004: 290).
17. Nietzsche (1995 [1872]: 76 and 86).
18. Nietzsche (1995 [1872]: 79).
19. Fox and Miller-Idriss (2008); see Zubrzycki (2011: 32) for the crown of thorns example.
20. See von der Goltz (2009: 6).
21. Attebery (2014: 21).
22. Kershaw (1987: 253).
23. Liulevicius, Vejas Gabriel. 2009. *The German Myth of the East: 1800 to the Present.* New York: Oxford University Press, p. 2.
24. Eliade (1957: 209).
25. I am indebted to Roger Griffin for linking Eliade and Becker in his September 25, 2014, lecture at Panteon University in Athens, Greece. Ernest Becker's ideas about myth and what he calls "hero-systems" are explored, among other places, in his 1971 book *The Birth and Death of Meaning: An Interdisciplinary Perspective on the Problem of Man.* New York: Free Press.
26. McIlwain, Charlton. 2003. *Death in Black and White: Death, Ritual and Family Ecology.* New York: Hampton, p. 80.
27. Von der Goltz (2009: 8).
28. Griffin (2008b: 81). *Volksgemeinschaft*, which translates as the "national" or "people's community," was a key concept for the Third Reich. See, for example, Welch, David. 2004. "Nazi Propaganda and the *Volksgemeinschaft*: Constructing a People's Community." *Journal of Contemporary History* 39(2): 213–38.
29. Von der Goltz (2009: 5).
30. Smith, Anthony. 2000a. *Myths and Memories of the Nation.* Oxford: Oxford University Press.
31. In recent months, the apocalyptic and mythic fantasies espoused by the Islamic State have proven appealing to thousands of young men in Europe, Australia, and North America, who have rushed to take up brutal arms in an effort to restore a utopian Islamic caliphate through literal interpretation of the Koran. As Graeme Wood explains, "For certain true believers—the kind who long for

epic good-versus-evil battles—visions of apocalyptic bloodbaths fulfill a deep psychological need." Wood, Graeme. 2015. "What ISIS Really Wants." *Atlantic*. March 2015, https://www.theatlantic.com/magazine/archive/2015/03/what-isis-really-wants/384980/, accessed May 5, 2017.

32. Hall, Stuart 1999–2000. "Whose Heritage? Un-settling 'The Heritage,' Reimagining the Post-nation." *Third Text* 49: 3–13, p. 5.

33. Eliade (1957: 25).

34. Zubrzycki (2011: 22; also see p. 24).

35. Zubrzycki (2011: 24).

36. Von der Goltz (2009: 115).

37. Von der Goltz (2009: 116–21). Paul Von Hindenburg was a leading German World War I military commander who was elected president of the German Weimar Republic in 1925, and then reelected in 1932; it was Hindenburg who appointed Adolf Hitler as Reich Chancellor in 1933 (Von der Goltz 2009: 1–2).

38. Barthes (1972: 126).

39. Zubrzycki (2011: 37), citing Victor Turner. 1967. *The Forest of Symbols: Aspects of Ndembu Ritual*. Ithaca, NY: Cornell University Press.

40. Barthes (1972 [1956]).

41. Also see Attebery (2014: 37).

42. Patterson (2014: 11).

43. Zubrzycki (2011).

44. Zubrzycki (2011: 52).

45. Zubrzycki (2011: 52).

46. Benz, Wolfgang, and Peter Reif-Spirek. 2003. *Geschichtsmythen: Legenden über den Nationalsozialismus*. Berlin: Metropol Verlag; Bleckmann, Bruno. 2009. *Die Germanen: Von Ariovist bis zu den Wikingern*. München: Verlag C. H. Beck oHG; Hattenhauer, Hans. 1990. *Geschichte der deutschen Nationalsymbole: Zeichen und Bedeutung*. Munich: Olzog Verlag; Hattenhauer, Hans. 2006. *Deutsche Nationalsymbole: Geschichte und Bedeutung*. München: Olzog Verlag GmbH; Koop, Andreas. 2008. *NSCI: Das visuelle Erscheinungsbild der Nationalsozialisten 1920–1945*. Mainz: Verlag Hermann Schmidt; Münkler, Herfried. 2010. *Die Deutschen und ihre Mythen*. Bonn: Bundeszentrale für politische Bildung; Reichel, Peter. 2005. *Schwarz-Rot-Gold: Kleine Geschichte deutscher Nationalsymbole*. Bonn: Bundeszentrale für politische Bildung; Reichel, Peter. 2006. *Der schöne Schein des Dritten Reiches: Gewalt und Faszination des deutschen Faschismus*. Hamburg: Ellert & Richter Zeitgeschichte; Weißmann, Karlheinz. 2007. *Deutsche Zeichen: Symbole des Reiches, Symbole der Nation*. Schnellroda: Edition Antaios.

47. Heller, Friedrich Paul, and Anton Maegerle. 2001. *Die Sprache des Hasses: Rechtsextremismus und völkische Esoterik*. Stuttgart: Schmetterling Verlag; Speit, Andreas, ed. 2010. *Ohne Juda, ohne Rom: Esoterik und Heidentum im subkulturellen Rechtsextremismus; Konzepte für Demokratie und Toleranz Band 8*. Braunschweig: Bildungsvereinigung Arbeit und Leben Niedersachsen Ost GmbH; Strohmeyer, Arn. 2005. *Von Hyperborea nach Auschwitz: Wege eines antiken Mythos*. Cologne: PapyRossa Verlags GmbH.

48. For a notable exception, see Goodrick-Clarke, Nicholas. 2002. *Black Sun: Aryan Cults, Esoteric Nazism and the Politics of Identity*. New York: New York University Press.

49. Knudsen, Daniel C., Jillian Rickly-Boyd, and Charles Greer. 2014. "Myth, National Identity and the Contemporary Tourism Site: The Case of Amalienborg and Frederiksstaden." *National Identities* 16(1): 53–70; Knudsen, Rickly-Boyd, and Greer (2014); Laruelle, Marlene. 2007. "The Return of the Aryan Myth: Tajikistan in Search of a Secularized National Identity." *Nationalities Papers* 35(1): 51–70; Smith, Anthony. 1996. "LSE Centennial Lecture: The Resurgence of Nationalism? Myth and Memory in the Renewal of Nations." *British Journal of Sociology* 47(4): 575–98.

50. See Williamson 2004: 6.

51. Miller-Idriss (2009); Smith (1991).

52. Smith (2000a: 807); Smith, Anthony. 2000b. "The 'Sacred' Dimension of Nationalism." *Millenium: Journal of International Studies* 29(3): 791–814.

53. McIlwain 2003.

54. Mosse, George L. 1985. *Nationalism and Sexuality: Respectability and Abnormal Sexuality in Modern Europe.* New York: Howard Fertig.

55. Smith (2000a, 2000b).

56. Griffin (2008b).

57. Griffin (2008a, 2008b).

58. I thank Joan Ramon Resina for the phrase "restoration to a past utopia," which he used to describe the Spanish case (public lecture at Morphomata Kolleg, University of Cologne, June 2014).

59. Smith (2000b: 808).

60. As Will Baldet has noted, a cluster of elements (doomsday framing, radical action, and a moral or social or religious obligation to follow through on beliefs) is likely to lead to violent extremist action. I would suggest that this cluster of elements is significantly aided when integrated with aspects of sacred origin narratives as outlined above. Baldet presentation, "The Hate Equation," from the ESRC Seminar "Right Wing Extremism in Contemporary Europe: Issues of Policy and Practice," Wiener Library for the Study of the Holocaust and Genocide, November 13, 2015.

61. The Aryan racial myth tells the story of a tribe called "Aryans" who invaded India sometime during the pre-Christian era. See Dunlap, Knight. 1944. "The Great Aryan Myth." *Scientific Monthly* 59(4): 296–300, p. 296. No historical evidence of such a group is available; the first mentions of Aryan "racial stock," Dunlap points out, show up in the mid-nineteenth century, meaning that the Aryan myth "is a modern invention" (p. 296). Related slippages between ethnicity and language were taking place even earlier; the term *deutsch*, for example, which is used in modern times to convey both German citizenship or ethnicity and German language, was originally used exclusively as a linguistic term but began to be used as a term to denote an entire people (the Germans) in the fifteenth century (Liulevicius 2009: 32).

62. Dunlap (1944: 296–97; also see Williamson (2004: 212–13).

63. Dunlap (1944: 297).

64. Liulevicius (2009: 114).

65. Dunlap (1944: 297).

66. Liulevicius (2009: 117).

67. Dunlap (1944: 299).

68. Liulevicius (2009: 122). The Nordics were known to the Greeks as Hyperboreans but were called "Germans" by the Romans (Dunlap 1944). Modern historians have sometimes identified the "Swedish Vikings," or Varangians, as a "Germanic" group, along with other early Germanic tribes like the Saxons, Frisians, Franks, and Carolingians and in contrast to other regional groups like the Slavs (Liulevicius 2009: 18–19).

69. Liulevicius (2009: 122).

70. The pre–World War I *völkish* movement blended esoteric and occult ideas with a "defensive ideology of 'Aryan' German folk identity" (Goodrick-Clarke 2002: 2 and 258).

71. Williamson (2004: 286); Liulevicius (2009).

72. See the extensive discussion in Christopher Krebs's 2012 treatise *A Most Dangerous Book: Tacitus' Germania from the Roman Empire to the Third Reich*. New York: W. W. Norton. As Krebs points out, the notion of Nordic descent is based at least in part on the manuscript of a Roman scribe (Tacitus) who likely never set foot in Germania but instead compiled an "armchair ethnography" of the Germanic tribes for political reasons and gathered details from literary sources, merchants, soldiers, and a general "mosaic of Greek and Roman stereotypes" (Krebs 2012: 49).

73. See p. 1002 of Bernal, Martin. 1995. "Race, Class and Gender in the Formation of the Aryan Model of Greek Origins." In "Nations, Identities, Cultures." Special issue, *South Atlantic Quarterly* 94(4): 987–1008.

74. Krebs (2012: 49). Notably, Tacitus described Germanic tribes as characterized by moral and linguistic purity (which later became intertwined with purity of blood) — what Christopher Krebs refers to as the "Tacitean myth of the indigenous and pure German people" (Krebs 2012: 114).

75. Krebs (2012: 183).

76. Williamson (2004: 2).

77. Krebs (2012: 128).

78. Krebs (2012: 175).

79. Nietzsche (1995 [1872]: 90–91).

80. Varshizky, Amit. 2012. "Alfred Rosenberg: The Nazi Weltanschauung as Modern Gnosis." *Politics, Religion and Ideology* 13(3): 311–31.

81. Eller (2013: 200).

82. Varshizky (2012: 321).

83. Varshizky (2012: 329), citing Whisker, James. 1990. *The Philosophy of Alfred Rosenberg*. Costa Mesa, CA: Noontide, p. 274.

84. S. Heller (2000: 63).

85. Dunlap (1944: 297).

86. Griffin (2008b: 81). Notably, the expulsion of all who were deemed not to belong to such a German utopia — including Jews, homosexuals, the disabled, and others — is consistent with mythical and fantastical thinking; Eliade notes that the expulsion of "foreigners" was a primordial impulse of traditional societies, in part because territories were thought of as consecrated, sacred spaces to be protected from invasion and incursion by outsiders, which would ultimately lead to chaos (1957: 29–47).

87. Williamson (2004: 293).

88. Williamson (2004: 294).

89. Krebs (2012: 218).

90. Weißmann, Karlheinz. 2006. *Das Hakenkreuz: Symbol eines Jahrhunderts.* Schnellroda: Edition Antaios; Weißmann (2007).

91. The swastika is one of the oldest known symbols; evidence of its use has turned up across multiple continents in carvings, gravestones, mosaics, ceramics, and other art forms (see Weißmann 2006). For example, it was an ancient symbol of life in Indian culture (see Williamson 2004: 292) and appears in nineteenth-century American iconography as a symbol of good luck (Weißmann 2006: 49). Weißmann notes that the political decision to deploy the swastika was a strategic choice that enabled Hitler to appeal to multiple interpretations simultaneously: for some, it is seen as an ancient Aryan symbol while for others it is an "emblem of anti-Semites," a holy Germanic sign of salvation, or a symbol of nature (Weißmann 2006: 101).

92. See Williamson (2004: 290–91).

93. See plate 21 for details. The image is part of a series of propaganda slides from a Hitler Youth educational presentation entitled "5000 years of German Culture."

94. Guerlain, Sarah. 2010. "Geheimer Orden und dunkle Sonnen—Mythen um die Schutzstaffel." Pp. 75–104 in *Ohne Juda, ohne Rom: Esoterik und Heidentum im subkulturellen Rechtsextremismus; Konzepte für Demokratie und Toleranz Band 8,* edited by Andreas Speit. Braunschweig: Bildungsvereinigung Arbeit und Leben Niedersachsen Ost GmbH.

95. Krebs (2012: 228, 233, 241); also see Reitzenstein (2014).

96. Williamson (2004: 299).

97. Krebs (2012: 217, 224).

98. Krebs (2012: 227).

99. Paul (1995); Steinmetz (1997).

100. Sawyer, Peter. 1997. *The Oxford Illustrated History of the Vikings.* Oxford: Oxford University Press, p. 210.

101. Agentur für soziale Perspektiven (2009).

102. Schuppener, Georg. 2010. *Sprache des Rechtsextremismus: Spezifika der Sprache rechtsextremistischer Publikationen und rechter Musik. 2. Auflage.* Leipzig: Edition Hamouda, Wissenschaftsverlag; also see Schuppener (2007).

103. Goodrick-Clarke (2002).

104. Mediatex, the parent company of the Thor Steinar brand, was bought out in 2008 by a conglomerate based in Dubai; the products continue to use coded far right symbols.

105. See, e.g., Rogers (2015).

106. See, e.g., Scholte, Jan. 2005. *Globalization: A Critical Introduction.* New York: Palgrave Macmillan; Bauman (2000).

107. Klinenberg, Eric. 2013. *Going Solo: The Extraordinary Rise and Surprising Appeal of Living Alone.* New York: Penguin Books.

108. Sheldrake, Philip. 2001. *Spaces for the Sacred: Place, Memory, and Identity.* Baltimore: Johns Hopkins University Press, p. 8.

109. The discussion in this and subsequent paragraphs of Griffin's theory comes from his September 25, 2014, lecture at the Economic and Social Research Council seminar on right-wing extremism, held at Pantheon University in

Athens, Greece; published works outlining elements of the theory and related arguments can be found in Griffin 2014, 2008a, and 2008b.

110. Griffin lecture, 2014; the phrase "sacred canopy" is attributed to Berger, Peter L. 1967. *The Sacred Canopy: Elements of a Sociological Theory of Religion*. New York: Anchor Books.
111. Bauman (2007b: 98).
112. Varshizky (2012: 330).
113. Sheldrake (2001: 19).
114. Sheldrake (2001); also see Miller-Idriss (2009) on taboos on German national pride.
115. Sheldrake (2001: 94).
116. See Hell, Julia. 1997. *Post-fascist Fantasies: Psychoanalysis, History, and the Literature of East Germany*. Durham, NC: Duke University Press. It is important to note that there is a distinction between folklore and fantasy and that there are historical elements to the history of the Germanic tribes that help lay the groundwork for the fantasy of Nordic inheritance. Indeed, the fact that fantasies draw on some elements of historical fact might make them more powerful. See Kamentsky, Christa. 1977. "Folktale and Ideology in the Third Reich." *Journal of American Folklore* 90(356): 168–78.
117. McIlwain (2003: 80).
118. Goodrick-Clarke (2002: 145).
119. Gibbs, David. 2011. "See How You Feel." Pp. 7–11 in *Symbol*, edited by Angus Hyland and Steven Bateman. London: Laurence King, p. 7.
120. Miller-Idriss, Cynthia. 2006. "Everyday Understandings of Citizenship in Germany." *Citizenship Studies* 10: 541–70.
121. Of Germany's 2013 population, 20.5 percent had a migrant background. https://www.destatis.de/EN/FactsFigures/SocietyState/Population/Population.html, accessed July 1, 2015.
122. Statistics cited in Hebel, Christina, Benjamin Knaack, and Christoph Sydow. 2014. "Pegida Faktencheck: Die Angstbürger." *Spiegel Online*. December 14, http://www.spiegel.de/politik/deutschland/pegida-die-thesen-im-faktencheck-a-1008098-druck.html, accessed July 1, 2015.
123. Krebs (2012: 134).
124. Michaelis, Arno. 2015. "This Is How You Become a White Supremicist." *Washington Post*. June 25, https://www.washingtonpost.com/posteverything/wp/2015/06/25/this-is-how-you-become-a-white-supremacist/?utm_term=.cdd0c3b2f71c.
125. Michaelis (2015).
126. Fiske, Alan Page, and Tage Shakti Rai. 2015. *Virtuous Violence: Hurting and Killing to Create, Sustain, End, and Honor Social Relationships*. Cambridge: Cambridge University Press.
127. Agentur für soziale Perspektiven (2009).
128. See, e.g., Griffin (2014).
129. By way of comparison with the U.S. case, as I have noted elsewhere, for the German far right, the aspirational nation comes first, and racial purity is implied, while for U.S. right-wing extremists, racial separation comes first, and national purity is implied.

Chapter 4. Dying for a Cause, Causing Death: The Threat of Violence

1. Epigraph: Hesse, Hermann. 1965 [1919]. *Demian*. New York: Harper and Row, pp. 14–15; as cited in Hunt, Maurice. 2015. *The Divine Face in Four Writers: Shakespeare, Dostoyevsky, Hesse, and C. S. Lewis*. London: Bloomsbury, p. 97.
2. The burgeoning subfield of medical sociology and in particular end-of-life research is one exception; see, e.g., Luth, Elizabeth. 2017. "Social and Health Determinants of End-of-Life Care Quality: A Multidimensional Approach." Ph.D. diss., Rutgers University.
3. See, e.g., F. Heller and Maegerle (2001); Speit (2010); Strohmeyer (2005).
4. See especially extended discussion of Köhler (2017a) of the ritualization of violence in far right extremism and right-wing terrorism.
5. Panofsky (1955: 308).
6. I owe Daniel Köhler tremendous thanks for providing a detailed written explanation of the historical use of the death's head by the SS-Totenkopf and its meaning and for several other points about the connection between death, violence, and far right ideology, which have much enriched this chapter.
7. Panofsky (1955: 300).
8. Seale, Clive. 1998. *Constructing Death: The Sociology of Dying and Bereavement*. Cambridge: Cambridge University Press.
9. Wolfgang Braungart's treatment of Rilke's words in his November 2013 lecture at Morphomata, University of Cologne, was a critical source for this chapter. Quotations from Rilke are from an English translation of "The Ninth Elegy," pp. 198–203, in Stephen Mitchell, ed. and trans. 1982. *The Selected Poetry of Rainer Maria Rilke*. New York: Random House, p. 199.
10. See McIlwain (2003).
11. Panofsky (1955: 309).
12. I am indebted to Daniel Köhler for this point.
13. Gorer, Geoffrey. 1967. *Death, Grief and Mourning*. New York: Anchor/Doubleday.
14. Quoted in Didion, Joan. 2005. *The Year of Magical Thinking*. London: Fourth Estate, p. 60; also see Aries, Philippe. 1981. *Hour of Our Death*. Oxford: Oxford University Press; Becker, Ernest. 1973. *The Denial of Death*. New York: Free Press; Glaser, Barney, and Anselm Strauss. 1965. *Awareness of Dying*. Piscataway, NJ: Transaction; Harrison, Robert Pogue. 2003. *The Dominion of the Dead*. Chicago: University of Chicago Press; Wong, Paul T., Gary T. Reker, and Gina Gesser. 1994. "Death Attitude Profile—Revisited: A Multidimensional Measure of Attitudes toward Death." Pp. 121–48 in *Death Anxiety Handbook: Research, Instrumentation, and Application*, edited by Robert Niemeyer. London: Routledge.
15. According to McIlwain (2003: 20–21); see also Gorer's original essay: Gorer, Geoffrey. 1955. "The Pornography of Death." *Encounter*. October, p. 50.
16. As cited by McIlwain (2003: 23).
17. Wallace and Kovacheva (1996).
18. Hebdige (1979).
19. Van der Valk, Ineke, and Willem Wagenaar. 2010. *The Extreme Right: Entry and Exit*. Leiden: Anne Frank House/Leiden University, p. 47.
20. Unfortunately, there is little empirical research tracing the use of death iconography in youth subcultures. This is a rich potential area for future research,

particularly as it would help tease out what is unique about the far right's use of these symbols compared to other youth subcultural groups' use of death symbols. I thank an anonymous reviewer for pointing this out.

21. Personal correspondence from Daniel Köhler.
22. For example, the political cartoonist Arthur Szyk used images of the skull and crossbones, as well as skulls more generally, in several of his cartoons about the Nazi era. See the bibliography and images available at the U.S. Holocaust Memorial Museum, https://www.ushmm.org/collections/bibliography/arthur-szyk, accessed May 7, 2017.
23. See McConnell, Winder, and Werner Wunderlich. 2015. *The Nibelungen Tradition: An Encyclopedia.* New York: Routledge.
24. I thank Daniel Köhler for reminding me of this point.
25. Köhler (2017a: 55–56).
26. Köhler (2017a).
27. See, for example, the detailed account of the NSU murders detailed in Deutsche Welle. 2013. "Chronicle of the NSU Murders." April 16, http: //www.dw.com/ overlay_media/chronicle-of-the-nsu-murders/g-16743396, accessed April 21, 2016.
28. For more on the name change, see *Spiegel Online.* 2012a. "Fashion Faux Pas: Controversial 'Brevik' Clothing Store Changes Name." March 8, http: //www .spiegel.de/international/germany/fashion-faux-pas-controversial-brevik-clothing -store-changes-name-a-820080.html, accessed January 15, 2014.
29. Because spätzle is traditionally rooted in the southwestern German state of Baden-Württemberg, the term itself acts as a symbol for this region and its people (Swabians). Using a symbol of this pasta on a sign at a far right event therefore indicates that the group is based in the Baden-Württemberg region. I am indebted to Daniel Köhler for this information (personal correspondence).
30. See Wallace and Kovacheva (1996) on performative messaging. I would note that such specific death symbols might simultaneously serve the same kinds of functions as the death's head, since observers may react to the slight of a bloody ax or a noose in a similar way (provoking anxiety or fear). But their primary aim, I would suggest, is more specific.
31. This has come up periodically in Germany in a variety of contexts. See, e.g., Wittrock, Philipp. 2006. "Umstrittener Vergleich: Häuptling Koch und die Indianer." *Spiegel Online.* May 29, http: //www.spiegel.de/politik/deutschland/um strittener-vergleich-haeuptling-koch-und-die-indianer-a-418605.html, accessed January 16, 2014.
32. Sawyer (1997: 2).
33. See Smith (2000a, 2000b, 2003).
34. See discussion of the Phalanx Europa brand in the Amadeu Antonio Foundation's digital platform *Belltower News*: Garrel (2015). Garrel identifies the brand as Austrian and part of the Identitäre movement—the Identitäre are typically characterized as a modern, young movement within the far right spectrum. For a fuller discussion, see Hafeneger, Benno. 2014. "Die Identitären: Vorüberge-hendes Phänomen oder neue Bewegung?" Published by the Friedrich Ebert Stiftung, available at http: //library.fes.de/pdf-files/dialog/10649.pdf.
35. Original German: "Weil Todesbereitschaft nur aus den Augen der Masse aus-sieht wie Todessehnsucht. Weil ein Leben auf der Suche nach Schicksal nur aus

den Augen unserer Eltern aussieht wie eine gescheiterte Existenz. Weil unser gefährliches Denken nur aus den Augen der Kleingeister aussieht wie Extremismus. Weil unsere Haltung nur von unten aussieht wie Arroganz. Deshalb sind wir nicht nur Gast auf der Erde, sondern Leben nach Goethes Worten: Stirb und Werde."

36. Sawyer (1997: 217).
37. I thank Daniel Köhler for feedback about the role of violence as it relates to far right ideology. Also see Schuppener (2007: 97).
38. Two of the NPD's election posters were initially banned in Berlin's Kreuzberg district, but the Kreuzberg district office (Bezirksamt) overturned this decision and permitted the posters to be used. See *Die Welt*, "NPD-Wahlplakate sind nicht rechtswidrig." July 9, http: //www.welt.de/regionales/berlin/article13591648/NPD -Wahlplakate-sind-nicht-rechtswidrig.html, accessed May 21, 2016.
39. See especially Köhler (2017a).
40. See for example Köhler and Speransky (forthcoming). It's worth noting as well that two of the youth mentioned experiences where they or others had dressed up as or imitated Hitler as a joke. Hayri noted, "OK, but I'd say, who hasn't done that [dressed up as Hitler]. Everyone's shaved [a mustache] or something for fun at some point." Julian described a Halloween party he had been to the year before where the DJ was dressed up as Adolf Hitler, with breasts, "doing Sieg Heil, Sieg Heil the whole time . . . but that's funny . . . these days that's not serious."
41. For information about the concert, see the website of the Anti-racist Initiative Rostock (*Antirassistische Initiative Rostock*) at https: //systemausfall.org/anti ra/?q=node/530, accessed May 24, 2016. The concert "Dancing in the Air" is described on the website as having opened the ninth Anti-racist Action Week.
42. I thank Annett Graefe for very helpful discussions on this point as well as on the interpretation of the image of the Twin Towers, discussed below.

Chapter 5. Global Symbols, Local Bans: Transnational Nationalist Symbols

1. Epigraph: Gleiser, Marcelo. 2014. "Globalization: Two Visions of the Future of Humanity." Pp. 7–9 in *Globalization: A Reader for Writers*, edited by Maria Jerskey. Oxford: Oxford University Press, p. 9.
2. For a more detailed discussion, see the recent opinion essay in which a German colleague and I elaborate on the extensive civic education resources in German aimed at combating extremism. See Köhler, Daniel, and Cynthia Miller-Idriss. 2017. "The Most Dangerous National Security Threat That Donald Trump Is Ignoring." Fortune.com. February 13, http://fortune.com/2017/02/13/donald -trump-national-security-cve-right-wing-extremism-terrorism-germany/, accessed May 8, 2017.
3. As discussed in Köhler and Miller-Idriss (2017).
4. See Shoshan (2016) for a discussion of what he calls the "management of hate"—the broad combination of legal and penal codes, state surveillance, interventions, regulations, and initiatives that target the far right in Germany.

5. See the extensive materials available at each of the Landeszentrale für politische Bildung (State Center for Political Education) and the Bundeszentrale für politische Bildung (Federal Center for Political Education), for example at https: // www.bpb.de/, accessed January 10, 2017.

6. See Cherian George's analysis of how "cross-border hate propaganda" has spread globally, in his chapter "God, Google, and the Globalization of Offendedness." George, Cherian. 2016. *Hate Spin: The Manufacture of Religious Offense and Its Threat to Democracy.* Cambridge, MA: MIT Press.

7. See, e.g., Berezin (1997); Copsey, Nigel, and John Richardson. 2015. *Cultures of Post-war British Fascism.* New York: Routledge; Copsey, Nigel and Graham Macklin (eds.). 2011. *British National Party: Contemporary Perspectives.* London: Routledge; Molnár (2016); Pilkington, Hilary. 2016. *Loud and Proud: Passion and Politics in the English Defence League.* Manchester, UK: Manchester University Press; Simi and Futrell (2010).

8. See, e.g., Semyonov, Raijman, and Gorodzeisky 2006; Thorisdottir, Hulda, John T. Jost, Ido Liviatan, and Patrick E. Shrout. 2007. "Psychological Needs and Values Underlying Left-Right Political Orientation: Cross-National Evidence from Eastern and Western Europe." *Public Opinion Quarterly* 71(2): 175–203; Wilkes, Guppy, and Farris 2007.

9. Scholte (2005).

10. Casey (2009: 299).

11. Anderson (1991).

12. I thank Jonathan Friedman for this point.

13. Langebach and Raabe (2011).

14. See the post and discussion on the right-wing extremist web forum Stormfront, at https: //www.stormfront.org/forum/t538924/, accessed March 10, 2016. The original post was dated November 8, 2008 and was posted in response to other comments, in the context of a discussion in the wake of the U.S. election (in which the first African American president, Barack Obama, was elected).

15. I am indebted to Larissa Förster for her feedback on the idea of traveling or circulating images.

16. Morgan (2005: 147–87).

17. Krasinski, Jennifer. 2015. "In a Captivating Show, Hito Steyerl Vivisects the Veracity of Video." *Village Voice.* April 22, http://www.villagevoice.com/arts/in-a-captivating-show-hito-steyerl-vivisects-the-veracity-of-video-7194669, accessed May 9, 2017.

18. Morgan (2005: 187).

19. Casey (2009: 262).

20. Casey (2009: 260).

21. Khatib (2013: 12), citing Hemphill, David F. 2001 "Incorporating Postmodernist Perspectives into Adult Education." Pp. 15–28 in *Making Space: Merging Theory and Practice in Adult Education*, edited by Peggy Sheared and Vanessa Sissel. Westport, CT: Greenwood.

22. O'Carroll, Eoin. 2011. "Political Misquotes: The 10 Most Famous Things Never Actually Said." *Christian Science Monitor.* June 3, http://www.csmonitor.com/USA/Politics/2011/0603/Political-misquotes-The-10-most-famous-things-never-actually-said/I-can-see-Russia-from-my-house!-Sarah-Palin, accessed May 9, 2017.

23. Michael (2009: 56), citing Kaplan, Jeffrey, and Leonard Weinberg. 1998. *The Emergence of a Euro-American Radical Right*. New Brunswick, NJ: Rutgers University Press.

24. As described in the Anti-defamation League (ADL)'s Hate Symbols Database; see the description of the blood drop cross at http: //www.adl.org/combating -hate/hate-on-display/c/blood-drop-cross.html, accessed March 10, 2016.

25. Kidd (2015).

26. The large imperial eagle (*Reichsadler*) was "the most common Nazi symbol aside from the swastika" and became the national emblem of the Third Reich (S. Heller 2008: 29–30).

27. *Volk* translates as "the national people," so using it as an adjective translates loosely as "nationalist." But the specific adjective "völkish" also refers to a particular group of political and youth movements, with origins in the late nineteenth and twentieth centuries, that blended Nordic, Aryan, Germanic, and pagan myths and ideals into a specific form of nationalism. See chapter 3 for a lengthier discussion. Also see Goodrick-Clarke (2002), Liulevicius (2009), and Williamson (2004).

28. Rogers (2015).

29. Kidd (2015).

30. Osuch and Eluek (2016).

31. See the Dortrix website at http: //www.dortrix.com/, accessed March 24, 2016.

32. Hannes, Heine. 2009. "Rechte Szene: Thor Steinar will weltweit expandieren." In *Der Tagesspiegel*. March 23, http://www.tagesspiegel.de/berlin/rechte-szene -thor-steinar-will-weltweit-expandieren/1480814.html, accessed May 9, 2017.

33. Berliner Morgenpost. "Arabischer Investor kauft Thor Steinar," 24. März 2009, http: //www.morgenpost.de/berlin/article1058671/Arabischer_Investor_kauft _Thor_Steinar.html, accessed January 11, 2011.

34. Rogers (2015).

35. Cruzcampo, Oliver. 2011. "Berliner 'Erik & Sons'-Laden macht dicht." *Endstation Rechts*. February 11, http: //www.endstation-rechts.de/news/kategorie/ nazilaeden-1/artikel/berliner-erik-sons-laden-macht-dicht.html, accessed April 7, 2016.

36. Hannemann (2016).

37. The court did in fact ban the symbol. This opened the door to the banning of symbols that express neo-Nazi or right-wing extremist ideology, even if they have not previously been connected to a banned organization. In such cases, courts rely on their ability to ban symbols because of the meaning (*Sinnverhalt*) contained in the symbol, rather than because the symbols represent a re-creation of a symbol connected to the banned organization. With thanks to colleagues at apabiz for discussions of this case. For a recent description of legally banned symbols, including the Celtic cross, see Günter, Christian. 2014. "Rune, Hakenkreuz: Welche Symbole und Zeichen sind Verboten?" *Kölnische Rundschau*. June 25, http://www.rundschau-online.de/ratgeber/finanzen/recht/symbole-zeichen-verbo ten-hakenkreuz-fdj-verbot-verfassungswidrig-849462, accessed May 9, 2017.

38. Knapp, Ursula. 2009. "Ein Schlupfloch für Naziparolen." *Frankfurter Rundschau*. August 13, http://www.fr.de/importe/fr-online/home/bundesgericht shof-urteil-zu-blood-honour-ein-schlupfloch-fuer-naziparolen-a-1087491.

39. Southern Poverty Law Center. 2009. "Germans OK Nazi Signs, in Other Languages." *Intelligence Report.* November 30, https://www.splcenter.org/fighting-hate/intelligence-report/2009/germans-ok-nazi-signs-other-languages.
40. Knapp (2009).
41. Kidd (2015).
42. "The White Continent" is a phrase that commonly refers to the continent of Antarctica. See, e.g., Gurney, Alan. 2002. *The Race to the White Continent: Voyages to the Antarctic.* New York: W. W. Norton.
43. There are clear social class and educational differences in Germany in terms of English language ability. The interview sample has a clear bias in this regard because I focused on youth training for construction trades, who spend less time learning English than students in traditional or academic high schools. If I had conducted interviews with a group of *Gymnasium* students, it is much more likely that interviewees would have understood these foreign language references; this may also be true for some of the historical references in the coded symbols. I thank Daniel Köhler for pointing this out.
44. Gereluk, Dianne. 2008. *Symbolic Clothing in Schools: What Should Be Worn and Why.* New York: Continuum, p. 1.
45. Gereluk (2008); Goldstein, Arnold, and Donald Kadlubov. 1998. *Gangs in Schools: Signs, Symbols and Solutions.* Champaign, IL: Research Press.
46. Miller-Idriss (2009).
47. Anti-antifa activities and subgroups are highly ideologically committed, typically senior members of far right organizations with specialized skills in counterintelligence or information technology. They have a reputation for being brutal and militant. I thank Daniel Köhler for this information (personal correspondence).
48. A derogatory term for Turks.
49. Concrete boat competitions are held regularly in Germany and Europe; typically, teams of students who are training in construction or engineering fields construct a fully concrete boat and compete in a race or series of races. See, e.g., https: //www.beton.org/inspiration/betonkanu-regatta/ or http: //www .betonboot.de/, accessed January 12, 2017.
50. A colleague from an antifascist organization reported in summer 2010 that the deployment of the Che Guevara shirts was fiercely contested in the far right scene and had not been seen in months or even years.

Chapter 6. Soldier, Sailor, Rebel, Rule Breaker: Embodying Extremism

1. Epigraph: Vinken, Barbara. 2016. *Die Angst vor der Kastration: Über rechtsradikale Mode.* Hamburg: Sven Murmann Verlagsgesellschaft mbH, p. 173.
2. The peculiarities of the German context and the historical intertwining of nationalism, patriotism, and racism mean that all three concepts are linked within the broad spectrum of far right ideology, particularly as applied to subcultural style and groups as opposed to formal political movements. Nationalism is thus—at times—evidenced in this case through instances including calls to Nordic origins or to being proud of being German (see Miller-Idriss 2009 for

more detail). I thank Hilary Pilkington and an anonymous reviewer for helping me articulate this point.

3. Connell, R. W. 1995. *Masculinities*. Berkeley: University of California Press.

4. Meuser, Michael. 1998. *Geschlect und Männlichkeit: Soziologische Theorie und kulturelle Deutungsmuster*. Opladen: Leske & Budrich; Virchow, Fabian. 2008. "Die Bedeutung von Männlichkeitsstereotypen im Rechtsextremismus." Manuscript prepared for Brave Mädels und echte Kerle? Theorie und Praxis von Geschlecterrollen im Rechtsextremismus. Conference held by Friedrich Ebert Stiftung. January 23, 2008, Berlin, http://www.fes-gegen-rechtsextremismus.de/pdf_08/080123_virchow.pdf, accessed May 21, 2017.

5. Mosse, George. 1998. *The Image of Man: The Creation of Modern Masculinity*. New York: Oxford University Press; Joane Nagel. 1998. "Masculinity and Nationalism: Gender and Sexuality in the Making of Nations." *Ethnic and Racial Studies* 21(2): 242–69.

6. Nagel (1998: 251).

7. Anand, Dibyesh. 2007. "Anxious Sexualities: Masculinity, Nationalism, and Violence." *British Journal of Political and International Relations* 9: 257–69, p. 257.

8. Waetjen, Thembisa. 2001. "The Limits of Gender Rhetoric for Nationalism: A Case Study from Southern Africa." *Theory and Society* 30(1): 121–52, p. 23.

9. Tumblety, Joan. 2012. *Remaking the Male Body: Masculinity and the Uses of Physical Culture in Interwar and Vichy France*. Cambridge: Oxford University Press, p. 4; also see Anand (2007: 260–61) on Hindu nationalists' emphasis on physical exercise for boys.

10. Tumblety (2012: 4).

11. Also see Vlossak, Elizabeth. 2010. *Marianne or Germania? Nationalizing Women in Alsace, 1870–1946*. Cambridge: Oxford University Press.

12. Bernal (1995: 1008).

13. Caplan, Gregory A. 2003. "Militarism and Masculinity as Keys to the 'Jewish Question' in Germany." Pp. 175–90 in *Military Masculinities: Identity and the State*, edited by Paul R. Higate. Westport, CT: Praeger, p. 177; Mosse (1985).

14. Linke, Uli 1999. *German Bodies: Race and Representation after Hitler*. New York: Routledge; Mosse (1985).

15. Linke, Uli. 1997. "Gendered Difference, Violent Imagination: Blood, Race, Nation." *American Anthropologist* 99(3): 559–73, p. 564.

16. Patterson (2014: 10); Richardson, Niall, and Adam Locks. 2014. *Body Studies: The Basics*. New York: Routledge, p. ix.

17. Dussel, Inés. 2004. "Fashioning the Schooled Self through Uniforms: A Foucauldian Approach to Contemporary School Policies." Pp. 85–116 in *Dangerous Coagulations: The Uses of Foucault in the Study of Education*, edited by Bernadette Baker and Katharina M. Heyning. New York: Peter Lang, p. 89.

18. Ghannam, Farha. 2013. *Live and Die Like a Man: Gender Dynamics in Urban Egypt*. Stanford, CA: Stanford University Press, p. 5; Richardson and Locks (2014: 23).

19. Quotes in this sentence and the previous one are from Richardson and Locks (2014: 24). Also see Swain, Jon. 2002. "The Right Stuff: Fashioning an Identity through Clothing in a Junior School." *Gender and Education* 14(1): 53–69, for a related example.

20. See also Pilkington (2010a and 2010b).
21. See Adelman, Miriam, and Linnita Ruggi. 2015. "The Sociology of the Body." *Current Sociology* 64(6): 1–24.
22. Ghannam (2013: 6).
23. Richardson and Locks (2014: 37). (See Messner, Michael. 1990. "Boyhood, Organized Sports and the Construction of Masculinities." *Journal of Contemporary Ethnography* 18[4]: 416–44; and Way [2011] on idealized manliness and appropriate masculine behavior). Also see also see Nagel, Joane. 2010. "Ethnicities and Sexualities." Pp. 188–220 in *The SAGE Handbook of Race and Ethnic Studies*, edited by John Solomos and Patricia Hill Collins. Thousand Oaks, CA: SAGE, especially on the issue of performativity and the body.
24. Richardson and Locks (2014: 37), citing Pope, Harrison, Kate Phillips, and Roberto Olivardia. 2000. *The Adonis Complex: The Secret Crisis of Male Body Obsession*. London: Simon and Schuster.
25. Richardson and Locks (2014: 24).
26. Nayak, Anoop. 2005. "White Lives." Pp. 141–62 in *Racialization: Studies in Theory and Practice*, edited by K. Murji and J. Solomos. Oxford: Oxford University Press, p. 150, cited in Pilkington (2010a: 156).
27. On physical strength and working-class style, see especially Pilkington (2010a and 2010b); and Halkitis, Perry N. 2000. "Masculinity in the Age of AIDS: HIV-Seropositive Gay Men and the 'Buff Agenda.'" *Research on Men and Masculinities Series* 12: 130–51; for a discussion of economic disenfranchisement, see Kimmel, Michael S. 2005. "Globalization and Its Mal(e)contents: The Gendered Moral and Political Economy of Terrorism." Pp. 414–31 in *Handbook of Studies on Men and Masculinities*, edited by Michael S. Kimmel, Jeff Hearn, and R. W. Connell. Thousand Oaks, CA: Sage. Pascoe (2007) discusses issues of heterosexual masculinity, as does Pilkington (2010a and 2010b). On questions of lack of opportunity and marginalization, see Rios, Victor, and Rachel Sarabia. 2016. "Synthesized Masculinities: The Mechanics of Manhood among Delinquent Boys." Pp. 166–77 in *Exploring Masculinities: Identity, Inequality, Continuity, and Change*, edited by C. J. Pascoe and Tristan Bridges. New York: Oxford University Press.
28. Ghannam (2013: 22).
29. Pilkington (2010a).
30. Tumblety (2012).
31. Adelman and Ruggi (2015); Surak (2013: 5).
32. Miller-Idriss (2006, 2009).
33. Surak (2013: 5).
34. Surak (2013: 6).
35. See, e.g., Enloe, Cynthia 2001. *Bananas, Beaches and Bases: Making Sense of International Politics*. Berkeley: University of California Press; Kanaaneh, Rhoda Ann. 2002. *Birthing the Nation: Strategies of Palestinian Women in Israel*. Berkeley: University of California Press; Kimmel, Michael 2013. *Angry White Men: American Masculinity at the End of an Era*. New York: Nation Books; Linke (1997, 1999); Nagel, Joane. 1998. "Masculinity and Nationalism: Gender and Sexuality in the Making of Nations." *Ethnic and Racial Studies* 21(2): 242–69; Yuval-Davis, Nira, and Floya Anthias. 1989. *Women-Nation-State*. New York: St. Martin's.

36. See especially work by Ferber, Abby L. 1998. *White Man Falling: Race, Gender, and White Supremacy.* Lanham, MD: Rowman and Littlefield; Ferber, Abby L. and Michael S. Kimmel. 2008. "The Gendered Face of Terrorism." *Sociology Compass* 2(3): 870–87; Kimmel (2005); Simi, Bubolz, and Hardman (2013); and Virchow (2008). Gender differences in right-wing extremist engagement have been well documented cross-culturally, particularly in voting patterns and in acts of violence. See, e.g., Rippl, Susanne, and Christian Seipel. 1999. "Gender Differences in Right-Wing Extremism: Intergroup Validity of a Second-Order Construct." *Social Psychology Quarterly* 62: 381–93.

37. Pilkington (2010b: 189).

38. See the short essay by Barbara Vinken (2016) on right-wing radical fashion for a recent exception to the gap in the literature in this area.

39. Virchow (2008).

40. Virchow (2008: iv); also see Hopton, John. 2003. "The State and Military Masculinity." Pp. 111–24 in *Military Masculinities: Identity and the State*, edited by Paul R. Higate. Westport, CT: Praeger.

41. Virchow (2008: v).

42. Kimmel (2005: 422).

43. Simi, Bubolz, and Hardman (2013).

44. For more on the Tibet expedition, see Monika Köhler's 1989 discussion in her review of the film *Terra X*, "Wissenschaft im Dienst der Nazis: Professor Ernst Schäfer; Neues vom Nichtwissen." *Die Zeit*, http: //www.zeit.de/1989/04/ neues-vom-nichtwissen.

45. Caiani, Manuela, Donatella della Porta, and Claudius Wagemann. 2012. *Mobilizing on the Extreme Right: Germany, Italy and the United States.* Oxford: Oxford University Press, p. 122.

46. Hammerbacher (2015).

47. Importantly, this phrase is associated with a football team in Liverpool, UK. I thank Hilary Pilkington for reminding me of this connection.

48. Omel'chenko, Elena. 2010. "In Search of Intimacy: Homosociality, Masculinity and the Body." Pp. 166–86 in *Russia's Skinheads: Exploring and Rethinking Subcultural Lives*, edited by Hilary Pilkington, Elena Omel'chenko, and Al'bina Garifzianova. London: Routledge.

49. Kimmel (2005: 424), citing Bjørgo, Tore. 1997. *Racist and Right-Wing Violence in Scandinavia: Patterns, Perpetrators, and Responses.* Leiden: University of Leiden, p. 136.

50. Pilkington (2010a, 2010b).

51. As seen on the now broken link of the Reconquista website, http: //www.rcqt .de/Laden/, accessed 27 September 2011. As chapter 5 noted, the brand name Reconquista itself is a code, in reference to the Christian pogrom against Muslims in Andalusia in the Middle Ages. The Reconquista website was taken off line in November following a police search of the company after Reconquista advertised a T-shirt with a coded symbolic reference to the migrant murder victims of the right-wing terrorist cell that was broken up in November 2011. It is not clear whether and when Reconquista will resume sales (see Kunow, Fabian. 2011. "Volksverhetzung—Polizei durchsucht Büros der Nazimarke 'Reconquista.'"

Zeit Online. November 30, http://blog.zeit.de/stoerungsmelder/2011/11/30/re
conquista-neue-nazimode-aus-berlin_7686#comments, accessed May 19, 2017).

52. Messerschmidt, James W. 1993. *Masculinities and Crime: Critique and Reconceptualization of Theory*. Lanham, MD: Rowman and Littlefield, pp. 94–95.

53. Simi, Bubolz, and Hardman (2013).

54. Pilkington (2010a, 2010b).

55. Rios and Sarabia (2016: 168), citing Pyke, K. D. 1996. "Class-Based Masculinities:
The Interdependence of Gender, Class and Interpersonal Power." *Gender and
Society* 10: 527–49.

56. Rios and Sarabia (2016: 168 and 175).

57. Kimmel (2005: 415); also see Messerschmidt, James. 2000. *Nine Lives: Adolescent
Masculinities, the Body, and Violence*. Boulder, CO: Westview, p. 10.

58. Statistics on employment and a host of other data are available through the
publications of the regional Statistics Office Berlin-Brandenburg (Amt für
Statistik Berlin-Brandenburg), available through the website, https://www.
statistik-berlin-brandenburg.de/, accessed May 10, 2017. The statistics cited
here come from the following reports on the construction trades in Berlin
and Brandenburg: *Statistischer Bericht—Baugewerbe in Berlin 2011, SB E II 2 / E
III 2—j / 11—Berlin*, available at https://www.statistik-berlin-brandenburg.de/
publikationen/stat_berichte/2011/SB_E2-2_E3-2_j01-11_BE.pdf, and *Statistischer
Bericht-Baugewerbe im Brandenburg 2012, E II 2 / E III 2—j / 12*, available at
https://www.statistik-berlin-brandenburg.de/Publikationen/Stat_Berichte/2013/
SB_E02-02-00_2012j01_BB.pdf, both published by the Amt für Statistik
Berlin-Brandenburg.

59. Deissinger, Thomas. 2015. "The German Dual Vocational Education and Training System as 'Good Practice'?" *Local Economy* 30(5): 557–67.

60. Miller-Idriss, Cynthia, and Annett Graefe. 2017. "Fitting In, Standing Out: Ambivalence and Multivocality in Far Right German Youth Style." Paper presented
at the American Sociological Association 112th Annual Meeting in Montreal,
Canada, August.

61. Simi, Bubolz, and Hardman (2013: 662); also see Cohen, Albert K. 1955. *Delinquent Boys: The Culture of the Gang*. New York: Free Press.

62. Michaelis (2015).

63. Rios and Sarabia (2016: 174).

64. Rios and Sarabia (2016: 175); also see p. 173, citing Harris, Angela. 2000. "Gender, Violence, Race, and Criminal Justice." *Stanford Law Review* 52(4): 777–807.
Also see Willis (1981).

65. Rios and Sarabia (2016: 168).

66. Rios and Sarabia (2016: 175).

67. Messerschmidt (2000: 13).

68. It is also important to note that articulations of masculinity are also deeply embedded in social contexts that are much broader than what I have been able to
detail here. Young people position themselves against police actions, aggression
from left-wing groups, or changing state policies on immigration, for example,
in ways that link themselves more strongly to others within their group even
as they are expressing anger or frustration against others. I am grateful to Will
Baldet for pointing this out in his presentation "The Hate Equation," from

the ESRC Seminar "Right Wing Extremism in Contemporary Europe: Issues of Policy and Practice," Wiener Library for the Study of the Holocaust and Genocide, November 13, 2015.

69. Also see Claus et al. (2010); Virchow (2010).
70. Kimmel (2005); also see Nagel, Joane. 2005. "Nation." Pp. 397–413 in *Handbook of Studies on Men and Masculinities*, edited by Michael S. Kimmel, Jeff Hearn, and R. W. Connell. Thousand Oaks, CA: Sage.

Conclusion. Mainstreaming the Extreme

1. Mishak, Michael J. 2015. "Are Donald Trump's Supporters Racist?" *Atlantic.* December 7, https://www.theatlantic.com/politics/archive/2015/12/are-donald -trumps-supporters-racist/450927/, accessed May 12, 2017.
2. Quote from Berenson, Tessa. 2016. "David Duke Says He and Donald Trump Have the Same Message." *Time Magazine.* September 30, http://time.com/4514350/da vid-duke-donald-trump-senate-louisiana/, accessed May 12, 2017; also see Holley, Peter. 2016. "KKK's Official Newspaper Supports Donald Trump for President." *Washington Post.* November 2, https://www.washingtonpost.com/news/post-pol itics/wp/2016/11/01/the-kkks-official-newspaper-has-endorsed-donald-trump-for -president/?utm_term=.e13bd1b737a6, accessed May 12, 2017.
3. Wemple, Erik. 2016. "PBS Issues Second Editor's Note on Trump-Supporter's White Supremacist Tattoos." *Washington Post.* March 17. https://www.washington post.com/blogs/erik-wemple/wp/2016/03/17/pbs-issues-second-editors-note -on-trump-supporters-white-supremacist-tattoos/?utm_term=.5138af4f7085, accessed May 12, 2017.
4. Moyer, Justin Wm. 2016. "D.C. Restaurant Apologizes after Hosting Alt-Right Dinner with 'Sieg Heil Salute.'" *Washington Post.* November 21, https://www .washingtonpost.com/news/local/wp/2016/11/21/d-c-restaurant-apologizes-after -hosting-alt-right-dinner-with-sieg-heil-salute/?utm_term=.5fe11209e546, ac- cessed May 12, 2017.
5. Hellmuth, Dorle. 2016. "Of Alienation, Association, and Adventure: Why Ger- man Fighters Join ISIL." *Journal for Deradicalization* (6): 24–50, p. 28.
6. For an exception, see Pilkington (2010a and 2010b) on Russian skinheads.
7. Picart, Caroline Joan S. 2015. "'Jihad Cool/Jihad Chic': The Roles of the Internet and Imagined Relations in the Self-Radicalization of Colleen LaRose (Jihad Jane)." *Societies* 5: 354–83, p. 361.
8. Picart (2015: 362).
9. Picart (2015: 362, citing Katz, Jack. 1988. *Seductions of Crime: Moral and Sensual Attractions in Doing Evil.* New York: Basic Books, p. 80, for quote about how, for many youth, being a badass and other symbols of deviance are a "good thing").
10. I am indebted to Daniel Köhler for this point.
11. See, e.g., Scott (1985: 38).
12. Gans (2012).
13. Patterson (2014).
14. Bartmański and Alexander (2012, especially p. 4); Durkheim (1995 [1915]); Kopytoff, Igor. 1988. "The Cultural Biography of Things: Commoditization as

Process." Pp. 64–91 in *The Social Life of Things: Commodities in Cultural Perspective*, edited by Arjun Appadurai. Cambridge: Cambridge University Press, p. 85.

15. Marx, Karl. 2017 [1867]. "Capital and the Values of Commodities." Pp. 40–46 in *Social Theory: The Multicultural, Global and Classic Readings*, 6th ed., edited by Charles Lemert. Boulder, CO: Westview, p. 45.

16. Bourdieu (1984). For a discussion of the embodiment of cultural capital, also see Shamus Khan's 2011 book *Privilege: The Making of an Adolescent Elite at St. Paul's School*. Princeton, NJ: Princeton University Press.

17. Kopytoff's contention is that because "commoditization homogenizes value, while the essence of culture is discrimination, excessive commoditization is anti-cultural," thereby excluding the possibility that commodities are also cultural objects. See Kopytoff (1988: 73); also see Durkheim (1995 [1915]) on the sacred nature of objects.

18. February 2, 2004, interview with Douglas Atkin on PBS Frontline, http://www.pbs.org/wgbh/pages/frontline/shows/persuaders/interviews/atkin.html, accessed June 9, 2016.

19. Atkin (2004: 199).

20. Molotch (2005); Zelizer (2011: 373).

21. Zelizer (2011: 402).

22. See Aronczyk (2013) on branding nations; Comaroff and Comaroff (2009) on marketing ethnicity; on fashion models and the VIP party circuit, see Mears, Ashley. 2011. *Pricing Beauty: The Making of a Fashion Model*. Berkeley: University of California Press; and Mears, Ashley. 2014. "Who Runs the Girls?" *New York Times*. September 20, https://www.nytimes.com/2014/09/21/opinion/sunday/who-runs-the-girls.html, accessed May 12, 2017.

23. Lamont and Molnár (2001); Todd (2004).

24. Zelizer (2011: 375, also see p. 429).

25. Molotch (2005: 8).

26. Griffin (2008b: 77).

27. As cited by Paul du Gay in his analysis of Willis and Hebdige's work on youth subcultures. Du Gay, Paul. 1996. *Consumption and Identity at Work*. Thousand Oaks, CA: Sage, p. 86.

28. Du Gay (1996), pp. 86–87.

29. Zelizer (2011: 399). Zelizer cites Putnam, Robert. 2000. *Bowling Alone: The Collapse and Revival of American Community*. New York: Simon and Schuster.

30. See Swidler (1986) on cultural "tool-kits."

31. Chan (2012).

32. I am indebted to Daniel Köhler for this astute observation (personal correspondence).

33. Sageman, Marc. 2004. *Understanding Terror Networks*. Philadelphia: University of Pennsylvania Press, p. 97.

34. See "Mit der freiwilligen Feuerwehr gegen Extremismus," *Deutsche Welle*. July 13, 2016, http://www.dw.com/de/mit-der-freiwilligen-feuerwehr-gegen-extremismus/a-19398283, accessed 4 November 4, 2016.

35. See Caelin, Derek. 2016. "Can Your Playstation Stop a War?" *Foreign Policy*. February 8, http://foreignpolicy.com/2016/02/08/can-your-playstation-stop-a-war-videogames-peace/, accessed May 12, 2017. Also see the website of the in-

ternational nongovernmental organization Search for Common Ground for more on their efforts to launch Battle for Humanity, at https: //www.sfcg.org/ tag/battle-for-humanity/, accessed January 23, 2017, and https://www.sfcg.org/ wp-content/uploads/2016/04/Search-Proposal-Battle-for-Humanity.pdf, accessed May 12, 2017.

36. For a comprehensive discussion of deradicalization work, see Köhler, Daniel. 2017b. *Understanding Deradicalization: Methods, Tools and Programs for Countering Violent Extremism*. New York: Routledge.
37. Way (2011).
38. George (2016: 25).
39. See a detailed explanation of Storch Heinar and the varied uses of the stork humor and parody at http://www.storch-heinar.de/about/, accessed May 12, 2017.
40. See "Trojan T-shirt Targets German Right-Wing Rock Fans," BBC News, http: //www.bbc.com/news/world-europe-14465150, accessed 25 October, 2016.
41. Worden and Miller-Idriss (2016).
42. See Nayak (2005).
43. See especially Schedler and Häusler (2011).

Methodological Appendix: Narrative Account of Research Methods

1. Panofsky (1955: 29).
2. Panofsky (1955: 31). Panofsky does not cite a specific reference from Ernst Cassirer's work in attributing the phrase "symbolical" values to Cassirer, but he is likely referring to Cassirer's three-volume work *The Philosophy of Symbolic Forms*, 1965, New Haven, CT: Yale University Press, in which Cassirer articulates this concept. See Holly, Michael Ann. 1985. *Panofsky and the Foundations of Art History*. Ithaca, NY: Cornell University Press, p. 12 and chapter 5, for a lengthier discussion of the use of Cassirer's work by Panofsky.
3. Thus Panofsky helpfully distinguishes between *iconography* (which he notes is a description of image or form, a classification) and *iconology* (which he notes is an interpretation — the suffix "logy" denotes interpretation, while the suffix "graphy" denotes description, based on original Greek verbs *graphien* (to write) and *logos* (to think or reason) (see Panofsky 1955: 31–32).
4. An image that references Tibet, for example, may seem like a simple tourist-style T-shirt, but it takes on a different connotation in the context of the brand Thor Steinar, which has a strong far right consumer base, as well as in the context of the history of the official Nazi expedition(s) to Tibet in the late 1930s.
5. Miller-Idriss (2009).
6. In an seminar in Athens, Greece, as part of the Economic and Social Research Council–funded research network, "Right-Wing Extremism in Contemporary Europe," September 2014.
7. One interview was conducted in spring 2012, prior to the full data collection, owing to an impending retirement.
8. Charmaz, Kathy. 2006. *Constructing Grounded Theory: A Practical Guide through Qualitative Analysis*. Thousand Oaks, CA: Sage; Corbin, Juliet, and Anselm

Strauss. 1997. *Basics of Qualitative Research: Techniques and Procedures for Developing Grounded Theory*. 3rd ed. Thousand Oaks, CA: Sage.
9. Birks, Melanie, and Jane Mills. 2011. *Grounded Theory: A Practical Guide*. Thousand Oaks, CA: Sage; Lofland, John, David Snow, Leon Anderson, and Lyn H. Lofland. 2006. *Analyzing Social Settings: A Guide to Qualitative Observation and Analysis*. Belmont, CA: Wadsworth.

REFERENCES

Adelman, Miriam, and Linnita Ruggi. 2015. "The Sociology of the Body." *Current Sociology* 64(6): 1–24.

Agentur für soziale Perspektiven e.V., Hg. 2009, 2011. *Versteckspiel: Lifestyle, Symbole und Codes von neonazistischen und extrem rechten Gruppen.* Antifaschistisches Pressearchiv und Bildungszentrum Berlin.

Alexander, Jeffrey C. 1990. "Analytic Debates: Understanding the Relative Autonomy of Culture." Pp. 1–27 in *Culture and Society: Contemporary Debates*, edited by Jeffrey C. Alexander and Steven Seidman. Cambridge: Cambridge University Press.

———. 2012. "Iconic Power and Performance: The Role of the Critic." Pp. 25–35 in *Iconic Power: Materiality and Meaning in Social Life*, edited by Jeffrey C. Alexander, Dominik Bartmański, and Bernhard Giesen. New York: Palgrave Macmillan.

Alexander, Jeffrey C., Dominik Bartmański, and Bernhard Giesen, eds. 2012. *Iconic Power: Materiality and Meaning in Social Life.* New York: Palgrave Macmillan.

Altman, Anna. 2014. "Radical Chic." *New York Times.* July 2, https://op-talk.blogs.nytimes.com/2014/07/02/radical-chic/.

Anand, Dibyesh. 2007. "Anxious Sexualities: Masculinity, Nationalism, and Violence." *British Journal of Political and International Relations* 9: 257–69.

Anderson, Benedict. 1991. *Imagined Communities: Reflections on the Origin and Spread of Nationalism.* New York: Verso.

Andreasch, Robert. 2016. "Widerstandsschritte: Die radikale Rechte in der Bundesrepublik, zwei Jahre nach dem ersten PEGIDA-Spaziergang in Dresden; Ein Ein- und Ausblick." *Lernen aus der Geschichte- Magazin* 09/2016 (November 23). Brandenburgische Landeszentrale für politische Bildung.

Appadurai, Arjun. 1990. "Disjuncture and Difference in the Global Cultural Economy." *Theory, Culture and Society* 7(2): 295–310.

Aries, Philippe. 1981. *Hour of Our Death.* Oxford: Oxford University Press.

Aronczyk, Melissa. 2013. *Branding the Nation: The Global Business of National Identity.* New York: Oxford University Press.

Aronczyk, Melissa, and Devon Powers. 2010. "Introduction: Blowing Up the Brand." Pp. 1–28 in *Blowing up the Brand: Critical Perspectives on Promotional Culture*, edited by Melissa Aronczyk and Devon Powers. New York: Peter Lang.

Atkin, Douglas. 2004. *The Culting of Brands: When Consumers Become True Believers.* New York: Portfolio.

Attebery, Brian. 2014. *Stories about Stories: Fantasy and the Remaking of Myth.* New York: Oxford University Press.

BBC News. 2011. "Trojan T-shirt Targets German Right-Wing Rock Fans." August 9, http://www.bbc.com/news/world-europe-14465150.

———. 2016. "German Far-Right Pegida Founder Bachmann in Race Trial." April 19, http://www.bbc.com/news/world-europe-36079533.

Bacher, Johann. 2001. "In welchen Lebensbereichen lernen Jugendliche Ausländer-feindlichkeit? Ergebnisse einer Befragung bei Berufsschülerinnen und Berufs-schülern." *Kölner Zeitschrift für Soziologie und Sozialpsychologie* 53: 334–49.

Baier, Dirk, Christian Pfeiffer, and Susann Rabold. 2009. "Jugendgewalt in Deutschland: Befunde aus Hell- und Dunkelfelduntersuchungen unter be-sonderer Berücksichtigung von Geschlechterunterschieden." *Kriminalistik* 6: 323–33.

Barthes, Roland. 1972. *Mythologies*. New York: Farrar, Straus, and Giroux.

——. 1974. *S/Z: An Essay*. New York: Hill and Wang.

Bartmański, Dominik, and Jeffrey C. Alexander. 2012. "Materiality and Meaning in Social Life: Toward an Iconic Turn in Cultural Sociology." Pp. 1–12 in *Iconic Power: Materiality and Meaning in Social Life*, edited by Jeffrey C. Alexander, Dominik Bartmański, and Bernhard Giesen. New York: Palgrave Macmillan.

Baudrillard, Jean. 1998. *The Consumer Society: Myths and Structures*. Thousand Oaks, CA: Sage.

Bauman, Zygmunt. 2000. *Liquid Modernity*. Malden, MA: Polity.

——. 2007a. *Consuming Life*. Malden, MA: Polity.

——. 2007b. *Liquid Times: Living in an Age of Uncertainty*. Malden, MA: Polity.

Bay, Ann-Helen, and Morten Bleksaune. 2014. "Youth, Unemployment and Political Marginalization." Pp. 21–35 in *Youth and the Extreme Right*, edited by Cas Mudde. New York: IDebate.

Becker, Ernest. 1971. *The Birth and Death of Meaning: An Interdisciplinary Perspective on the Problem of Man*. New York: Free Press.

——. 1973. *The Denial of Death*. New York: Free Press.

Beifuss, Artur, and Francesco Trivini Vellini. 2013. *Branding Terror: The Logo-types and Iconography of Insurgent Groups and Terrorist Organizations*. London: Merrell.

Benhabib, Seyla. 2002. *The Claims of Culture: Equality and Diversity in the Global Era*. Princeton, NJ: Princeton University Press.

Benz, Wolfgang, and Peter Reif-Spirek. 2003. *Geschichtsmythen: Legenden über den Nationalsozialismus*. Berlin: Metropol Verlag.

Berenson, Tessa. 2016. "David Duke Says He and Donald Trump Have the Same Message." *Time Magazine*. September 30, http://time.com/4514350/david-duke-donald-trump-senate-louisiana/.

Berezin, Mabel. 1997. *Making the Fascist Self: The Political Culture of Interwar Italy*. Ithaca, NY: Cornell University Press.

Berger, Peter L. 1967. *The Sacred Canopy: Elements of a Sociological Theory of Religion*. New York: Anchor Books.

Berliner Morgenpost. 2009. "Arabischer Investor kauft Thor Steinar." March 20, http://www.morgenpost.de/berlin/article1058671/Arabischer_Investor_kauft_Thor_Steinar.html.

Bernal, Martin. 1995. "Race, Class and Gender in the Formation of the Aryan Model of Greek Origins." In "Nations, Identities, Cultures." Special issue, *South Atlantic Quarterly* 94(4): 987–1008.

Betz, Hans-Georg. 1993. "The New Politics of Resentment: Radical Right-Wing Pop-ulist Parties in Western Europe." *Comparative Politics* 25(4): 413–27.

Billig, Michael. 1995a. *Banal Nationalism*. Thousand Oaks, CA: Sage.

————. 1995b. "Rhetorical Psychology, Ideological Thinking, and Imagining Nationhood." Pp. 64–81 in *Social Movements and Culture*, edited by Hank Johnston and Bert Klandermans. Minneapolis: University of Minnesota Press.

Birks, Melanie, and Jane Mills. 2011. *Grounded Theory: A Practical Guide.* Thousand Oaks, CA: Sage.

Bjørgo, Tore. 1997. *Racist and Right-Wing Violence in Scandinavia: Patterns, Perpetrators, and Responses.* Leiden: University of Leiden.

Bleckmann, Bruno. 2009. *Die Germanen: Von Ariovist bis zu den Wikingern.* München: Verlag C. H. Beck oHG.

Blee, Kathleen. 2003. *Inside Organized Racism: Women in the Hate Movement.* Berkeley: University of California Press.

Bleich, Erik. 2011. *The Freedom to Be Racist? How the United States and Europe Struggle to Preserve Freedom and Combat Racism.* New York: Oxford University Press.

Bonikowski, Bart. 2016. "Nationalism in Settled Times." *Annual Review of Sociology* 42: 427–49.

Bourdieu, Pierre. 1984. *Distinction: A Social Critique of the Judgement of Taste.* Cambridge, MA: Harvard University Press.

Bovier, Elke, and Klaus Boehnke. 1999. "Do Liberal Teachers Produce Violent and Xenophobic Students? An Empirical Study of German Ninth Graders and Their Teachers." *Teaching and Teacher Education* 15: 815–27.

Bowler, Wendy. 2012. "Seeing Tragedy in the News Images of September 11." Pp. 85–99 in *Iconic Power: Materiality and Meaning in Social Life*, edited by Jeffrey C. Alexander, Dominik Bartmański, and Bernhard Giesen. New York: Palgrave Macmillan.

Braun, Stephan, Alexander Geisler, and Martin Gerster. 2009. "Die extreme Rechte: Einleitende Betrachtungen." Pp. 9–20 in *Strategien der extremen Rechten: Hintergründe, Analysen, Antworten*, edited by V. S. Verlag für Sozialwissenschaften. Wiesbaden: VS Verlag für Sozialwissenschaften.

Brown, Timothy. 2004. "Subcultures, Pop Music and Politics: Skinheads and 'Nazi Rock' in England and Germany." *Journal of Social History* 38: 157–78.

Caelin, Derek. 2016. "Can Your Playstation Stop a War?" *Foreign Policy.* February 8, http://foreignpolicy.com/2016/02/08/can-your-playstation-stop-a-war-video games-peace/.

Caiani, Manuela, Donatella della Porta, and Claudius Wagemann. 2012. *Mobilizing on the Extreme Right: Germany, Italy and the United States.* Oxford: Oxford University Press.

Caicedo, Martha Marín, ed. 2012. *Subculture.* New York: Routledge.

Calhoun, Craig. 2007. *Nations Matter: Culture, History, and the Cosmopolitan Dream.* New York: Routledge.

Campbell, Colin. 1996. "The Meaning of Objects and the Meaning of Actions." *Journal of Material Culture* 1(1): 93–105.

————. 2004. "I Shop Therefore I Know That I Am: The Metaphysical Basis of Modern Consumerism." Pp. 27–44 in *Elusive Consumption*, edited by Karin M. Ekström and Helene Brembeck. New York: Berg.

Caplan, Gregory A. 2003. "Militarism and Masculinity as Keys to the 'Jewish Question' in Germany." Pp. 175–90 in *Military Masculinities: Identity and the State*, edited by Paul R. Higate. Westport, CT: Praeger.

Casey, Michael. 2009. *Che's Afterlife: The Legacy of an Image*. New York: Vintage.

Cassirer, Ernst. 1965. *The Philosophy of Symbolic Forms*. 3 vols. New Haven, CT: Yale University Press.

Cerulo, Karen. 1993. "Symbols and the World System: National Anthems and Flags." *Sociological Forum* 8(2): 243–71.

Chan, Cheris Shun-ching. 2012. *Marketing Death: Culture and the Making of a Life Insurance Market in China*. New York: Oxford University Press.

Charmaz, Kathy. 2006. *Constructing Grounded Theory: A Practical Guide through Qualitative Analysis*. Thousand Oaks, CA: Sage.

Clarke, John. 2007. "Style." Pp. 147–61 in *Resistance through Rituals: Youth Subcultures in Post-war Britain*, 2nd ed., edited by Stuart Hall and Jefferson Tony. New York: Routledge.

Claus, Robert, Esther Lehnert, and Yves Müller. 2010. *"Was ein rechter Mann ist . . .": Männlichkeiten im Rechtsextremismus*. Berlin: Karl Dietz Verlag.

Cohen, Albert K. 1955. *Delinquent Boys: The Culture of the Gang*. New York: Free Press.

Cohen, Roger. 2001. "Schroeder Joins Debate, Taking Side of Pride in Germany." *New York Times*. March 20, http://www.nytimes.com/2001/03/20/world/schroder-joins-debate-taking-side-of-pride-in-germany.html.

Comaroff, John, and Jean Comaroff. 2009. *Ethnicity, Inc*. Chicago: University of Chicago Press.

Connell, R. W. 1995. *Masculinities*. Berkeley: University of California Press.

Connolly, Kate. 2012. "Anger after German Shop Allegedly Namechecks Norwegian Mass Murderer." *Guardian*. March 6, https://www.theguardian.com/world/2012/mar/06/germany-far-right.

Cooper, Marta. N.d. "The 'Romantic' and 'Distorted' Language of Campaigners Who Want Britain to Leave the EU." https: //qz.com/703078/language-experts-say-the-rhetoric-of-campaigners-who-want-britain-to-leave-the-eu-is-romantic-and-distorted/, accessed February 3, 2017.

Copsey, Nigel, and Graham Macklin (eds). 2011. *British National Party: Contemporary Perspectives*. London: Routledge.

Copsey, Nigel, and John Richardson. 2015. *Cultures of Post-war British Fascism*. New York: Routledge.

Corbin, Juliet, and Anselm Strauss. 1997. *Basics of Qualitative Research: Techniques and Procedures for Developing Grounded Theory*. 3rd. ed. Thousand Oaks, CA: Sage.

Cruzcampo, Oliver. 2011. "Berliner 'Erik & Sons'-Laden macht dicht." *Endstation Rechts*. February 11, http: //www.endstation-rechts.de/news/kategorie/nazilaeden-1/artikel/berliner-erik-sons-laden-macht-dicht.html.

Daniels, Stephen, and Denis Cosgrove. 1988. "Introduction: Iconography and Landscape." Pp. 1–10 in *The Iconography of Landscape: Essays on the Symbolic Representation, Design, and Use of Past Environments*, edited by Stephen Daniels and Denis Cosgrove. New York: Cambridge University Press.

Davies, Douglas. 1988. "The Evocative Symbolism of Trees." Pp. 32–42 in *The Iconography of Landscape: Essays on the Symbolic Representation, Design, and Use of Past Environments*, edited by Stephen Daniels and Denis Cosgrove. New York: Cambridge University Press.

Decker, Oliver, Johannes Kiess, Eva Eggers, and Elmar Brähler. 2016. "Die 'Mitte' Studie 2016: Ergebnisse und Langzeitverlauf." Pp. 23–66 in *Die enthemmte Mitte:*

Autoritäre und rechtsextreme Einstellung in Deutschland, edited by Oliver Decker, Johannes Kiess, and Elmar Brähler. Giessen: Psychosozial Verlag.

Deissinger, Thomas. 2015. "The German Dual Vocational Education and Training System as 'Good Practice'?" *Local Economy* 30(5): 557–67.

Deutsche Welle. 2013. "Chronicle of the NSU Murders." April 16, http: //www .dw.com/overlay_media/chronicle-of-the-nsu-murders/g-16743396.

Didion, Joan. 2005. *The Year of Magical Thinking*. London: Fourth Estate.

Die Welt. "NPD-Wahlplakate sind nicht rechtswidrig." July 9, http: //www.welt.de/ regionales/berlin/article13591648/NPD-Wahlplakate-sind-nicht-rechtswidrig.html.

DieWeltOnline. 2010. "Universität verbietet 'Thor Steinar'-Kleidung." *Welt Online*. September 10, https://www.welt.de/vermischtes/article9521785/Universitaet-ver bietet-Thor-Steinar-Kleidung.html.

DiMaggio, Paul. 1997. "Culture and Cognition." *Annual Review of Sociology* 23: 263–87.

Dinas, Elias. 2013. "Opening 'Openness to Change': Political Events and the Increased Sensitivity of Young Adults." *Political Research Quarterly* 66(4): 868–82.

du Gay, Paul. 1996. *Consumption and Identity at Work*. Thousand Oaks, CA: Sage.

Dunlap, Knight. 1944. "The Great Aryan Myth." *Scientific Monthly* 59(4): 296–300.

Durkheim, Emile. 1995 [1915]. *The Elementary Forms of Religious Life*. New York: Free Press.

Durso, Rachel M., and David Jacobs. 2013. "The Determinants of the Number of White Supremacist Groups: A Pooled Time-Series Analysis." *Social Problems* 60(1): 128–44.

Dussel, Inés. 2004. "Fashioning the Schooled Self through Uniforms: A Foucauldian Approach to Contemporary School Policies." Pp. 85–116 in *Dangerous Coagulations: The Uses of Foucault in the Study of Education*, edited by Bernadette Baker and Katharina M. Heyning. New York: Peter Lang.

Eagleton, Terry. 2000. *The Idea of Culture*. Malden, MA: Blackwell.

Eliade, Mircea. 1957. *The Sacred and the Profane: The Nature of Religion*. San Diego: Harvest/HBJ.

Eller, Cynthia. 2013. "Matriarchy and the Volk." *Journal of the American Academy of Religion* 81(1): 188–221.

Enloe, Cynthia 2001. *Bananas, Beaches and Bases: Making Sense of International Politics*. Berkeley: University of California Press.

Ferber, Abby L. 1998. *White Man Falling: Race, Gender, and White Supremacy*. Lanham, MD: Rowman and Littlefield.

Ferber, Abby L., and Michael S. Kimmel. 2008. "The Gendered Face of Terrorism." *Sociology Compass* 2(3): 870–87.

Fiske, Alan Page, and Tage Shakti Rai. 2015. *Virtuous Violence: Hurting and Killing to Create, Sustain, End, and Honor Social Relationships*. Cambridge: Cambridge University Press.

Fox, Jon, and Cynthia Miller-Idriss. 2008. "Everyday Nationhood." *Ethnicities* 8: 536–62.

Fuchs, Marek. 2003. "Right-Wing Attitudes among Adolescents: Testing the Explanatory Power of Theoretical Concepts." *Kölner Zeitschrift für Soziologie und Sozialpsychologie* 55(4): 654–78.

Fuchs, Thorsten. "Der Neonazi neben mir." *Hannoversche Allgemeine*. September 16, 2016, http: //www.haz.de/Sonntag/Top-Thema/Der-Neonazi-neben-mir-Was -tun-mit-Rechtsextremen.

Funke, Hajo. 2011. "Rechtsextreme Ideologien, strategische Orientierungen und Gewalt." Pp. 21–44 in *Strategien der extremen Rechten: Hintergründe—Analysen—Antworten*, edited by Stephan Braun, Alexander Geisler, and Martin Gerster. Wiesbaden: VS Verlag.

Futrell, Robert, and Pete Simi. 2004. "Free Spaces, Collective Identity, and the Persistence of U.S. White Power Activism." *Social Problems* 51: 16–42.

Gabriel, Thomas. 2014. "Parenting and Right-Wing Extremism: An Analysis of the Biographical Genesis of Racism among Young People." Pp. 36–47 in *Youth and the Extreme Right*, edited by Cas Mudde. New York: IDebate.

Gans, Herbert J. 2012. "Against Culture versus Structure." *Identities: Global Studies in Culture and Power* 19(2): 125–34.

Garrel, Théo. 2015. "Phalanx Europa: Kleidung von Identitären für Identitäre." *Belltower News: Netz für digitale Zivilgesellschaft*. January 26, http://www.belltower .news/artikel/phalanx-europa-kleidung-von-identit%C3%A4ren-f%C3%BCr-iden tit%C3%A4re-10007.

George, Cherian. 2016. *Hate Spin: The Manufacture of Religious Offense and Its Threat to Democracy*. Cambridge, MA: MIT Press.

Gereluk, Dianne. 2008. *Symbolic Clothing in Schools: What Should be Worn and Why*. New York: Continuum.

Ghannam, Farha. 2013. *Live and Die Like a Man: Gender Dynamics in Urban Egypt*. Stanford, CA: Stanford University Press.

Gibbs, David. 2011. "See How You Feel." Pp. 7–11 in *Symbol*, edited by Angus Hyland and Steven Bateman. London: Laurence King.

Gigengil, Elisabeth, Matthew Henniger, Andre Blais, and Neil Nevitte. 2005. "Explaining the Gender Gap in Support for the New Right: The Case of Canada." *Comparative Political Studies* 38(10): 1171–95.

Gilliard-Matthews, Stacia. 2011. "The Impact of the Economic Downturn, Immigrants, and Political Representation on White Supremacist Group Organization in the United States." *Sociological Focus* 44(3): 255–79.

Glaser, Barney, and Anselm Strauss. 1965. *Awareness of Dying*. Piscataway, NJ: Transaction.

Gleiser, Marcelo. 2014. "Globalization: Two Visions of the Future of Humanity." Pp. 7–9 in *Globalization: A Reader for Writers*, edited by Maria Jerskey. Oxford: Oxford University Press.

Goffman, Erving. 1967. *Interaction Ritual: Essays in Face to Face Behavior*. Piscataway, NJ: Aldine Transaction.

Goldstein, Arnold, and Donald Kadlubov. 1998. *Gangs in Schools: Signs, Symbols and Solutions*. Champaign, IL: Research Press.

Goodrick-Clarke, Nicholas. 2002. *Black Sun: Aryan Cults, Esoteric Nazism and the Politics of Identity*. New York: New York University Press.

Goodwin, Jeff, and James Jasper. 2004. *Rethinking Social Movements: Structure, Meaning, and Emotion*. New York: Rowman and Littlefield.

Gorer, Geoffrey. 1955. "The Pornography of Death." *Encounter*. October, p. 50.

———. 1967. *Death, Grief and Mourning*. New York: Anchor/Doubleday.

Greenfeld, Liah. 1992. *Nationalism: Five Roads to Modernity*. Cambridge, MA: Harvard University Press.

Griffin, Roger. 2008a. "Fascism's New Faces (and New Facelessness) in the 'Post-fascist' Epoch." Pp. 181–202 in *A Fascist Century: Essays by Roger Griffin*, edited by Matthew Feldman. New York: Palgrave Macmillan.

———. 2008b. "Fatal Attraction: Why Nazism Appealed to Voters." Pp. 71–82 in *A Fascist Century: Essays by Roger Griffin*, edited by Matthew Feldman. New York: Palgrave Macmillan.

———. 2014. "Fixing Solutions: Fascist Temporalities as Remedies for Liquid Modernity." *European Journal of Modern History* 13(1): 5–23.

Guerlain, Sarah. 2010. "Geheimer Orden und dunkle Sonnen—Mythen um die Schutzstaffel." Pp. 75–104 in *"Ohne Juda, ohne Rom"*: *Esoterik und Heidentum im subkulturellen Rechtsextremismus; Konzepte für Demokratie und Toleranz Band 8*, edited by Andreas Speit. Braunschweig: Bildungsvereinigung Arbeit und Leben Niedersachsen Ost GmbH.

Günter, Christian. 2014. "Rune, Hakenkreuz: Welche Symbole und Zeichen sind Verboten?" *Kölnische Rundschau*. June 25, http://www.rundschau-online.de/rat geber/finanzen/recht/symbole-zeichen-verboten-hakenkreuz-fdj-verbot-verfas sungswidrig-849462.

Gurney, Alan. 2002. *The Race to the White Continent: Voyages to the Antarctic*. New York: W. W. Norton.

Hafeneger, Benno. 2014. "Die Identitären: Vorübergehendes Phänomen oder neue Bewegung?" Published by the Friedrich Ebert Stiftung, available at http: //library .fes.de/pdf-files/dialog/10649.pdf.

Hagan, John, Hans Merkens, and Klaus Boehnke. 1995. "Delinquency and Disdain: Social Capital and the Control of Right-Wing Extremism among East and West Berlin Youth." *American Journal of Sociology* 100: 1028–52.

Hagan, John, Susanne Rippl, Klaus Boehnke, and Hans Merkens. 1999. "The Interest in Evil: Hierarchic Self-Interest and Right-Wing Extremism among East and West German Youth." *Social Science Research* 28: 162–83.

Halkitis, Perry N. 2000. "Masculinity in the Age of AIDS: HIV-Seropositive Gay Men and the 'Buff Agenda.'" *Research on Men and Masculinities Series* 12: 130–51.

Hall, Stuart. 1973. *Encoding and Decoding in the Television Discourse*. Birmingham: Centre for Contemporary Cultural Studies.

———. 1999–2000. "Whose Heritage? Un-settling 'The Heritage,' Re-imagining the Post-nation." *Third Text* 49: 3–13.

Hall, Stuart, Dorothy Hobson, Andrew Lowe, and Paul Willis, eds. 1991 [1980]. *Culture, Media, Language: Working Papers in Cultural Studies, 1972–79*. London: Routledge.

Hall, Stuart, and Tony Jefferson, eds. 2007. *Resistance through Rituals: Youth Subcultures in Post-war Britain*. 2nd ed. New York: Routledge.

Hammerbacher, Michael, ed. 2015. *Kennzeichen und Symbole der rechtsextremen Szene: Bausteine der Prävention von Rechtsextremismus und Gruppenbezogener Menschenfeindlichkeit in der beruflichen Bildung Nr. 6; Eine Handreichung für Demokratie und Vielfalt*. OSZ für Demokratie und Vielfalt. Berlin: DEVI e.V. Verein für Demokratie und Vielfalt in Schule und beruflicher Bildung.

Hannemann, Jana. 2016. "Wie Dortmunder Neonazis das Run-DMC-Logo missbrauchen." *WAZ- Westdeutsche Allgemeine Zeitung*. June 9, https://www.derwesten

.de/politik/wie-dortmunder-neonazis-das-run-dmc-logo-missbrauchen-id1190 1373.html.

Hannes, Heine. 2009. "Rechte Szene: Thor Steinar will weltweit expandieren." In *Der Tagesspiegel*. March 23, http://www.tagesspiegel.de/berlin/rechte-szene-thor-stein ar-will-weltweit-expandieren/1480814.html.

Harris, Angela. 2000. "Gender, Violence, Race, and Criminal Justice." *Stanford Law Review* 52(4): 777–807.

Harris, David. 1996. *A Society of Signs?* New York: Routledge.

Harrison, Robert Pogue. 2003. *The Dominion of the Dead*. Chicago: University of Chicago Press.

Hattenhauer, Hans. 1990. *Geschichte der deutschen Nationalsymbole: Zeichen und Bedeutung*. Munich: Olzog Verlag.

———. 2006. *Deutsche Nationalsymbole: Geschichte und Bedeutung*. München: Olzog Verlag GmbH.

Hebdige, Dick. 1979. *Subculture: The Meaning of Style*. New York: Methuen.

Hebel, Christina, Benjamin Knaack, and Christoph Sydow. 2014. "Pegida Faktencheck: Die Angstbürger." *Spiegel Online*. December 14, http://www.spiegel.de/ politik/deutschland/pegida-die-thesen-im-faktencheck-a-1008098-druck.html.

Heitmeyer, Wilhelm. 1988. *Rechtsextremistische Orientierungen bei Jugendlichen*. 2nd ed. Weinheim: Juventa.

———. 1999. "Sozialräumliche Machtversuche des Ostdeutschen Rechtsextremismus." Pp. 47–79 in *Rechtsextremistische Jugendliche — Was Tun?*, edited by Karin Sitte, Peter E. Kalb and Christian Petry. Weinheim: Beltz Verlag.

Heitmeyer, Wilhelm, Heike Buhse, Joachim Liebe-Freund, Kurt Möller, Joachim Müller, Helmut Ritz, Gertrud Siller, and Johannes Vossen. 1992. *Die Bielefelder Rechtsextremismus-Studie: Erste Langzeituntersuchung zur Politischen Sozialisation männlicher Jugendlicher*. Munich: Juventa Verlag.

Hell, Julia. 1997. *Post-fascist Fantasies: Psychoanalysis, History, and the Literature of East Germany*. Durham, NC: Duke University Press.

Heller, Friedrich Paul, and Anton Maegerle. 2001. *Die Sprache des Hasses: Rechtsextremismus und völkische Esoterik*. Stuttgart: Schmetterling Verlag.

Heller, Steven. 2000. *The Swastika: Symbol beyond Redemption?* New York: Allworth.

Hellmuth, Dorle. 2016. "Of Alienation, Association, and Adventure: Why German Fighters join ISIL." *Journal for Deradicalization* (6): 24–50.

Hemphill, David F. 2001 "Incorporating Postmodernist Perspectives into Adult Education." Pp. 15–28 in *Making Space: Merging Theory and Practice in Adult Education*, edited by Peggy Sheared and Vanessa Sissel. Westport, CT: Greenwood.

Herf, Jeffrey. 2006. *The Jewish Enemy: Nazi Propaganda during World War II and the Holocaust*. Cambridge, MA: Belknap Press of Harvard University Press.

Hesse, Hermann. 1965 [1919]. *Demian*. New York: Harper and Row.

Higgins, Andrew, and James Kanter. 2014. "Fringe Groups Gain in European Voting." *New York Times*. May 25, https://www.nytimes.com/2014/05/26/world/europe /turnout-in-european-parliament-election-hits-record-low.html?_r=0.

Holley, Peter. 2016. "KKK's Official Newspaper Supports Donald Trump for President." *Washington Post*. November 2, https://www.washingtonpost.com/news /post-politics/wp/2016/11/01/the-kkks-official-newspaper-has-endorsed-donald -trump-for-president/?utm_term=.e13bd1b737a6.

Holly, Michael Ann. 1985. *Panofsky and the Foundations of Art History*. Ithaca, NY: Cornell University Press.

Hopton, John. 2003. "The State and Military Masculinity." Pp. 111–24 in *Military Masculinities: Identity and the State*, edited by Paul R. Higate. Westport, CT: Praeger.

Hunt, Maurice. 2015. *The Divine Face in Four Writers: Shakespeare, Dostoyevsky, Hesse, and C. S. Lewis*. London: Bloomsbury.

Kamentsky, Christa. 1977. "Folktale and Ideology in the Third Reich." *Journal of American Folklore* 90(356): 168–78.

Kanaaneh, Rhoda Ann. 2002. *Birthing the Nation: Strategies of Palestinian Women in Israel*. Berkeley: University of California Press.

Kang, Milaan, and Katherine Jones. 2007. "Why Do People Get Tattoos?" *Contexts* 6(1): 42–47.

Kaplan, Jeffrey, and Leonard Weinberg. 1998. *The Emergence of a Euro-American Radical Right*. New Brunswick, NJ: Rutgers University Press.

Katsourides, Yiannos. 2013. "Determinants of Extreme Right Reappearance in Cyprus: The National Popular Front (ELAM), Golden Dawn's Sister Party." *South European Society and Politics* 18(4): 567–89.

Katz, Jack. 1988. *Seductions of Crime: Moral and Sensual Attractions in Doing Evil*. New York: Basic Books.

Kershaw, Ian. 1987. *The "Hitler Myth": Image and Reality in the Third Reich*. New York: Oxford University Press.

Khan, Shamus. 2011. *Privilege: The Making of an Adolescent Elite at St. Paul's School*. Princeton, NJ: Princeton University Press.

Khatib, Lina. 2012. *Image Politics in the Middle East: The Role of the Visual in Political Struggle*. New York: I. B. Tauris.

Kidd, Laura Klosterman. 2015. "The Nazi Aesthetic in Fashion." In *Berg Encyclopedia of World Dress and Fashion*: Berg Fashion Library. New York: Berg.

Kimmel, Michael S. 2005. "Globalization and Its Mal(e)contents: The Gendered Moral and Political Economy of Terrorism." Pp. 414–31 in *Handbook of Studies on Men and Masculinities*, edited by Michael S. Kimmel, Jeff Hearn, and R. W. Connell. Thousand Oaks, CA: Sage.

———. 2013. *Angry White Men: American Masculinity at the End of an Era*. New York: Nation Books.

Klinenberg, Eric. 2013. *Going Solo: The Extraordinary Rise and Surprising Appeal of Living Alone*. New York: Penguin Books.

Knapp, Ursula. 2009. "Ein Schlupfloch für Naziparolen." *Frankfurter Rundschau*. August 13, http://www.fr.de/importe/fr-online/home/bundesgerichtshof-urteil-zu-blood-honour-ein-schlupfloch-fuer-naziparolen-a-1087491.

Knudsen, Daniel C., Jillian Rickly-Boyd, and Charles Greer. 2014. "Myth, National Identity and the Contemporary Tourism Site: The Case of Amalienborg and Frederiksstaden." *National Identities* 16(1): 53–70.

Köhler, Daniel. 2015. "Contrast Societies: Radical Social Movements and Their Relationships with Their Target Societies; A Theoretical Model." *Behavioral Sciences of Terrorism and Political Aggression* 7(1): 18–34.

———. 2017a. *Right-Wing Terrorism in the 21st Century: The "National Socialist Underground" and the History of Terror from the Far Right in Germany*. New York: Routledge.

Köhler, Daniel. 2017b. *Understanding Deradicalization: Methods, Tools and Programs for Countering Violent Extremism*. New York: Routledge.

Köhler, Daniel, and Cynthia Miller-Idriss. 2017. "The Most Dangerous National Security Threat That Donald Trump Is Ignoring." *Fortune*. February 13, http://fortune.com/2017/02/13/donald-trump-national-security-cve-right-wing-extremism-terrorism-germany/.

Köhler, Daniel, and Chilja Speransky. Forthcoming. "Humour and the Extreme Right." In *Cultural Dimensions of Far Right Politics*, edited by Fabian Virchow and Cynthia Miller-Idriss. Wiesbaden: VS Verlag.

Kohlstruck, Michael. 2005. " 'Ich bin stolz, ein Deutscher zu sein': Zur Entstehung und Verbreitung eines politischen Symbols." Pp. 53–76 in *Stolz deutsch zu sein? Aggressiver Anspruch und selbstverständlicher Patriotismus*, edited by Ute Benz and Benz Wolfgang. Berlin: Metropol Verlag.

Koop, Andreas. 2008. *NSCI: Das visuelle Erscheinungsbild der Nationalsozialisten 1920–1945*. Mainz: Verlag Hermann Schmidt.

Kopytoff, Igor. 1988. "The Cultural Biography of Things: Commoditization as Process." Pp. 64–91 in *The Social Life of Things: Commodities in Cultural Perspective*, edited by Arjun Appadurai. Cambridge: Cambridge University Press.

Krasinski, Jennifer. 2015. "In a Captivating Show, Hito Steyerl Vivisects the Veracity of Video." *Village Voice*. April 22, http://www.villagevoice.com/arts/in-a-captivating-show-hito-steyerl-vivisects-the-veracity-of-video-7194669.

Krebs, Christopher. 2012. *A Most Dangerous Book: Tacitus' Germania from the Roman Empire to the Third Reich*: New York: W. W. Norton.

Kunow, Fabian. 2011. "Volksverhetzung — Polizei durchsucht Büros der Nazimarke 'Reconquista.'" *Zeit Online*. November 30, http://blog.zeit.de/stoerungsmelder/2011/11/30/reconquista-neue-nazimode-aus-berlin_7686#comments.

Lamont, Michèle 1994. *Money, Morals, and Manners: The Culture of the French and the American Upper-Middle Class*. Chicago: University of Chicago Press.

———. 2002. *The Dignity of Working Men: Morality and the Boundaries of Race, Class and Immigration*. Cambridge, MA: Harvard University Press.

Lamont, Michèle, and Virág Molnár. 2001. "How Blacks Use Consumption to Shape Their Collective Identity." *Journal of Consumer Culture* 1(1): 31–45.

Langebach, Martin. 2016. "Rechtsextremismus und Jugend." Pp. 375–440 in *Handbuch Rechtsextremismus*, edited by Fabian Virchow, Martin Langebach, and Alexander Häusler. Wiesbaden: VS Verlag.

Langebach, Martin, and Jan Raabe. 2011. "Die Genese einer extrem rechten Jugendkultur." Pp. 154–66 in *Autonome Nationalisten: Neonazismus in Bewegung*, edited by Jan Schedler and Alexander Häusler. Wiesbaden: VS Verlag.

———. 2016. "Die 'Neue Rechte' in der Bundesrepublik Deutschland." Pp. 561–92 in *Handbuch Rechtsextremismus*, edited by Fabian Virchow, Martin Langebach, and Alexander Häusler. Wiesbaden: VS Verlag.

Laruelle, Marlene. 2007. "The Return of the Aryan Myth: Tajikistan in Search of a Secularized National Identity." *Nationalities Papers* 35(1): 51–70.

Leach, Darcy K., and Sebastian Haunss. 2009. "Scenes and Social Movements." In *Culture, Social Movements, and Protest*, edited by Hank Johnston. Burlington, VT: Ashgate.

Lee, Benjamin, and Edward LiPuma. 2002. "Cultures of Circulation: The Imaginations of Modernity." *Public Culture* 14: 191–213.

Liulevicius, Vejas Gabriel. 2009. *The German Myth of the East: 1800 to the Present.* New York: Oxford University Press.

Linden, Annette, and Bert Klandermans. 2006. "Stigmatization and Repression of Extreme-Right Activism in the Netherlands." *Mobilization: An International Journal* 11: 213–28.

Linke, Uli. 1997. "Gendered Difference, Violent Imagination: Blood, Race, Nation." *American Anthropologist* 99(3): 559–73.

———. 1999. *German Bodies: Race and Representation after Hitler.* New York: Routledge.

linksunten. 2010. "Erik & Sons weiter im Berlin Europacenter." linksunten.indymedia.org. December 29, https://linksunten.indymedia.org/de/node/31207.

Lofland, John, David Snow, Leon Anderson, and Lyn H. Lofland. 2006. *Analyzing Social Settings: A Guide to Qualitative Observation and Analysis.* Belmont, CA: Wadsworth.

Lucassen, Geertje, and Marcel Lubbers. 2012. "Who Fears What? Explaining Far-Right-Wing Preference in Europe by Distinguishing Perceived Cultural and Economic Ethnic Threats." *Comparative Political Studies* 45(5): 547–74.

Luschen, Kristen. 2012. "Style." Pp. 268–72 in *Keywords in Youth Studies: Tracing Affects, Movements, Knowledges,* edited by Nancy Lesko and Susan Talburt. New York: Routledge.

Luth, Elizabeth. 2017. "Social and Health Determinants of End-of-Life Care Quality: A Multidimensional Approach." Ph.D. diss., Rutgers University.

MacInnis, Deborah, C. W. Park, and Joseph Priester, eds. 2009. *Handbook of Brand Relationships.* New York: M. E. Sharpe.

Marcks, Holger. 2016. "Don't Call Me Right! The Strategy of Normalization in German Right-Wing Extremism." Pp. 65–72 in *Trouble on the Far Right: Contemporary Right-Wing Strategies and Practices in Europe,* edited by Maik Fielitz and Laura Laloire. Bielefeld: Transcript Verlag.

Margaronis, Maria. 2012. "Fear and Loathing in Athens: The Rise of Golden Dawn and the Far Right." October 26, http: //www.theguardian.com/world/2012/oct/26/golden-dawn-greece-far-right.

Martin, Andres. 1997. "On Teenagers and Tattoos." *Journal of the American Academy of Child and Adolescent Psychiatry* 36: 860–61.

Marx, Karl. 2017 [1867]. "Capital and the Values of Commodities." Pp. 40–46 in: *Social Theory: The Multicultural, Global and Classic Readings,* 6th ed., edited by Charles Lemert. Boulder, CO: Westview.

McConnell, Winder, and Werner Wunderlich. 2015. *The Nibelungen Tradition: An Encyclopedia.* New York: Routledge.

McIlwain, Charlton. 2003. *Death in Black and White: Death, Ritual and Family Ecology.* New York: Hampton.

McLaren, Lauren M. 1999. "Explaining Right-Wing Violence in Germany: A Time-Series Analysis." *Social Science Quarterly* 80: 166–80.

McVeigh, Brian. 2015. "Wearing Ideology: How Uniforms Discipline Minds and Bodies in Japan." *Fashion Theory* 1(2): 189–213.

Mears, Ashley. 2011. *Pricing Beauty: The Making of a Fashion Model*. Berkeley: University of California Press.

———. 2014. "Who Runs the Girls?" *New York Times*. September 20, https://www.nytimes.com/2014/09/21/opinion/sunday/who-runs-the-girls.html.

Messerschmidt, James W. 1993. *Masculinities and Crime: Critique and Reconceptualization of Theory*. Lanham, MD: Rowman and Littlefield.

———. 2000. *Nine Lives: Adolescent Masculinities, the Body, and Violence*. Boulder, CO: Westview.

Messner, Michael. 1990. "Boyhood, Organized Sports and the Construction of Masculinities." *Journal of Contemporary Ethnography* 18(4): 416–44.

Meuser, Michael. 1998. *Geschlecht und Männlichkeit: Soziologische Theorie und kulturelle Deutungsmuster*. Opladen: Leske & Budrich.

Michael, George. 2009. "David Lane and the Fourteen Words." *Totalitarian Movements and Political Religions* 10: 43–61.

Michaelis, Arno. 2015. "This Is How You Become a White Supremicist." *Washington Post*. June 25, https://www.washingtonpost.com/posteverything/wp/2015/06/25/this-is-how-you-become-a-white-supremacist/?utm_term=.cdd0c3b2f71c.

Miklavcic, Alessandra. 2008. "Slogans and Graffiti: Postmemory among Youth in the Italo-Slovenian Borderland." *American Ethnologist* 35: 440–53.

Miller, Daniel. 2010. *Stuff*. Boston: Polity.

Miller-Idriss, Cynthia. 2005. "Citizenship Education and Political Extremism in Germany: An Ethnographic Account." Pp. 101–22 in *Political and Citizenship Education: International Perspectives*, edited by Stephanie Wilde. Wallingford, U.K.: Symposium.

———. 2006. "Everyday Understandings of Citizenship in Germany." *Citizenship Studies* 10: 541–70.

———. 2009. *Blood and Culture: Youth, Right-Wing Extremism, and National Belonging in Contemporary Germany*. Durham, NC: Duke University Press.

———. Forthcoming. "Youth and the Radical Right." In *The Oxford Handbook of the Radical Right*, edited by Jens Rydgren. Oxford University Press.

Miller-Idriss, Cynthia, and Annett Graefe. 2017. "Fitting In, Standing Out: Ambivalence and Multivocality in Far Right German Youth Style." Paper presented at the American Sociological Association 112th Annual Meeting in Montreal, Canada, August.

Miller-Idriss, Cynthia, and Elizabeth Knauer. Forthcoming. "Buying into the Far Right: Material Culture and Right-Wing Consumption." In *The Cultural Dimensions of Far Right Politics*, edited by Fabian Virchow and Cynthia Miller-Idriss. Wiesbaden: VS Verlag.

Miller-Idriss, Cynthia, and Bess Rothenberg. 2012. "Ambivalence, Pride, and Shame: Conceptualizations of German Nationhood." *Nations and Nationalism* 18(1): 132–55.

Milner, Murray. 2006. *Freaks, Geeks, and Cool Kids: American Teenagers, Schools, and the Culture of Consumption*. New York: Routledge.

Mishak, Michael J. 2015. "Are Donald Trump's Supporters Racist?" *Atlantic*. December 7, https://www.theatlantic.com/politics/archive/2015/12/are-donald-trumps-supporters-racist/450927/.

Mitchell, Stephen, ed. 1982. *The Selected Poetry of Rainer Maria Rilke*. New York: Random House.

Mitchell, W.J.T. 2005. *What Do Pictures Want? The Lives and Loves of Images*. Chicago: University of Chicago Press.

Mock, Steven. 2014. *Symbols of Defeat in the Construction of National Identity*. Cambridge: Cambridge University Press.

Möller, Kurt. 2000. *Rechte Kids: Eine Langzeitstudie über Auf- und Abbau rechtsextremistischer Orientierungen bei 13- bis 15jährigen*. Weinheim: Juventa Verlag.

Molnár, Virág. 2016. "Civil Society, Radicalism and the Rediscovery of Mythic Nationalism." *Nations and Nationalism* 22(1): 165–85.

Molotch, Harvey. 2005. *Where Stuff Comes From: How Toasters, Toilets, Cars, Computers, and Many Other Things Come to Be as They Are*. New York: Routledge.

Morgan, David. 2005. *The Sacred Gaze: Religious Visual Culture in Theory and Practice*. Berkeley: University of California Press.

Mosse, George L. 1985. *Nationalism and Sexuality: Respectability and Abnormal Sexuality in Modern Europe*. New York: Howard Fertig.

———. 1998. *The Image of Man: The Creation of Modern Masculinity*. New York: Oxford University Press.

Moyer, Justin Wm. 2016. "D.C. Restaurant Apologizes after Hosting Alt-Right Dinner with 'Sieg Heil Salute.'" *Washington Post*. November 21, https://www.washingtonpost.com/news/local/wp/2016/11/21/d-c-restaurant-apologizes-after-hosting-alt-right-dinner-with-sieg-heil-salute/?utm_term=.082a41182d0b.

Mudde, Cas. 2005. "Racist Extremism in Central and Eastern Europe." *East European Politics and Societies* 19(2): 161–84.

———. 2014. "The Far Right in the 2014 European Elections: Of Earthquakes, Cartels and Designer Fascists." *Washington Post*. May 30, https://www.washingtonpost.com/news/monkey-cage/wp/2014/05/30/the-far-right-in-the-2014-european-elections-of-earthquakes-cartels-and-designer-fascists/?utm_term=.ce2e036d5c86.

———, ed. 2017. *The Populist Radical Right: A Reader*. New York: Routledge.

Muggleton, David. 2000. *Inside Subculture: The Postmodern Meaning of Style*. New York: Berg.

Münkler, Herfried. 2010. *Die Deutschen und ihre Mythen*. Bonn: Bundeszentrale für politische Bildung.

Nagel, Joane. 1998. "Masculinity and Nationalism: Gender and Sexuality in the Making of Nations." *Ethnic and Racial Studies* 21(2): 242–69.

———. 2005. "Nation." Pp. 397–413 in *Handbook of Studies on Men and Masculinities*, edited by Michael S. Kimmel, Jeff Hearn, and R. W. Connell. Thousand Oaks, CA: Sage.

———. 2010. "Ethnicities and Sexualities." Pp. 188–220 in *The SAGE Handbook of Race and Ethnic Studies*, edited by John Solomos and Patricia Hill Collins. Thousand Oaks, CA: Sage.

Nayak, Anoop. 2003. *Race, Place and Globalization: Youth Cultures in a Changing World*. New York: Berg.

———. 2005. "White Lives." Pp. 141–62 in *Racialization: Studies in Theory and Practice*, edited by K. Murji and J. Solomos. Oxford: Oxford University Press.

Nietzsche, Friedrich. 1995 [1872]. *The Birth of Tragedy*. Mineola, NY: Dover.

Nolan, Rachel. 2008a. "Neo-Nazi Fashion: Thor Steinar and the Changing Look of the German Far Right." *Spiegel Online.* November 20, http://www.spiegel.de/international/germany/neo-nazi-fashion-thor-steinar-and-the-changing-look-of-the-german-far-right-a-587746.html.

————. 2008b. "Wearing Identity on Its Sleeve, German Far Right Gets a Makeover." Forward.com. May 8, http://forward.com/news/13346/wearing-identity-on-its-sleeve-german-far-right-g-01822/.

O'Carroll, Eoin. 2011. "Political Misquotes: The 10 Most Famous Things Never Actually Said." *Christian Science Monitor.* June 3, http://www.csmonitor.com/USA/Politics/2011/0603/Political-misquotes-The-10-most-famous-things-never-actually-said/I-can-see-Russia-from-my-house!-Sarah-Palin.

Omel'chenko, Elena. 2010. "In Search of Intimacy: Homosociality, Masculinity and the Body." Pp. 166–86 in *Russia's Skinheads: Exploring and Rethinking Subcultural Lives,* edited by Hilary Pilkington, Elena Omel'chenko, and Al'bina Garifzianova. London: Routledge.

Oschlies, Renate. 2001. "Hinter die 'ideologische Kostümierung' schauen." *Berliner Zeitung* 69 (March 22): 6.

O'Shaugnessy, Nicholas. 2016. *Selling Hitler: Propaganda and the Nazi Brand.* London: C. Hurst.

Osuch, Florian, and Moritz Eluek. 2016. " 'Thor Steinar' mit Millionenumsatz." *Antifa Infoblatt.* January 25, https://www.antifainfoblatt.de/artikel/%E2%80%9Ethor-steinar%E2%80%9C-mit-millionenumsatz.

Panofsky, Erwin. 1955. *Meaning in the Visual Arts.* Chicago: University of Chicago Press.

Parade, Heidi. 2001. "Ungebetene Mitstreiter." *Der Tagesspiegel* 17358 (March 23): 5.

Pascoe, C. J. 2007. *Dude, You're a Fag: Masculinity and Sexuality in High School.* Berkeley: University of California Press.

Patterson, Orlando. 2014. "Making Sense of Culture." *Annual Review of Sociology* 40: 1–30.

Paul, Gerhard. 1995. "Rechtsextremismus im vereinten Deutschland." Pp. 33–46 in *Gewalt unter Jugendlichen, Rechtsextremismus und Fremdenfeindlichkeit.* Erfurt: Friedrich Ebert Stiftung.

Peters, Jürgen, and Christoph Schulze, eds. 2009. *Autonome Nationalisten: Die Modernisierung neofaschistischer Jugendkultur.* Munich: Unrast Verlag.

Picart, Caroline Joan S. 2015. " 'Jihad Cool/Jihad Chic': The Roles of the Internet and Imagined Relations in the Self-Radicalization of Colleen LaRose (Jihad Jane)." *Societies* 5: 354–83.

Pientka, Claudia, and Martin Knobbe. 2008. "Die Klamotte der Neonazis." *Stern.* December 21, http://www.stern.de/panorama/gesellschaft/thor-steinar-die-klamotte-der-neonazis-3747124.html.

Pilkington, Hilary. 2010a. "No Longer 'on Parade': Style and the Performance of Skinhead." Pp. 143–65 in *Russia's Skinheads: Exploring and Rethinking Subcultural Lives,* edited by Hilary Pilkington, Elena Omel'chenko, and Al'bina Garifzianova. London: Routledge.

————. 2010b. "No Longer 'on Parade': Style and the Performance of Skinhead in the Russian Far North." *Russian Review* 69(2): 187–209.

————. 2016. *Loud and Proud: Passion and Politics in the English Defence League.* Manchester, UK: Manchester University Press.

Pilkington, Hilary, and Cynthia Miller-Idriss, eds. 2017. "Gender and the Radical and Extreme Right: Mechanisms of Transmission and the Role of Educational Interventions." Special issue, *Gender and Education* 29(2).

Pilkington, Hilary, Elena Omel'chenko, and Al'bina Garifzianova. 2010. *Russia's Skinheads: Exploring and Rethinking Subcultural Lives*. London: Routledge.

Polletta, Francesca. 1999. "'Free Spaces' in Collective Action." *Theory and Society* 28: 1–38.

————. 2001. "Collective Identity and Social Movements." *Annual Review of Sociology* 2001(27): 283–305.

Pope, Harrison, Kate Phillips, and Roberto Olivardia. 2000. *The Adonis Complex: The Secret Crisis of Male Body Obsession*. London: Simon and Schuster.

Potok, Mark. 2010. "Rage on the Right." *Intelligence Report*. Southern Poverty Law Center. March 2, https://www.splcenter.org/fighting-hate/intelligence-report/2010/rage-right.

————. 2013. "The Antigovernment 'Patriot' Movement Expands for the Fourth Year in a Row as Hate Groups Remain at Near-Historic Highs." In *Intelligence Report*. Southern Poverty Law Center. March 4, https://www.splcenter.org/fighting-hate/intelligence-report/2013/year-hate-and-extremism.

Putnam, Robert. 2000. *Bowling Alone: The Collapse and Revival of American Community*. New York: Simon and Schuster.

Pyke, K. D. 1996. "Class-Based Masculinities: The Interdependence of Gender, Class and Interpersonal Power." *Gender and Society* 10: 527–49.

Quinn, Malcolm. 1994. *The Swastika: Constructing the Symbol*. New York: Routledge.

Radke, Johannes. 2008. "Hausverbot im Bundestag." *Der Tagesspiegel*. March 16, http://www.tagesspiegel.de/berlin/hausverbot-im-bundestag/1189634.html.

Rauer, Valentin. 2012. "The Visualization of Uncertainty: HIV Statistics in Public Media." Pp. 139–54 in *Iconic Power: Materiality and Meaning in Social Life*, edited by Jeffrey C. Alexander, Dominik Bartmański, and Bernhard Giesen. New York: Palgrave Macmillan.

Reichel, Peter. 2005. *Schwarz-Rot-Gold: Kleine Geschichte deutscher Nationalsymbole*. Bonn: Bundeszentrale für politische Bildung.

————. 2006. *Der schöne Schein des Dritten Reiches: Gewalt und Faszination des deutschen Faschismus*. Hamburg: Ellert & Richter Zeitgeschichte.

Reitzenstein, Julian. 2014. *Himmlers Forscher: Wehrwissenschaft und Medizinverbrechen im "Ahnenerbe" der SS*. Paderborn: Ferdinand Schöningh.

Richardson, Niall, and Adam Locks. 2014. *Body Studies: The Basics*. New York: Routledge.

Richey, Lisa Ann, and Stefano Ponte. 2011. *Brand Aid: Shopping Well to Save the World*. Minneapolis: University of Minnesota Press.

Rios, Victor, and Rachel Sarabia. 2016. "Synthesized Masculinities: The Mechanics of Manhood among Delinquent Boys." Pp. 166–77 in *Exploring Masculinities: Identity, Inequality, Continuity, and Change*, edited by C. J. Pascoe and Tristan Bridges. New York: Oxford University Press.

Rippl, Susanne, and Dirk Baier. 2005. "Das Deprivationskonzept in der Rechtsextremismusforschung." *KZfSS Kölner Zeitschrift für Soziologie und Sozialpsychologie* 57(4): 644–66.

Rippl, Susanne, and Christian Seipel. 1999. "Gender Differences in Right-Wing Extremism: Intergroup Validity of a Second-Order Construct." *Social Psychology Quarterly* 62: 381–93.

Rogers, Thomas. 2014. "Heil Hipster: The Young Neo-Nazis Trying to Put a Stylish Face on Hate." *Rolling Stone*. June 24, http://www.rollingstone.com/culture/news /heil-hipster-the-young-neo-nazis-trying-to-put-a-stylish-face-on-hate-20140623.

———. 2015. "Authoritarian Outfitters." *New Republic*. https://newrepublic.com /article/121199/germanys-thor-steinar-neo-nazis-favorite-clothing-brand.

Rommelspacher, Birgit. 2006. *"Der Hass hat uns geeint": Junge Rechtsextreme und ihr Ausstieg aus der Szene.* Frankfurt: Campus Verlag.

Rydgren, Jens. 2007. "The Sociology of the Radical Right." *Annual Review of Sociology* 33: 241–62.

———. Forthcoming. *The Oxford Handbook of the Radical Right.* Oxford: Oxford University Press.

Saal, Oliver. 2016. "On Patrol with the New German Vigilantes." Pp. 73–78 in *Trouble on the Far Right: Contemporary Right-Wing Strategies and Practices in Europe*, edited by Maik Fielitz and Laura Laloire. Bielefeld: Transcript Verlag.

Sageman, Marc. 2004. *Understanding Terror Networks.* Philadelphia: University of Pennsylvania Press.

Sawyer, Peter. 1997. *The Oxford Illustrated History of the Vikings.* Oxford: Oxford University Press.

Schedler, Jan. 2011. "Style Matters: Inszenierungspraxen 'Autonomer Nationalisten.' " Pp. 67–89 in *Autonome Nationalisten: Neonazismus in Bewegung*, edited by Jan Schedler and Alexander Häusler. Wiesbaden: VS Verlag.

Schedler, Jan, and Alexander Häusler, eds. 2011. *Autonome Nationalisten: Neonazismus in Bewegung.* Wiesbaden: VS Verlag.

Schnabel, Kai, and Dietrich Goldschmidt. 1997. "Ausländerfeindlichkeit bei Auszubildenden-ein Handlungsfeld für Berufsschullehrer?" *Zeitschrift für Berufs- und Wirtschaftspädagogik* 93: 607–29.

Schnabel, Kai U. 1993. "Ausländerfeindlichkeit bei Jugendlichen in Deutschland: Eine Synopse empirischer Befunde seit 1990." *Zeitschrift für Pädagogik* 39: 799–822.

Scholte, Jan. 2005. *Globalization: A Critical Introduction*: New York: Palgrave Macmillan.

Schubarth, Wilfried, and Richard Stöss, eds. 2001. *Rechtsextremismus in der Bundesrepublik Deutschland: Eine Bilanz.* Opladen: Leske und Budrich.

Schuppener, Georg. 2007. *Spuren germanischer Mythologie in der deutschen Sprache: Namen, Phraseologismen und aktueller Rechtsextremismus.* Leipzig: Edition Hamouda, Wissenschaftsverlag.

———. 2010. *Sprache des Rechtsextremismus: Spezifika der Sprache rechtsextremistischer Publikationen und rechter Musik. 2. Auflage.* Leipzig: Edition Hamouda, Wissenschaftsverlag.

Scott, James C. 1985. *Weapons of the Weak: Everyday Forms of Peasant Resistance.* New Haven, CT: Yale University Press.

Seale, Clive. 1998. *Constructing Death: The Sociology of Dying and Bereavement.* Cambridge: Cambridge University Press.

Semyonov, Moshe, Rebeca Raijman, and Anastasia Gorodzeisky. 2006. "The Rise of Anti-foreigner Sentiment in European Societies, 1988–2000." *American Sociological Review* 71(3): 426–49.

Shafer, Joseph A. 2002. "Spinning the Web of Hate: Web-Based Hate Propagation by Extremist Organizations." *Journal of Criminal Justice and Popular Culture* 9(2): 69–88.

Sheldrake, Philip. 2001. *Spaces for the Sacred: Place, Memory, and Identity.* Baltimore: Johns Hopkins University Press.

Sherwin, Adam. 2014. "Outrage as Far-Right's Favourite Outfitter 'Thor Steinar' Opens Shop in Heart of London's Jewish Community." *Independent.* April 16, http://www.independent.co.uk/news/uk/home-news/outrage-as-far-rights-favour ite-outfitter-thor-steinar-opens-shop-in-heart-of-londons-jewish-9265311.html.

Shoshan, Nitzan. 2016. *The Management of Hate: Nation, Affect, and the Governance of Right-Wing Extremism in Germany.* Princeton, NJ: Princeton University Press.

Siedler, Thomas. 2011. "Parental Unemployment and Young People's Extreme Right-Wing Party Affinity: Evidence from Panel Data." *Journal of the Royal Statistical Society: Series A (Statistics in Society)* 174: 737–58.

Simi, Pete. Forthcoming. "The Culture of Violent Talk: An Interpretive Approach." In *Cultural Dimensions of Far Right Politics*, edited by Fabian Virchow and Cynthia Miller-Idriss. Wiesbaden: VS Verlag.

Simi, Pete, Bryan F. Bubolz, and Ann Hardman. 2013. "Military Experience, Identity Discrepancies, and Far Right Terrorism: An Exploratory Analysis." *Studies in Conflict and Terrorism* 36(8): 654–71.

Simi, Pete, and Robert Futrell. 2009. "Negotiating White Power Activist Stigma." *Social Problems* 56(1): 89–110.

———. 2010. *American Swastika: Inside the White Power Movement's Hidden Spaces of Hate.* New York: Rowman and Littlefield.

Smith, Anthony. 1989. "The Origins of Nations," *Ethnic and Racial Studies* 12(3): 340–67.

———. 1991. *The Ethnic Origin of Nations.* Hoboken, NJ: Wiley-Blackwell.

———. 1996. "LSE Centennial Lecture: The Resurgence of Nationalism? Myth and Memory in the Renewal of Nations." *British Journal of Sociology* 47(4): 575–98.

———. 2000a. *Myths and Memories of the Nation.* Oxford: Oxford University Press.

———. 2000b. "The 'Sacred' Dimension of Nationalism." *Millenium: Journal of International Studies* 29(3): 791–814.

———. 2003. *Chosen Peoples: Sacred Sources of National Identity.* Oxford: Oxford University Press.

———. 2008. *The Cultural Foundation of Nations: Hierarchy, Covenant, and Republic.* Hoboken, NJ: Wiley-Blackwell.

Soep, Elisabeth. 2012. "Resistance." Pp. 126–30 in *Keywords in Youth Studies: Tracing Affects, Movements, Knowledges*, edited by Nancy Lesko and Susan Talburt. New York: Routledge.

Southern Poverty Law Center. 2009. "Germans OK Nazi Signs, in Other Languages." *Intelligence Report.* November 30, https://www.splcenter.org/fighting-hate/intel ligence-report/2009/germans-ok-nazi-signs-other-languages.

Speit, Andreas, ed. 2010. *Ohne Juda, ohne Rom: Esoterik und Heidentum im subkulturellen Rechtsextremismus: Konzepte für Demokratie und Toleranz Band 8.* Braunschweig: Bildungsvereinigung Arbeit und Leben Niedersachsen Ost GmbH.

Spiegel Online. 2012a. "Fashion Faux Pas: Controversial 'Brevik' Clothing Store Changes Name." March 8, http: //www.spiegel.de/international/germany/fashion -faux-pas-controversial-brevik-clothing-store-changes-name-a-820080.html.

———. 2012b. "Neo-Nazi Fashion: Thor Steinar Names New Store after Norwegian Killer." March 6, http://www.spiegel.de/international/germany/neo-nazi-fashion -thor-steinar-names-new-store-after-norwegian-killer-a-819611.html.

Staecker, Joern. 2003. "The Cross Goes North: Christian Symbols and Scandanavian Women." Pp. 464–82 in *The Cross Goes North: Processes of Conversion in Northern Europe, AD 300–1300*, edited by Martin Carver. York: York Medieval Press, University of York.

Staud, Toralf. 2005. *Moderne Nazis: Die neuen Rechten und der Aufstieg der NPD*. Köln: Verlag Kiepenheuer & Witsch.

Steinmetz, George. 1997. "Social Class and the Reemergence of the Radical Right in Contemporary Germany." Pp. 335–68 in *Reworking Class*, edited by John Hall. Ithaca, NY: Cornell University Press.

———. 1999. *State/Culture: State-Formation after the Cultural Turn*. Ithaca, NY: Cornell University Press.

Stevens, Mitchell, Cynthia Miller-Idriss, and Seteney Shami. Forthcoming. *Seeing the World: How Universities Make Knowledge in a Global Era*. Princeton, NJ: Princeton University Press.

Stiehm, Enno. 2012. *Rechtsextreme Jugendliche: Erkennungsmerkmale, Begriffe, Erklärungsansätze und schulische Handlungsmöglichkeiten*. Hamburg: Diplomica Verlag.

Strohmeyer, Arn. 2005. *Von Hyperborea nach Ausschwitz: Wege eines antiken Mythos*. Cologne: PapyRossa Verlags GmbH.

Surak, Kristin. 2013. *Making Tea, Making Japan: Cultural Nationalism in Practice*. Stanford, CA: Stanford University Press.

Swain, Jon. 2002. "The Right Stuff: Fashioning an Identity through Clothing in a Junior School." *Gender and Education* 14(1): 53–69.

Swidler, Ann. 1986. "Culture in Action: Symbols and Strategies." *American Sociological Review* 5: 273–86.

Thorisdottir, Hulda, John T. Jost, Ido Liviatan, and Patrick E. Shrout. 2007. "Psychological Needs and Values Underlying Left-Right Political Orientation: Cross-National Evidence from Eastern and Western Europe." *Public Opinion Quarterly* 71(2): 175–203.

Todd, Anne Marie. 2004. "Environmental Consumer Ethics of Natural Care Products." *Ethics and the Environment* 9(2): 86–102.

Traynor, Ian. 2015. "Europe's Far Right Gets the Attention, but the Left Is Making the Political Running." *Guardian*. January 17, https://www.theguardian.com /world/2015/jan/18/europe-greece-far-right-anti-austerity-left-power-syriza-podemos.

Tumblety, Joan. 2012. *Remaking the Male Body: Masculinity and the Uses of Physical Culture in Interwar and Vichy France*. Cambridge: Oxford University Press.

Turner, Victor. 1967. *The Forest of Symbols: Aspects of Ndembu Ritual*. Ithaca, NY: Cornell University Press.

Van der Valk, Ineke, and Willem Wagenaar. 2010. *The Extreme Right: Entry and Exit*. Leiden: Anne Frank House/Leiden University.

Varshizky, Amit. 2012. "Alfred Rosenberg: The Nazi Weltanschauung as Modern Gnosis." *Politics, Religion and Ideology* 13(3): 311–31.

Vinken, Barbara. 2016. *Die Angst vor der Kastration: Über rechtsradikale Mode*. Hamburg: Sven Murmann Verlagsgesellschaft mbH.

Virchow, Fabian. 2008. "Die Bedeutung von Männlichkeitsstereotypen im Rechtsextremismus." Manuscript prepared for Brave Mädels und echte Kerle? Theorie und Wirklichkeit von Geschlectsrollen im Rechtsextremismus. Conference held by the Friedrich Ebert Stiftung. January 23, Berlin, http://www.fes-gegen-rechtsex tremismus.de/pdf_08/080123_virchow.pdf.

———. 2010. "Tapfer, stolz, opferbereit—Überlegungen zum extrem rechten Verständnis 'idealer Männlichkeit.'" Pp. 39–52 in *"Was ein rechter Mann ist . . ." Männlichkeit im Rechtsextremismus*, edited by Robert Claus, Esther Lehnert, and Yves Müller. Berlin: Karl Dietz Verlag.

Vlossak, Elizabeth. 2010. *Marianne or Germania? Nationalizing Women in Alsace, 1870–1946*. Cambridge: Oxford University Press.

Von der Goltz, Anna. 2009. *Hindenburg: Power, Myth, and the Rise of the Nazis* New York: Oxford University Press.

Vozella, Laura, and Jenna Portnoy. 2015. "Virginia's McAuliffe Plans to Phase Out Confederate Flag License Plate." *Washington Post*. June 23, http: //www.washington post.com/local/virginia-politics/virginias-mcauliffe-plans-to-phase-out-confederate -flag-license-plate/2015/06/23/bb8a1738-19b0-11e5-93b7-5eddc056ad8a_story.html.

Waetjen, Thembisa. 2001. "The Limits of Gender Rhetoric for Nationalism: A Case Study from Southern Africa." *Theory and Society* 30(1): 121–52.

Wallace, Clare, and Sijke Kovacheva. 1996. "Youth Cultures and Consumption in Eastern and Western Europe: An Overview." *Youth and Society* 28: 189–214.

Watts, Meredith W. 2001. "Aggressive Youth Cultures and Hate Crime: Skinheads and Xenophobic Youth in Germany." *American Behavioral Scientist* 45: 600–15.

Way, Niobe. 2011. *Deep Secrets: Boys' Friendships and the Crisis of Connection*. Cambridge, MA: Harvard University Press.

Wedeen, Lisa. 1999. *Ambiguities of Domination: Politics, Rhetoric, and Symbols in Contemporary Syria*. Chicago: University of Chicago Press.

Wedekamp, Johannes. 2008. "Tønsberg macht zu, Tønsberg macht auf." *Zeit Online blog Störungsmelder*. February 4, http://blog.zeit.de/stoerungsmelder/2008/02/04 /t%C3%B8nsberg-macht-zu-t%C3%B8nsberg-macht-auf_223.

Weißmann, Karlheinz. 1991. *Schwarze Fahnen, Runenzeichen: Die Entwicklung der politischen Symbolik der deutschen Rechten zwischen 1890 und 1945*. Duesseldorf: Droste Verlag.

———. 2006. *Das Hakenkreuz: Symbol eines Jahrhunderts*. Schnellroda: Edition Antaios.

———. 2007. *Deutsche Zeichen: Symbole des Reiches, Symbole der Nation*. Schnellroda: Edition Antaios.

Welch, David. 2004. "Nazi Propaganda and the *Volksgemeinschaft*: Constructing a People's Community." *Journal of Contemporary History* 39(2): 213–38.

Wemple, Erik. 2016. "PBS Issues Second Editor's Note on Trump-Supporter's White Supremacist Tattoos." *Washington Post*. March 17, https://www.washingtonpost.com /blogs/erik-wemple/wp/2016/03/17/pbs-issues-second-editors-note-on-trump-suppor ters-white-supremacist-tattoos/?utm_term=.5138af4f7085.

Whisker, James. 1990. *The Philosophy of Alfred Rosenberg*. Costa Mesa, CA: Noontide.

Wilkes, Rima, Neil Guppy, and Lily Farris. 2007. "Comment on Semyonov, Raijman, and Gorodzeisky, ASR, June 2006: Right-Wing Parties and Anti-foreigner Sentiment in Europe." *American Sociological Review* 72(5): 831–40.

Williams, J. Patrick. 2011. *Subcultural Theory: Traditions and Concepts*. Malden, MA: Polity.

Williams, Raymond. 1985. *Keywords: A Vocabulary of Culture and Society*. New York: Oxford University Press.

Williamson, George S. 2004. *The Longing for Myth in Germany: Religion and Aesthetic Culture from Romanticism to Nietzsche*. Chicago: University of Chicago Press.

Willis, Paul. 1981. *Learning to Labor: How Working-Class Kids Get Working-Class Jobs*. New York: Columbia University Press.

Wittrock, Philipp. 2006. "Umstrittener Vergleich: Häuptling Koch und die Indianer." *Spiegel Online*. May 29, http: //www.spiegel.de/politik/deutschland/umstrittener -vergleich-haeuptling-koch-und-die-indianer-a-418605.html.

Wong, Paul T., Gary T. Reker, and Gina Gesser. 1994. "Death Attitude Profile — Revisited: A Multidimensional Measure of Attitudes toward Death." Pp. 121– 48 in *Death Anxiety Handbook: Research, Instrumentation, and Application*, edited by Robert Niemeyer. London: Routledge.

Wood, Graeme. 2015. "What ISIS Really Wants." *Atlantic*. March 2015, https://www .theatlantic.com/magazine/archive/2015/03/what-isis-really-wants/384980/.

Worden, Elizabeth Anderson, and Cynthia Miller-Idriss. 2016. "Beyond Multiculturalism: Conflict, Co-existence, and Messy Identities." Pp. 289–311 in *Annual Review of Comparative and International Education 2016: International Perspectives on Education and Society*, vol. 30, edited by Alexander Wiseman. Bingley, UK: Emerald Group.

Yuval-Davis, Nira, and Floya Anthias. 1989. *Women-Nation-State*. New York: St. Martin's.

Zacharoff, Lucien. 1934. "Angola Again Being Discussed as Possible Haven for Jewish Exiles." *Jewish Daily Bulletin*. May 6. Jewish Telegraphic Agency, http: //www.jta.org /1934/05/06/archive/angola-again-being-discussed-as-possible-haven-for-jewish-exiles.

Zelizer, Viviana A. 2011. *Economic Lives: How Culture Shapes the Economy*. Princeton, NJ: Princeton University Press.

Zubrzycki, Geneviève. 2006. *The Crosses of Auschwitz: Nationalism and Religion in Post-Communist Poland*. Chicago: University of Chicago Press.

———. 2011. "History and the National Sensorium: Making Sense of Polish Mythology." *Qualitative Sociology* 34(1): 21–57.

———. 2013. "Aesthetic Revolt and the Remaking of National Identity in Québec, 1960–1969." *Theory and Society* 42(5): 423–75.

———. 2016. *Beheading the Saint: Nationalism, Religion and Secularism in Quebec*. Chicago: University of Chicago Press.

INDEX

 **PRINCETON STUDIES IN CULTURAL SOCIOLOGY**
Paul J. DiMaggio, Michèle Lamont,
Robert J. Wuthnow, and Viviana A. Zelizer,
Series Editors